A COMPLETE GUIDE

Palm Springs & Desert Resorts

Andreas Canyon. Palm Springs Desert Resorts Conventions & Visitors Authority

A COMPLETE GUIDE

FIRST EDITION

Palm Springs & Desert Resorts

Christopher P. Baker

The Countryman Press
Woodstock, Vermont

Dedication

This book is dedicated to my sister, Alison, and her wonderful husband, Steven, both of whom I admire and love very much.

First Edition

ISBN 978-1-58157-048-9

Cover and interior photos by the author unless otherwise specified
Book design by Bodenweber Design
Page composition by Susan McClellan
Maps by Mapping Specialists Ltd., Madison, WI © The Countryman Press

Published by The Countryman Press, P.O. Box 748, Woodstock, Vermont 05091

Distributed by W. W. Norton & Company, Inc., 500 Fifth Avenue, New York, NY 10110

Manufactured in the United States of America

10 9 8 7 6 5 4 3 2 1

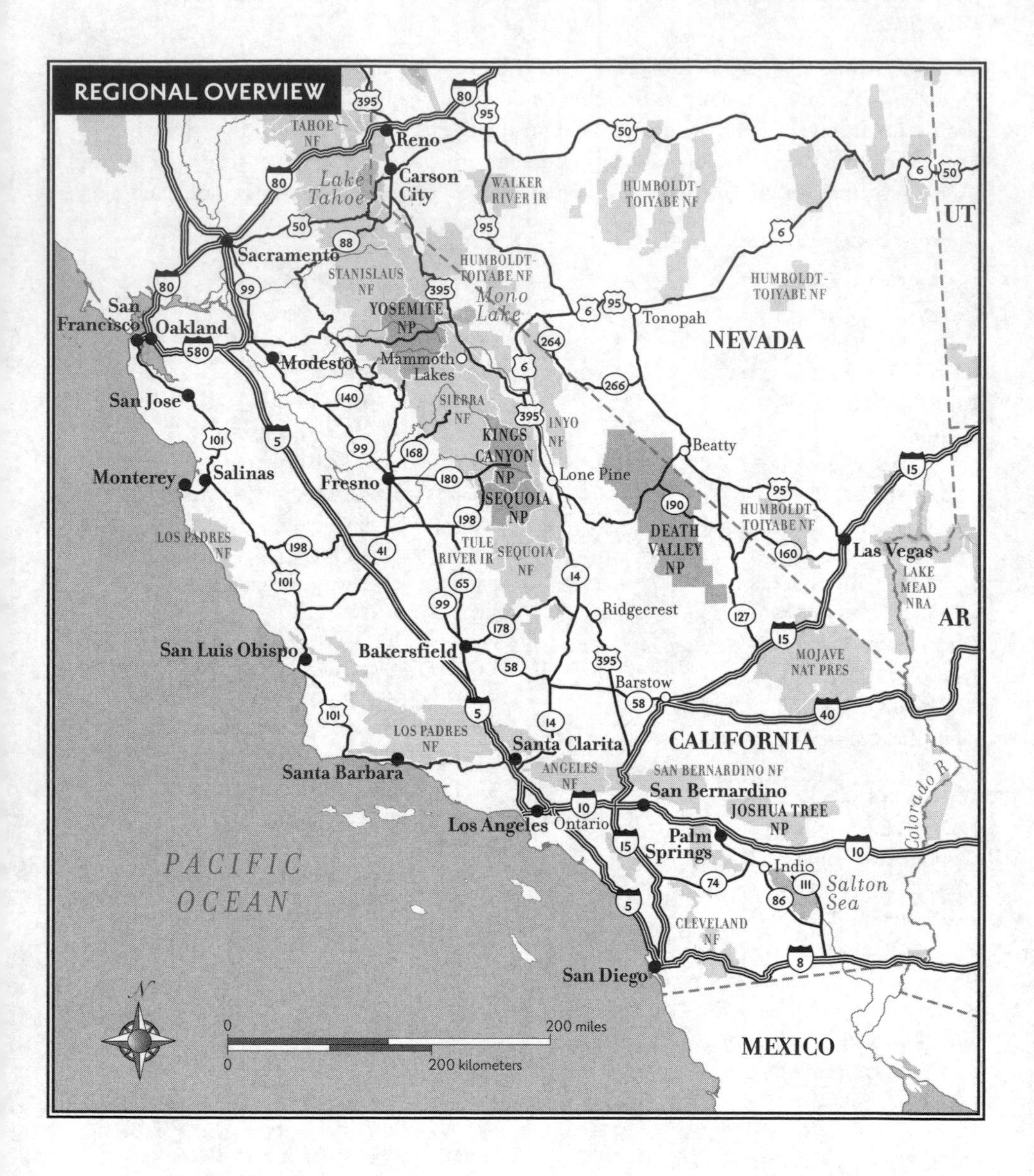

REGIONAL OVERVIEW
TAHOE NF
Lake Tahoe
Reno
Carson City
WALKER RIVER IR
HUMBOLDT-TOIYABE NF
UT
Sacramento
STANISLAUS NF
HUMBOLDT-TOIYABE NF
Mono Lake
YOSEMITE NP
San Francisco
Oakland
Tonopah
NEVADA
Modesto
Mammoth Lakes
San Jose
SIERRA NF
INYO NF
KINGS CANYON NP
Beatty
Monterey
Salinas
Fresno
Lone Pine
SEQUOIA NP
HUMBOLDT-TOIYABE NF
LOS PADRES NF
DEATH VALLEY NP
Las Vegas
TULE RIVER IR
SEQUOIA NF
LAKE MEAD NRA
Ridgecrest
AR
San Luis Obispo
Bakersfield
MOJAVE NAT PRES
Barstow
CALIFORNIA
LOS PADRES NF
Santa Clarita
Santa Barbara
ANGELES NF
SAN BERNARDINO NF
San Bernardino
JOSHUA TREE NP
Colorado R.
Los Angeles
Ontario
Palm Springs
Indio
Salton Sea
PACIFIC OCEAN
CLEVELAND NF
San Diego
N
0
200 miles
0
200 kilometers
MEXICO

Contents

Acknowledgments

I could not have prepared this book without the help of a coterie of other people.

Particular thanks go to Mark Graves, of the Palm Springs Desert Resorts Convention & Visitors Authority; to Mary Perry, of the Palm Springs Bureau of Tourism; and to Lena Zimmerschied, of Palm Springs Aerial Tramway.

I also wish to acknowledge the following for miscellaneous assistance: Bob Bogard, of Palm Springs Art Museum; Kimberly Bowers and Peter Siminski, of The Living Desert; Bill Davis, of Celebrity Tours; Mary Dungans, of Desert Adventures; Therese Everett-Kerley, of the Agua Caliente Band of Cahuilla Indians; Mark Farley, of Elite Tours; Robert Imber, of PS Modern Tours; Kristy Kneiding, of the City of Palm Desert; Patrick Milson, of Fleming's Restaurant; Greg Purdy, of Fabulous Palm Springs Follies; Larry Rener, of Homes Run; Rick Seidner, of Rick's; Evan Trubee, of Big Wheel Touring; Dan Westfall, of C.H.E.E.T.A. Primate Sanctuary; and Stephen and Cynthia Wilkinson, of Fantasy Balloon Flights.

Finally, I'd like to hear from you if you have suggestions for ways to improve this book. Also, please let us know about your experiences, both good and bad, with hotels, restaurants, and other businesses listed. If they don't live up to their recommendations, let me know.

Snow-capped Mount San Jacinto rises in the distance. Palm Springs Desert Resorts Conventions & Visitors Authority

Date palms.

Introduction

In the 1950s and '60s, Frank Sinatra and his Rat Pack made Palm Springs the definition of cool. Palm Springs' Hollywood-tinged hedonism began in the 1930s, when the arrival of stars and starlets turned the area from a sleepy desert outpost into a world-famous winter retreat. "The season" traditionally kicked off in late October with a party at the Racquet Club, where Sinatra, Sammy Davis Jr., Bing Crosby, and "Honorary Mayor" Bob Hope warmed up their fellow stars. Sinatra and Hope eventually settled here, while scores of their Hollywood peers, from Elvis Presley and Dean Martin to Lucille Ball and Liberace, bought homes in which to winter and play.

The stars' modernist homes defined the vernacular style of the city and were an ideal complement to the elegantly informal (and often debauched) desert lifestyle. The mountains and desert sands attracted architects now recognized as modern masters, such as Richard Neutra, John Lautner, William Cody, E. Stewart Williams, and Albert Frey, whose spare, sharp-lined, and sensuously curved designs found their full and iconoclastic blossoming amid the stark desert landscape. Modernism's place in the sun lasted two decades, then waned, along with the city's own fortunes. By the late 1970s the Hollywood set had moved on, and the town went into decline. The money moved down valley to newer cities, such as Palm Desert and Rancho Mirage, with their lush golf courses and country clubs exuding luxury beyond the dreams of Croesus.

Recently considered outdated and déclassé, Palm Springs has since staged an impressive comeback. Nostalgia is a major factor. Unlikely as it may seem, this desert oasis is ground zero in the worldwide modernist revival that is influencing everything from architecture and furniture to fashion and graphic design. Palm Springs' stock of more than two thousand Midcentury Modernist homes and public buildings—one of the most important concentrations of modernist architecture in the world—has been rediscovered. The architectural gems are being spruced up, while many owners of modernist homes have gone so far as to park Thunderbird convertibles and other automotive exemplars of space-age retro chic in the driveway, adding to the impression of Palm Springs as the prototypical early-sixties American Dream come to life. Meanwhile, many of the city's modernist motels have been transformed into chic boutique hotels furnished with retro kitsch and classic period pieces by famous modernist designers—Saarinen, Noguchi, Eames. Ol' Blue Eyes himself would feel right at home.

Newly fresh and compelling, this desert hot spot exudes contemporary cool. No surprise, then, that a whole new generation of Hollywood stars is flocking to where it's 1967 all over again. On weekends the sidewalks on Palm Canyon Drive are packed with beautiful people sipping lattés and shopping for Bertoia bikini chairs.

An easy 90-minute drive from L.A., "Palm Springs" is actually understood as the entire Coachella Valley, comprising eight "desert resort communities" (Desert Hot Springs, Palm Springs, Cathedral City, Rancho Mirage, Palm Desert, Indian Wells, La Quinta, and Indio) clustered at the foot of the San Jacinto Mountains. They merge into one another along California Highway 111, one of America's great scenic drives. The physical setting is out of this world. Majestic mountains soar on three sides, glistening with snow in the winter sunshine. The vistas are so dramatic that locals, supported by city ordinances, guard them with gusto.

The desert resorts region has lured visitors for more than a century to bask in its year-round warmth and enjoy its hot mineral springs, lush palm oases, and serene desert and mountain landscapes. Today the region retains a magical hold on visitors, who always come back, many to make it their home. The figures for both off-season tourism and year-round residents are soaring, with the population in the Coachella Valley projected to reach half a million by 2015—almost double what it is now. Palm Springs' jocular title as "God's waiting room" is now outdated. Today more Palm Springs residents are age 25 to 44 than 65 plus. Gays have flocked, bringing their own aesthetic. So, too, artists and techie hipsters, along with young couples arriving, according to official statistics, at the rate of 42 families per day. And many among the Hollywood and cultural A-list, such as Anne Rice and Barry Manilow, still choose to reside here full-time for the peace and seclusion it offers. So great is the demand to live here that real estate prices in the region rose at a faster rate than anywhere else in the nation 2001–2005.

Contrary to the myth that the majority of visitors are golfers, gamblers, or creaky retirees, today's typical visitor is surprisingly youthful. The region has transformed itself from a seasonal resort to a year-round vacation destination that is much more than a "hideaway for martini soaked celebrities in the land of a thousand golf pros." There's no shortage of activities and attractions. The dining is fabulous. The spas are among California's best. And the region boasts several ritzy casinos. Museums cater to aviation buffs, art fans, and nature lovers keen to learn about and experience desert ecology. El Paseo gives Beverly Hills' Rodeo Drive a run for its money in the quality and range of boutiques. Its numerous jazz, film, and art festivals have earned acclaim. More than two million visitors come annually to play golf on the more than 110 rolling green courses. And almost as many arrive to hike the palm canyons, alpine summits of the San Jacintos, or the spectacular desert landscapes of Anza-Borrego Desert State Park and Joshua Tree National Park. Palm Springs even caters to nudists.

There aren't many places where you can golf in the morning, go skiing or snowshoeing in the afternoon, and enjoy a cocktail by the pool in the evening. Which explains why in 2007, almost five million visitors descended on Palm Springs and the surrounding region, where the summer never dies, the architecture is retro-cool, and the reinvigorated spirit feels as refreshing as an iced martini.

The Way This Book Works

This book is divided into nine chapters. Entries within each chapter are first divided into "Palm Springs," "Palm Springs Vicinity," and "Southern Desert Resorts," and, where relevant, each area is then broken down geographically according to the names of towns, moving generally from north to south.

Some entries include specific information—telephone numbers, Web sites, addresses, business hours, and the like—organized for easy reference in blocks at the top of each entry. All information was checked as close to the publication date as possible. Even so, since details can change without warning, it is always wise to call ahead.

For the same reasons, we have routinely avoided listing specific prices, indicating instead a range. Lodging price codes are based on a per-room rate, double occupancy during winter months (high season). Off-season rates are often cheaper. Restaurant price ratings indicate the cost of an individual meal, including appetizer, entrée, and dessert but not cocktails, wine, tax, or tip.

Price Codes

	Lodging	*Dining*
Inexpensive	Up to $100	Up to $10
Moderate	$100 to $150	$10 to $20
Expensive	$150 to $250	$20 to 35
Very Expensive	Over $250	$35 or more

Credit Cards

AE—American Express | CB—Carte Blanche | D—Discover Card
DC—Diners Club | MC—MasterCard | V—Visa

Towns in the Desert Resorts Region

Palm Springs and the desert resort communities occupy the western half of the Coachella Valley, which slopes gradually southward and is enclosed by the Little San Bernardino Mountains to the east and the San Jacinto and Santa Rosa mountain chains to the north and west. The city of Palm Springs is at the northern end of the valley, with most of the other desert resort cities merging one into the next, in order southward: Cathedral City, Rancho Mirage, Palm Desert, Indian Wells, and La Quinta. Farther south comes Indio and, finally, Coachella. All lie west of Interstate 10 (I-10) and are connected by CA 111, the main thoroughfare, known locally as Highway 111. The city of Desert Hot Springs lies apart, on the east side of the valley. The term "Palm Springs" is often used to refer to the entire region.

Beyond the valley, to the northeast, the high-desert communities of Yucca Valley, Joshua Tree, and Twentynine Palms form their own enclave on the periphery of Joshua Tree National Park.

View of Coachella Valley from atop the Palm Springs Aerial Tram.

Mountain lions still prowl secluded canyons. Bert Buxbaum

History

The Voice of the Desert

Nearly every striking feature of this special world . . . goes back ultimately to the grand fact of dryness—the dryness of the ground, of the air, of the whole sum-total.

—Joseph Wood Krutch

Natural History

The Coachella Valley belongs to the "low desert" or, more properly, the Colorado Desert, part of the greater Sonoran desert system that covers much of Arizona, northwestern Mexico, and southeastern California. The "low desert" mostly lies below 1,000 feet. To the northeast is the "high desert," or Mojave Desert, covering an area of 35,000 square miles, mostly at an elevation above 2,000 feet, extending into Nevada and southern Utah. The distinction between "low" and "high" deserts lies primarily in the vegetation.

The valley extends for approximately 45 miles along a northwest-southeast axis and is approximately 15 miles wide for most of its length. It is framed on the west by the San Jacinto Mountains and, farther south, by the Santa Rosa Mountains, with Mount San Jacinto rising to nearly 11,000 feet. The Little San Bernardino Mountains rise along the north and east side of the valley; the San Andreas fault runs at its feet, spawning hot springs at major fissures. Over the aeons, tectonic activity has dropped the eastern end of the valley to well below sea level. Thus, the valley slopes eastward from the San Gorgonio Pass to the Salton Sea, where some 100,000 acres of fertile alluvial lands are irrigated by waters supplied by the Coachella Canal—a concrete-lined aqueduct completed in 1948 to feed water from the Colorado River. Palm Springs sits at the base of Mount San Jacinto, at the northwest end of the valley.

At dawn a rubicund radiance mantles the eastern mountains. As the sun rises above the horizon, it ignites the cactus and tinges the spindly palm tops with saffron. Burning sunlight splashes the mountains with violet and fiery vermilion, and for a moment it seems as if the desert is truly ablaze. Then the sun shoots skyward and the sublime conflagration is extinguished with magical swiftness, leaving only a memory of the evanescent enchantment of the desert at dawn. Because there is little moisture in the air to refract and reflect light, darkness comes equally swiftly at sundown, with the oranges and reds and purples melting away rapidly once the sun sinks from view.

Nowhere does rainfall exceed 8 inches a year, except atop the towering San Jacinto Mountains, where temperatures are typically 20 degrees Fahrenheit less than on the valley

Jeep adventures in the canyons of the Coachella Valley.

floor and abundant winter rains crown the peaks with soft blankets of snow. The summits can remain dazzlingly snowcapped into late spring, offering a remarkable contrast to the valley far below, where Palm Springs sizzles in microwave heat.

As the snows melt, water percolates into the mountains and follows the dictates of gravity. Eventually it seeps out into springs that gush from the base of the mountains, and drops down through rocky ravines where thirsty plant life take up the surface water, with any surplus being lost again underground. Even in the heart of summer, water is usually always present in *tinajas*, natural tanks scoured into the bedrock, and in ravines whose running streams metamorphose into thunderous waterfalls after storms. Then, flash floods can sluice out of the mountain canyons with savage fury, surging downstream with such a load of mud, gravel, and rock that they bury trees up to their necks or tear them asunder, adding them to the stony rubble forming vast alluvial fans at the base of the mountains.

After thousands of years of being grilled by sun and frozen at night, even the toughest mountain granite begins to crack and flake. Year by year it is eroded into ever finer grains that are eventually washed down by creeks onto the desert flats. Thus, most of the Coachella Valley bottom is composed of sand many hundreds of feet thick. Winds tear through the San Gorgonio Pass (one of the windiest places on earth), scouring the valley, pushing the sand up against the base of the mountains or shaping it into sensuous dunes and even, on occasion, whipping the desert dust into dense sandstorms.

Although the winter clime is idyllic, temperatures in the valley are extreme in the brutal heat of midsummer. By noon the air shimmers like a sort of dreamworld between hallucination and reality, and the rocks are so hot that you can fry an egg on them. Nothing moves unless it has to. Only the most dedicated of desert creatures venture out at midday during June through August, when surface temperatures can reach 200 degrees Fahrenheit. Although the surface can become broilingly hot, just a few inches down it is surprisingly cool, permitting animals to live comfortably in burrows where relative humidity is two to five times that of outside. The absence of clouds not only denies shade by day, but also by night any blanket to retain the heat. Searingly hot by day, the desert can freeze by night.

In the longer-term geological time frame, the region is in the grip of a dry phase.

During the last ice age, beginning several million years ago, the landscape resembled that of the Pacific Northwest. Large lakes studded the region. About 12,000 years ago, the lakes dried out. In wetter times, pine and fir forests were found at lower elevations than today. They have since retreated to the tops of the mountains, while thorny scrub and cacti have advanced north from the desert highlands south of the Mexican border. The ebb and flow, the expansion and contraction of desert, takes place over an immensity of time.

Desert Flora

Despite little rain and temperatures well into the hundreds, the parsimonious desert brims with the glories of nature. The valley is home to at least 100 rare species of desert plants. The varied flora ranges from the delicate white desert lilies, apricot-colored desert mallow, and brilliant orange of the California poppy to the intense blue of lupine, scarlet torches of ocotillo, and magnificent magenta of owl's clover. Most species lie dormant for long periods before exploding in riotous color with the onset of rain. The bloom is usually short lived, coming in waves that can run from January through July. As April turns into May, the moisture is gone, the seeds are set, and the flowers shrivel and die. Even a little rain at the right time can draw forth a spectacular palette of desert blooms. It is impossible to say when spring wildflowers will reach their peak, as desert springs vary from year to year. Sometimes there is no bloom at all. El Niño years, marked by wetter-than-normal winters and springs, give rise to spectacular displays, while colder, drier winters presage a lack of wildflowers. The past three decades have witnessed a more than average number of spectacular blooms.

California fan palms.

An hour-long deluge can resurrect desert flora from sun-scorched torpor, although the temperature at the times of the rains may determine which species bloom (desert sunflower and chia, for example, require searing summer heat in order to germinate the following winter). And many plant species' seeds are able to resist the temptation to germinate at the first drop of rain. The rains could be a false start, and seeds can't risk the threat of desiccation and death in the dry spell to follow. Like time-release medications, their coats have an inhibitor to prevent germination unless rainfall is sufficiently heavy to wash the coating away (an inch of rain will do the trick if it falls between late September and early December).

Desert plants, or xerophytes (plants capable of withstanding long periods of drought without ill effects), are adapted in other ingenious ways. To reduce loss of water through evaporation, the American holly, for example, grows its leaves at 70 degrees to the vertical so that the sun strikes only the edge of the leaves for most of the day. It also excretes salt through its leaves, layering them with fine white crystals that help reflect sunlight. By contrast, the hardy creosote is coated with a waxy layer that keeps in moisture. Most xerophytes also spread their roots wide and far to soak up a maximum of moisture in the quick-draining desert soil. Hence, each plant is well separated from its neighbors to ration water equally. In contrast, some cacti send roots 30 feet or more downward to tap underground water, while the mesquite root can bore down 100 feet to reach the water table.

Wild fan palms—named for the shape of their long fronds—grow on the sunny, south-facing side of deep, shady mountain canyons, forming shady oases wherever sufficient water exists. Of the two species, the California fan palm is most numerous and is easily recognizable by the long curly fibers fraying from the edges of its fronds. As the palm fronds die they slowly wilt, dry, and dangle down the trunk, building up with the years to form a thick skirt. In favored conditions, the palm can grow to 60 feet tall and live in excess of 200 years. It is the only native palm to the desert and propagates in late spring by producing small black berries.

Cottonwoods, tamarisk, and willows also flourish along canyon watercourses, as does arrow weed, a thick shrub that creates an effective windbreak. Come spring, the canyon bottoms hum with bees gathering pollen amid the new-blooming pale green paloverde, dark green mesquite, and gray-green ironwoods. The smoke tree also flourishes along the riparian banks, seeming to float on the air, hence its name. It grows only in washes, where the rough and tumble of flash floods cascading over sandy surfaces can break open the tough seeds and offer the sustained water that they need to germinate. Hikers entering the canyons delight, too, to discover marshes of bright green rushes and cattails flourishing around bodies of standing water. An astonishing amount of aquatic insect life darts about busily in the limpid spring-fed pools, including the predaceous diving beetle, which feeds on snails, tadpoles, and tiny fish. Frogs hop about the marshes, too, drawing garter snakes and innumerable birds.

Vegetation changes dramatically with elevation. At about 4,000 feet elevation, desert scrub gives way to open woodland, and the air is sweetened with the aromatic, resinous scent of piñon pine. Higher still, sugar, pitch, lodgepole, and Jeffrey pines mingle with sycamore, aspen, fir, incense cedar, live oak, California juniper, and cypress. Thick, twisted tree roots push through the sun-baked rocks, widening cracks and tilting boulders as they grope downward for underground moisture.

The Hardy Cactus

The cactus is the quintessential desert plant. Coming in a wide range of shapes and sizes, the cactus family has reached a pinnacle of diversification in the Sonoran Desert, where more than 140 species exist (not all can be found in the Coachella region, however). These range from pincushion cacti barely 2 inches tall to ponderous and columnar cardóns, a crude hulking brute of a cactus growing up to 60 feet tall and looking, thought desert sage Edward Abbey, "as if they'd been hammered out of bronze and old iron by some demented junkyard genius." (The cardón is the world's tallest cacti and grows to be 200 years old, supporting its bulk with stiff rods that grow inside the ridges between its vertical pleats.)

Cacti have literally reshaped themselves to fit their arid environment. A few cacti have tiny leaves. However, because leaves increase a plant's surface area and can be extremely spendthrift with water, most cacti have evolved to deal with the problem of evaporation by ridding themselves of leaves altogether and by increasing their bulk, thus reducing the relative surface area exposed to the desiccating elements. Their stems have evolved into succulent structures that have taken over the role of photosynthesis (a plant's sun-powered food-making process), while the leaves have evolved into spines that serve to protect the fleshy plant from nibbling grazers and also break up desiccating air currents passing over the skin, which is thick and waxy. Drawing energy from year-round sunshine and their water-storing interior pulp, cacti can function year-round, even flowering in times of drought.

Cactus spines range from tiny hairlike glochids that penetrate into the skin like invisible splinters to stiff, needlelike spikes that can easily pierce a boot or tire. The stiff spines of the hedgehog cactus are so brutally long that the plant could be more appropriately

The thorny ocotillo appears dry and lifeless much of the year.

called the porcupine cactus. In spring, it blooms spectacularly with huge satiny blossoms that, depending on the species, vary from white through pink and purple. When fully opened, the flower of the comb hedgehog may span 6 inches (the cacti themselves rarely exceed 10 inches tall). Some species may have dozens of stems, each decorated with numerous effulgent blooms.

Ubiquitous in gardens, the barrel cactus is thick and squat and named for its shape. Barrel cacti are able to contract and expand their pleated trunks with the seasons in response to the supply of moisture, like a bellows or concertina. They wither during drought and swell during rains, when their widespread roots sup up rainfall almost as fast as it falls. When swollen, the plant may consist of as much as 95 percent water, stored within millions of tiny pores in the species' spongelike flesh. Thus gorged, and by making only sparing use of its stored-up moisture, these expansible organisms can live for several years of complete drought. The thirsty traveler, when he cuts open and squeezes the plant, will be disappointed to find a bitter-tasting, viscous liquid (the flesh, however, can be boiled in sugar syrup to make a delicious preserve). Barrel cactus can reach 6 feet tall and naturally lean toward the sunny southwest.

The yin to the barrel cactus's yang is the snakelike ocotillo, which appears dry and lifeless for much of the year. A "weird, Martian, spidery thing . . . like squid or octopus buried head downward in the sand," thought Abbey. After moderately heavy rains, however, the multiple, thorn-clad, gray, slender stems that grow to 15 feet high become sheathed in bright green leaves. It may bear five or six short-lived crops every year. In springtime each stem is tipped as if with flames by a clutch of small scarlet flowers.

The hardiest and most adaptable plants in the cacti family are the prickly pears, fast-growing even in the poorest of desert soil. They grow in a succession of fleshy oval pads, protected by long spines and short barbed glochids. The plant is anchored by a deep-reaching taproot. Other wide-spreading roots near the surface soak up light rains. In winter these roots take up the role of the pads by storing water, thus minimizing the risk from aboveground freezing. Prickly pears come in a variety of forms, all of which burst into glorious bloom (from yellow to deep carmine, depending on species) and give off a seedy and nutritious pomegranate-like purplish fruit.

The shrubby and exquisite teddy bear cholla cactus is so thickly tufted with microscopically barbed glochids that it looks as if it is covered in yellowing fur, especially when haloed in slanting sunlight. Its sprawling branches grow in loosely attached, sausagelike joints that break off and impale victims so easily that some species are known as "jumping" chollas. The ease with which the barbs attach themselves to passing animals and humans helps propagate the species. When the joint eventually falls to the ground, it takes root as a new cactus. The spines are no hardship, however, to pack rats, which like to use them to fortify their nests, while the wily cactus wren even builds its nest securely atop the plant.

Some cactus species grow horizontally instead of vertically, such as the creeping devil cactus, or caterpillar cactus, whose fiercely barbed wormlike stems underfoot are as tangled and impenetrable as barbed wire. The sinister-looking plant crawls relentlessly across the desert floor, over any obstacles in its path. Periodically the branches put down stems that take on new life as the older growth gradually withers and dies. Freed from its parent, the stem crawls across the desert floor and propagates itself in a kind of creeping immortality, with multiple generations forming a huge tangled colony that edges forward at about 1 inch a year.

Agaves and Yuccas

Another cliché of the desert is the spiky agave, which comes in several variations. Unlike cacti, which store water in the stems, agaves store water in their thick leaves (it can even be drunk fresh). Known as the "century plant," the agave grows gradually around a tightly wrapped artichoke-like heart from which branch swordlike blades fringed with barbs and tipped with needle-sharp points. When the plant is fully grown, the inner heart suddenly opens and sends up a single thick stalk that shoots up to 15 feet skyward in a matter of days. At its climax the stalk produces efflorescing blossoms of brassy gold—its only flowering in its life. The prodigious burst of energy entirely depletes the plant, which, having flowered, then dies and withers, leaving seed pods as spawn for the next generation. If the stalk is cut off before it flowers, the sap (known as *aguamiel*, or honey water) that has been produced as a fuel for the sudden growth can be distilled to produce mescal, while the heart can be roasted on slow coals and eaten (it apparently tastes especially good with garlic).

The yucca, a relative of the agave, is another classic—and finicky—desert plant that comes in many forms, from ground hugging to the towering Joshua tree, which when fully mature can reach up to 20 feet, with trunks up to 2 feet in diameter. Growing abundantly in the Mojave Desert yet absent in the drier, hotter, lower Colorado Desert, the Joshua tree is distinguished by its awry branches. Explorer John C. Frémont wrote of "their stiff and ungraceful forms . . . the most repulsive tree in the vegetable kingdom." Despite its rough-barked and gnarled appearance, the yucca is actually a member of the lily family. In spring the plant sends up stalks of tight-fisted white flowers like chandeliers. It is entirely dependent on the night-flying yucca moth for propagation, and vice versa—only this single moth species pollinates yucca flowers, while its caterpillars eat only yucca seeds. After mating, the female moth collects pollen from the dill-scented blossoms. This she packs into a ball to carry off to another plant, where she lays up to six eggs in the flower ovary and deposits the pollen onto the stigma (thus transferring male gametes to the female reproductive organ and permitting seeds to develop). The caterpillars hatch at the same time that seeds develop—fortunately, in far greater number than the caterpillars can eat, thus ensuring survival of the plant.

The Creosote Bush

The creosote bush—the most abundant and drought-tolerant shrub of the desert—can go for a year or longer without rain, although even it can succumb to the most severe drought. Clonal colonies of the bush can live for many thousands of years. Nonetheless, the species is notoriously resistant to germination, requiring a substantial autumnal rainstorm when the temperature is neither too hot nor too cold. If seedlings win the lotto, they put down roots very quickly (desert shrub seedlings tend not to waste energy on foliage until they have secured a water supply), although creosote bush roots fan out rather than grow downward. The plant relies on the thin film of dew that forms at night around rock particles just below the surface. Its roots are so extensive that virtually every available molecule of water is extracted, robbing potential competitors of sustenance (as an insurance, the plant also gives off a toxic substance that poisons the soil around it; it gets its name from its pungent odor, which is so unpleasant that few creatures will eat the blooms). It grows in the desert at mathematically precise intervals and propagates by sending out new stems around its base. Eventually the central stem dies of old age, with each generation of new stems sprouting farther from the original source. In time, the creosote bush forms an ever-expanding ring that might be as much as 10,000 years old.

Bighorn sheep can sometimes be seen on golf fairways. Bert Buxbaum

Desert Fauna

Despite the seemingly inimical heat and lack of water, the desert teems with animals and birds. Most reptile and mammal species are pale in color, often similar to that of the predominant terrain in which each lives—usually in varying shades of fawn, brown, or gray. Whether bird, insect, or mammal, all desert creatures go to great lengths to conserve water. Many species never drink water, relying on special adaptive techniques and the manufacture internally of "metabolic water" processed from solid food. Coyotes and other carnivores get water from the blood of their prey. Herbivores, such as jackrabbits, derive moisture from plants.

From rodents to porcupines and skunks, there's no shortage of mammals. They're just hard to see, at least by day. Since they must deal with extremes of temperature, most creatures are nocturnal and shelter in burrows throughout the day, husbanding their energies for nighttime foraging. Their refuges are pleasantly cool, while the humidity is also high, not least thanks to the occupant's own breath. At dusk the creatures timidly venture out. After a few hours of active foraging to appease their hunger, they retire again as the temperature continues to fall. They are usually asleep again in their dens well before sunup. Some rodents, such as ground squirrels, become torpid during the extremes of summer and estivate inside their deep burrows (their body temperatures drop to that of the surrounding air, and respiration and other physiological processes slow down).

Seed-eating rodents are especially numerous, from cactus mice and rock squirrels to pocket gophers and pack rats—the presence of the latter is betrayed by their middens built of bark, sticks, bottle tops, and other scavenged miscellany. Kangaroo rats are common, too. Their long hind legs, resembling those of their namesake, are capable of generating prodigious leaps in any direction, including straight up—a handy defense against predators. The diminutive critter measures about 3 inches long, trailing a 7-inch-long tail that helps provide the balance that this acrobat requires when performing its leaps. In the desert the use of water to help rid the body of soluble waste is a potentially deadly extravagance. Hence the kangaroo rat has evolved kidneys capable of concentrating urine into paste. It also has an especially adapted nasal passage at a lower temperature than the rest of the body. When warm exhalations pass through the passage, the air is cooled and the water content condenses and is retained inside the body instead of being lost at the tip of the nose. Thus the kangaroo rat can retain virtually all the moisture inside its body and has no need to drink water (it will even shun water when it is available). It can survive indefinitely on dry food, although it also eats plants, which contain a small amount of water. Kangaroo rats even have an uncanny ability to synthesize and secrete salt.

Antelope jackrabbits are often seen bounding about in broad daylight, their gray and brown coats blending seamlessly into the desert landscape. While their 8-inch-long ears are handy for detecting sounds and thus for avoiding predators, they have evolved principally to aid in keeping cool: Hot blood from the body runs through the veins in the transparent-thin ears, from which the heat dissipates into the air. Curiously, the mechanism works only if the animal faces north (a rabbit facing south *absorbs* heat through its ears). The rabbit can also change the color of either flank in an instant from tan to white to befuddle pursuers. Moreover, it can streak across the desert at 35 miles per hour, zigzagging like a football halfback and jumping like its namesake antelope to confuse and outpace predators such as coyotes.

Although often heard, the wily coyote is rarely seen, betraying itself solely by the tracks

Bobcat.

it leaves at night. The kit fox is another master of nocturnal concealment. It forages with its pointed snout close to the ground, checking for scents while its huge ears are cocked and alert to every sound. Secluded mountain canyons are prowled by bobcats and mountain lions. Bighorn sheep also make their homes amid the remote mountain canyons. Lean and muscular, a full-grown ram can grow to 5 feet long and 3 feet high at the shoulders, its massive horns curling back, around, and forward in a full spiral. The sheep sometimes emerge from the mountains at dusk and dawn to nibble the nourishing grass of golf fairways. They usually take off at the slightest approach of humans, however, springing away sure-footedly across the rocks. Though protected by law, the animal suffers from poaching by unscrupulous hunters, who contribute doubly to the demise of the bighorn by targeting the largest rams. The bighorn's natural enemies—mountain lions and coyotes—have also been reduced in numbers, so that the rule of the survival of the fittest no longer applies. Weak, ill, less competent and less alert animals who would otherwise fall prey to predators survive longer, passing their genes down the line so that the bighorn stock as a whole is inferior to prior generations, contributing to its further decline.

The desert is also home to bats, who emerge at night to feast on insects, which they echo-locate in the darkness by emitting an ultrasonic squeak whose echo is picked up by their oversize ears.

Avians of Arid Climes

Birds are well represented. The mellifluous notes of the mockingbird start up with the first hint of dawn. The lyrical chimes of the canyon wren enliven the canyons, while the spotted brown cactus wren stutters from its nest in the midst of cactus branches (the spinier the

Roadrunners include rattlesnakes in their diet. Bert Buxbaum

A great horned owl peers down from a palm tree.

better). Within an hour or two of dawn, the bird chorus dwindles down to occasional singular calls. The nervous clucking of desert quail. The *Urk! Urk!* of ravens. The alarm call of a Gambel's quail warning of the presence of a rattlesnake or coyote.

Most desert birds feed actively in the early morning hours. Later in the day, large birds tend to circle in the sky, cooling on the breezes, while smaller birds shelter in trees and bushes, often with their wings held wide and beaks open. Though a bird's feathers give the impression that the creatures will overheat, in fact they are extremely efficient insulators that keep external heat out just as effectively as they keep body heat in. Birds also have a higher body temperature than mammals and are able to withstand body temperatures as high as 116.5 degrees Fahrenheit. For that reason many birds can sit in the desert sun all day long without ill effect, though they often need to assist cooling by fluttering their throats to create a flow of air across the moist insides of their mouths. Hence, the existence in the desert of "nondesert" birds such as the mourning dove, one of the most common birds of the Palm Springs desert region. Alas, the shade trees planted in urban settings have drawn less benign aliens such as sparrows and starlings, which displace native birds by tearing apart their nest sites to establish their own. The raven population has also soared, much to the detriment of young desert tortoises, whose soft scutes can be penetrated by the ravens' big, hard black beaks.

The ladderback woodpecker can be heard chiseling holes in cardón cacti. When it moves on to another home, its abandoned hole provides a shady lodging for such species as flycatchers, tiny elf owls, and sparrow hawks. The quintessential desert bird is the jaunty, snake-hunting roadrunner, or chaparral cock, often seen racing across the desert floor on its long legs. Though it can fly if needed, its preferred locomotion is to trot tirelessly across the ground on X-shaped clawed feet that provide excellent traction on the desert floor. The roadrunner can get up to 15 miles per hour, employing its foot-long tail as a kind of rudder for turning or as a flap, raised upright like that of an aircraft wing, for sudden stops. Roadrunners typically nest in tall cactus or thorn bush and produce broods of two or three youngsters. It doesn't drink, but gets its water from its omnivorous diet. The bird, which is a cousin to cuckoos, is even capable of killing and eating rattlesnakes. The roadrunner relies on its tremendous agility to dance around the rattler. When the snake has expended its venom striking uselessly at the nimble bird, the roadrunner hops over the snake, kills it with powerful stabs with its beak, and then stuffs the snake whole down its gullet.

Born with a Watertight Skin

Rattlesnakes, stout-bodied with wedge-shaped heads, are ever-present. A vital part of the desert ecosystem, these ruthlessly efficient killers help keep the rodent population within wholesome limits. Five major species of rattlesnakes inhabit cactus country. Most common is the dangerous and wide-ranging Mojave (or ringtail) rattler. The largest rattler is the western diamondback, which can grow to 6 feet in length and injects venom capable of swiftly killing a full-grown man. The blacktail rattler and small tiger rattler are relatively rare. The smallest is the mild-mannered sidewinder rattlesnake (averaging only 18 inches long). Bleached, sand-colored reptiles that blend in with their background, they are masters of concealment and often bury themselves curled up in the soft sand to form an insulating layer overhead—a deadly inconvenience for hikers!

Rattlesnakes hunt mostly at night with the aid of a sensory device in a pit between the eyes and nostril (hence the family name, "pit vipers"). This unique instrument comprises elaborate blood vessels and sensory nerves capable of detecting infrared radiation (heat) and the precise direction and point of the source. Thus, a ground squirrel crouching motionless a meter away in complete darkness is visible to the snake, which glides silently across the sand to strike its prey. The prey usually takes a while to die and often goes staggering away until it succumbs to the viperine venom. Rattlesnakes trail their victims by means of the "Jacobson's organ," a specialized sense organ that tracks the scent particles

Sidewinder Motion

Sidewinder rattlesnakes move forward in a wavelike sideways motion that has evolved as a means to get traction in loose sand. This it achieves by flexing its flank muscles to produce a flowing S-shaped contraction that travels in waves down the body. Having carved a diagonal channel in the sand with its upper body, the snake then slides its lower body into the channel, which acts like a hollowed-out step on which to push itself forward. The upper body lifts in the other direction, then drops to repeat the process. Thus, the body touches the ground at only two points. The snake's motion can be tracked by the ladderlike succession of parallel lines orientated at 45 degrees to the direction of travel.

Mojave rattlesnake. Bert Buxbaum

that the snake's forked tongue picks up. The rattle is composed of interlocking horny pieces, which, when rapidly vibrated, produce an angry buzz that serves as a warning when the snake feels threatened. Every time a rattlesnake sheds its skin, a special hollow scale remains fixed to its tail. A fully mature rattler may have as many as 20 rattles. Unlike most other snakes, rattlesnakes protect their eggs by retaining them inside the body. The babies emerge from the mother's body fully formed.

Since reptiles absorb the sun's energy directly and have no need to convert food into heat, their food requirements are small, as is their need for water, thanks to their thick, watertight skins. Nonetheless, since reptiles' metabolism increases with an increase in temperature, the baking deserts can become too hot even for reptiles. Because they have no physiological way of losing heat, they can keep cool in lethal heat only by hiding from it inside cool, humid burrows. Lizards can withstand much greater temperatures than snakes, which have a thermal optimum better adjusted to the desert night. Thus, lizards are active throughout the day, darting in chase of grasshoppers, flies, and other succulent insect prey.

Hikers should look for the fat chuckwalla lizard, which reaches a length of 18 inches and sheds its skin in patches, as if suffering from a bad sunburn. It inhabits rocky canyons with plentiful shade, and when threatened backs into a crevice and inflates its body to wedge itself in place. It is such a prodigious drinker that it can store water in built-in sacs and even gurgles when it walks, like a hot-water bottle. Like many desert species, it even has its own built-in desalination plant to process briny water during droughts.

The Desert Tortoise

Count yourself very lucky to see a California desert tortoise, the state reptile. This nomadic and solitary reptile shared the earth with the dinosaurs. Today it is protected as an endangered species, and its future is highly uncertain. Although the desert tortoise passes the heat of midafternoon tucked inside its burrow, it tolerates heat well and even on the hottest days can be seen roaming across the flat desert atop its stumplike, scaly legs. It feeds primarily on grasses, desert flowers, and juicy cactus pads, which it chomps with a scissorlike jaw like a cookie cutter. It can go an entire year without drinking water, which it can reabsorb from its oversize bladder (like the kangaroo rat and rattlesnake, it concentrates uric acids and excretes a semisolid acidic paste). When their bodies exceed 105 degrees Fahrenheit, they wet their heads, necks, and front legs with saliva and can even release urine over their back legs to maintain their temperature below that level.

Unlike most vertebrates, which have an internal skeleton, tortoises wear their skeletons like armor plating on the outside of their bodies to protect the vital organs and flesh within. The shell also helps to keep evaporation to a minimum. The males have a prolonged spur on their undershell, used like a lance for jousting with rivals during mating season with the intent of flipping the rival onto its back. The animal uses its large, flattened forelimbs for digging burrows, while females use their hind legs to scoop out nests in which to lay eggs. Intriguingly, the entire brood of hatchlings from any one nest will be of the same sex, depending on the temperature of the sandy soil (cooler for males; warmer for females). Females lay their eggs in early summer. Hatchlings emerge about four months later, but young tortoises take five years or so to develop their hard shell and do not reach maturity for 15 or 20 years, although an adult tortoise may grow to no more than 9 inches long.

Desert tortoise. Bert Buxbaum

Arachnids, Insects, and Relatives

The desert is abuzz with bees, wasps, and flies. Dragonflies flit back and forth across the surface of pools. Butterflies—morning cloaks, painted ladies, monarchs and their cousins, the reddish queen butterfly—brighten the desert, dancing like floating leaves on the wind. At night desert crickets emerge with probing antennae, as do cockroaches, venomous centipedes, and the flightless, 1-inch-long cactus beetle, which feeds on the succulent tissues of cacti, thanks to a tough exoskeleton immune to the stabbing points of the spines. Tiny cactus flies also land to drink at exuding sap and lay their eggs among the spines, where hatching larvae can burrow into the flesh.

Termites and ants are abundant. Cold-blooded creatures, they emerge when temperatures rise above 60 degrees Fahrenheit and retreat to their underground nests when temperatures top 110 degrees. Two of the most common desert ants are the harvesters, which feed on seeds, and the ferocious and omnivorous fire ants (named for the burning sensation their bites inflict), which boil from the ground when their nests are disturbed.

Anyone with a home in the desert can attest to the presence of black widow spiders, easily identified by their large, gloss-black bodies and bright red hourglass belly (the half-size male is brown with no hourglass marking). Since the females hang upside down from their nests, the red markings are underneath to serve as a warning to predators: The black widow's venom is 15 times more potent than that of rattlesnakes and can be fatal to humans. The spider's sticky silk has amazing tensile strength and is highly effective at ensnaring insect prey. In contrast, the green lynx spiders and burrowing wolf spiders spin no webs, preferring to pounce on bees and beetles as they hover in search of pollen. Tarantulas operate the same way. Big as your hand and furry as a teddy bear, this near-sighted nocturnal prowler feeds mostly on insects, small lizards, and even tiny mammals. Despite its reputation, the tarantula is virtually harmless to humans and will bite only if provoked. The chief enemy of the tarantula (besides humans with egos and guns) is the enormous tarantula hawk wasp, unmistakably adorned with brilliant orange wings. Though they feed on nectar, the females paralyze tarantulas with their powerful sting. Dragging the paralyzed spider into her burrow, she then lays an egg upon it and seals the entrance to the hole. When the larvae hatch, they eat the inert yet still-alive host.

Probing around with your hands amid rocks is never a good idea in the desert, where scorpions spend the daylight hours hiding in shady crevices. They stir around dusk, when they emerge to hunt crickets, cockroaches, and other insects, which they subdue with a venomous sting. With their fearsome-looking claws and sharp, curving stinging tail, scorpions are regarded with undue trepidation by humans. Some scorpion species are virtually harmless to humans; others have venom as deadly as any viper. The desert has several

Scorpion Sex

Scorpion sex is a potentially deadly affair. The male stands a real risk of being regarded not as a mate but a meal. Thus, he approaches the female with deliberate caution. First, he grabs her pincers in his. Safely neutralized, she is then hauled around in a shuffling dance that clears the ground of debris. The male then deposits a packet of sperm on the ground and, still grasping the female with their tails intertwined, he waltzes her backward and forward until her sexual opening is directly over his treasure. She picks it up. The two disengage. The male scurries off. And she is left to hatch the eggs inside a pouch. The newborns emerge and clamber onto her back, where they are carried around until mature enough to fend for themselves.

species, running from black to sand-colored and reddish brown, including the vinegaroons, a large species of stingless whip scorpion that lives in deep, moist burrows and is named for the vinegary acid it emits when threatened.

SOCIAL HISTORY

First Inhabitants

The region is full of romantic litter, what author Edward Abbey called "the rust and silence and echoes of human history along dusty desert roads." That history echoes back more than 15,000 years to the arrival of the first "newcomers" to cross the land bridge that once connected Asia to America. Gradually their descendants moved south. The first known occupants of the Palm Springs region arrived about 2,000 years ago. They evolved complex communities in the canyons, where an abundant water supply provided nourishment year-round. The shady canyons provided an escape from the summer heat, and hot springs provided warmth on cold winter nights.

The first visitors came for the curative powers of the desert climate and hot springs that are still owned by the Agua Caliente ("Hot Water") band of Cahuilla Indians. The men hunted quail and rabbit and mountain goat, and even trapped fish in the lakes and streams, and the women gathered acorns, berries, and seeds, and made flour and tortillas from mesquite beans. The mesquite, which can tolerate salty soils as long as they are damp, retains its leaves long after most desert plants. Its edible bean was a staple of the Agua Caliente Indians, who also made liquor from its sugary fruit and used the stalks to

Indian artifacts at the Palm Springs Art Museum.

Agua Caliente Hot Springs historical marker: "The original Palm Springs."

erect their papago homes. Other shrubs from which the Indians derived food, clothing, medicine, and shelter included agave, cat's claw (acacia), the chuparosa, the encilia, desert lavender, yucca, and numerous cacti and wildflowers. Peaceful and full of integrity, these industrious and creative peoples had a reputation as skilled agriculturalists who irrigated fertile land by diverting streams. Their irrigation ditches, dams, and house pits can still be seen in Tahquitz, Chino, and Indians canyons, as can rock art comprising symbolic pictographs and petroglyphs painted and etched, respectively, onto stone.

After possession of California passed from Mexico to the United States, prospectors came to extract what they could from the land and move on. The hills echoed, wrote Edward Abbey, "to the sound of the prospector's pick and the bray of his burro." (Mules were called "Arizona nightingales" for their high-pitched bray.) A fortunate few got lucky panning gravel from streambeds in hopes of finding some "color." Silver miners hacked tunnels out of solid rock. The tunnels were treacherous places; wooden beams were erected along their length to prevent cave-ins. By the mid-1800s the veins had run out and the mines were forsaken and left to the bats.

In the mid-19th century plans were evolved to irrigate the area of today's Palm Springs as an agricultural valley to be named Palm Valley. In 1876 the U.S. government deeded 32,000 acres in trust to the Cahuilla Indians, while the Southern Pacific Railroad Company was given land as an inducement to build a railroad. The Southern Pacific and the Indians got alternating plots in a checkerboard to each side of the tracks. (The U.S. government promised the Southern Pacific every other section of land for 12 miles on either side of the railway line at the completion of the railroad project. In time, the Indian lands turned out to be the most valuable real estate in the region. However, federal law prohibited them from leasing or selling the land to derive income from it; not until President Eisenhower signed the Equalization Act in 1959 were the tribes able to realize a profit.) In 1877 the Southern Pacific Railroad was built, linking Yuma, Arizona, with Los Angeles and running through the Cahuilla Indian reservation. The members of the Cahuilla Nation were placed on various reservations.

Birth of a Playground

In 1853 a U.S. railroad engineer had "discovered" bubbling mineral springs, which he called Agua Caliente. With the railroad in place, visitors soon began to arrive for their health, to hike the canyons, and to learn about Native American culture (an Indian Pageant was eventually started in 1921). Soon enough, crude structures were erected. Palm Springs was born.

The earliest pioneer families clustered their basic wood-and-canvas huts together. The first permanent structure was erected in 1884 by settler "Judge" John Guthrie McCallum, who arrived in search of a hot climate that might cure his young son's tuberculosis. McCallum, a former U.S. Indian agent in San Bernardino, bought 320 acres from a local Indian and opened a general store (he also attempted to divert the Whitewater River 13 miles across searing sands). McCallum's early homestead still stands on Palm Springs Drive alongside Miss Cornelia White's "Little House," made entirely of railroad ties in 1893. A short while later, "Doctor" Welwood Murray, a Scottish-born botanist and pharmacist, built the Palm Springs Hotel—the region's first. He dressed a local Indian as an Arab and had him ride a camel out to the railroad watering stop, 7 miles away, to lure passengers to his hotel, initiating Palm Springs' humble birth as the eventual ultimate American oasis. German-born illustrator Carl Eytel and scenic photographer Stephen Willard fell in love with the landscapes, and their works helped promote Palm Springs.

A decade-long drought that lasted until 1905 (the year Scottish naturalist John Muir arrived in the heat of summer) dashed early hopes, however, and Palm Springs' debut had to await the arrival, in 1908, of "Mother" Nellie Coffman. Finding Murray's hotel rather dour, she opened the society-oriented Desert Inn across the street in 1915. Most of her early guests came for their health, arriving only in the winter months. Thus, Nellie's inn operated initially as a sanatorium. One of her regulars was Fatty Arbuckle, who rented a bungalow for the season. The turn-of-the-century settlement was able to transform itself from humble beginnings into international fame in a relatively short time, thanks to Arbuckle and other stars of the silent screen, who quickly cottoned on to Palm Springs' possibilities as a celebrity hideaway. Among them was the dashing Rudolph Valentino, who galloped over Palm Springs' dunes in *The Sheik* (1921). Directors in jodhpurs with megaphones descended on the desert, making the 100-mile drive through the windswept sands on a rough road to establish a mini movie industry. Palm Springs became a favorite location for desert-themed movies: Theda Bara starred in *Salome* (1910), while Valentino played the part of a legionnaire in *The Foreign Legion* (1928). Frank Capra even filmed *Lost Horizon* here in 1937. It also served well for Wild West shootouts and exotic battlefields halfway around the world.

In 1924 some 30,000 car-mobile tourists arrived to find that streets formerly named North, South, West, and East had been changed to ethnic appellations such as Amado, Baristo, Caballeros, and Tachevah. That year the transition from sleepy desert outpost to glamorous getaway was given a boost when Pearl McCallum McManus (Judge John's daughter) built the Oasis Hotel (designed by Lloyd Wright, eldest son of Frank Lloyd Wright) with the first swimming pool in town. In 1928 Coloradan cattle baron Prescott W. Stevens

La Quinta Resort & Club, circa 1938. La Quinta Resort

added the El Mirador with an eye on the celluloid stars. The Spanish-Moorish-style Mirador, in the north end of town, was managed by Frank Bogert, who later became "cowboy mayor" of Palm Springs (Bogert was a master of publicity, releasing photos of each Hollywood star patron, with the name of the hotel clearly visible). The hotel proved so popular with Hollywood personalities that the residential area around it became known as Movie Colony. The 1920s also saw the opening of two guest ranches—Smoke Tree and Deep Well—that catered to the evolving taste for the dude ranch experience. The ranch hotels were notably unpretentious for the region and time, despite the presence of Walt and Lillian Disney, who bought a home here and were regular figures at Smoke Tree. And in 1927 a developer named Walter H. Morgan initiated expansion of the greater Palm Springs realm by building a secluded resort—it would eventually evolve into the world-renowned La Quinta Resort & Club—30 miles south in the desert.

Within a few short years, celebrities such as Marlene Dietrich, Clark Gable, Bette Davis, Carole Lombard, and Errol Flynn had become regular fixtures alongside Hollywood moguls Darryl Zanuck, Samuel Goldwyn, and Walt Disney. For five decades Palm Springs was a privileged playground to the stars. Locals—and the media—looked the other way at the indiscretions of Hollywood idols, who had found a demure hideaway at the foot of the mountains for their wild parties and peccadilloes. The Kelloggs, Maytags, and Marses were among the many plutocrat families who also made Palm Springs their winter home.

Palm Springs' prominence was boosted during World War II, when General George S. Patton chose the area down valley to train his tank regiments in the desert (the cul-de-sac configuration of much of Palm Springs also dates from World War II, when lollipop-shaped hard-stands—parking places with an approach road—were built for warplanes). The war provided a bit of a boom for hotels, bars, and, of course, prostitution. Thousands of maids, cooks, gardeners, and chauffeurs were employed as a whole new industry took hold and the playground of the wealthy in the 1920s and 1930s reconfigured itself as increasing numbers of middle-class vacationers flocked after 1945 with the advent of air service.

Hollywood Heyday

Meanwhile, the arrival of air-conditioning presaged a boom in the residential population. Before refrigerated air-conditioning became standard, architects could go only so far in controlling heat, and most residents were seasonals who packed up and returned to cooler climes in summer. President Dwight Eisenhower unwittingly added to the real estate boom when he arrived for vacation in February 1954. Eisenhower's trip coincided with the infancy of television, which showcased the sunny desert playground to the entire nation. (Eisenhower retired here in 1962, living at the Eldorado Country Club in Indian Wells until his death in 1969.)

After World War II local architectural tastes began to change, too, as the Spanish-style village of stucco, adobe, and ranch styles evolved into a city of tomorrow, with new banks, shops, offices, homes, and hotels in modernist style. "The MODERN CITY in the Desert," proclaimed a postcard by the City National Bank of the eccentric atomic age buildings constructed in the desert sand by such leading young architects as Albert Frey, John Lautner, and Richard Neutra. Although the movement took flight across the nation, nowhere did modernism take wing with such impact. The stark, empty desert provided a more dramatic backdrop than anywhere else, while, suggested writer Alan Hess, "the eerie visual echoes of atomic bomb blasts in the Nevada desert . . . added to the futurism associated with the desert and modernism in the public eye." Palm Springs' handsome modernist buildings, both private and public, were showcased in movies and magazines, while the fame of Palm Springs' residents gave the town nationwide prominence and luster as a retreat of the wealthy. Carefully considered publicity shots also helped shape the public image.

Palm Springs became the very epitome of glamour, wealth, and relaxation as the influence and power of Hollywood blossomed after World War II, along with that of the TV and recording industries. "At weekends, a stream of besotted lovers, transients, and misfits streamed to Palm Springs, where a colony of drunks and fornicators had been founded," commented British actor Patrick Macnee, who made Palm Springs his home. The right money ensured that the police looked the other way. The "really juicy stuff was covered up, suppressed," claimed writer Ray Mungo. "In Palm Springs they can party all weekend, let their hair down, drink into oblivion, easily obtain all drugs, keep their mistresses and boyfriends, go gay or bi- or pansexual, hide from the law or the press, and have it all without the glare of publicity, without the risk of exposure." It was here, on March 24, 1962, for example, that President John F. Kennedy and Marilyn Monroe made love at Bing Crosby's home.

"The season" traditionally kicked off in late October with a party at the Racquet Club, where Frank Sinatra, Sammy Davis Jr., Bing Crosby, and Bob Hope—a long-term resident, Hope was named an honorary mayor—performed for their peers. Crosby, who played piano, was known for pouring Glenlivet Scotch into everyone's drink. The infamous members-only Racquet Club, with state-of-the-art tennis courts at the north end of town, was owned by soft-spoken actor Charlie Farrell and his partner Ralph Bellamy. The club had no liquor license when it first opened on Christmas Day 1933, so it sold Coca-Cola, and the beer and liquor were on the house. Later, guests could sip a Bloody Mary at the Bamboo Lounge, where the drink was created. The Racquet Club rapidly became *the* place to see and be seen among the elite, who paid a $650 annual membership and whose party antics here rose to the status of legend. (If ever the bedroom antics were exposed, "We'd all be in San Quentin or divorced," quipped Farrell, whose sitcom, "The Charles Farrell Show," was loosely based on the goings on at the club.) It was here, in 1948, that Hollywood photographer Bruno Bernard and agent Johnny Hyde "discovered" 22-year-old Norma Jeane Mortenson, whom Hyde, after an exchange of sexual favors, according to author Howard Johns, renamed and launched to stardom as blond bombshell Marilyn Monroe. The club later promoted itself shamelessly, proclaiming that patrons could "Swim in the same Olympic-size pool where Marilyn Monroe was discovered." (Marilyn became a regular to Palm Springs and even honeymooned in the area with hubby Joe DiMaggio in January 1954.) Many a famous Hollywood couple had their first sexual encounters together here. "Racquet Club guests liked to play musical bedrooms," claimed Johns. "Marie McDonald and Harry Karl, Harry Karl and Debbie Reynolds, Debbie Reynolds and Eddie Fisher, Eddie Fisher and Elizabeth Taylor." Secret lovers Spencer Tracy and Katharine Hepburn assumed a cloak of invisibility that the club was happy to help maintain. And actress Jamie Lee Curtis was supposedly conceived here when Tony Curtis and Janet Leigh made out at the Racquet Club. Stars and starlets vied for attention, indulging their fancies, with the staff at their beck and call. Al Jolson. John Barrymore. Rita Hayworth. Clark Gable and Carole Lombard. Douglas Fairbanks. Jean Harlow. Spencer Tracy. Jane Russell. Rock Hudson. And presidents, and even Prince Philip, were guests.

Scores of celebrities bought homes in Palm Springs during the postwar era, including Elvis Presley and, most notoriously, Liberace, who arrived in Palm Springs in 1952 and lived a life of utter decadence behind the gates of his various local homes. "There are enough famous people in the desert that it's no longer about being famous. I would see Greta Garbo window shopping," noted Robert Wagner.

One name above all, however, stood out. Frank Sinatra's move to Palm Springs in 1947 signaled the beginning of "the Sinatra era," which lasted half a century, until he moved to Rancho Mirage shortly before his death. Throughout the 1950s and '60s, the city was closely associated with the vibe of the "Rat Pack," who considered it their favorite retreat. Sinatra, Sammy Davis Jr., and Dean Martin were famous for nonstop nightclubbing at the Chi Chi Club and the Doll House, where the bar stools were equipped with seat belts. Entertainers such as Nat King Cole, Lena Horne, Louis Armstrong, and Peggy Lee regularly warmed up their fellow stars at these supper clubs when the Rat Pack weren't stealing the limelight.

However, by the 1960s, glamour and business were moving "down valley" to Rancho Mirage, Palm Desert, and Indian Wells, where the craze for golf had usurped tennis as the game of choice. Golf courses became the great hallmark of the recreation culture of the second half of the 20th century and never more so than in the Coachella Valley. The era saw emerald fairways spread across the valley floor as dozens of country club homes went up inside gated communities. The concept of the "fairway home" began at the Thunderbird Country Club, where the electric golf cart was invented. Thunderbird had been converted from a western-style horse ranch to a more sophisticated golf club in 1951, beginning the post–World War II golf boom and, along with it, the concept of financing the technically complex golf course construction by real estate sales. The idea took off like a long drive when Hoagy Carmichael, Bing Crosby, Bob Hope, and Lucille Ball and Desi Arnaz all bought Thunderbird homes.

Decline and Revival

As the energy (and money) moved to newer communities down valley, Palm Springs began to be considered outdated and déclassé. The city suffered an economic downturn and fell into a state of decay. A layer of dust gathered on the bric-a-brac that filled the thrift and consignment stores. By the eighties, half the storefronts in Palm Springs were empty. "FOR LEASE" signs flapped in the wind. The town developed a seedy image, not least thanks to its raunchy side as *the* West Coast "spring-break party hole," drawing beer-guzzling frat boys and butt-baring babes. Spring break came to the town in the wake of the movie *Palm Springs Weekend*, when blond heartthrob Troy Donahue got ripped by the pool. It was a fitting moment for Jim and Tammy Faye Bakker, who briefly brought Palm Springs back into the national limelight with their farcical religious soap-opera that ended when Jim, the televangelist with a taste for kink and Rolex watches, received a 45-year prison term and a $500,000 fine for defrauding investors. Meanwhile, long-term resident and keen Palm Springs advocate Kirk Douglas helped the city cling to a modicum of respectability as a philanthropic patron to the arts.

In 1988 songwriter Sonny Bono (the male half of Sonny and Cher; the couple divorced in 1974) was elected mayor. Bono had moved to Palm Springs in 1986 and had opened Bono's Racquet Club Restaurant, while his wife Mary ran Mary's Nightclub. Although derided by many at the time, Bono is credited with having cleaned up and revived Palm Springs. In 1991 he passed his famous "anti-thong ordinance" in a successful effort to tone

Sinatra's Palm Springs

PALM SPRINGS CONFIDENTIAL

When the skinny Columbia recording artist, MGM movie star, and teenage bobby-soxer idol first hit Palm Springs, the place was already jumping. After he arrived, things really started to hop.

—Howard Johns

Sinatra's first Palm Springs home was "Twin Palms" (1148 E. Alejo Rd., Palm Springs, CA 92262; www.sinatrahouse.com), purpose-built for the singer in 1947 by Palm Springs architect E. Stewart Williams; the location was apparently chosen so that "The Voice" could be close to the downtown action. Built at a cost of $110,000, the four-bedroom house—a classic of "desert modern" architecture—featured electronically operated automated gates, a movie projection room, and an intercom system, and was named for the two tall slender palm trees that still stand in the yard. A floor-to-ceiling, retractable sliding wall opened to the piano-shaped pool. Twin Palms was "a house at ease, with right angles tempered by oblique angles and curves," wrote author Alan Hess, and perfectly captured "the smooth craft and the informality of the client. It is the pinnacle of hip." This, despite its surprisingly small master bedroom (though with a magnificent view over the pool to the mountains).

The house, and the Sinatra lifestyle with which it became associated, helped define the glamorous image of Palm Springs. Sinatra lived here with his first wife, Nancy Barbato (they divorced in 1951), and, later, Ava Gardner, his second wife, whom he met in 1950 at the legendary Chi Chi Club in Palm Springs (the club formerly stood at 271 North Palm Canyon Dr., but was torn down in 1977). He was dancing with Lana Turner at the time, and Gardner was with eccentric billionaire Howard Hughes. The bandleader apparently said "Change partners!" and Frank and Ava waltzed all the way back to Frank's pad. Sinatra and Gardner married in November 1951.

Each afternoon Sinatra would hoist a flag bearing the Jack Daniel's logo, signaling to friends that it was time for martinis. In his early years the Chairman of the Board was a fixture of the local bar scene and

down the party. He famously rode around town on a black Harley-Davidson to help enforce the law. He also established the Palm Springs Film Festival and brought the Virginia Slims Classic Tennis Tournament to town (his plans for a Grand Prix motorcar race through the town never succeeded, however). Meanwhile, with Palm Springs in a tailspin, city fathers looked for a quick fix through gambling. Easily done. The Agua Caliente Indian tribe owned half the town. Permitted to have legal gambling as a "sovereign nation," they opened a cash-generating Vegas-style downtown casino. Other casinos soon followed.

By the mid-1990s the city had initiated an impressive comeback. Fortunately, there's nothing like decades in the doldrums to keep history intact: The city's unique modernist architecture was actually preserved by its 1970s tailspin. Gays flocked to snap up distressed modernist homes on the cheap, restore them, and turn many into trendy restaurants and boutique hotels. Newspapers and magazines began to report on the "retro chic" appeal of a historic town rediscovering itself while preserving the atmosphere of America's glory years. The Hollywood set began to return, drawn by Palm Springs' retro-chic character and the new breed of hip hotels. By the millennium, Palm Springs was sufficiently back in the international limelight to proclaim itself a year-round destination. Today winter brings the likes of Chris O'Donnell and Donatella Versace, while Brad Pitt and Angelina Jolie fly in their own planes to hang out. The wind turbines northwest of town supply much of the valley's electricity. The rest is supplied by an energetic young group of permanent residents—primarily gays—who have put an invigorating new spark back in town.

drank at clubs like Pal Joey's, the Chi Chi Club, and Ruby's Dunes. Sinatra usually arrived with an entourage, including his bodyguards (among them, "Jerry the Crusher," named for his habit of crushing Coca-Cola bottles with his bare hands). Sinatra apparently never sat with his back to the door; instead, he sat in a corner and even had his own corner booth at Ruby's Dunes, plus a red telephone for his personal use. Sinatra tipped big. A major patron of the Desert Hospital and Eisenhower Medical Center, he is also remembered for his philanthropy. Often, when he read in the newspaper about someone having difficulty or trouble, he would pop an anonymous check in the mail to the person.

Frank Sinatra's recording studio in his Palm Springs house.

Sinatra was "Mr. Palm Springs," considered a local hero despite his frequent public tantrums and drunkenness, resulting in some famous scenes. On October 21, 1952, for example, Sinatra rowdily threw both Lana Turner and Gardner into the street (though Sinatra and Gardner separated the following year, she remained his friend); a crack in the bathroom sink was supposedly caused by a champagne bottle that Sinatra threw at Gardner during the fight.

In 1957 Sinatra moved to "The Compound," in Rancho Mirage (see the special topic, The Compound, in the Culture chapter). After he died in 1998, Sinatra received a star-spangled funeral in Los Angeles, then was flown back to Palm Springs. As his plane approached, air traffic controllers were heard to say: "You're clear for landing—welcome home, Mr. Sinatra." He was buried at Desert Memorial Park, in Cathedral City. He is commemorated with a boulevard named for Ol' Blue Eyes in Rancho Mirage.

Eagle Rider motorcycle rentals, Palm Springs International Airport.

2

Transportation

Get the Top Down!

One look at a map should be sufficient for most people to get a good sense of the layout and to find their way around the Palm Springs region, at least in broad terms. The Coachella Valley is framed on the east by Interstate 10 and on the west by California Highway 111, the main thoroughfare, running parallel to the freeway. Between them the valley is laid out in a checkerboard grid of north-south and east-west boulevards connecting the highway and freeway.

Most traffic moving "down valley" or "up valley" flows along these two routes. Interstate 10 is preferred for rapid transit, but Highway 111 is a far more rewarding drive. Edged on its west by rugged mountains, this winding, palm-lined route is a scenic stunner, with dips, rises, and sweeping bends adding to the fun. It's also the valley's commercial thoroughfare: Many of the region's key hotels, restaurants, and shopping malls line the route. Anyone who last knew the highway a decade ago won't recognize it today. More and more traffic lights have gone up to regulate the ever-increasing traffic flows, and what was once a carefree drive can be a crawling stop-and-go experience at certain times of day, although fortunately L.A.-style gridlock there is not. During rush hour, savvy locals know to take to the less-trafficked boulevards—even the zigzag route that this may require can cut down on the time it takes to get from one end of the valley to the other at rush hour.

Given the region's relative affluence, it's perhaps no surprise that the private plane is a popular way of arriving and departing. The valley has several small airstrips in addition to Palm Springs International Airport, superbly situated so close to downtown that the city's town hall is literally across the street.

There are numerous ways to get to and around the Palm Springs region. Let us be your guide.

Getting to Palm Springs and the Desert Resorts

By Air

Most air travelers to Palm Springs arrive at and depart from **Palm Springs International Airport (PSP)**, which is mere minutes from downtown and within easy driving distance of other Coachella Valley cities. During peak winter months, 13 airlines offer nonstop flights to Palm Springs from 18 destinations throughout the United States and Canada. Many

other travelers utilize **Los Angeles International Airport (LAX)** or **Los Angeles / Ontario International Airport (ONT)**, 35 miles east of Los Angeles.
Bermuda Dunes Regional Airport (UDD), in Bermuda Dunes, 13 miles southeast of Palm Springs, and **Desert Resorts Regional Airport (TRM)**, in Thermal, 20 miles southeast of Palm Springs, have small-plane charter service.
Palm Springs International Airport: 760-318-3800; 3400 E. Tahquitz Canyon Way; www.palmspringsairport.com.

By Car

Although aircraft and buses will bring you to the valley, a car is a virtual necessity once you arrive. Public transportation is somewhat limited, especially to outlying attractions, and distances in this part of California are considerably greater than many visitors may imagine. Traffic along Highway 111 is fairly heavy during weekday rush hours and on weekends in winter months. Fortunately, there isn't a public parking meter in the valley, except for a single meter within the Blue Skies Mobile Home Park (see Historic Sites, in the Culture chapter).

Renting a Car or Motorcycle

Since a car is almost a requirement in the Desert Resorts region, visitors arriving by air inevitably rent a vehicle. Most major rental companies are represented at the international airports and are usually helpful in plotting routes as well as providing maps. Just in case, a few directions:
Los Angeles International Airport: To find your way to Palm Springs from Southern California's largest airport, take N. Sepulveda Boulevard south to I-105. Take this freeway eastbound to connect with I-605 northbound. Stay on I-605 to I-10. Take I-10 eastbound all the way to the Palm Springs exits, or those serving cities farther down-valley. Miles: 122 to downtown Palm Springs. Time: 2.5 hours minimum, depending on traffic.
Ontario International Airport: To reach the Palm Springs region, take E. Airport Drive east to S. Haven Avenue; turn left and follow the signs for I-10 eastbound. Stay on I-10 until you see the Palm Springs exits. Miles: 70 to downtown Palm Springs. Time: 1 hour.

You can also rent a car after arriving in the area. Reservations up to a week in advance are recommended during busy winter months. Local information and reservations numbers are listed below.
Alamo Rent-a-Car: 760-778-6271 or 1-800-327-9633; www.alamo.com
Avis: 760-778-6300 or 1-800-331-1212; www.avis.com
Aztec Rent-a-Car: 760-325-2294
Budget Rent-a-Car: 760-778-1960 or 1-800-221-1203; www.budget.com
Dollar Rent-a-Car: 760-325-7333 or 1-800-800-4000; www.dollar.com
Enterprise Rent-a-Car: 760-778-0054 or 1-800-261-7331; www.enterprise.com
Hertz: 760-778-5100 or 1-800-654-3131; www.hertz.com
National Rent-a-Car: 760-327-1438 or 1-800-227-7368; www.nationalcar.com
Palm Springs is a popular destination with motorcyclists, many of whom choose to rent a motorcycle when they arrive. You can rent Harley-Davidsons at the Palm Springs International Airport from **Eaglerider Motorcycle Rentals**: 760-251-5990; www.eaglerider.com

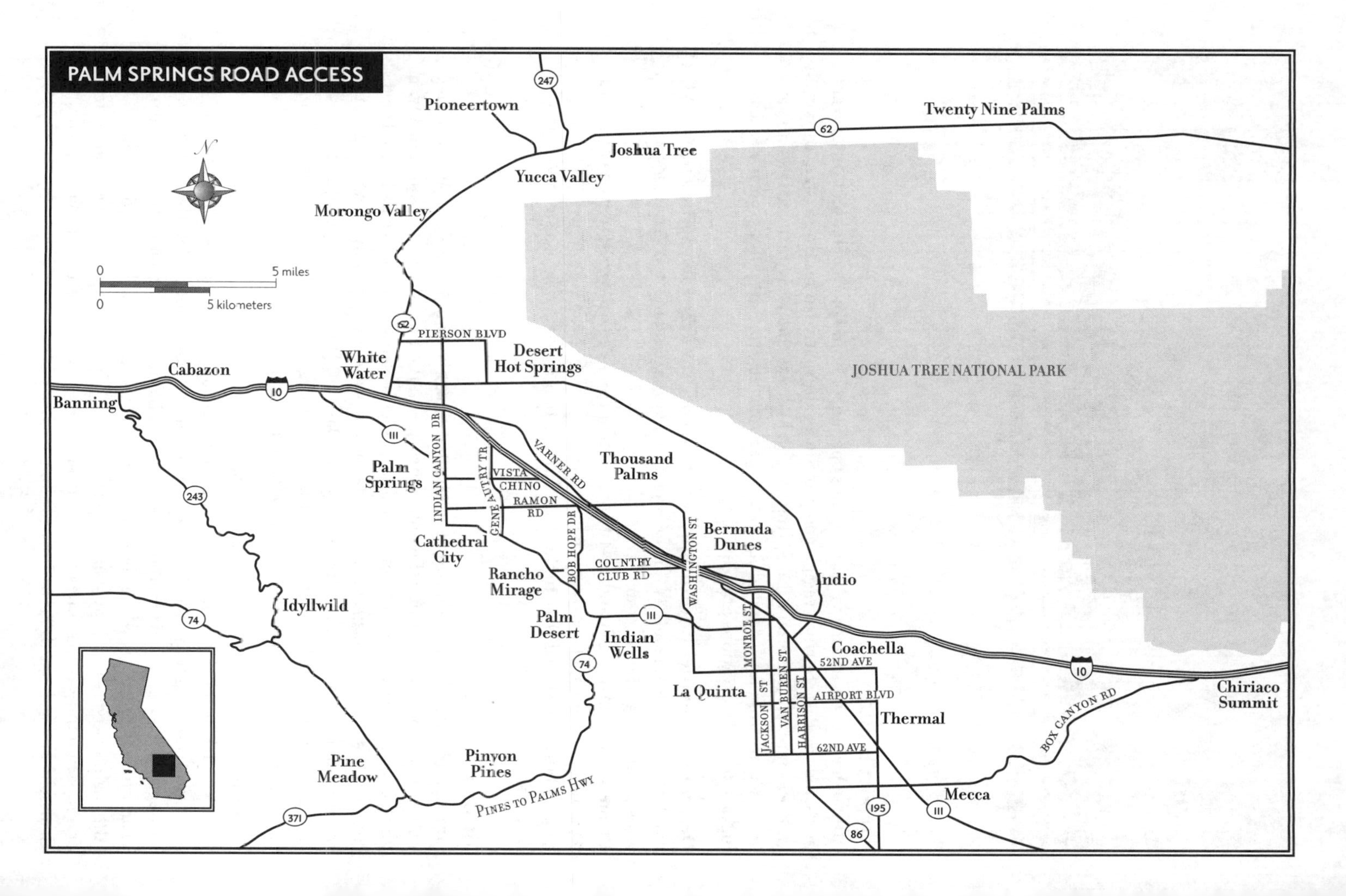
PALM SPRINGS ROAD ACCESS
N
0
5 miles
0
5 kilometers
Pioneertown
Twenty Nine Palms
Joshua Tree
Yucca Valley
Morongo Valley
PIERSON BLVD
White Water
Desert Hot Springs
JOSHUA TREE NATIONAL PARK
Cabazon
Banning
INDIAN CANYON DR
VARNER RD
Thousand Palms
Palm Springs
GENE AUTRY TR
VISTA CHINO
RAMON RD
BOB HOPE DR
WASHINGTON ST
Bermuda Dunes
Cathedral City
COUNTRY CLUB RD
Rancho Mirage
Indio
Idyllwild
Palm Desert
Indian Wells
MONROE ST
Coachella
52ND AVE
La Quinta
JACKSON ST
VAN BUREN ST
HARRISON ST
AIRPORT BLVD
Thermal
62ND AVE
BOX CANYON RD
Chiriaco Summit
Pine Meadow
Pinyon Pines
PINES TO PALMS HWY
Mecca
247
62
10
111
243
74
371
195
86

Palm Springs International Airport.

Airport Shuttle

Although relatively expensive, shuttle vans operate to/from Los Angeles and Ontario airports and the Palm Springs region and provide an alternative to renting a car at the airport. One-way fares to/from the Palm Springs region begin at about $65 to/from ONT and at about $85 to/from LAX, depending on the operator, the drop-off point, and any excess luggage fees. Reservations are required.

Desert Valley Shuttle: Twice-daily scheduled service from the Palm Springs region to ONT and LAX, plus nonscheduled "floater" vans, 760-251-4020 or 1-800-413-3999; www.palmspringsshuttle.com
Prime Time Shuttle: LAX and ONT to the Palm Springs region, 310-536-7922 or 1-800-733-8267; www.primetimeshuttle.com
SuperShuttle: LAX and ONT to the Palm Springs region, 909-984-0040 or 760-320-6600; www.supershuttle.com

By Bus

Greyhound buses serve Indio from Los Angeles, Phoenix, San Bernardino, and San Diego, with connecting service from other cities throughout the United States. Unfortunately, in 2006 Greyhound was evicted from its Palm Springs locale and has since had trouble getting permits to establish a replacement station. At press time the only Greyhound station in the Coachella Valley was in Indio, at 45-525 Oasis St. However, in spring 2008 Greyhound announced plans to utilize the Palm Springs train station, on Garnet Station Road, at the north end of Indian Canyon Road, near I-10.

Greyhound: 1-800-231-2222; www.greyhound.com
Once you are inside the Palm Springs region, public bus service is available through **Sunline Transit Agency**, which operates modern, air-conditioned "SunBus" vehicles throughout the valley. This method of travel could be indispensable for the Palm Springs visitor on a tight budget. Buses have wheelchair lifts and bike racks. One drawback: Although relatively numerous, many bus stops are not sheltered, and it can be an ordeal in summer months waiting beneath the brutal blitz of the midday sun. SunBus 111 connects Coachella and Indio with Palm Springs along Highway 111.

Air-conditioned SunBus vehicles operate throughout the Coachella Valley.

One-way fares cost $1, regardless of distance traveled (transfers for a multiple route cost 25 cents). Exact fares are required, as drivers do not give change. Sunline's Web site provides complete information, including a detailed route map.

For schedules and information, call 760 343-3456 or 1-800-347-8628, or check their Web site at www.sunline.org.

By Train

Amtrak's Sunset Limited operates three days a week between Los Angeles and New Orleans, stopping at the unstaffed Palm Springs station at the north end of Indian Road, about 6 miles north of Palm Springs and just south of I-10. However, the only service here is a public phone, and the station is isolated. It's wise to make prior arrangements for pick-up upon arrival.

Amtrak California Motor Coach operates daily between Bakersfield and Indio (Jackson St. and Indio Blvd.) and stops in Palm Desert (Westfield Shopping Center) and Palm Springs (Palm Springs International Airport) en route. The *San Joaquin* train service linking Bakersfield with San Francisco and Sacramento allows for trips to northern and central California without having to drive through Los Angeles.

For Amtrak information and reservations call 1-800-872-7245, or check their Web site at www.amtrakcalifornia.com.

By Limousine

For many visitors to the Palm Springs region, chauffeured travel goes hand in hand with the luxury lifestyle with which the area is synonymous. For others, a limousine ride through Palm Springs and the Desert Resorts can be a romantic and unforgettable luxury

Palm Springs and Desert Resorts Access

Approximate mileage and times by car between towns and cities:

Palm Springs to:	Time	Miles
Cabazon	15 min	17
Cathedral City	10 min	5
Coachella	37 min	30
Desert Hot Springs	18 min	12
Idyllwild	1 hr 15 min	48
Indio	33 min	26
Laguna Beach	2 hr	108
La Quinta	30 min	24
Las Vegas	4 hr 15 min	279
Los Angeles	2 hr	107
Mexicali	2 hr	109
Oceanside	2 hr	112
Phoenix	4 hr	269
Rancho Mirage	22 min	12
Riverside	1 hr	52
Sacramento	8 hr	489
San Diego	2.5 hr	120
San Francisco	8 hr	487
Tucson	6 hr	385
Yucca Valley	35 min	26

that represents the ultimate in personal transportation.

The region has an abundance of professional limousine services. Most offer daylong, fixed-rate touring packages, as well as customized itineraries. Per-hour rates range from $60, depending on the limo and the tour. That doesn't include taxes, driver's gratuities, parking fees, or any miscellaneous extra charges. Reservations are required at least two or three days in advance, and as much as a week or longer during winter months.
For your added safety, ensure that the limousine service you book with is licensed and insured. Your hotel concierge should be able to recommend a reputable company. A few of the area's most respected companies are listed below:

Cardiff Limousine: 760-568-1403 or 1-800-669-0355; www.cardifflimo.com
Limo 4U: 760-322-1881 or 1-888-546-6148; www.limo4ups.com
Palm Springs Limo: 760-320-0044 or 1-800-355-7302; www.palmspringslimo.com

By Taxi

Taxis are a staple of transport in and around Palm Springs. The standard of service is very high, and a large number of taxis serve the city and Desert Resorts. However, hailing a taxi on the street is nigh impossible; instead, except at the airport and in downtown Palm Springs, expect to have to call a taxi company. The cab companies below operate around the clock, seven days a week, but some companies close down during summer months, when the wait for a taxi can be longer. The airport drop fee is $3.75, and fares average $3 per mile.

Airport Taxi: 760-862-9000; www.airporttaxips.com
City Cab: 760-416-2594
Classic Cab: 760-322-3111
United Taxi: 760-866-9262; www.unitedtaxips.com
VIP Express Taxi: 760-322-2264

Within the Valley

The Palm Springs region stretches from Cabazon (known for its Desert Hills Premium Outlet) to Coachella, a distance of some 50 miles. Moving through the valley is easy going. Highway 111 runs along the western foothills of the San Jacinto and Santa Rosa mountains and is the main boulevard linking all the cities. Most of the region's traffic takes this route, which has dozens of stoplights and can be slow going during rush hour. The route, however, is winding and superbly scenic, and most of the valley's important restaurants, shopping malls, and other facilities (including hotels) line the route.

If speed is of the essence, Interstate 10 (I-10), which connects Los Angeles with Arizona, will whisk you from one end of the valley to the other in no time at all. The freeway runs northwest-southeast clean through the center of the valley, well east of most towns (Desert Hot Springs and Thousand Palms are the exceptions; they lie to the east of the freeway) before turning east at Coachella for Arizona. High winds sometimes scour the valley, kicking up fierce dust storms that can obliterate drivers' vision.

Within Palm Springs, Highway 111 becomes Palm Canyon Drive, lined with boutiques, art galleries, restaurants, and bars. The 2-mile-long main drag, known as "the Strip," runs north-south through the heart of town and connects all the districts before turning east for Cathedral City and the desert resorts beyond.

On a macro level, the Coachella Valley is laid out in a large grid, with major thoroughfares named for luminaries in the region's history: Gerald Ford Drive, Frank Sinatra Drive, Bob Hope Drive, Barbara Stanwyck Road. These two- or three-lane boulevards run north-south and east-west, connecting Highway 111 to I-10.

From the north: Travelers from the north, including Los Angeles, have only one option, as the only entry to the valley is via I-10, which channels downhill through the San Gorgonio Pass. There's always a strong tailwind, which combines with the gradient to keep drivers on their toes in an effort to control their speed. Highway 111, the first exit for the valley, leads 10 miles along the base of Mount San Jacinto before becoming Palm Canyon Drive, leading through the heart of Palm Springs. This remote, unlit, virtually unpopulated section of Highway 111 is often patrolled by police on the lookout for speedsters. Incredibly strong gusts of wind sometimes sweep down the mountain valleys with sufficient force to push cars clean across the road. Drive with caution! If you stay on I-10, you can follow it southeast to Indian Road, which leads (east) to Desert Hot Springs and (west) to Palm Springs. Other exits off I-10 are clearly marked for each of the major cities in the valley.

From the east: Drivers arriving from Phoenix, Arizona, do so on I- 10, which runs through Chiriaco Summit and along the southern border of Joshua Tree National Park, then drops into the Coachella Valley just north of the Salton Sea. Paralleling I-10 farther south is I-8, which connects Tucson, Arizona, with San Diego and runs just north of the Mexican border for much of the way. To reach the Coachella Valley and Palm Springs from I-8, exit at El Centro and follow either Highway 111 along the east shore of the Salton Sea or Highway 78 and then Highway 86 along the west shore.

From the west and southwest: San Diego and the beaches of Orange County are separated from the Coachella Valley by rugged mountains. From San Diego you can take I-8 to El Centro, then take either Highway 111 or 78 (see above). A more scenic route, handy for residents of Oceanside, is to take Highway 78 east via Anza-Borrego Desert State Park, then turn north at the junction with Highway 86. The most scenic route, if you have the time, is to follow I-15 to Temecula and cut east through lush wine country along Highway 79. At Aguanga turn north onto Highway 371, which climbs into the San Jacinto Mountains; turn right at the junction with Highway 74 and follow this scenic route—known as the "Palms to Pines Highway"—until it switchbacks downhill to connect with Highway 111 in Palm Desert.

The Hyatt Grand Champions.

Palm Springs Desert Resorts Conventions & Visitors Authority

3

LODGING

Home Away from Home

Desert hoteliers love to brag about the stars who spent a night under their roofs. "Sinatra slept here" is no idle chatter. Palm Springs alone has more than 130 hotels, and almost every one has played host to a coterie of the rich and famous. There's something for everyone, from intimate bed-and-breakfast inns and slightly jaded classics to ritzy spa-resorts and retro-hip exemplars of the modernist motel style.

In Palm Springs especially, a new generation of hoteliers has been transforming midcentury motels into stylish boutique retreats. Most tend toward the high end. The city's social waters teem again at the pools of Midcentury Modern motels that have been revived with a twist of kitsch. Many are furnished by modernist purists with top-dollar retro pieces. Some simulate the house-party atmosphere, enabling you to feel like an old-time movie star as you sip your martini poolside. Most of the city's new crop of boutique hotels and inns congregate around the Tennis Club district, which begins one block west of Palm Canyon Drive—right in the heart of downtown. Palm Springs doesn't lack for large-scale hotels, either. And at press time, work was under way on a string of new superchic hotels, including the 200-room Mondrian Hotel and 490-room Hard Rock Hotel.

Desert Hot Springs is known for its intimate spa hotels, where guests check in to receive therapeutic treatments and laze by the thermal pools with martinis, or at least sparkling water, at hand. Down valley, Palm Desert, Indian Wells, and La Quinta are venues for a mix of roadside motels and large-scale deluxe resorts, most with their own golf courses and sumptuous spas.

Although the desert communities boast world-class deluxe resorts and literally thousands of condos and villas for private rental, they also serve budget tastes. If all you seek is a motel chain, you'll find all the familiar names represented, along with a wide range of independent motels, many of which promote themselves with fanciful names. Within the city of Palm Springs, the title "motel" is not permitted, so it pays to check carefully to ascertain that the "inn" or "bed & breakfast" is what it claims to be. A true Palm Springs B&B is an intimate, serene, and sometimes luxurious (and pricey) family-run hotel. Many of the finest are run by—and principally for—gays and concentrate in the Warm Springs district. Here again, you should check carefully, as many gay-focused establishments are sexually permissive and promiscuous places. There's also no shortage of clothing-optional spa resorts, many still catering to a randy clientele as in days of yore. But nude recreation has also gone mainstream, and there are more than 30 clothing-optional and naturist resorts in the valley, placing the Palm Springs region at the forefront in the nation.

The Palm Springs Bureau of Tourism publishes a 60-page guide, *Historic Inns of Palm Springs*.

Lodging Notes

Minimum Stay: A majority of inns and B&Bs require a two-night minimum on weekends. A three-night stay may be required on holiday weekends, while private condo/villa rentals often require a minimum one-week stay during peak season.
Reservations/Cancellations: Reservations are advisable (even essential for some resorts) during "the season," which runs January through April, when it's wise to reserve as far in advance as possible. A deposit by credit card for the first night is usually required. Expect a charge for last-minute cancellations.
Restrictions: Smoking is not permitted in most inns and hotels, although the casino hotels are an exception. A few small boutique hotels permit pets, and a small fee usually applies. As a general rule, children under 12 are discouraged, but many properties welcome children, even infants. The major resorts usually furnish room service, often around the clock, and WiFi or high-speed Internet is more or less standard, along with direct-dial telephones and cable TV. B&Bs and small inns may offer limited room service.
Rates and Credit Cards: Sure, it's hot in summer, May to November. But that also means bargain time, with some accommodations offering savings up to 50 percent over high-season rates. Likewise, midweek rates may be significantly less than weekend rates. Hotels (and most vacation rentals) add a Transient Occupancy Tax (TOT) to your room rate for stays of less than 29 days. The TOT rate varies by city and hotel type (from 9 percent in Palm Desert to 13.5 percent for convention hotels in Palm Springs). Some hotels also add on a "utility surcharge" and often a "resort charge" (for parking facilities, the morning paper, etc.).

Lodging Price Codes

Inexpensive:	Up to $100
Moderate:	$100 to $150
Expensive:	$150 to $250
Very Expensive:	Over $250

Credit Cards

AE—American Express
DC—Diners Club
CB—Carte Blanche
MC—MasterCard
D—Discover Card
V—Visa

LODGING IN PALM SPRINGS

Bed-and-Breakfast Inns / Boutique Hotels

BALLANTINE'S ORIGINAL

Innkeepers: Marty and Barb Cohen
760-320-1178 or 1-800-485-2808;
fax: 760-320-5308
www.ballantineshotels.com
E-mail: info@ballantineshotels.com
1420 N. Indian Canyon Dr., Palm Springs, CA 92262
Price: Very Expensive
Credit Cards: AE, D, MC, V
Special Features: Pool, massage, concierge service

Emphasizing vintage fifties kitsch, this chic boutique retreat was one of the first Palm Springs hotels to lead the city's Midcentury Modernism revival. With their spectacular contemporary conversion of an earlier hotel, the two English owners have created a visual stunner that melds clinical whites with blinding flashes of color. No wonder it's been featured in top magazines, from *Elle* to *Vogue*. The intimate hotel has a total of 14 rooms, all differently themed: Maxfield Parrish blues in the Audrey Hepburn Room, leopard prints in the African Room, and lipstick pink in the Marilyn Suite, with its voluptuous couches and rose-tinted rotary phone, chenille bedspread, and walls hung with a reproduction of Warhol's famous painting. Yes, Marilyn *did* stay here. So, too, Gloria Swanson and Veronica Lake. Some suites have kitchens. The rooms overlook an inauspicious quadrangle with a tiny pool ringed with bright blue Astroturf. Cocktails are served poolside, where free wines are served at sunset, adding to the house party atmosphere.

CALLA LILY INN

Innkeepers: Alan and Leslie Dunn
760-323-3654 or 1-888-888-5787;
fax: 760-323-4964
www.callalilypalmsprings.com
E-mail: info@callalilypalmsprings.com
350 S. Belardo Rd., Palm Springs, CA 92262
Price: Moderate to Very Expensive
Credit Cards: AE, MC, V
Special Features: Wireless Internet

With just nine poolside, nonsmoking units, this intimate gem in the heart of the Tennis Club district feels just like home away from home. It started life in 1950 as La Riviera Apartment Hotel. After falling into disuse, this Midcentury Modern facility was restored and reinvented with chic panache by owners Anne and Leslie Dunn. They also run it themselves. Sophistication is the watchword. All rooms feature tile floors, chocolate and cream color schemes, king beds with plump duvets, plus TVs and VCRs and DVD players, in-room refrigerators, coffeemakers, hair dryers, irons and ironing boards, and robes. Some have private patios overlooking the heated pool and Jacuzzi, floodlit at night—a perfect place for guests to congregate over complimentary evening cocktails. The location is dandy, being just one block from South Palm Canyon Drive.

CASA CODY

Innkeepers: Frank Tyson and Terese Hayes
760-320-9346 or 1-800-231-2639;
fax: 760-325-8610
www.casacody.com
E-mail: casacody@aol.com
175 S. Cahuilla Rd., Palm Springs, CA 92262
Price: Moderate to Very Expensive
Credit Cards: AE, D, DC, MC, V
Special Features: Fireplaces in some rooms

Billing itself as a "Country Bed and Breakfast Inn," this romantic retreat harks back to the 1920s, when the bed-and-breakfast was built for Hollywood pioneer Harriet Cody. Its 23 rooms are in five hacienda-style adobe structures festooned with bougainvillea. Choose from studios to

The Del Marcos Hotel.

two-bedroom suites, all furnished Santa Fe style with timber-framed sofas, leather-and-wood seats, handwoven dhurrie rugs, and North African and Turkish wall hangings. Some have wood-burning fireplaces and private patios. Continental breakfast is served poolside; the inn has two heated pools, plus a whirlpool.

DEL MARCOS HOTEL

Manager: Joe Kelley
1-800-676-1214; fax: 760-325-6905
www.delmarcoshotel.com
E-mail: info@delmarcoshotel.com
225 W. Baristo Rd., Palm Springs, CA 92262
Price: Moderate to Very Expensive
Credit Cards: AE, D, MC, V
Special Features: Midcentury Modern styling

A Tennis Club district hotel with heaps of Rat Pack style, this 1947 Midcentury Modern classic was designed by William Cody and is a Palm Springs architectural landmark, not least for its angular stone walls and purposely skewed doorway and asymmetrical rooflines. The exterior has a timeless beauty that melds seamlessly into the San Jacinto Mountain backdrop. Recently spectacularly renovated and fitted with period furniture, it exudes yesteryear chic, from the glass-walled lobby to the 16 individually furnished rooms arranged in a U-shape around a huge swimming pool. Most rooms look onto the pool through shuttered walls of glass, and suites come with kitchens. Who can resist ordering a killer martini to sip poolside while enjoying Sinatra classics? Feeling active? Then hop aboard one of the hotel's vintage bicycles, or take to the shuffleboard court.

THE HORIZON HOTEL

Manager: Jodee Smith
760-323-1858 or 1-800-377-7855;
fax: 760-327-2933
www.thehorizonhotel.com
E-mail: info@thehorizonhotel.com
1050 E. Palm Canyon Dr.,
Palm Springs, CA 92264
Price: Expensive
Credit Cards: AE, D, MC, V

Swimming pool, the Horizon Hotel.

Special Features: Poolside bar with Jacuzzi and fire pit

Originally a "personal motel," the Horizon was designed as a bungalow court in 1952 by William Cody for oil magnate / producer Jack Wrather and his B-movie actress wife, Benita Granville, as a retreat for their family and Hollywood friends. Cody designed it on 2.5 grassy acres with glorious mountain views and a collection of seven modern, flat-roofed, wide-eaved bungalows set on an oblique grid. Alan Hess, in his co-authored book *Palm Springs Weekend,* noted, "You think it's just a rectilinear flat-roofed series of bungalows, but then you realize all the buildings have these amazing acute angles that create a rhythm and very dramatic interior and exterior spaces." A Who's Who of Hollywood stars, including Lassie, the dog, slept here. Marilyn Monroe preferred the sole bungalow without an outdoor shower (presumably as protection against the paparazzi).

After a careful restoration, the Horizon reopened as a 22-room hotel in 2006. The stunning, iconic Midcentury Modern architecture remains, but thankfully Wrather's taste for coral pink walls and bright green carpets has been replaced with chic whites, glamorous tile floors, sparkling walls of glass, and tasteful contemporary art. Other highlights: flat-screen TVs, Italian linens and robes, and garden showers. Also offered: Wrather's zigzag-shaped main house with a sunken living room, martini bar, and a lavish pool in its private garden. And everyone is welcome to linger by the poolside bar with fire pit flaming at night. Somehow it still seems to always be 1960 at this ultra-hip spot described in *Travel & Leisure* as having "innumerable boldfaced names on its well-guarded guest list."

INGLESIDE INN

General Manager: Brian Ellis
706-325-0046; fax: 706-325-0710
www.inglesideinn.com
E-mail: contact@inglesideinn.com
200 W. Ramon Rd., Palm Springs, CA 92262
Price: Very Expensive

Credit Cards: AE, D, MC, V
Special Features: A timeless bar
A Palm Springs institution for four decades, the Ingleside—a luxury compound featured as "One of the Ten Best" by *Lifestyles of the Rich & Famous*—guarantees a flavor of the old Hollywood lifestyle. The Spanish-style, antique-filled hacienda hotel one block from the main downtown drag began life as the Twin Palms, a private residence built in 1922 by the widow of George Birge, president of the Pierce-Arrow Motor Car Company. The original building was converted to a 29-room hotel in 1935. In ensuring decades it drew a Who's Who of celebrities, from Greta Garbo and Gary Cooper to John Wayne and Salvador Dalí. Billionaire Howard Hughes and actress Ava Gardner famously tried to sneak in under assumed names on October 12, 1946 (Hughes used the names of his mechanic, Earl Martyn, and his secretary, Mrs. Clark). New York businessman Melvyn Haber bought the old inn in 1975 and restored it, adding a gourmet restaurant that became a favorite of Frank Sinatra. One year later, Ol' Blue Eyes chose it for his prewedding dinner before saying "I do!" with Barbara.

The inn retains its Old World charm in its 30 suites, "mini-suites," and villas sprinkled amid lush, well-manicured lawns. Regal furnishings and decor hark back to a time when mahogany antiques and heavy brocades and chintz were in favor, so this is one place where the modernist set will *not* feel at home. The intimate Casablanca Room piano bar is a throwback to the 1950s, packing in monied residents of a certain age.

The Korakia Pensione.

KORAKIA PENSIONE

General Manager: Paul Monarrez
760-864-6411; fax: 760-864-4147
www.korakia.com
227 S. Patencio Rd., Palm Springs, CA 92262
Price: Very Expensive
Credit Cards: AE, MC, V
Special Features: Pool

A vision of Beau Geste perfectly suited to the desert setting, this Moroccan-style inn is one of Palm Springs' most charming boutique hotels. The original owner, Scottish painter Gordon Coutts, attempted to re-create the romance he had experienced in Tangiers with crenellated, brilliantly whitewashed walls, a keyhole-shaped grand entrance with ornately carved wooden double doors, turret windows, and high ceilings adorned with Moorish tiles. In 1992 architect preservationist Douglas Smith restored the 1924 villa to its original splendor and infused it with a Grecian flavor in homage to his own fondness for the Greek isles. In 1997 Smith bought the 1930s Mediterranean villa across the street, formerly owned by early screen star J. Carrol Naish, and melded it seamlessly with his own Dar Maroc villa.

Functioning as a bed-and-breakfast, the inn has 27 individually themed rooms. Rattan chairs and an eclectic sprinkling of Moroccan chests, writing desks, wrought-iron or antique hardwood beds sit upon pine floors spread with North African throw rugs. The Mediterranean Villa evokes southern France with its high wood-beam ceilings and tawny yellows and ocher earth tones. The highlight is an impossibly romantic five-room suite with massive fireplace and a two-person stone bathtub. Some rooms are in individual bungalows.

The Movie Colony Hotel.

Guests get to splash around in a mosaic-tiled pool in which Rudolph Valentino splashed with Natascha Rambova. The palm-shaded garden blazes with bougainvillea and oleander and is scented by citrus blossoms and olive trees and studded with Moroccan fountains.

The Korakia is favored by the literati and glitterati, and is a preferred location for fashion shoots. Winston Churchill, who had a great fondness for Morocco, relaxed here with his easel and paints. Alicia Silverstone, Chris O'Donnell, and Andy Garcia count among more recent guests, reflecting the inn's steadfast reputation as an *en vogue* retreat for the rich and famous.

MOVIE COLONY HOTEL
General Manager: Bruce Abney
760-320-6340 or 1-888-953-5700;
fax: 760-320-1640
www.moviecolonyhotel.com
E-mail: info@ballantineshotels.com
726 N. Indian Canyon Dr.,
Palm Springs, CA 92262
Price: Very Expensive
Credit Cards: AE, D MC, V
Special Features: Pool

Situated one block from the Strip, on the edge of the Movie Colony area, this contemporary stunner is where many of Hollywood's hottest hang out when they come to town. Oozing modernist attitude, the Bauhaus-style boutique hotel would look right at home on the French Riviera. Dating back to 1935, it originated as the three-townhouse, Albert Frey–designed San Jacinto. The current owners recently restored the original town homes and two adjacent 1930s and '40s buildings, which modernist architect Frank Urrutiathey then furnished with impeccably chosen minimalist period furnishings and fabrics, such as Bertoia chairs and Noguchi tables. Effortlessly chic!

Beyond the plate glass and brushed steel double doors, the 17 rooms and three two-story town home suites are a mélange of soothing whites, eggshells, and golds. All have king beds with Knoll throw pillows and duvets as soft as a cloud. Cable TV, DVD/CD players, plus wireless Internet access are standard, as are stainless steel bars with fully stocked minibars. Delightful period touches include the fully functioning vintage radios and in-house 1950s' classic and B movies. One of the rooms is a tribute to Jackson Pollock, complete with floor-to-ceiling painting splotches. White plantation shutters keep as much sun at bay as you wish.

The three buildings are staggered alongside a pool into which Jim Morrison is said to have leapt from his balcony! Don your strongest sunglasses and laze the day away on your patio shielded from your neighbor by yellow canvas drapes.

Guests gather in the early evening at the alfresco marble-and-stainless-steel bar serving "Dean Martinis" at cocktail hour, and for the sunset wine hour around a poolside fire pit. The hotel has no restaurant or room service.

ORBIT IN

Innkeepers: Christy Eugenis and Stan Amy
760-323-3585 or 1-877-996-7248;
fax: 760-323-3599
www.orbitin.com
E-mail: mail@orbitin.com
562 W. Arenas Rd., Palm Springs, CA 92262
Price: Very Expensive
Credit Cards: AE, D, MC, V
Special Features: Pool

A modernist courtyard motel in the Tennis Club district, the ultra-chic Orbit Inn opened in early 2001 after a two-year renovation of the former 1957 Oasis motel—a classic example of desert modern architecture of the fifties, with low-pitched, almost flat roof-lines, deep overhangs and extensive glass, and a sienna and olive green color scheme. If Sinatra or Sammy Davis Jr. were to walk between the perforated-metal gates and step into the lobby, they'd feel right at home.

The nine rooms, with names like the Martini Room, Bossanovaville, and the Leopard Lounge, are tricked out in retro-kitsch decor by famous modernist designers (think Saarinen, Noguchi, Eames), including Bertoia's sensual bikini chairs. Lava lamps ooze in slow motion. And framed pages from *Life* and *McCall's* adorn the walls. Some rooms have kitchens (replete with polished fifties stoves). The hotel is centered on an intimate courtyard, where it's a sheer pleasure to lie by the pool under a lifesaving mist. To one side, a custom terrazzo boomerang-shaped pool bar inlaid with glass is known for its Arnold Palmers (half lemonade, half iced tea) and sake cocktails—everything from an Orbitini (a sake martini) to an Atomic Cosmo (cosmopolitan with sake). Guests get free use of vintage-style bikes.

The Orbit In, Palm Springs.

THE PARKER

General Manager: Thomas Meding
760-770-5000; fax: 760-324-2188
www.theparkerpalmsprings.com
E-mail: reservations@theparkerpalmsprings.com
4200 E. Palm Canyon Dr., Palm Springs, CA 92264
Price: Very Expensive
Credit Cards: AE, D, DC, MC, V
Special Features: Full-service spa

The Parker Palm Springs, formerly Gene Autry's Melody Ranch and Merv Griffin's Resort.

Recently reincarnated by wizard designer Jonathan Adler, the jet-set revival Parker began life in 1959 as California's first Holiday Inn. Later it became Gene Autry's Melody Ranch, then the luxury Merv Griffin's Resort, where Barbra Streisand knocked down a wall to connect her two villas. In its new vogue, Adler's groovy digs cater to the retro-hip culture after a $27 million makeover that turned the ornateness of Griffin's Resort on its head. The 13 acres of formal gardens, for example, were replaced with desert flora. And beyond the breeze-block facade with orange-lacquered lobby doors (attended by bellboys in snappy pink jackets), the interiors are now a chic fusion of cultures and eras that embraces elements from Edwardian chairs to Peruvian rugs. Adler's tongue-in-cheek "hippy chic" design isn't to everyone's tastes, especially the Moroccan-inspired "hookah chill-out zone" (a perfect setting, however, for the Moroccan tea served on arrival) near the bar. Frankly, many of the pieces look like they were picked up at a garage sale. But the overall effect is magnificent.

The 144 rooms blend minimalist high design: Think cubist canopy beds, wire-based Warren Platner chairs, zebra-patterned rugs, vases inspired by Picasso paintings, plus sisal floors and sea-grass ceilings. All the cozy comforts are here, from 400-count Egyptian cotton sheets to Hermès and Molton Brown toiletries. For the best value, take the Lanai king rooms with private patios overlooking the pool.

The hotel draws the young monied crowd to dine at mister parker's (flooded with natural light through the wall of glass) and Norma's (spilling onto a terrace with a wraparound poured concrete sofa). Lounge chairs are sprinkled throughout the gar-

The lounge at the Parker Palm Springs.

The grounds at the Parker Palm Springs. The Parker Palm Springs

dens, which even has lawn games: Order a Pimm's before learning to play croquet like an Englishman, or a Pernod as prelude to playing pétanque. Paths lead to classic red-clay tennis courts. And the 16,500-square-foot Palm Springs Yacht Club spa has 19 indoor and 2 outdoor treatment rooms.

RUBY MONTANA'S CORAL SANDS INN

Innkeeper: Ruby Montana
760-325-4900 or 1-866-820-8302
www.coralsandspalmsprings.com
E-mail: coralsands@email.msn.com
210 W. Stevens Rd., Palm Springs, CA 92262
Price: Moderate to Expensive
Credit Cards: AE, MC, V
Special Features: Kitschy decor and colorful owner

This one-of-a-kind, flamingo-pink boutique hotel is a 1950s Midcentury Modern classic as famous for its eccentric and lovable owner—Ruby Montana—as for its chic and kitschy whimsy. The seven guest rooms are each uniquely themed. Dog-lovers will appreciate the Poodle Room. Cowboys-at-heart might opt for the Roy Rogers and Dale Evans Suite, or even the Yiddish Cowgirl Room.

Here's Ruby's partial (but says-it-all) description of the adorably gauche Liberace Room: "If anyone has ever said you have Attention Deficit Disorder, book this room immediately. It cannot disappoint you. There is flamboyance reminiscent of the room's eponymous entertainer but there are also hints of musicality along with a complete redefinition of masculinity. Can we start with the leopard print California king size bed? On the nightstand beside it, a turban-wearing blackamoor in pantaloons and a golden earring holds a torch lamp to his naked chest." What more is there to say?

The kidney-shaped pool with loungers is the perfect spot to relax. Ruby loves her hounds! Pets welcome.

SAN GIULIANO

General Manager: Marina Rossi
760-325-7100 or 1-877-897-7100; fax: 760-325-7221
www.sangiulianohotel.com
E-mail: customerservice@sangiulianohotel.com
375 W. Arenas Rd., Palm Springs, CA 92262
Price: Moderate to Expensive
Credit Cards: AE, D, MC, V
Special Features: Massages

A lovely marriage of Spanish colonial architecture and contemporary decor, this bed-and-breakfast set in vibrant gardens is a break from the retro-modernist themed hotels typical of the Tennis Club district. Rooms are individually styled, though all offer luxury linens, goose-down duvets, flat screen TVs, stereo and DVD players, WiFi Internet, and bathrooms with granite tops, Jacuzzi tubs, and Gilchrist & Soames toiletries. Most rooms face the pool and courtyard, while others have private patios with Jacuzzis. The rooms vary immensely in style, and it pays to study the hotel's Web site to select a room that best appeals: The Velvet Room is almost baroque with its dark blue walls, red velvets, and gilt mirror, while the more airy white-themed Glass Suite will appeal if you appreciate contemporary decor.

VILLA ROYALE INN

General Manager: Clark Tylee
760-327-2314 or 1-800-245-2314; fax: 760-322-3794
www.villaroyale.com
E-mail: Info@villaroyale.com
1620 S. Indian Trail, Palm Springs, CA 92262
Price: Expensive
Credit Cards: AE, D, MC, V
Special Features: Restaurant

This historic boutique resort hotel exudes all the charm of a Mediterranean *auberge*, especially at night when the warm glow of candlelight sparkles in the award-winning restaurant. Tucked discreetly off East Palm Canyon Drive, this former hideaway for 1950s Hollywood stars was recently renovated. The romance remains. Bougainvillea spill into the tranquil, terra-cotta courtyards with tinkling fountains and palm-shaded ponds. Bouquets of citrus, jasmine, and lavender scent the air. It's a quite lovely combination, tempting guests to lounge by the two heated pools or in the whirlpool, perfect for luxuriating beneath the stars.

Each of the 31 beamed guests rooms and suites is furnished with antiques, oriental rugs, and cozy sofas atop terra-cotta floors. All come with herbal toiletries, thick robes, and down duvets as soft as a sigh. Some rooms evoke a western ranch; others lean toward a Tuscan villa. Choose from Hideaway Guestrooms; Royale Guestrooms with king beds, cozy fireplaces, and private patios; or sumptuous villas.

VICEROY PALM SPRINGS

General Manager: Jonathan Heath
760-320-4117; fax: 760-323-3303
www.viceroypalmsprings.com
E-mail: reservations@viceroypalmsprings.com
415 S. Belardo Rd., Palm Springs, CA 92264
Price: Very Expensive
Credit Cards: AE, CD, D, DC, MC, V
Special Features: Full-service spa

An astonishingly distinctive resort that exudes class and manages to recapture Hollywood's golden age, this hotel makes you shout "Wow!" The former Estrella Inn was recently invigorated by owner Kelly

Wearstler and her husband, Brad Korzen, and is now especially popular with gay fashionistas. The 68 guest rooms and bungalows, which once housed the likes of Clark Gable and Carole Lombard, surround three separate pools and are done up in the signature black, white, and lemon-yellow house motif. Decor is best described as retro Regency-style. The white and yellow bar, with its long countertop and sixties-style high chairs, tempts you to linger over the signature Le Citron Bleu martini. The Estrella Spa is one of the valley's finest. And the inn's Citron restaurant, serving California modern cuisines, is peerless. The Viceroy also has two adults-only pools and offers full valet and bellman service.

A guest room at the Viceroy Palm Springs. Viceroy Palm Springs

This is one romantic valley venue guaranteed to melt your sweetie's heart. A special "Retreat to Romance" package for loving couples includes strawberries plus a bottle of Moët champagne upon arrival, plus a couples massage, and dinner at Citron. Oh, and dogs are welcome.

THE WILLOWS

General Manager: Kimberly Tucker
760-320-0771, 1-800-966-9597;
fax: 760-320-0780
www.thewillowspalmsprings.com
E-mail: stay@thewillowspalmsprings.com
412 W. Tahquitz Canyon Way, Palm Springs, CA 92262
Price: Very expensive
Credit Cards: AE, D, DC, MC, V
Special Features: Peaceful garden

This graceful Mediterranean-style villa with an updated spin on yesteryear posh was once owned by former New York attorney and U.S. Secretary of the Treasury Samuel Untermyer and was a magnet for society figures, including Clark Gable and Albert Einstein (in 1933). It still exudes timeless romance with its gorgeous antique furnishings, hardwood floors, and mahogany-beamed frescoed ceilings, married to modern amenities such as cable TV and data ports. The eight guest rooms indulge guests with sumptuous linens, fireplaces, and luxurious bathrooms. A swimming pool is set in a lovely hillside garden with waterfall and superb mountain views. It enjoys a quiet location tucked at the base of the mountains behind the Palm Springs Art Museum.

Resort Hotels and Spas

CALIENTE TROPICS RESORT

General Manager: Randy Rasmussen
760-327-1391 or 1-888-277-0999;
fax: 760-318-1883
www.calientetropics.com
E-mail: questions@calientetropics.com
411 E. Palm Canyon Dr., Palm Springs, CA 92264
Price: Moderate to Expensive
Credit Cards: MC, V
Special Features: Pool, spa

The Caliente Tropics.

A true Palm Springs icon that first opened in 1964, this classic Polynesian-styled motel with its A-frame entrance was one of the hippest hotels of the era. The Rat Pack partied here. Elvis Presley and Nancy Sinatra hung out by the pool. And Victor Mature had "his" table in the Congo Room. Like most hotels of that epoch, by the 1980s the property went into decline and became a favored spring break hangout and a suitably risqué setting for the Miss Hawaiian Tropics Pageant. After a period as a less-than-salubrious motel, the beat is back. Still clinging to its sixties Polynesian pop-culture theme, the motel was recently restored as a chic boutique hotel. The 90 guest rooms are custom-furnished in classic Midcentury Modern style and come with complimentary in-room beverages, daily newspaper, and desktop data ports. All are nonsmoking and pet-friendly (rooms even feature pet dishes and pet beds). Guests can choose a variety of bed configurations that include king, two queens, or two doubles. The swimming pool stretches for 65 feet and has a broad sundeck perfect for tanning by day and, in the evening, for relaxing with cocktails while surrounded by the warm light of tiki torches. The Tropics Retreat spa offers a complete menu, from heated stone treatments to pumpkin peels. There's a steakhouse, coffee shop, and a cocktail lounge where the Rat Pack would still feel right at home. We have found the front desk understaffed at times, and the welcome isn't always the friendliest.

THE CHASE HOTEL AT PALM SPRINGS

General Manager: Jonathan Childe
760-320-8866, 1-877-532-4273;
fax: 760-323-1501
www.chasehotelpalmsprings.com
E-mail: chasehotelps@aol.com
200 W. Arenas Rd., Palm Springs, CA 92262
Price: Moderate

Credit Cards: AE, MC, V
Special Features: Heated saltwater pool

Tastefully decorated in conservative contemporary style, this classic Midcentury Modern remake is a popular bargain-price option for discerning cognoscenti who don't want to break the bank. A casual gem of the Tennis Club district, this enclave of structures has 26 nonsmoking rooms, some with kitchenettes and dining areas. Brown, cream, and taupe combos sooth the senses, although furnishings are somewhat sedate: no Eames and Saarinen pieces here. In-room DVDs and VCRs are provided for, er, rainy days. But most folk prefer to linger on the sundeck by the large saline pool—a venue for continental breakfasts and, in the evening, the hotel's signature fresh-baked chocolate chip cookies.

HOTEL ZOSO

General Manager: Lee Utley
760-325-9676; fax: 760-969-6600
www.hotelzoso.com
E-mail: info@hotelzoso.com
150 S. Indian Canyon Dr., Palm Springs, CA 92262
Price: Moderate to Expensive
Credit Cards: AE, D, DC, CB, MC, V
Special Features: Enticing pool

Aiming to please the "discriminatingly hip" when it opened in 2005, this 21st-century, retro-themed hotel is perfectly positioned in the heart of downtown. The entire place is done up in warm desert colors melding into blacks and creams, with Samuel Starkman–designed decor, replicated-snakeskin furniture, and faux fur throws on the beds. The 163 rooms come with 350-thread-count Frette sheets, 42-inch flat-screen TVs, and a work station with high-speed data port and WiFi. The backlit onyx bar with pool table is a tad aloof and fails to draw much of a clientele. The fine-dining restaurant, "eatz. at Hotel Zoso," is a chic venue for enjoying fusion cuisine, and a spa was due to open in 2008.

Conventioneers are drawn to the 20,000 square feet of meeting space. If the trendy decor doesn't lure you, then come for the pool, tricked out with red cabanas and double chaise longues, and a misting system for hot summer days and a quartzite fire pit to heat cool winter nights.

PALM MOUNTAIN RESORT & SPA

General Manager: Tim Ellis
760-325-1301, 1-800-622-9451; fax: 760-323-8937
www.palmmountainresort.com
E-mail: timellis@palmmountain.com.
155 S. Belardo Rd., Palm Springs, CA 92262
Price: Inexpensive
Credit Cards: AE, MC, V
Special Features: Full-service spa

This blazing white, contemporary Mediterranean-style hotel is conveniently located in the Tennis Club district and is one of Palm Springs' better bargains. The highlight here is the expansive palm-shaded courtyard with lounge chairs, pool, and separate whirlpool. And Miko's Spa & Salon tempts patrons to lie back and enjoy a range of treatments. There's no on-site restaurant, but more than a dozen options are mere steps away. Rooms are cavernous, but, alas, decor is institutional and uninspired—a serious weak link in an otherwise pleasant property.

PALM SPRINGS TENNIS CLUB RESORT

General Manager: Jeannetta Dal
760-325-1441 or 1-800-854-2324; fax: 760-327-0234
http://palmspringstennisclub.net
E-mail:tennisclub@tricommanagement.com
701 W. Baristo Rd., Palm Springs, CA 92262
Price: Moderate to Expensive
Credit Cards: AE, MC, V
Special Features: Fine-dining restaurant

One of Palm Springs' iconic historic hotels, the Tennis Club has seen its fair share of

The Palm Springs Tennis Club Resort.

glamour. Marilyn Monroe's famous *Playboy* shoot was here—surely you'll recognize the oval-shaped swimming pool pinned by twin palms. You sense something special as you ascend the stairs (landscaped with water cascades) of the 1937 modernist main building nudging up against the rock-strewn base of Mount San Jacinto. Tennis buffs can use the 11 night-lit courts. There are three pools and five whirlpools. And Spencer's at the Mountain is one of Palm Springs' classiest places to dine. Today the Tennis Club primarily functions as a time-share condo, but it also doubles as a hotel. Choose from nonsmoking studios and one- and two-bedroom suites with kitchens, all soothingly decked out Tommy Bahama style.

RIVIERA RESORT & SPA

760-327-8311
www.psriviera.com
1600 N. Indian Canyon Rd., Palm Springs, CA 92262
Price: Expensive
Credit Cards: Unknown
Special Features: Exotic spa

Modeled after its Las Vegas cousin when it opened in 1959 as the city's first resort hotel, the Riviera boasted an 18-hole golf course (now the Riviera Gardens) and Olympic-size pool. In its day it hosted movie stars, presidents, and entertainers, and parts of the movie *Palm Springs Weekend* were shot here. The iconic hotel closed in 2006, lay fallow for a while, and at press time was undergoing an exciting $70 million overhaul. It was slated to reopen in late 2008 as a truly deluxe resort hotel and spa with a fine-dining restaurant, 406 sumptuous guest rooms featuring marble-clad bathrooms, widescreen plasma TVs, and luscious linen-covered beds with mountains of pillows. Expect this hotel to shine!

SMOKE TREE RANCH

General Manager: Lisa Bell
760-327-1221, 1-800-787-3922; fax: 760-327-9490
www.smoketreeranch.com
E-mail: reservations@smoketreeranch.com

1850 Smoke Tree Lane, Palm Springs, CA 92264
Price: Moderate to Expensive
Credit Cards: D, MC, V
Special Features: Horse-riding stables

A rambling, informal Old West–style desert sanctuary hidden behind a curtain of oleander, the venerable Smoke Tree Ranch retains the character of Palm Springs in the 1930s and is the last of the traditional ranch-style hotels to offer a true western desert experience. Opened in 1936 as an enclave of homes and guest cottages (now totaling 85) on 375 acres of pristine desert, it became an unpretentious retreat for the likes of Cary Grant and Walt Disney. Disney had his designers build six cottages, which can be rented today. Every timber-beamed cottage has a TV, telephone, Internet access, refrigerator, and stone fireplace. Albeit expensive, in all other regards the cottages are homely and may disappoint guests seeking luxe. Ranch life is kept simple, with no effort made to impress. Meals are served in a western-style log lodge containing a cozy lounge and library, and there are live cowboy crooners. There's a western-style gatehouse, and lanes without curbs meld into open sandy desert studded with cactus and tamarisk. Rabbits and quail add to the enjoyment of the natural desert. There are nature trails, a tennis clinic, and a stable offering trail rides into the canyons.

THE SPA HOTEL & CASINO

General Manager: Scott Cooper
760-883-1000 or 1-800-999-1995; fax: 760-325-3344
www.sparesortcasino.com
E-mail: scooper@accmail.net
100 N. Indian Ave., Palm Springs, CA 92262
Price: Moderate to Expensive
Credit Cards: AE, DC, D, MC, V
Special Features: Casino

This downtown hotel, originally designed in 1955, is intricately linked to the casino. The 228 rooms on five levels are surprisingly tasteful, with subdued desert color schemes and stylish contemporary fittings. Hallways can echo with noisy revelers. We like the two heavenly hot outdoor mineral pools and the eucalyptus steam rooms, and the adjacent casino offers a counterpoint to too much relaxing. The hotel is slated to receive a $500 million remake beginning in 2008, with two new hotel towers, a Vegas-style showroom, and a climate-controlled shopping gallery modeled on Milan's Galleria Vittorio Emanuele linking the hotel directly to Indian Canyon Drive.

THE SPRINGS OF PALM SPRINGS HOTEL & SPA

General Manager: Marilu Rogers
760-327-5701 or 1-888-327-5701; fax: 760-327-6291
www.thespringsofps.com
E-mail: stay@thespringsofps.com
227 N. Indian Canyon Dr., Palm Springs, CA 92262
Price: Moderate to Expensive
Credit Cards: AE, D, DC, MC, V
Special Features: On-site spa

Built in 1935 in Spanish-colonial style as the Royal Palms Hotel, this two-story property was upgraded by new owners in 2004. Beyond its new Tuscan front, it centers on an Olympic-length pool complex. All 25 rooms and suites evoke an elegant classical European theme and have fireplaces, plus kitchenettes with microwaves, fridges, and coffeemakers, and white, cream, and purple decor. Many rooms have king beds with wrought-iron headboards. And separate walk-in showers and Jacuzzi tubs are a plus in the bathrooms. The spa offers skin care, massages, and body treatments, and the stone-lined lounge with fireplace is a cozy spot to relax.

Generic Hotels

COURTYARD MARRIOTT

General Manager: Vanessa Perera
760-322-6100 or 1-800-321-2211;
fax: 760-322-6091
www.marriott.com/pspch
1300 Tahquitz Canyon Way, Palm Springs, CA 92262
Price: Moderate
Credit Cards: AE, CB, D, DC, MC, V
Special Features: Pay-per-view movies

On a relatively undeveloped tract of Palm Springs, this cookie-cutter, midprice hotel is within a 15-minute walk of downtown (complimentary shuttles are also provided). A plus is that it is entirely non-smoking. Rooms here are sharp, with contemporary decor featuring polished hardwoods and dark blue carpeting. Business travelers will appreciate the work stations. No pets allowed.

HOLIDAY INN PALM SPRINGS

General Manager: John Wzaguirre
760-323-1711 or 1-888-465-4329;
fax: 760-416-3071
www.holidayinn.com/palmspringsca
1800 E. Palm Canyon Dr., Palm Springs, CA 92264
Price: Moderate to Expensive
Credit Cards: AE, CB, D, DC, MC, V
Special Features: Two-acre pool courtyard

Originally built in 1969 and reopened in 2008 after a lengthy remake, this three-star budget property (formerly the Ramada) is now a flagship Holiday Inn that boasts a snazzy new frontage and hip, all-new interior. The 249 guest rooms are on three levels in a quadrant surrounding an Olympic-size pool studding lush palm-shaded lawns. The hotel has a fitness center, plus public whirlpool, WiFi connections, and a business center, plus Billie D's restaurant. Several other restaurants are within a few minutes' walk.

The Holiday Inn Palm Springs.

HYATT REGENCY SUITES

General Manager: Robert Kallmeyer
760-322-9000 or 1-800-233-1234;
fax: 760-322-6009
www.palmsprings.hyatt.com
E-mail: qualitypalm@hyatt.com.
285 N. Palm Canyon Dr., Palm Springs, CA 92262
Price: Moderate to Expensive
Credit Cards: AE, CB, D, DC, MC, V
Special Features: Tremendous views

Most Palm Springs hotels like to boast of their views of the San Jacinto Mountains, but few can compare to the grandstand views from the Hyatt. Sure, this slanted six-story hotel is an architectural ugly duckling, but its prime position offers the best of both worlds: just steps from the heart of affairs, and unassailed vistas of the mountains. The 194 guest rooms (refurbished in 2006) boast tasteful contemporary furnishings in a pastel of soft desert colors, and all rooms have balconies and sitting areas with pull-out sofas. Take a west-facing room for the views. The glitzy atrium lobby is a tremendous venue for the Palm Court Café.

The trapezoid pool is a tad small, but still sufficient for laps. Other facilities include a gym, small spa, business center, and even a putting green. Pets are accepted.

WYNDHAM PALM SPRINGS HOTEL
General Manager: Duane Rohrvaugh
760-322-6000 or 1-800-996-3426;
fax: 760-322-5351
www.wyndham-palmsprings.com
888 E. Tahquitz Canyon Way, Palm Springs, CA 92262
Price: Moderate to Expensive
Credit Cards: AE, D, DC, MC, V
Special Features: Health club

The carpeted rooms at this pet-friendly hotel four blocks from the downtown Strip are predictably institutional yet pleasantly stylish and perfectly suited to visitors not too fussy about luxury or modernist chic. Each has a work desk and WiFi and high-speed Internet access. South- and west-facing rooms offer great mountain views. Recreational and leisure amenities include a health club and spa—you can even enjoy an outdoor massage beside the "oasis-style" pool with whirlpool. The hotel's Café Terraza offers indoor and outdoor dining, and plenty of fine-dining options are within a 10-minute stroll.

Clothing-Optional Resorts

DESERT SHADOWS RESORT & SPA
General Manager: Michael Williams
760-325-6410, 1-800-292-9298;
fax: 760-327-7500
www.desertshadows.com
E-mail: relax@desertshadows.com
1533 Chaparral Rd., Palm Springs, CA 92262
Price: Expensive
Credit Cards: AE, DC, MC, V
Special Features: Nude resort

This is not a clothes-optional facility: You *have* to be nude. Billing itself as a full-service resort for the "discerning naturist," the facility—identifiable to everyone by the Lee R. Baxandall Bridge spanning Indian Canyon Drive—features secluded, palm-shaded gardens landscaped with lagoons, water cascades, and citrus. Guest rooms are surprisingly stylish, with desert color schemes; choose from four room types, including one- and two-bedroom Mediterranean-style villas, which have high-speed Internet access. It has two pools: A "quiet" pool and a heated activity pool, and a restaurant that serves ho-hum fare. However, the entire facility is a tad run-down, for which reason the loyal, fun-loving repeat clientele has begun to drift away. New owners took over in late 2007, and at press time a gradual renaissance was under way.

MORNINGSIDE INN
Innkeepers: Jill and Vern Sorenson
760-325-2668, 1-800-916-2668;
fax: 760-322-1532
www.morningsideinn.com
E-mail: jill@morningsideinn.com
888 N. Indian Canyon Dr., Palm Springs, CA 92262
Price: Inexpensive to Moderate
Credit Cards: MC, V
Special Features: Whirlpool

This nude and clothing-optional resort makes first-time "social" nudists feel right at home. The uninspired decor, alas, is a tad frumpy and old-fashioned, but the repeaters who love this place are here for the camaraderie that is integral to naturism. All rooms have refrigerators, microwaves, cable TV and VCR, and suites have full kitchens. Facilities include a cool plunge pool, and a whirlpool perfect for cool desert nights.

TERRA COTTA INN
Innkeepers: Tom and Mary Clare
760-322-6059 or 1-800-786-6938;
fax: 760-322-4169

http://sunnyfun.com
E-mail: info@sunnyfun.com
2388 E. Racquet Club Rd., Palm Springs, CA 92262
Price: Moderate to Expensive
Credit Cards: AE, MC, V
Special Features: Whirlpool spa

This relaxing and friendly clothing-optional resort has its own loyal clientele, much thanks to the pampering attention of the owners. The 17 spacious rooms have bamboo-and-wicker furnishings and lively fabrics, plus king-size beds, and coffeemakers, mini-fridges, and TVs and VCRs. Deluxe rooms have kitchens. Massages and other spa treatments are offered. There's a pool and whirlpool in pleasant gardens, with a fire pit to temper the evening chill.

Especially for Gays and Lesbians

Many of the dozen or so gay resorts are clothing optional and intended for the promiscuous-minded and include **Camp Palm Springs** (760-322-2267; www.camp-palm-springs.com); **Exile Inn** (760-327-6413; www.innexile.com; 545 Warm Sands Dr., Palm Springs, CA 92264); and **Triangle Inn** (1-800-732-7555; www.triangle-inn.com).

INNDULGE

Innkeepers: John Williams and Jean-Guy Lachance
760-327-1408 or 1-800-833-5675
www.inndulge.com
E-mail: info@inndulge.com
601 Grenfall Rd., Palm Springs, CA 92264
Price: Moderate to Expensive
Credit Cards: AE, D, MC, V
Special Features: Whirlpool

Among the most tasteful of the many clothing-optional, gay-oriented hotels that concentrate in the Warm Sands district, this inn, built in 1958, is a classic Midcentury Modern gem. The lobby, with its original brick fireplace, gets things off to a cozy start, while the courtyard boasts the original kidney-shaped pool—now heated year-round. The 24 guest rooms (which include some two-bedroom apartments with kitchens and private patios) are furnished in southwestern fashion with pine and wrought-iron pieces, including king beds. The inn's health-conscious clientele make good use of the on-site gym, and guests can tune in to the outside world with WiFi Internet.

QUEEN OF HEARTS

Innkeeper: Michelle Secor
760-322-5793, 1-888-275-9903; fax: 760-322-5795
www.queenofheartsps.com
E-mail: jmichelle@queenofheartsps.com
435 Avenida Olancha, Palm Springs, CA 92264
Price: Moderate
Credit Cards: AE, D, DC, MC, V
Special Features: Lesbians only

In 1969 actress Eadie Adams partnered with female friend Pat McGrath and founded Palm Springs' first lesbian hotel, the Desert Knight. Gloria Swanson was supposedly among the early visitors. Now the

Clothing is optional at Inndulge.

Queen of Hearts, and gleaming from a recent renovation, it offers lesbians-only a calming and pampering place to relax with like-minded souls. The nine air-conditioned rooms surround a heated pool, where misters cool things down in summer. Each individually styled room is "feminine" in style and offers fluffy robes, plus cable TV and VCR. The outdoor Jacuzzi is shaded by a gazebo.

SANTIAGO

General Manager: David Geraci
760-322-1300 or 1-800-710-7729;
fax: 760-322-6121
www.santiagoresort.com
E-mail: santiagoresort@aol.com
650 San Lorenzo Rd., Palm Springs, CA 92264
Price: Moderate to Expensive
Credit Cards: AE, D, DC, MC, V
Special Features: Exciting decor

With its gorgeous aesthetic, this clothing-optional resort for gays exudes sophistication. Set in lush gardens, this pampering hotel even offers complimentary lunch as well as breakfast, and iced teas and lemonades are on the house, too. The rooms here, newly refurbished in 2006, are highlighted by plump pillows, designer fabrics, 37-inch TVs plus VCR/DVD players, and luxurious bathrooms fixtures. The 50-foot diving pool is kept at a perpetual 85 degrees year-round, and a highlight is the 12-man whirlpool.

VISTA GRANDE RESORTS

Innkeeper: Bob Mellen
760-322-2404; fax: 760-320-1667
www.mirage4men.com
E-mail: mirage4men@aol.com
574 Warm Sands Dr., Palm Springs, CA 92262
Price: Moderate to Expensive
Credit Cards: AE, D, NC, V
Special Features: Adult channels

For nudes, not prudes, this exuberant resort is distinctly adult-oriented and proudly proclaims its provocative image. The jungly landscaping here sets the tone for wild times. Actually, the resort is three hotels in one: the Avalon, Mirage, and Vista Grande. The choice of rooms is equally varied, from studios to the Royal Waterfall Suite. Facilities include three pools and three whirlpool spas.

Motels

Cambridge Inn (760-325-5574 or 1-877-325-5574, fax: 760-327-2020; www.cambridgeinnpalmsprings.com; 1277 S. Palm Canyon Dr., Palm Springs, CA 92264; Inexpensive to Moderate; AE, MC, V) No-frills motel with functional furnishings. The Cedar Creek Inn is adjacent and there are restaurants close by. At least the 66 rooms have coffeemakers and refrigerators, and you get 70 cable channels, if that's your thing.

Comfort Inn (760-778-3699 or 1-888-322-1997, fax: 760-322-8789; www.palmspringscomfortinn.com; 390 S. Indian Canyon Dr., Palm Springs, CA 92262; Inexpensive; AE, CB, D, DC, MC, V) Cozy three-story motel close to downtown with 130 spacious rooms, some with king beds and refrigerators. Large swimming pool plus whirlpool.

Travelodge (760-327-1211 or 1-877-544-4446; www.palmspringstravelodge.com; 333 E. Palm Canyon Dr., Palm Springs, CA 92264; Inexpensive; AE, D, DC, MC, V) Offers 155 rooms, some with king beds; free Internet; shuffleboard and badminton courts plus two outdoor heated pools.

Vagabond Inn (760-325-7211 or 1-800-522-1555; www.vagabondinn.com; 1699 S. Palm Canyon Dr., Palm Springs, CA 92262; Inexpensive; AE, D, DC, MC, V) At the far south end of Palm Springs, a 20-minute walk from downtown. The 120 guest rooms are simply furnished in desert tones. Heated pool, whirlpool. Restaurants close by.

Recreational Vehicle Resorts

Emerald Desert Golf & RV Resort (760-345-4770; www.emeralddesert.com; 76-000 Frank Sinatra Dr., Palm Desert, CA 92211) Full-service resort with 760 sites; fitness center, mini-market, laundry.

Indian Wells RV Park (760-347-0895; www.carefreervresorts.com; 47-340 Jefferson St., Indian Wells, CA 92201) Three pools, two whirlpool spas, gym, clubhouse.

Shadow Hills RV Resort (760-360-4040; www.shadowhillsrvresort.com; 40-655 Jefferson St., Indian Wells, CA 92203) This premier RV park has 100 paved sites, plus clubhouse, pool, spa and fitness center. Free WiFi and satellite TV.

Horizon Mobile Home Village.

Lodging in Palm Springs Vicinity

Desert Hot Springs' biggest asset could well be its wealth of midcentury motels, many of them saved from the wrecking ball by the post-1970s economic slump. In fact, most hostelries in town are motels. Virtually every one sits atop a mineral spa and has its own well. Thus they bill themselves as spas, though most could equally be considered boutique hotels: We've classed them accordingly. A few are world-class. Others are quite undistinguished. That "inn," "lodge," or "resort" might just be an ugly duckling of cinder block and stucco. *Caveat emptor!*

Rancho Mirage is known for its large scale, ritzy resort hotels.

Bed-and-Breakfast Inns / Boutique Hotels

EL MOROCCO INN AND SPA

Innkeeper: Bruce Abney
760-288-2527 or 1-888-288-9905;
fax: 760-288-2523
www.elmoroccoinn.com
E-mail: info@elmoroccoinn.com
66-810 E. Fourth St., Desert Hot Springs, CA 92240
Price: Expensive
Credit Cards: D, MC, V
Special Features: Mineral spa

You can't help but frown and do a double-take as you approach this hotel in the midst of an ugly suburban area far from any attractions or amenities. Fortunately, once you get through the door things improve dramatically. "Exotic" perfectly suits to describe this lavish Moroccan-themed lair, wrapping around a mineral pool and whirlpool. It's easy to imagine Rudolph Valentino seducing sultry maidens on the chaise longues festooned with carnal red cushions. In fact, the whole place is done up like a fantasy from *Beau Geste*. Plenty of luxuries are provided, including king beds with exotic fabrics, fancy toiletries, terry robes, CD/DVD players, and WiFi Internet. The main reason to indulge here, of course, is the natural mineral spa. At night relax with a Moroccotini in the Kasbah lounge. After all, it's a long drive to any other nightspot. Still, it's a bit pricey, all things considered.

HOPE SPRINGS

General Manager: Chloe Peppas
760-329-4003; fax: 760-329-4223
www.hopespringsresort.com
E-mail: manager@hopespringsresort.com
68-075 Club Circle Dr., Desert Hot Springs, CA 92240
Price: Expensive
Credit Cards: AE, D, MC, V
Special Features: Spa services

Another Zen-like fifties-redux gem, Hope Springs is owned by two fans of Midcentury Modernism. The motel, which began life as the Cactus Springs, is shaped like a boomerang and has 10 rooms that are a testament to the fine taste of former Los Angeles–based graphic designers Mick Haggerty and Steve Samiof. The chic, laid-back retro style is epitomized by low-slung platform king beds, M&M-colored Saarinen chairs, Flokati rugs on waxed concrete floors, utilitarian bathrooms, and colorful contemporary art. No dressers or closets here. Just shelves and hangers on a rod. No TV, either. Nor phones. The fabulous circular lobby lounge with terrazzo floor spins around a central fire pit with conical suspended chimney. It has WiFi connectivity, plus three hot mineral pools and a mosaic goldfish pond. No children. No pets.

MIRACLE MANOR RETREAT

General Manager: Tony Merchell
760-329-6641 or 1-877-329-6641; fax: 760-329-9962
www.miraclemanor.com
E-mail: miraclemanorretreat@yahoo.com
12-589 Reposa Way, Desert Hot Springs, CA 92240
Price: Expensive
Credit Cards: AE, MC, V
Special Features: Mineral spa

This low-slung 1948 modernist motel had gone to seed when it was bought in 1997 by L.A. designers April Greiman and Michael Rotondi, who restored it as one of the first motels to be reincarnated as a modernist desert retreat. It's a classic exemplar of sensual, almost ascetic, "desert zen." Think floors of varnished concrete, a Plexiglas-and-steel enclosure, and bare walls (not even plastered) without artwork. And no TVs, nor phones or clocks in the six rooms that overlook a small courtyard. It's intended more for souls seeking a total escape for silent contemplation. However, the place throbs with exciting color and irresistible contemporary touches. Linens of gauzy organic cotton. Giddy curtains of East Indian fabrics. Sage soap in the bathrooms with stylish contemporary basins. Panoramic windows grant expansive views of the desert. Of course, Miracle Manor sits atop a steaming mineral well that feeds the hot tub and spa (actually, it's a single "healing room"), which specializes in organic essential-oil treatments.

SAGEWATER SPA

Innkeepers: Rhoni Epstein and Cristina Pestana
760-220-1554; fax: 760-251-1553
www.sagewaterspa.com
E-mail: sagewater.spa@verizon.net
12-697 Eliseo Rd., Desert Hot Springs, CA 92240
Price: Expensive
Credit Cards: MC, V
Special Features: Fabulous mountain vistas

Yes, yet another superb example of restful minimalist retro chic! This one, a streamlined L-shaped modernist building dating from 1954 and surrounded by a wall of sandblasted glass, blazes snow white through and through. Energizing light pours in through aluminum-framed walls of glass, enlivening blood-red chairs and red and green pillows for chromatic highlights. Simplicity reigns. The seven small rooms are filled with simple IKEA pieces (including armchairs in waterproof fabrics so you can lounge fresh from the pool) and custom beds with Egyptian cotton comforters and Frette linens as soft as a sigh. All rooms have kitchens. Owners Rhoni Epstein and Cristina Pestana greet guests with a pot of tea or a refreshing glass of cucumber water. Two mineral pools are fed by the area's celebrated hot springs, and a wide range of spa treatments are offered. Prudes take note: Midnight skinny-dipping is welcomed. Poolside caipirinhas (free on Sundays) are served, courtesy of Brazilian-born Pestana. No children. No pets.

Resort Hotels and Spas

DESERT HOT SPRINGS SPA HOTEL

General Manager: David Malstan
760-329-6000 or 1-800-808-7727; fax: 760-329-6915
www.dhsspa.com
E-mail: info@dhsspa.com
10-805 Palm Dr., Desert Hot Springs, CA 92240
Price: Inexpensive to Moderate
Credit Cards: AE, CB, D, DC, MC, V
Special Features: Vast pool complex

If lounging in thermal water is paramount, check into this family-friendly spa hotel with *eight* separate mineral-water pools (ranging in temperature from 70 to 104 degrees Fahrenheit) in a huge palm-fringed courtyard. This 50-room midcentury motel has been drawing spa-goers for five decades. Spacious guest rooms offer a choice of king or queen beds and homely decor. It has its own restaurant and sports bar, plus dry sauna.

RANCHO LAS PALMAS MARRIOTT RESORT & SPA

General Manager: Victor Woo
760-568-2727; fax: 760-862-4521
www.rancholaspalmas.com
41-000 Bob Hope Dr., Rancho Mirage, CA 92270
Price: Expensive
Credit Cards: AE, D, DC, MC, V
Special Features: Water park

Sprawling over 240 acres of lushly landscaped grounds, handily close to The River, this ritzy resort reopened in 2007 fresh from a $35 million renovation (it was formerly Marriott's Rancho Las Palmas Resort). A complete (and sophisticated) resort, it appeals to everyone, from families to spa-goers and the active minded. The 444 guestrooms and 22 suites are in Spanish-style structures with exposed wooden beams and red tile roofs and graceful arches. Rooms cluster around courtyards. The decor throughout is stylishly contemporary, combining desert color schemes with dark hardwoods, plus plush, top-quality bedding, and all the modern conveniences you could wish for. The resort makes a unique splash with Splashtopia, a huge water feature with waterslides and pool with faux beach. The bluEmber restaurant has quickly established itself as one of the valley's premier fine-dining options. And Rancho Las Palmas boasts a 27-hole Ted Robinson golf course, 25 tennis courts, and four pools, plus the 20,000-square-foot Spa Las Palmas, with 26 treatment rooms and a sensational gym.

RITZ CARLTON RANCHO MIRAGE

General Manager: To be announced
760-321-8282; fax: 760-318-4258
www.ritzcarlton.com
68-900 Frank Sinatra Dr., Rancho Mirage, CA, 92270
Price: Very expensive
Credit Cards: AE, CB, D, DC, MC, V
Special Features: Mountaintop location

This supremely deluxe and secluded resort (formerly The Lodge at Rancho Mirage) has changed hands several times in recent years, and in August 2006 it closed for a total remodel at the hands of RockResorts. Then, in 2007, it reverted to the Ritz-Carlton, which promises to pump $500 million into a remake. It is slated to open in late 2008. The result promises to be absolutely sensational, as you'd expect from Ritz-Carlton. The Web site suggests contemporary decor themed to desert colors and unparalleled in sophistication, and sure to have politicians and Hollywood stars flocking back. The two restaurants promise to up the ante on the competition. Facilities will include a deluxe spa, a swimming pool, and 10 tennis courts (eight lit).

Perched high, 650 feet above the valley, with sweeping views, its location is one of a kind. (In fact, it's high enough that it's in bighorn sheep territory. Supposedly when permits were first issued after a lengthy battle with environmentalists, it was stipulated that a wall not be built so as to permit bighorn sheep free range. The result was that the sheep discovered the swimming pool. A fence was eventually permitted.)

TWO BUNCH PALMS RESORT & SPA

General Manager: Mark Eads
760-329-8791 or 1-800-472-4334;
fax: 760-329-1317
www.twobunchpalms.com
E-mail: reservations@twobunchpalms.com
67-425 Two Bunch Palms Trail, Desert Hot Springs, CA 92240
Price: Very expensive
Credit Cards: AE, DC, MC, V, D
Special Features: High-class spa

Nestled on a berm overlooking the craggy desert floor, this sprawling, ultra-private, world-renowned spa hotel is one of the valley's most exclusive and sought-after digs. Initiated almost a century ago (although it has periodically added new guest rooms), it quickly established itself as a serene and veiled retreat for Hollywood celebrities, beginning with Rudolph Valentino and Charlie Chaplin. The owners also like to promote Two Bunch as Al Capone's "West Coast capital" (they've even named Al Capone's Suite), but biographers believe that Capone never set foot here. No matter.

A room at Two Bunch Palms Resort & Spa. Two Bunch Palms Resort & Spa

The place still draws celebrities. Absolute privacy is the watchword. No children are allowed. Nor pets or cell phones!

Its 44 rooms, suites, and villas, all with private patios, are sprinkled throughout meticulously manicured grounds with a landscaped, waterfall grotto. They're done up in a traditional Europcan fashion. Very elegant. Very suave. No modernism here, thank you! Some rooms have their own patio whirlpool tubs. Two Bunch is acclaimed for its mud treatments and peaceful spa with hot mineral pools, where guests can steep like steaming tea bags. Tai chi classes are among the specialties, but more than 45 treatments are offered. Other facilities include the Casino Restaurant, plus two lighted tennis courts, a swimming pool, and nude sun-bathing bins.

THE WESTIN MISSION HILLS RESORT
General Manager: Ken Pilgrim
760-328-5955 or 1-800-228-3000; fax: 760-770-2199
www.starwoodhotels.com
E-mail: ranch@westin.com
71-333 Dinah Shore Dr., Rancho Mirage, CA 92270
Price: Expensive
Credit Cards: AE, D, DC, MC, V
Special Features: Rooms have fireplaces

With its formal courtyards and arches adapted from a Moroccan design, the pubic arenas at this spa resort fit right in to the desert, though the grounds are lushly landscaped and planted with perennials. Call it an oasis! The 512 spacious guest rooms are in 16 two-story contemporary buildings. All have wet bar, fireplace, whirlpool tubs, and private patios. Some have cathedral ceilings, and the furnishings and decor are refined. No surprise, the beds here are top-class, as are the linens and fittings. The hotel has a kids club, seven tennis courts, a world-class spa, a health and fitness center, and three swimming pools (one with a 60-meter waterslide). And the Pete Dye–designed Mission Hills Course is here.

Westin Mission Hills Resort.

Clothing-Optional Resorts

LIVING WATERS SPA
Innkeepers: Jeff and Judy Bowman
760-329-9988 or 1-866-329-9988
www.livingwatersspa.com
E-mail: info@livingwatersspa.com
13-340 Mountain View Rd., Desert Hot Springs, CA 92240
Price: Moderate to Expensive
Credit Cards: MC, V
Special Features: Pool, spa

Nestled high above the valley floor with fabulous mountain views, this is the nicest non-gay clothing-optional resort in the valley. Sheltered by white walls, the modernist gem is a restored 1950s "spa-tel" with two natural hot mineral pools (one at 100 degrees, the other at a pleasant 88 degrees) in a cozy courtyard. The intimate family atmosphere provides an unselfconscious, accepting environment where first-timers can feel comfortable. It has just nine rooms, all but two with fully furnished kitchens (there are also two two-bedroom condos). Furnishings are from IKEA, and there are no phones or TVs. It has free WiFi connection, however. The small lounge has a fireplace, and guests here make their own entertainment.

SEA MOUNTAIN INN

Innkeepers: Dewey and Julie Wohl
760-251-1230, 1-877-928-2827;
fax: 818-576-9800
www.nudespa.com
E-mail: info@seamountaininn.com
66-540 San Marcus Rd., Desert Hot Springs, CA 92240
Price: Very expensive
Credit Cards: AE, D, DC, MC, V
Special Features: Parties

More adventurous than Desert Shadows or the Morningside Inn, this racy place is "lifestyles" (aka swingers) friendly. It's also more tasteful. Asian art and artifacts grace the hacienda-style property with a delightful courtyard featuring a circular mineral water whirlpool spa and thatched umbrellas. The 15 rooms offer understated contemporary decor, down duvets, Egyptian linens, and robes, plus flat-screen TVs, DVD players and DVDs, and WiFi Internet access. It has a sauna, and a 24-hour lounge club (Taboo Gardens) where saucy parties and events are held nightly. Sorry, gents . . . It's for single women and couples only. Reservations are a must.

Especially for Gays and Lesbians

OZZ RESORT

General Manager: Greg Mitchell
760-324-3000 or 1-866-247-7443
www.ozzresortps.com
E-mail: info@ozzresortps.com
67-580 Hwy. 111, Cathedral City, CA 92234
Price: Moderate
Credit Cards: AE, D, DC, MC, V
Special Features: Superb restaurant

The former Desert Palms Inn, where the campy movie *Palm Springs Weekend* was filmed in 1963, is today a gay- and lesbian-oriented resort. The place may have changed, but for gays this chic retro modernist retreat remains a tempting place to spend their own Palm Springs Weekend.

The 29 guest rooms are done in a ghastly outdated decor that's retro 1980s, melding pink and purple fabrics and chintzy gray plastic pieces. What were they thinking? Fortunately, all have private patios or balconies looking onto the delightful lawn and sundeck, where Balinese beds by the Jacuzzi tempt lazing the day away. Why is the pool shaped like a keyhole? It was built for filming of the movie *Through the Keyhole* in 1983. The lively little palapa bar off the patio is a place to warm up for recherché dishes at Plum, a splendid restaurant that was formerly one of the top dining spots in Palm Springs. The party scene here hops, not least thanks to the free-flowing martinis at the hip nightclub with pool table, TVs, and lots of gay erotica.

Lodging in the Southern Desert Resorts

Bed-and-Breakfast Inns / Boutique Hotels

CASA LARREA INN

Innkeepers: Frank and Kim Schuler
760-235-4304 or 1-877-261-8474;
fax: 760-568-9587
http://casalarrea.com
E-mail: casalarreainn@aol.com
73-771 Larrea St., Palm Desert, CA 92260
Price: Inexpensive to Expensive
Credit Cards: AE, MC, V

This quaint and homely, immaculately kept B&B enjoys a fabulous position one block from El Paseo. All rooms are individually furnished, although all are eclectic in decor, some with a real mishmash of styles.

All have WiFi access plus their own patios. Continental breakfast is served on the poolside sundeck, which has shade umbrellas and loungers. Pets welcome.

THE MOD RESORT
Innkeeper: Laura Slipak
760-674-1966 or 1-888-663-1970
www.modresort.com
E-mail: info@modresort.com
73-758 Shadow Mountain Dr., Palm Desert, CA 92260
Price: Moderate to Expensive
Credit Cards: MC, V
Special Features: Pool

A 1970s-throwback aesthetic to the days when Ol' Blue Eyes and other Hollywood sand-dabbers hung out in Palm Desert, this intimate retro-modernist creation of Argentinian-born fashion designer Laura Slipak has all the *pizzzazzz* of a finger-snapping Sinatra song. The groovy, sigh-inducing resort has a mere 14 rooms, all done up with light fabrics, stainless steels, sparkling mirrors, and funky flourishes that draw L.A. fashionistas. Down comforters. Flat LCD televisions, DVD and CD players, phone, and DSL and WiFi connections. Glass-tiled bathrooms with Frette terrycloth robes. All add to the immeasurable appeal. The rooms all face onto manicured lawns sprinkled with chaise lounges and patio tables around the pool.

MOJAVE
General Manager: Sheila Wheldon
760-346-6121 or 1-866-8-HOTEL-8; fax: 714-848-2223
www.hotelmojave.com
E-mail: sales@broughtonhospitality.com
73-721 Shadow Mountain Dr., Palm Desert, CA 92260
Price: Inexpensive to Expensive
Credit Cards: AE, D, DC, MC, V
Special Features: Private in-room spa treatments

Another retro-themed midcentury hotel, this one was renovated in 2001 and makes a lovely option for anyone seeking an intimate, small-scale abode with class. The 24 non-smoking rooms are graciously appointed in desert colors (taupes, tomato-soup orange) and tasteful contemporary teak and sisal furnishings, plus VCRs and luxurious bath amenities and robes. Some have fireplaces, kitchenettes, and private patios. Vintage photos adorn the walls. Unique features include a vintage video library, while a pool and spa are shaded by citrus and palms. El Paseo is just one block away.

TRES PALMAS BED & BREAKFAST
Innkeeper: Jean Whitney
760-773-9858 or 1-800-770-9858; fax: 760-776-9159
E-mail: jwacres1@hotmail.com
73-135 Tumbleweed Lane, Palm Desert, CA 92260
Price: Expensive
Credit Cards: AE, MC, V
Special Features: Breakfast alfresco

The gracious owner may be the top asset at this modern B&B—a somewhat nondescript interpretation of Spanish colonial—one block from El Paseo. The four guest rooms are exquisitely themed in southwestern style. Some have king beds; one is a four-poster. Your filling, health-conscious breakfast can be enjoyed by the pool or in the dining room.

Resort Hotels and Spas

DESERT SPRINGS JW MARRIOTT RESORT & SPA
General Manager: Ken Schwartz
760-341-2211 or 1-800-331-3112; fax: 760-341-1872
www.desertspringsresort.com
E-mail: desertspringsPVP@marriott.com
74-855 Country Club Dr., Palm Desert, CA 92260

Desert Springs JW Marriott Resort & Spa.

Price: Very Expensive
Credit Cards: AE, CB, D, DC, MC, V
Special Features: Spa, gondolas

Fresh from a $25 million renovation, this luxurious oasis known for its unique water features is more stylish than ever. The dramatic approach framed by palms is graced by a lake where flamingos parade around in hot pink. The massive, eight-story indoor atrium entrance features a vast wall of glass opening to Venetian-inspired waterways with gondolas and swans. Boats sail into the lobby to transport guests around the property. The lobby, with its snazzy new 60-foot bar backed by a water wall made of textured glass, even boasts a Starbucks with an outdoor fire pit.

This behemoth hotel boasts 884 guest quarters, including 65 suites (the largest are 3,100 square feet), all tastefully decorated with green carpet, teak furniture, king beds with thick duvets and heaps of fluffy pillows, plus deluxe marble-clad bathrooms with separate showers and tubs.

The five restaurants range from the superb Ristorante Tuscany to the Mikado

Guestroom at the Desert Springs JW Marriott Resort & Spa.

Japanese Steak House. The lobby bar is a sophisticated retreat for postprandial pleasure prior to kicking up your heels in Costas Nightclub. The coup de grâce is the hotel's 38,000-square-foot health spa, completely remodeled and expanded for 2007. Now offering 48 treatment rooms, a Turkish hammam, and private "spas within a spa," this sophisticated retreat is the largest spa facility in Southern California. Let's not forget the two swimming pools and 16 tennis courts. And two Ted Robinson–designed golf courses keep golfers in the swing.

HYATT GRAND CHAMPIONS RESORT & SPA

General Manager: Alan Farwell
760-341-1000; fax: 760-568-2236
www.grandchampions.hyatt.com
44-600 Indian Wells La., Indian Wells, CA 92210
Price: Expensive
Credit Cards: AE, D, DC, MC, V
Special Features: Huge spa

This world-renowned resort sprawls over 35 acres with a sparkling lake and celebrated art collection. It offers 428 luxurious "European-style" guest rooms, plus 26 lavishly appointed suites and 20 private villas, all furnished in stylish fashion and warm desert tones of taupe and gold. Feeling flush? Take a villa with fireplace and private courtyard garden with whirlpool. As you'd expect, a hotel this size doesn't lack for amenities, including seven pools, tennis, and a jogging trail. The vast Agua Serena Spa is one of the valley's premiere spas. And the Hyatt is big with conventioneers, thanks to 50,000 square feet of meeting space.

INDIAN WELLS RESORT HOTEL

General Manager: Brad Weimer
760-345-6466 or 1-800-248-3220; fax: 760-772-5083
www.indianwellsresort.com
E-mail: info@indianwellsresort.com
76-661 Hwy. 111, Indian Wells, CA 92210
Price: Inexpensive to Moderate
Credit Cards: AE, D, MC, V
Special Features: Heated swimming pool

A classic hotel founded by Lucille Ball and Desi Arnaz, this hotel boasts an elegant lobby with its arcing staircase and glittering gilt chandeliers. In 2007 the 126 rooms reemerged after a much-needed refurbishment and now boast an engaging pizzazz associated with that of competing hotels. Highlighted by checkered spreads and desert taupes, grays, and beiges, the carpeted rooms will appeal to traditionalists seeking subdued but tasteful decor. All have WiFi and private balcony or patio. A zigzag-shaped heated pool has a whirlpool, and you can make the most of a gym, tennis courts, and access to the Indian Wells Country Club, plus three restaurants.

LA QUINTA RESORT & CLUB

General Manager: Sergio Bocci
760-564-4111 or 1-877-527-7721; fax: 760-564-5718
www.laquintaresort.com
E-mail: inquiries@laquintaresort.com
49-999 Eisenhower Dr., La Quinta, CA 92253
Price: Very Expensive
Credit Cards: AE, CB, D, DC, MC, V
Special Features: Full spa, tennis courts

Built in 1926 and thereby the valley's oldest resort still in existence, this legendary spa resort—which lent its name to the town—sprawls over 900 acres and has drawn celebrities, society leaders, and others among the rich and famous since it opened with a mere 20 rooms in what was then pure desert. Nine decades and 776 rooms later, its commitment to guests' privacy and comfort is undiminished. The list of latter-day regulars is a Who's Who of the international A-list and includes every U.S.

La Quinta Resort & Club. La Quinta Resort & Club

president from Harry Truman to Bill Clinton.

Set amid citrus groves and lushly landscaped gardens, the resort is a classic of Spanish hacienda design. Though much expanded through the years, it still nurtures the mood of an exclusive country club. A posh clubhouse serves 23 tennis courts and two golf courses: the Dunes Course and the Mountain Course, both par 72 and both available for guest play. And the famous 23,000-foot Spa La Quinta is a sanctuary for recuperation, with a list of treatments as long as your arm. The seven restaurants include Azur, the signature fine-dining outlet, plus Mexican cuisine at the Adobe Grill, steak and American fare at Morgan's, and the new Twenty 6 American bistro. Classically elegant in tone, the 796 guest rooms and suites are tucked away in charming single-story Spanish-style casitas and privately owned condo villas in groupings, each surrounding a pool (41 in all, along with 53 whirlpools). The whole imparts a soothing sense of living the high life much as it was lived when Errol Flynn, Marlene Dietrich, Ginger Rogers, Greta Garbo, Clark Gable, et al. routinely made the trek over the mountains to relax here.

Spa Villa at the La Quinta Resort. La Quinta Resort & Club

MIRAMONTE RESORT & SPA

General Manager: Stan Kancowski
760-341-2200 or 1-877-716-7987;
fax: 760-568-0541
www.miramonteresort.com
E-mail: mcrawford@destinationhotels.com
45-000 Indian Wells La., Indian Wells, CA 92210
Price: Moderate to Expensive
Credit Cards: AE, D, DC, MC, V
Special Features: Spa

A Mediterranean-inspired sanctuary where citrus groves and olive trees scent the air, this romantic retreat has sumptuous public spaces and a gorgeous landscaped twin-level pool complex, plus a ballroom and heaps of meeting space. The Well Spa is well regarded, as is the Ristorante Brissago, the hotel's only restaurant. Although fresh from a $10 million renovation, however, this resort still shows some need for improvement. Despite lovely fabrics and furnishings, many of the 215 rooms show disturbing signs of age, with pitiful bathrooms, and the mood of a mediocre motel. Opt for the upgraded Dolce Suite accommodations.

RENAISSANCE ESMERALDA RESORT & SPA

General Manager: Bob Walsh
760-773-4444; fax: 760-346-9308
www.renaissanceesmeralda.com
44-400 Indian Wells La., Indian Wells, CA 92210
Price: Expensive to Very Expensive
Credit Cards: AE, D, DC, MC, V
Special Features: Kids club, spa, golf courses

At the base of the Santa Rosa Mountains, this recently remodeled resort has an exciting new aesthetic to go with its super location. We particularly like the sophisticated contemporary decor in the 560 oversize rooms on five levels. All rooms have balconies. The atrium lobby has a sweeping arced marble staircase. The expansive facilities include three restaurants, a lavish spa, vast meeting space, three heated pools, two renowned golf courses, and a kids club.

SHADOW MOUNTAIN RESORT & CLUB

General Manager: Cindy Calhoun
760-346-6123 or 1-800-472-3713; fax: 760-346-6518
www.shadow-mountain.com
E-mail: res@shadowmountain.com
45-750 San Luis Rey, Palm Desert, CA 92260
Price: Inexpensive to Expensive
Credit Cards: AE, D, MC, V
Special Features: Tennis clinic

This condo-hotel two blocks from El Paseo is well-suited to active travelers. Shadow Mountain is popular with tennis buffs: It has 16 courts, with free play. And volleyball, basketball, table tennis, and bicycle rentals keep visitors trim and amused. The high point is the lovely figure-eight pool—one of four heated pools—and there are five whirlpools and a spa. Guest rooms and studios to one-, two-, and three-bedroom condominiums and villas, all with fully equipped kitchens and a mix of Tommy Bahama and elegant contemporary furnishings.

Generic Hotels

COURTYARD BY MARRIOTT PALM DESERT

General Manager: Jim Zeltner
760-776-4150 or 1-800-321-2211; fax: 760-776-1816
www.courtyardpalmdesert.com
E-mail: helen.bonaddeio@marriott.com
74-895 Frank Sinatra Dr., Palm Desert, CA 92211
Price: Moderate to Expensive
Credit Cards: AE, CB, D, DC, MC, V
Special Features: Pay-per-view movies

A staid three-story property with 145 rooms appealing to the none-too-fussy traveler. Furnishings are pleasing and comfy, albeit a tad conservative despite a refurbishing in 2006. All the standard amenities are here, including free high-speed Internet, and TVs feature pay-per-view. However, this hotel has a breakfast-only café and few facilities. It's overpriced, given its lack of amenities and out-of-the-way locale (at least as far as activities are concerned) near the I-10 freeway.

EMBASSY SUITES PALM DESERT

General Manager: David Hirsch
760-340-6600 or 1-800-362-2779; fax: 760-340-9519
www.embassysuites.com
74-700 Hwy. 111, Palm Desert, CA 92260
Price: Moderate
Credit Cards: AE, D, DC, MC, V

Lively fabrics are a hallmark of this institutional, all-suite hotel with mass-market appeal. The 198 rooms have two televisions, refrigerator, microwave, coffeemaker, and a work table. Facilities include a fitness room, tennis court, and putting green.

HOMEWOOD SUITES BY HILTON

General Manager: Brad Poncher
760-391-4600; fax: 760-391-4601
www.homewoodsuites.com
45-200 Washington St., La Quinta, CA 92253
Price: Expensive
Credit Cards: AE, CB, D, DC, MC, V

Opened in 2007, this no-frills, three-story, cookie-cutter hotel close to the Indian Wells Tennis Garden has 130 comfy rooms, including studios and one-bedroom and two-bedroom suites, located on three floors. All offer views of the Santa Rosa Mountains, plus complimentary high-speed data ports, and two voice-mail telephones, and suites have full kitchens (the hotel includes free grocery shopping service). Facilities include a courtyard pool, gym, putting green, and business center.

INDIAN PALMS COUNTY CLUB RESORT

General Manager: Reggie Cox
760-775-4444 or 1-800-778-5288; fax: 760-775-4447
www.indianpalms.com
E-mail: info@indianpalms.com
48-630 Monroe St., Indio, CA 92201
Price: Inexpensive to Moderate
Credit Cards: AE, D, DC, MC, V
Special Features: Golf course

Set on the Indian Palms Golf Course, toward the southern end of the valley, this slightly staid option offers 59 comfy, well-equipped nonsmoking rooms, albeit with uninspired decor that includes taupe carpets, red- or green-painted walls, and pine furniture. You're offered a choice of king or two queen beds with comfy mattresses and quality linens. It also has three-bedroom condos, plus a clubhouse with restaurant and bar. The main draws here are the nine tennis courts (five lit for night play) and three nine-hole courses.

Motels

Best Western Palm Desert Resort
(760-340-4441 or 1-800-231-8675, fax: 760-773-9413; www.bestwestern.com; 74-695 Hwy. 111, Palm Desert, CA 92260; Inexpensive; AE, MC, V) No-frills chain motel with functional furnishings. Nonsmoking throughout. Pets are allowed.

The Inn at Deep Canyon
(760-346-8061 or 800-253-0004, fax: 760-341.9120; www.inn-adc.com; 74-470 Abonia Trail, Palm Desert, CA 92260; Inexpensive to Expensive; MC, V) It may project itself as a small-scale, homey B&B, but this resort is a motel by another name. Most of the 32 rooms overlook the pool and garden. Drab, outdated decor and furnishings. Some rooms have kitchenettes. No restaurant, but there's no shortage of options on nearby El Paseo.

Vacation Rentals

Hankering to put on your sunglasses, sit by the pool, and pretend you're a star in your very own pad? Easily done. Scores of modernist homes, plus condos and villas, are available for vacation rental.

Looking for a Midcentury Modern? Check out **Vacation Palm Springs** (760-778-7832 or 1-800-590-3110; www.vacationpalmsprings.com; 1276 N. Palm Canyon Dr., Suite 211, Palm Springs, CA 92262). About half its properties are Alexander-designed midcentury homes—collectible exemplars of fifties desert suburbia, often decorated with Eames chairs, Saarinen tables, and other furnishings of the era. All the houses have pools.

A similar service is offered by **McLean Company Rentals** (760-322-2500 or 1-800-777-4606; www.ps4rent.com; 477 S. Palm Canyon Dr., Palm Springs, CA 92262). Among its dozens of properties is the Marilyn Hideaway, lent to Monroe for weekend trysts. Built in the 1930s, it's a three-quarter-acre estate with tennis court, fountains, pool, five bedrooms, fireplaces, a baby grand piano, and a professional kitchen. The home is tastefully decorated with Marilyn photos and artwork. The Dinah Shore home, in contrast, is a California ranch with five themed bedrooms, including the Rat Pack Room, which has martini-decor rugs in the bath. Some of the rentals are Alexander-style three bedroom homes, furnished by their absentee owners with occasional period icons.

For the ultimate in luxury, check out the properties represented by **Time & Place Homes** (760-320-1058; www.timeandplace.com), which offers the Jack Warner estate and Twin Palms, the former home of Frank Sinatra, among its glittering villas.

Mesquite Realty & Rentals (760-322-0666 or 1-800-800-9303; www.mesquiterentals.com; 555 S. Sunrise Way, Palm Springs, CA 92264) specializes in condos and villas in six gated communities.

Bedroom in a vacation rental condo. www.laquintavillarentals.com

Danseur, *by Jean Louis Corby. El Paseo.*

4

Culture

Modernism's Place in the Sun

Bermuda shorts mingle with tuxes in the Coachella Valley, which is a desert only in name. The monied elite that pours in for winter, for example, is a major patron to the arts and has made fund-raising parties its own art form. There's so much to see and do it's quite stunning. The cultural life here is impressive, concentrated in **Palm Springs** (pop. 49,000), with its world-class museums, professional theaters, and piano bars recalling the days when Ol' Blue Eyes added a sparkle to the watering holes of the desert. Many of the singer's haunts are gone: Dominick's . . . Jilly's West . . . the Chi Chi Club . . . Romanoff's on the Rocks. But enough remain, alongside the fabulous modernist homes of the countless celebrities whose lingering presence still puts a shine on Palm Springs' cultural cachet. Nonetheless, the city has a youthful spring in its step, having emerged from its recent Republican, post-swinging-era past to see a new, more liberal—and heavily gay—generation take charge. And a spectacular $2.5 billion downtown redevelopment plan due to break ground in 2008 promises to invigorate Palm Springs even further, with at least two swank new hotels—the Mondrian and Hard Rock—plus a stunning new Agua Caliente Cultural Museum and a 300-foot-wide pedestrian walkway—"MuseumWay"—linking the world-class Palm Springs Art Museum to "The Strip."

To the north of Palm Springs and separated from it by the world's largest wind-turbine farm is the city of **Desert Hot Springs** (pop. 17,000), the only town on the east side of Interstate 10. Desert Hot Springs is famous for its hot mineral waters that bubble from underground to feed the thermal wells of more than 40 hotel spas dating from the 1940s and '50s. A decade ago, the city was strewn with burnt-out motel signs, but its "spa-tels" have since arisen like a phoenix from the desert dust. Nonetheless, the town itself is a true ugly duckling, with few other attractions of interest.

Adjoining Palm Springs to the south, "working class" **Cathedral City** (pop. 47,000) is known for its family entertainment, highlighted by the $5.1 million Desert IMAX Theater, the Camelot Park Family Entertainment Center, and the Big League Dreams Sports Park, comprising three baseball fields, a roller-hockey rink, soccer fields, and more. Half a century ago, casino gambling was a big part of the lure of Palm Springs, although the joints were discreetly over the town line in dusty Cathedral City, where the valley's brothels were also located. "Cat City," as it became known, has always played host to salacious clubs, and today hosts the Coachella Valley's only strip club, alongside such retro-hip venues as Buddy Greco's.

Desert Modernism

Modernist architecture had its roots in the Bauhaus school of 1920s' Germany. It took root in the United States in the 1930s and reached its zenith in the 1950s and '60s before falling from grace in the early '70s. The movement found a favorable setting in Palm Springs, which boasts an astonishing concentration of modernist gems for such a small region. Modernism became the vernacular style of the city, thanks to the architects who came to build homes for the rich and stayed because they fell in love with the weather and the lunarlike landscapes. As the newly arrived Swiss architect Albert Frey wrote in a 1935 letter to his former employer, Le Corbusier, "The sun, the pure air, and the simple forms of the desert create perfect conditions for architecture." Palm Springs was destined to become modernism's place in the sun, not least because the town's own fully fledged flourishing from the go-go 1940s to the 1960s coincided with that of the modernist movement. The result was one of the most important concentrations of modernist architecture in the world.

Modernist furniture inside a steel house.

Frey and fellow talented eccentrics interpreted the clean, angled austerity of the modernist style in ways that were appropriate for the mountains and desert sands: ground-hugging open-air designs, acres of glass beneath huge overhangs to capture the striking views, sun-resistant desert rocks, and shimmering pools amid Zen-like rock and cactus gardens. The style became known as desert modernism. Spare forms never looked better than they did in the desert's stark, elemental environment, their lines etched by the klieg-light sun.

The style perfectly suited the adventurous and elegantly informal desert lifestyle of Palm Springs'

Neighboring, upscale **Rancho Mirage** (pop. 14,000) is famous for its exclusive country clubs and world-class golfing. Frank Sinatra moved here in 1957 and made a large William Cody–designed house at Tamarisk Country Club, his home until his death. And Lucille Ball and Desi Arnaz, who lived in a private estate on Bob Hope Drive, were such regular habitués that they were as synonymous with the area as Sinatra, Crosby, and Hope. Rancho Mirage is most closely associated with Gerald and Betty Ford, whose public admission of her alcohol addiction led to the subsequent founding of the Betty Ford Center. The couple settled into retirement here, and until his death in 2007 the ex-president could be seen shopping just like any other retiree in Bermuda shorts.

The golf courses extend south into **Palm Desert** (pop. 43,000). A shopper's haven, the chic city is the Coachella Valley's equivalent of Beverly Hills, with its famous El Paseo shopping boulevard being its equivalent of Rodeo Drive. Palm Desert is a center for arts, with the region's most lavish performance venue plus many of its best galleries. Star-studded performances are held at the McCallum Theatre for the Performing Arts, while nature lovers are drawn to the Living Desert wildlife park and botanical gardens,

prominent personalities. Hollywood stars commissioned the leading modernist architects—L.A. imports like John Lautner and Richard Neutra, and locals like William Cody, Albert Frey, and E. Stewart Williams—to design their weekend getaway homes. Bullock's and Desmond's, I. Magnin's, and Saks Fifth Avenue also opened stores here in modernist style. Dozens of modernist commercial structures went up, including three important bank buildings—the Coachella Valley Bank (1960), Santa Fe Savings and Loan (1960), and the Ronchamp-inspired City National Bank (1959). Palm Springs also garnered one of the world's finest collections of commercially designed motels in the country: Cody, Frey, Krisel, Lautner, and Stewart Williams all produced spectacular designs of the genre, attesting to the respectability of motels at the time. And modernism flourishes even in Palm Springs' civic buildings, among them the city hall, the airport, and the Palm Springs Art Museum.

The mood had changed by the 1970s and '80s, when tastes turned toward Spanish revival, with its textured stucco, red-tile roofs, and ornamental frills. Modernist designs came to look plain. Many modernist gems, such as the elegant Bullock's Wilshire, were demolished as Palm Springs' city fathers envisioned an updated downtown in Santa Barbara's Spanish vernacular. Officials were slow to cotton on to the renewed appreciation for modernism that emerged about a decade ago as people with an eye for great design began rescuing architectural gems tarnished by time. Today Palm Springs is ground zero in a modernist revival that has parallels with the renaissance of Miami Beach's money-spinning art deco historic district. Although many gems are already lost, crushed beneath the bull-dozer's maw, others are now protected with National Historic status.

For further information contact the **Palm Springs Modern Committee** (www.psmodcom.org; P.O. Box 4738, Palm Springs, CA 92263), dedicated to maintaining the heritage of modern architecture and historic neighborhoods in Palm Springs and the Coachella Valley. The **Palm Springs Preservation Foundation** (www.pspf.net; P.O. Box 1122, Palm Springs, CA 92263) publishes *A Brief History and Architectural Guide*, listing 38 architectural jewels.

You can learn more about the masters of modernism through **PS Modern Tours** (760-318-6118, psmoderntours@aol.com), which offers guided tours by both minivan and Segways—the gyroscopically balanced two-wheelers. **Palm Springs Architectural Tours** (760-341-7330; segwayofthedesert@juno.com; 72-210 E-3 Hwy. 111, Palm Desert, CA 92260 also offer up-close and personal looks at the desert's most notable architecture, by appointment.

featuring ostrich, giraffe, and other desert wildlife.

Next comes **Indian Wells** (pop. 4,000), a high-income twin to Palm Desert with its surfeit of country clubs, golf courses, and upscale spa resort hotels. Also here is the world-class Indian Wells Tennis Garden, home to the Pacific Life Open. Likewise, neighboring **La Quinta** (pop. 28,000), the "Gem of the Desert," is home to some of the finest golf courses in the nation, including the world-class championship La Quinta Resort & Club (once home to Hollywood greats like Frank Capra, Bette Davis, and Clark Gable) and PGA West courses. The La Quinta Arts Festival draws top artists from across the nation. And Lake Cahuilla County Park is a bucolic escape, good for picnicking in the shadow of the Santa Rosa Mountains.

Indio (pop. 51,500), adjoining and southeast of La Quinta, is a heavily Latino working-class community that feels a universe away from the glitz of Palm Springs. Burgeoning today with residential development, it is still synonymous with its dwindling date groves (more than 90 percent of dates sold domestically are grown here). Also called the "City of Festivals," it has hosted the National Date Festival for more than 50 years. The annual Tamale Festival is held each December, and Indio hosts the Southwest Arts Festival, hot-air balloon festivals, plus polo matches and the largest annual rodeo west of the Mississippi at the Riverside County Fairground. Indio merges south into **Coachella** and **Thermal**, scruffy agricultural towns.

The following pages will give you some idea of the range of arts and entertainment possibilities, as well as key cultural sites from museums to nature attractions. The best place to find current happenings is the *Desert Entertainer*, distributed free at street stands, and the entertainment pages of the *Desert Sun*.

ARCHITECTURE

Palm Springs

Although plaques for local cosmetic surgeons are included in the downtown "Walk of Stars," the most noteworthy face-lift has been to the buildings. With its broad boulevards lined with landmark modernist and Spanish-Mediterranean houses hard up against the San Jacinto Mountains, Palm Springs is a trove of architectural jewels. The most obvious treasures are the modernist gems from the 1950s and early '60s. The following are among Palm Springs' exemplars:

BANK OF AMERICA

760-864-8616
588 S. Palm Canyon Dr., Palm Springs, CA 92262
Open: Mon.–Fri. 9–6, Sat. 9–1
Commanding the triangle at the junction of Palm Canyon, Indian Canyon, and Ramon roads, this freely expressionist structure was originally designed as the City National Bank Building in 1959 by Victor Gruen Associates, of Beverly Hills, in a dramatic, delightfully

Bank of America.

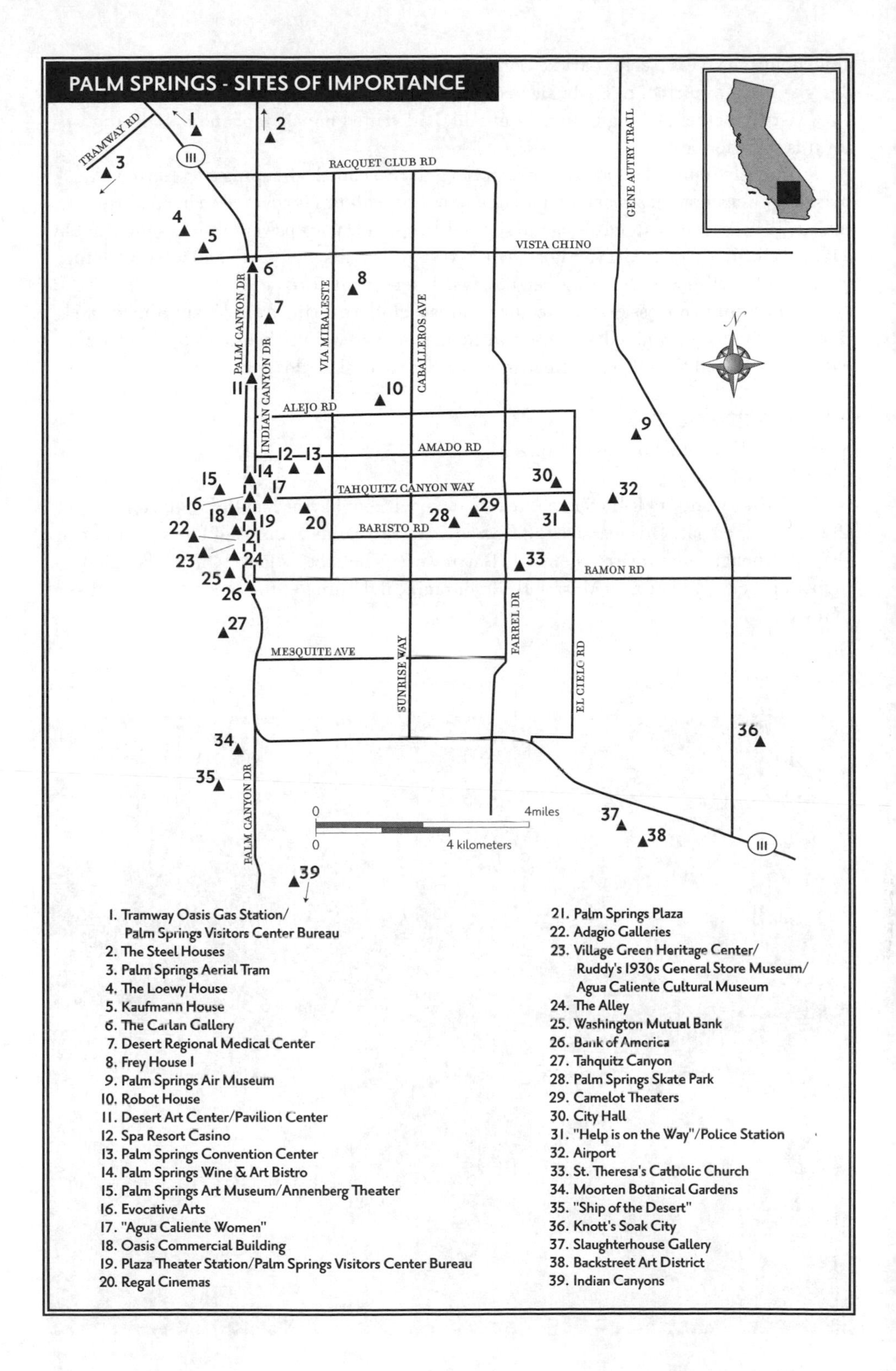

1. Tramway Oasis Gas Station/ Palm Springs Visitors Center Bureau
2. The Steel Houses
3. Palm Springs Aerial Tram
4. The Loewy House
5. Kaufmann House
6. The Carlan Gallery
7. Desert Regional Medical Center
8. Frey House I
9. Palm Springs Air Museum
10. Robot House
11. Desert Art Center/Pavilion Center
12. Spa Resort Casino
13. Palm Springs Convention Center
14. Palm Springs Wine & Art Bistro
15. Palm Springs Art Museum/Annenberg Theater
16. Evocative Arts
17. "Agua Caliente Women"
18. Oasis Commercial Building
19. Plaza Theater Station/Palm Springs Visitors Center Bureau
20. Regal Cinemas
21. Palm Springs Plaza
22. Adagio Galleries
23. Village Green Heritage Center/ Ruddy's 1930s General Store Museum/ Agua Caliente Cultural Museum
24. The Alley
25. Washington Mutual Bank
26. Bank of America
27. Tahquitz Canyon
28. Palm Springs Skate Park
29. Camelot Theaters
30. City Hall
31. "Help is on the Way"/Police Station
32. Airport
33. St. Theresa's Catholic Church
34. Moorten Botanical Gardens
35. "Ship of the Desert"
36. Knott's Soak City
37. Slaughterhouse Gallery
38. Backstreet Art District
39. Indian Canyons

amorphous form that seems part Le Corbusier, part Flintstones. In fact, the building was designed in the spirit of Le Corbusier's chapel at Ronchamp, France, which was built in 1954 (Gruen's chief of design, Rudi Baumfeld, had visited Ronchamp, and his admiration for it is plain to see).

Sensuously rounded pillars support an irregularly shaped, sweeping curved roof. A massively exaggerated, almost Stonehengian, corner column is covered in deep azure mosaic tiles that also extend along the south-facing wall. The upswept roof is supported by a long wall along Indian Canyon Road, while vast glass walls face north and west, with the west-facing wall shaded by a filigreed openwork screen anodized in gold.

The interior is no less exalted, featuring grass-cloth covering from Japan, Rhodesian lion-hair draperies, and teller cages of white marble and walnut. Sculptured chandeliers with pear-shaped Venini globes float above the German slate flooring.

BOB HOPE'S HOUSE

Southridge Dr., Palm Springs, CA 92264
Closed to visits
No first-time visitor to Palm Springs leaves town without having had the "Bob Hope House" pointed out. This massive (28,000 square feet) home with a roof like a giant turtle shell or (thought author Greg Nieman) "Darth Vader's helmet" is hard to miss. Perched high atop a craggy plateau of Murray Hill mountain, it dominates the scene at the south end of town.

Bob Hope's house.

The home, on 8 acres, was designed for Dolores Hope in 1973 by genius modernist architect John Lautner. Lautner had designed a house at 2175 Southridge Drive for Arthur Elrod that became the most photographed house in America, most famously in the James Bond movie *Diamonds are Forever* (released in 1971), where Bond gets his butt kicked by Amazonian sex-kitten gymnasts Thumper and Bambi. Dolores, apparently, wanted to one-up Elrod with her own Lautner home on Southridge Drive, sufficient for entertaining 300 people. Lautner came up with a great domed concrete roof with a huge hole in the middle. When shown the model for the home, Bob Hope quipped: "Well, at least when they come down from Mars, they'll know where to go." Dolores, however, kept tinkering with Lautner's designs. She also insisted on cheaper materials, such as plaster and a roof with plywood sheathing. Alas, on a searing July 24, 1973, a welder's torch set the plywood on fire and the house burned to the ground. Lawsuits followed. Reconstruction commenced only in 1977, and the house was completed in 1979.

Although the home can easily be seen from Highway 111, entry to the gated Southridge Community is barred. However, hikers can ascend the Araby Trail (see the Hiking section, in the Recreation chapter), which passes literally within a stone's throw of the house. You can make out the golf green, and there's a pool in the shape of Hope's familiar profile. Spectacular from a distance, the home is an inelegant monstrosity close up.

The exclusive Southridge estate has just 18 houses, owned at various times by Hollywood stars Ali McGraw, Joan Collins, Stefanie Powers, Steve McQueen, and William Holden.

CITY HALL

760-323-8299

3200 E. Tahquitz Canyon Way, Palm Springs, CA 92262

Combining the gravitas of a civic monument and the insouciant openness of the desert community, the Palm Springs City Hall is a utopian modernist gem designed in 1952 by a group of leading local architects, notably including Albert Frey. Standing directly opposite the airport, this single-story brick building receding rearward in lateral tiers provides visitors with their first vision of the city. The circular stepped entrance features a poured-concrete disc, or *tholos* (the circular temple of classical architecture), supported by four simple columns and engraved with the words "THE PEOPLE ARE THE CITY." Frey's design incorporated quintessential fifties institutional shapes, as well as unique conceptions such as metal piping cut at angles, providing both an artistic element as well as effective shields against the harsh morning sun.

A bronze statue of former mayor Frank Bogert riding a galloping steed was dedicated in 1991 on the palm-shaded lawn out front. (Bogert first moved to Palm Springs in 1927 and has ever since been a political fixture. Starting out as a horse wrangler, he was later named manager of the El Mirador Hotel and graduated to become a magazine publisher and twice-mayor of Palm Springs.) A bronze bust of regular Palm Springs visitor President John F. Kennedy rises from the center island of Tahquitz Canyon Way, in front of City Hall.

FREY HOUSE I

1210 N. Via Donna, Palm Springs, CA 92262

In 1940 acclaimed Swiss-born architect Albert Frey built a home in the desert for himself on a portion of the former El Mirador resort using plywood, corrugated aluminum sheeting, and other prefabricated materials, including vinyl padding for insulation—a poor choice in the torrid summer heat. The simple, diminutive (only 500 square feet) bungalow with floor-to-ceiling sliding-glass doors resembled something from a Flash Gordon movie. It comprised a collage of subtle indoor and outdoor spaces capped by a thin planar roof, with metal-clad walls arranged like shifting Japanese shoji screens. It was remodeled in 1953 with a circular second-story bedroom reached via a suspended staircase and upholstered in electric blue and yellow vinyl fabric and which author Alan Hess thought resembled a futuristic "Goffian spaceship," with a metal dining table suspended on wires "as if secured for intergalactic travel."

The house is now in the care of the Palm Springs Art Museum (760-322-4800; www.psmuseum.org). Visits are by appointment only.

KAUFMANN HOUSE

470 W. Vista Chino, Palm Springs, CA 92262
Closed to the public
Designed by world-acclaimed Los Angeles architect Richard Neutra in 1945–47 and the most celebrated of Neutra's forties postwar designs, this spectacular exemplar of modernism was commissioned by mercantile magnate Edgar Kaufmann (who earlier had commissioned Frank Lloyd Wright to design the epochal Fallingwater, near Pittsburgh). The house originally stood alone atop a boulder field at the foot of San Jacinto Mountain and was carefully aligned to maximize the stunning mountain vistas. The flat roofs seem to float atop polished glass walls with knife-edge lines sheathed in gray metal. Neutra's stunning exemplar of desert modernism was made famous by the iconographic photography of Julius Shulman. The house was later bought by Grammy-winning songwriter and singer Barry Manilow, who spent his winters here and in 1973 wrote his first hit, "Mandy," in the inspiring winter sun.

Over the decades the home became disfigured by ill-considered additions. In 1993 new owners, architectural historians Beth and Brent Harris, set out to painstakingly restore the house to its exact original specifications. In 2008 it was to be auctioned by Christie's as a work of art with an estimated value of $15–25 million!

THE STEEL HOUSES

Sunnyview Dr. between Simms Rd. and Molino Rd., Palm Springs, CA 92262
Closed to the public
Striking for their architectural simplicity, this cluster of seven steel-and-glass tract homes—including a now-famous model with a zigzag folded plate roof—were designed in 1961 and 1962 by Donald Wexler as prototype houses for developers George and Bob Alexander in conjunction with U.S. Steel, which wanted to promote the benefits of steel as a construction material. The prefabricated walls and core (two baths and a kitchen with living and dining rooms to each side) were erected on a concrete slab in less than four hours, and the entire house could be completed in three days for a cost of between $13,000 and 17,000 in 1962. Originally meant to be model homes for a larger development, the project was doomed when the costs of building with steel eventually became prohibitive. In 2001 the Historic Site Preservation Board declared the houses historic landmarks. Well-insulated and built of materials that better suited the desert environment than wood, the houses were incredibly energy efficient and look today as if they were built only yesterday.

The Alexander Company

In retro Palm Springs, "Alexander" is a key word, referring to major father-and-son developers George and Robert Alexander, who built more than 2,000 homes in Palm Springs in the 1950s and '60s. Delivering on the Bauhaus promise of progressive production housing, this was modernism for the middle-class masses. By ushering in the era of affordable air-conditioned tract housing, the Alexander company changed the face of the desert.

Utilizing designs by architects Dan Palmer and William Krisel, their fifties homes were open-plan, post-and-beam structures, typically with trademark butterfly roofs and clerestory and sweeping floor-to-ceiling windows adapted for the desert climate, with overhangs for shade. Some houses had natural stone walls; other had exposed concrete block. Most houses shared the same basic floor plans, though varying rooflines and the rotation of the plan on each lot lent a sense of diversity to individual neighborhoods. They had dual carports and often turned a windowless wall to the street, while glass walls opened up life to the pool to the rear. By the early 1960s the Alexanders had turned to a more conservative ranch-style home.

A-frame "Swiss Miss" Alexander home.

Hollywood celebrities were drawn to the posh yet simple designs of the typical Alexander home, which between 1955 and 1965 went for $20,000 to 50,000 and were bought up by everyone from Dean Martin to Debbie Reynolds. The homes created a comfortable and airy atmosphere that became as much a part of the persona of Palm Springs as the stars who bought them. In recent years the Alexander classic home has made a comeback as architectural collectibles of desert modernist vernacular at its best.

The Alexander family perished in a plane crash near Indio on November 14, 1965.

TRAMWAY OASIS GAS STATION

760-778-8418, 1-800-347-7746
2901 N. Palm Canyon Dr., Palm Springs, CA 92262
Open: Daily 9–5
Admission: Free

A visual exclamation point on the dusty desert road, this former gas station with the Space Age flying-wedge roof marks the entrance to the city 2 miles north of downtown, at Hwy. 111 and Tramway Road. Designed in 1965 in dramatic modernist style by noted architect Albert Frey, it features a now-famous and much-copied winglike roof that one critic likened to "a ninety-five-foot manta ray at liftoff." Frey called his wedge-shaped local icon

Albert Frey's Tramway Gas Station.

a "hyperbolic paraboloid." Jutting over the former gas pumps, the cantilevered kite of galvanized steel sheltered customers and attendants from the harsh sun, while seeming ready to soar up above the 10,000 foot peak behind it.

In 2000 Frey's iconic, much-copied masterpiece was restored and today is the home of the Palm Springs Visitors Center, providing a pointedly dramatic welcome at the unofficial gateway to town.

Other Architectural Sites

PALM SPRINGS

The Alley (333 S. Palm Canyon Dr., Palm Springs, CA 92262) Originally Robinson's department store, this striking Midcentury Modernist classic features a shady overhang with zigzag fascia supported on sculpturally tapering columns and a long wall of glass atop a raised pavilion.

Desert Regional Medical Center (1150 N. Indian Ave., Palm Springs, CA 92262) This modern hospital stands atop the site of the former El Mirador resort and retains the hotel's iconic three-story Spanish-revival-style bell tower striped in green, yellow, and blue (the tower, with wrought-iron balustrades plus Beaux-Arts touches, actually dates from 1991, after the original burned down). The tower and hotel were built in 1928 by Colorado cattleman Prescott Stevens, and through the years a never-ending parade of silver-screen idols passed through the door. Beginning in 1935, radio actors Freeman Gosden and Charles Correll broadcast their *Amos 'n' Andy* show from the tower.

The Loewy House (600 Panorama Rd., Palm Springs, CA 9262) Swiss architect Albert Frey designed a fabulous modernist home for commercial designer Raymond Loewy. One of Palm Springs' most celebrated homes, it features a pool easing into the living room, where one could simply slip off the couch for a dip. Loewy's most well-known designs include the Coca-Cola bottle, the silver Greyhound bus, and the Studebaker Avanti, as well as logos for Exxon and Shell.

The Oasis Commercial Building (Corner of Palm Canyon Drive and Tahquitz Canyon Way, Palm Springs, CA 92262) Originating as a swanky showroom with a grand staircase to the rear, this now legally protected historic site was designed in 1952 with austere atomic-age style by E. Stewart Williams, who had his office upstairs. The ground floor is now occupied by the prosaic Starbucks café.

St. Theresa's Catholic Church (760-323-2669; 2800 E. Ramon Rd., Palm Springs, CA 92264) Designed by William Cody in quasi-stupa form, this post-and-beam religious sanctuary is a modernist contemplation of a Gothic cathedral. Capped by a spreading pyramidal roof, it surrounds cloisterlike courtyards enclosed by curving walls and paved in packed sand.

Ship of the Desert (1995 Camino Monte, Palm Springs, CA 92262) A rare example of "Streamline Moderne," this private, ridgetop home designed by Earle Webster and Adrian Wilson features curvaceous, nautical contours and pipe railings denoting speed and efficiency.

Washington Mutual Bank (499 S. Palm Canyon Dr., Palm Springs, CA 92262) Originating as the Coachella Valley Savings, this E. Stewart Williams–designed building erected in 1960 features a dramatic facade exquisitely composed of inverted arches. On the side to the rear is a staircase, a classic Williams touch.

PALM SPRINGS VICINITY

Haleiwa Joe's (69-934 Hwy. 111, Rancho Mirage, CA 92270) Resembling some sort of prehistoric sea creature from an H. G. Wells novel, Haleiwa Joe's restaurant was designed by Kendrick Kellogg in 1978, when it was known as the Chart House. The building was unique for being earth-sheltered.

Haleiwa Joe's.

St. Louis Catholic Church (760-328-2398; 68-633 C St., Cathedral City, CA 92234) Visit this small church for the commemorative plaque to Frank Sinatra, to the rear, on the east side. It was a gift from Vice President Spiro Agnew, whose legal bills Sinatra helped pay.

Modernist Architects

Many of their finest designs come from the forties, fifties, and sixties, yet many of the architects below are only now being acknowledged. Palm Springs was a small town, and these architects not only competed for the same jobs—they often collaborated.

WILLIAM CODY Born in Dayton, Ohio, in 1916, Cody was raised in Los Angeles and moved to Palm Springs in 1942 to cure his asthma. He designed a wide variety of commercial and residential projects in Palm Springs. His most famous work was the now-extinct exuberantly designed Huddle Springs restaurant, built in 1957 on East Palm Canyon with soaring angled beams that reflected the "Googie-style" influence then popular in Southern California's roadside coffee shops. Cody was responsible, too, for St. Theresa's Catholic Church and much of the original Spa Hotel, in 1955. Later he concentrated his energies in designing country clubs, including the Eldorado Country Club (1957) in Indian Wells. Cody strove to reduce roof slabs and beams to the bare minimum: The roof on his own house at 1950 East Desert Palms Drive was a mere 4 inches thick. His colorful lifestyle, which earned him the nickname Wild Bill (he partied hard and slept late), eschewed promotion, and his name is little known beyond the valley.

ALBERT FREY Born in Switzerland in 1903, Frey became a disciple and friend of Le Corbusier. After establishing an architectural career in New York, he permanently relocated to Palm Springs in 1939, where he pursued his career largely unnoticed by the rest of the world until his ninth decade. The desert appealed to him, while the small community setting fit well with his lack of desire for preening and fame. Frey helped define Palm Springs modernism. He kept his minimalist buildings as close to the desert setting as possible, preferring to use cheap industrial materials such as corrugated metal, thin concrete panels, lots of glass to imbue qualities of simplicity and spareness, and blocks mixed with pulverized stone to give a pinkish, desert-like hue. Frey made 200-plus architectural contributions to the sun-blasted wasteland, including Palm Springs City Hall (1952), Tramway Valley Station (1963), the Tramway Gas Station (1965), and Frey's own metal home (1963)—all icons of the era.

JOHN LAUTNER Lautner was a protégé and former employee of Frank Lloyd Wright, who once called him the second-greatest architect in the world (after Wright himself). He preferred convoluted, organic designs over the boxy forms of his contemporaries. Lautner's most famous design was the turtle-shaped house he built for Bob and Dolores Hope atop the Southridge cliff, high above Highway 111, in southeast Palm Springs. His most stunning creation, however, is the neighboring house he designed for local interior designer Arthur Elrod in 1968. The circular concrete-and-glass aerie is essentially a vaulted cave built of poured concrete and incorporating the natural cliff-face as walls, topped by a curving, protective roof with alternating pie slices of cement and glass. It also featured a wall-to-wall curvilinear floor-to-ceiling glass window that offered a spectacular view and slid away to hide at the side of the house with the touch of a button. The space-age aerie was featured in the James Bond movie *Diamonds Are Forever* and was used regularly as a set for the naked models of *Playboy*.

DONALD WEXLER Wexler studied architecture at the University of Minnesota before settling in Los Angeles, where he was taken on by luminary architect Richard Neutra. Wexler developed an expertise in prefabricated steel construction, expressed in his famous "Steel Houses," built for developers George and Bob Alexander. These angular, 1,400-square-foot houses were extreme in their minimalist design. The Steel Development Houses project proved to be too expensive, and only seven homes were built along Sunny View Drive, just east of Indian Canyon Drive. Wexler also designed Palm Springs Airport (1965) and the Dinah Shore residence (1964).

E. STEWART WILLIAMS Emerson Stewart Williams studied architecture at Cornell and came to Palm Springs in 1946 to work in his family's architectural office. Williams's affinity for Scandinavian modern design was reflected in the wood and stone he used to root his houses in the desert landscape, such as in his first Palm Springs commission—the Frank Sinatra residence (1947), featuring natural stone and redwood. Tramway Mountain Station (1961), atop the tramway, is partly Williams's, as is the Palm Springs Art Museum (1970), a concrete building lifted above the street and sheathed in volcanic cinder. In 1964 Williams was asked to create a master plan for downtown Palm Springs, although shortsighted city fathers rejected his ambitious and orderly model to stick with their parochial small-town vision of scattered Spanish-style buildings.

SOUTHERN DESERT RESORTS

Palm Desert Community Presbyterian Church (760-346-8195; 47-321 Hwy. 74, Palm Desert, CA 92260) This dramatic modernist church was built in 1968 with a sweeping roof and soaring stained-glass facade between twin arcing frames. General Eisenhower and his wife, Mamie, were on the planning committee and presided at the ground-breaking. Note the bronze bust of Eisenhower by Cyria Henderson outside the south entrance.

William Boyd House (73-498 Joshua Tree St., Palm Desert, CA 92260) William who? You remember. He made 66 movies, 52 TV programs, and 104 radio shows as Hopalong Cassidy—the do-gooder cowboy who rode a white horse called Topper. Boyd and his wife, Grace, lived their winters between 1955 and 1971 in a low-slung, two-bedroom Midcentury Modernist home painted black and white. The house was recently restored to its original state with the help of the Palm Desert Historical Society. Boyd's original semicircular, black leather poolside bar still has his fixed bar-stools with saddle seats labeled for Gene Autry and Champion, Roy Rogers and Trigger, and other famous cowboys and their steeds. Now a private residence, it can be viewed from the outside only. Note the Mondrian-like wrought-iron sculptures framing the front door.

CASINOS

Since the valley's Cahuilla Indian territory is a sovereign nation, it is exempt from California's state ban on casinos. This isn't Monte Carlo, however. The casinos draw mostly from a lower-income bracket: Be prepared to share your space with an inordinate number of smokers (again, California's no-smoking laws don't apply). Some casinos thoughtfully provide no-smoking areas. No one under 21 years of age allowed.

Agua Caliente Casino (760-321-2000; www.hotwatercasino.com; 32-250 Bob Hope Dr., Rancho Mirage, CA 92270) This casino owned by the Agua Caliente Band of Cahuilla Indians has more than 1,000 slots and video machines, plus 49 gaming tables, including blackjack and poker. Also bingo six days a week. Live entertainment helps draw the punters, and there's a nonsmoking area, plus restaurants. It offers shuttles.

Augustine Casino (760-391-9500 or 1-888-752-2946; www.augustinecasino.com; 84-001 Ave. 54, Coachella, CA 92236) Operated by the Augustine Band of Cahuilla Indians, this casino has 750 slots and 10 table games. Open 24 hours.

Fantasy Springs Resort Casino (760-342-5000; www.fantasyspringsresort.com; 84-245

Speakeasy City

Illegal, albeit tolerated, gambling clubs operated in Cathedral City for decades beginning in the 1920s. Establishments ran the gamut from the no-class 139 Club to the Dunes Club, run by Detroit's notorious Purple Gang member Al Wertheimer. Big Al arrived in 1934, when Palm Springs was coming into its own as a playground of the stars. His entirely illicit casino in the midst of a sand-blown lot was lushly appointed in red velvet and chandeliers, and black-tie waiters served steaks and lobster to high-rollers. Pretty much everyone else was barred (a gun-toting watchman enforced the rules). Hollywood stars such as Marlene Dietrich, Clark Gable, and Errol Flynn were regulars. The 139 Club also drew Hollywood celebs, who mingled with the hoi polloi while a gunman looked down from a stone turret!

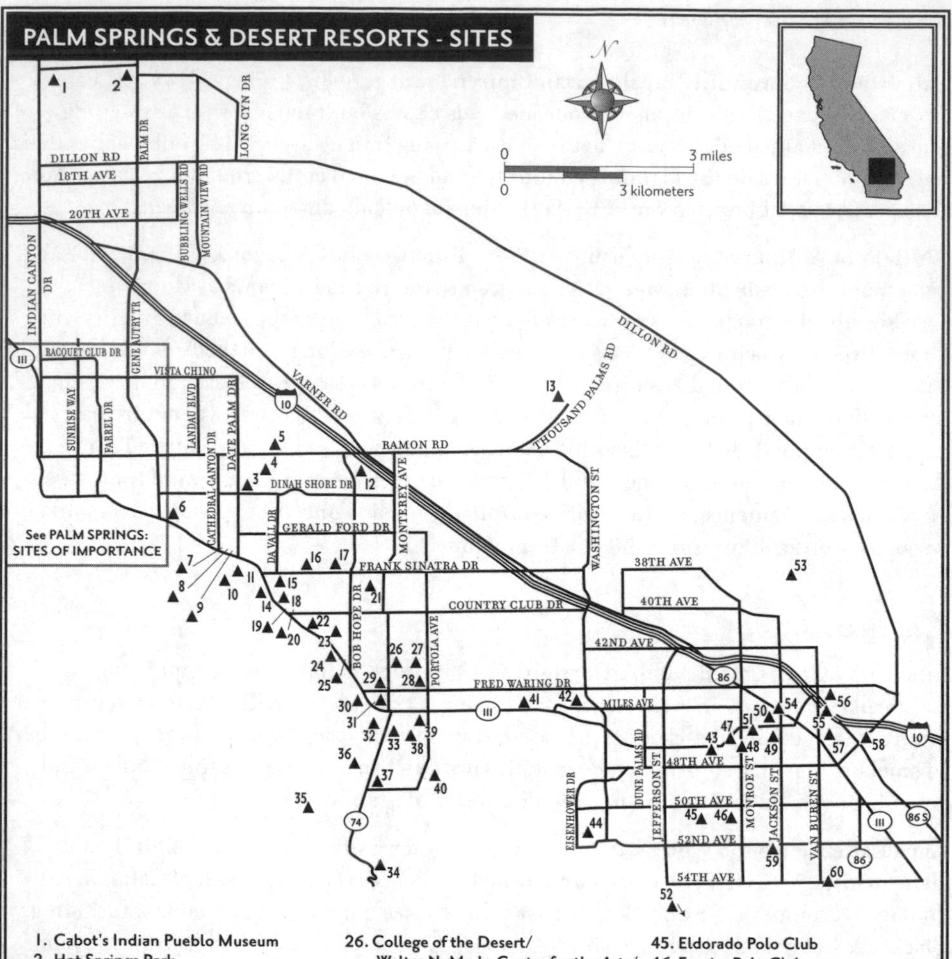

1. Cabot's Indian Pueblo Museum
2. Hot Springs Park
3. Patriot Park
4. Big League Dreams Sport Park
5. Desert Memorial Park
6. Boomers!
7. Desert IMAX
8. Town Square
9. Mary Pickford Theater
10. St. Louis Catholic Church
11. Buddy Greco's
12. Agua Caliente Casino
13. Coachella Valley Preserve
14. Cancer Survivor's Park
15. Michael S. Wolfson Park
16. Frank Sinatra's "The Compound"
17. Sunnylands Estate
18. Haleiwa Joe's
19. Palm Springs Desert Resort Convention & Visitors Authority
20. Blue Skies Village Mobile Home Park
21. Eisenhower Medical Center/Heartland
22. Rancho Mirage Public Library
23. Whitewater Park
24. Blixseth Mountain Park
25. The River at Rancho Mirage
26. College of the Desert/ Walter N. Marks Center for the Arts/ Jude E. Poynter Golf Museum
27. Civic Center Park
28. Desert Holocaust Memorial
29. The McCallum Theatre
30. Palm Desert Visitor Center
31. Cinema Palme d'Or/Westfield Shopping Plaza
32. Historical Society of Palm Desert Museum
33. Imago Galleries
34. Santa Rosa & San Jacinto Mountains National Monument Visitor Center
35. Aerie Art Garden
36. Cap Homme Ralph Adems Park
37. Palm Desert Community Presbyterian Church
38. William Boyd House
39. El Paseo
40. Living Desert Zoo & Gardens
41. Eisenhower Walk of Honor & Veterans Memorial
42. Indian Wells Tennis Garden
43. Shields Date Garden
44. Old Town La Quinta
45. Eldorado Polo Club
46. Empire Polo Club
47. Regal Metro 8 Cinema
48. John F. Kennedy Memorial Hospital
49. Riverside County Fairgrounds
50. Coachella Valley Museum & Cultural Center
51. Indio Fashion Mall
52. Lake Cahuilla
53. GarganOptics
54. Indio Performing Arts Center
55. Cabazon Band of Mission Indians Cultural Museum
56. Fantasy Springs Resort Casino
57. Coachella Valley Bird Center
58. Spotlight 28 Cinemas
59. Coachella Valley Cemetery Veterans Memorial
60. Augustine Casino

Morongo Casino.

Indio Springs Dr., Indio, CA 92203) This massive casino of the Cabazon Band of Mission Indians, just off I-10, has almost 2,000 slots and video machines, plus high-stakes bingo, blackjack, California craps, poker, and roulette, as well as off-track satellite horse wagering. It has five restaurants, live entertainment, plus bowling, and its Special Events Center hosts boxing tournaments, major entertainers, and conventions. It features a 12-story hotel. Free shuttles.

Morongo Casino Resort & Spa (1-800-226-2737; www.morongocasinoresort.com; 49-750 Seminole Dr., Cabazon, CA 92230) Attached to a soaring 27-story hotel with a spa, snazzy nightclubs, and restaurants, off I-10. With almost 150,000 square feet of casino space and 2,000 slots, it's one of the largest casinos in the U.S. It has two acclaimed nightclubs.

Spa Resort Casino (760-325-1461 or 1-800-854-1279, www.sparesortcasino.com; 401 E. Amado Rd., Palm Springs, CA 92262) This ritzy casino—owned by the Agua Caliente Band of Cahuilla Indians—in the heart of Palm Springs is open 24 hours. It has 1,000 slot machines, 30 gaming tables, and a private gaming room for high-rollers. Dining is first-class, and it has dancing and live entertainment nightly. Free shuttles to Agua Caliente Casino.

Spa Resort Casino.

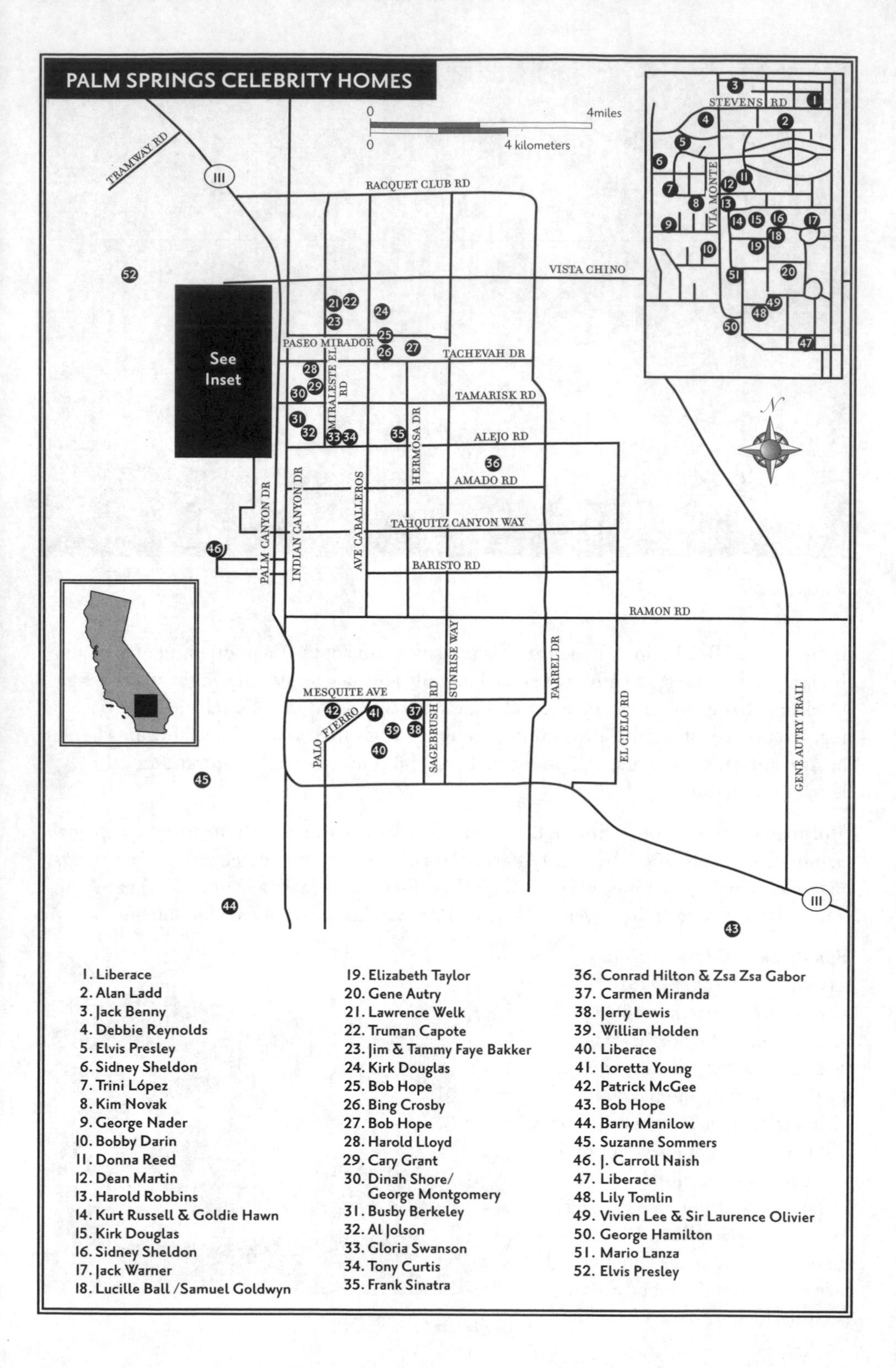
PALM SPRINGS CELEBRITY HOMES
0
4miles
0
4 kilometers
TRAMWAY RD
111
RACQUET CLUB RD
STEVENS RD
VIA MONTE
VISTA CHINO
See Inset
PASEO MIRADOR
TACHEVAH DR
MIRALESTE EL RD
TAMARISK RD
HERMOSA DR
ALEJO RD
AMADO RD
TAHQUITZ CANYON WAY
PALM CANYON DR
INDIAN CANYON DR
AVE CABALLEROS
BARISTO RD
RAMON RD
SUNRISE WAY
FARREL DR
MESQUITE AVE
PALO FIERRO
SAGEBRUSH RD
EL CIELO RD
GENE AUTRY TRAIL
N
111
1. Liberace
2. Alan Ladd
3. Jack Benny
4. Debbie Reynolds
5. Elvis Presley
6. Sidney Sheldon
7. Trini López
8. Kim Novak
9. George Nader
10. Bobby Darin
11. Donna Reed
12. Dean Martin
13. Harold Robbins
14. Kurt Russell & Goldie Hawn
15. Kirk Douglas
16. Sidney Sheldon
17. Jack Warner
18. Lucille Ball /Samuel Goldwyn
19. Elizabeth Taylor
20. Gene Autry
21. Lawrence Welk
22. Truman Capote
23. Jim & Tammy Faye Bakker
24. Kirk Douglas
25. Bob Hope
26. Bing Crosby
27. Bob Hope
28. Harold Lloyd
29. Cary Grant
30. Dinah Shore/ George Montgomery
31. Busby Berkeley
32. Al Jolson
33. Gloria Swanson
34. Tony Curtis
35. Frank Sinatra
36. Conrad Hilton & Zsa Zsa Gabor
37. Carmen Miranda
38. Jerry Lewis
39. Willian Holden
40. Liberace
41. Loretta Young
42. Patrick McGee
43. Bob Hope
44. Barry Manilow
45. Suzanne Sommers
46. J. Carroll Naish
47. Liberace
48. Lily Tomlin
49. Vivien Lee & Sir Laurence Olivier
50. George Hamilton
51. Mario Lanza
52. Elvis Presley

Spotlight 29 Casino (760-878-6729 or 1-866-377-6829, www.spotlight29.com; 46-200 Harrison St., Coachella, CA 92236). Not to be outdone, the Twenty-Nine Palms Band of Mission Indians operates this state-of-the-art casino, off I-10 at Dillon Rd. It has daily poker tournaments, 2,000-plus slots, 30 tables, and all the games from three-card poker to mini baccarat. The casino's Spotlight Showroom hosts boxing, as well as top entertainers.

CELEBRITY HOMES

Palm Springs

Perhaps apart from Beverly Hills, no other place on earth has so many famous names so closely associated with such a small space. The various neighborhoods evolved during different epochs, and their rise is closely associated with celebrity names of their specific eras. Even when seen from high above, the neighborhoods' distinct identities are discernible.

Celebrity Tours (760-770-2700 or 1-888-805-2700; www.celebrity-tours.com; 4751 E. Palm Canyon Dr., Palm Springs, CA 92264) offers guided motor coach tours. Reservations are required.

LAS PALMAS DISTRICT

The Las Palmas neighborhood, at the north end of town west of Palm Canyon Drive, has been home to more celebrities through the years than any other Palm Springs region. The older section, called Old Las Palmas, extends between Avenida Vista Chino and Alejo Road, and was first developed in the 1920s with grandiose estates in Spanish colonial and French provincial style. The newer section, Vista Las Palmas, rising west of Via Monte Vista to a granite escarpment called Tachevah, is studded with low-slung modernist villas—some of them desert midcentury classics built in the 1950s and 1960s by the Alexander Company for well-to-do winter residents. Every street has associations with at least one famous personality. The layout is a bit of a warren, and despite its condensed size (barely one mile north-south by three-quarters of a mile east-west), exploring can take up the better part of a day. The following barely scratches the surface of famous folks who once called Las Palmas home:

Radio and TV personality **Jack Benny** lived at 424 W. Vista Chino in a 1952 post-and-beam modernist home designed by William Cody, but later redesigned with a surfeit of steel and glass. Flamboyant entertainer **Liberace** loved Palm Springs and owned several homes here. His third home, at 1441 N. Kaweah Rd., was furnished in Liberace's trademark gauche French provincial style. Kaweah Road runs south into Camino Norte, lined with the former homes of Hollywood's high and mighty, such as **Alan Ladd**, who owned the five-bedroom modernist home (designed by Donald Wexler) at 323 Camino Norte, where he died from an overdose of alcohol and barbiturates on January 29, 1964. **Mary Martin**, of *South Pacific* and *The Sound of Music* fame, lived at 365 Camino Real, while **Joseph Barbera**, co-creator with William Hanna of *Yogi Bear*, *The Flintstones*, and *Tom and Jerry*, lived at 533 Camino Norte until his death in 2006.

Donna Reed, the Oscar-winning supporting actress in *From Here to Eternity*, lived off Camino Norte at 1184 Camino del Mirasol. Another famous Oscar-winning actress, **Claudette Colbert**, star of *It Happened One Night*, lived nearby at 1255 Camino del Mirasol. Camino del Mirasol curls south to Camino Sur, whose famous occupants include **Donald W. Douglas Sr.**, 377 Camino Sur, founder of Douglas Aircraft. Author **Harold Robbins** lived sexually debauched, and died, age 81, at 601 Camino Sur. Actor-singer **Tony Martin** and his ballet dancer-wife **Cyd Charisse** lived at 697 Camino Sur; blond bombshell **Kim**

Elizabeth Taylor's house.

Novak lived at 740 Camino Sur; and gay bronzed actor-pinup **George Nader** lived for many years at 893 Camino Sur, having bought it without knowing that the house had been the scene of an unsolved triple murder on the evening of October 3, 1978.

One block south, Via Lola perhaps has more names of the rich and famous associated with it than any other street in Palm Springs. **Jack Warner**, the much-feared founder of Warner Bros. Pictures, lived with his wife at 285 Via Lola (he supposedly bought another home nearby for his mistress). The lounge features hand-painted silk wallpaper of Captain Cook's voyages. Novelist **Sidney Sheldon** wintered at his home at 425 Via Lola until his death in January 2007. Labor lawyer **Sidney Korshak**, who famously defended Al Capone, lived in the six-bedroom home at 535 Via Lola. His neighbors included **Kurt Russell and Goldie Hawn** (550 Via Lola), and three-time Oscar nominee **Kirk Douglas**, who from 1957 lived at 515 Via Lola with his second wife, Anne Buydens, until ill health forced them to sell it in 1999. "Within two hours of arriving, Kirk and I rented bicycles, and we've never left," recalled Anne of her first vacation here, in the mid-fifties. The Douglases were highly respected members of the community, "humble enough to wait in line for a dinner table at Billy Reed's," claimed author Ray Mungo. Their stunning modernist post-and-beam home was designed by Donald Wexler and Richard Harrison and completed in 1954; when Douglas bought it in 1957 he added a gym, spa, and tennis court, plus a three-car motor court. They also filled their home with invaluable art and for four decades hosted a pantheon of Hollywood and Washington figures at relaxed parties for which they were famous.

For some reason, this lush Merito Vista subdivision of Las Palmas drew Hollywood moguls, including MCA chairman **Lew Wasserman**, who lived in an ultra-contemporary home at 295 W. Hermosa Pl. (one block south of Via Lola); and **Samuel Goldwyn**, who in 1960, after an esteemed career as a founder of Metro-Goldwyn-Mayer, Paramount, and Universal Artists, retired to spend the rest of his life at his Spanish estate at

Dean Martin's house.

334 W. Hermosa Pl. **Lucille Ball and Desi Arnaz** had lived in this home in 1953, and before them, effete British film director **Edmund Goulding**, who author Howard Johns, in *Palm Springs Confidential*, claims hosted bisexual orgies at which Errol Flynn and Tyrone Power once had sex with each other (Greta Garbo and Joan Crawford were among the other attendees). While we're on titillating trivia, it was at a party at 457 W. Hermosa Pl., then owned by spinning yo-yo innovator **Donald Duncan**, that Frank Sinatra slugged the bartender because his martini wasn't as ordered. And **Elizabeth Taylor** lived between 1956 and 1957 with then-husband Mike Todd in a 1930s classically Spanish estate at 417 W. Hermosa Pl. This lovely home was rented from movie mogul Leo Spitz, head of Universal Studios.

One of Palm Springs' legends, the singing cowboy and real-estate mogul **Gene Autry**, lived out his final years at the Moroccan-style manse at 328 W. Mountain View Place. (The home has a long list of illustrious owners: bandleader **Eddie LeBaron**; meteorologist **Irving P. Krick**, who selected the ideal weather conditions for the D-Day invasion of Europe; and TV producer **Glen A. Larson**.) In the late 1950s, sultry nightclub entertainer **Lena Horne** lived at 465 W. Merito Pl., although she had been forced to use an assumed name to purchase the home due to racial prejudice. Other famous Merito Place residents have included actors **Laurence Harvey** (300 W. Merito Pl.) and **Rod Taylor** (271 Merito Place), **Vivien Leigh and Sir Laurence Olivier** (401 W. Merito Pl.), plus Emmy-winning comedienne **Lily Tomlin** (443 W. Merito Pl.).

Running north to south, Via Monte Vista marks the dividing line between Old Las Palmas and Vista Las Palmas. The splendid Alexander-built home at 1123 Via Monte Vista belonged to martini-guzzling songster **Dean Martin**, who loved to spend time in the desert carousing with fellow Rat Packers Frank Sinatra, Peter Lawford, Sammy Davis Jr., plus Crosby and Hope. Actress **Debbie Reynolds** lived at 670 W. Stevens Rd. with her second husband, Harry Karl, whose high-stakes gambling habit left the couple $2 million in debt. Her neighbor at 695 W. Stevens Rd. was **John Phillips**, folk-rock leader of the Mamas and the Papas, who spent the last six years of his life here.

Stevens Road runs west, uphill, into Rose Avenue, with a security gate immediately on your right. Beyond, at 925 Coronado Ave., the palatial former home of Oklahoma oilman **Louis Taubman** was once known as the "Desert White House" following the stay of **President Lyndon B. Johnson** in February 1964; **Prince Philip** was another of a long list of prominent guests. The residents list of Rose Avenue reads like a veritable "Who's Who," including author **Sidney Sheldon** (1294 N. Rose Ave.) and **Maurice "Big Mac" McDonald** (1293 Rose Ave.), co-founder with his brother Richard of the world-famous hamburger chain. Perennially tanned, cigar-smoking actor **George Hamilton** lived just off Rose Avenue at 827 W. Via Vadera. Mexican American singer **Trini López**, one of the *Dirty Dozen*, still lives one block south at 1139 Abrigo Rd.

At the south end of Vista Las Palmas, pompadoured singer **Bobby Darin** lived at 845 N. Fair Circle; **George Hamilton** also lived in the Spanish manse at 591 N. Patencio Rd.; while heartthrob operatic tenor **Mario Lanza** lived at 784 N. Patencio Rd.; and sex-addicted millionaire author **Harold Robbins** also lived at 990 N. Patencio Rd. If the modernist home (designed by renowned architect A. Quincy Jones) at 993 N. Patencio Rd. looks familiar, it's because it was the setting for a Las Vegas mansion in the 2001 remake of *Ocean's 11* starring George Clooney, Matt Damon, Don Cheadle, Elliott Gould, and Brad Pitt.

THE CLOISTERS

501 N. Belardo Rd., Palm Springs, CA 92262
Closed to the public

Flamboyant *in extremis* describes Liberace's former mansion. The unrestrained entertainer, born with the unlikely name of Wladziu Valentino Liberace, arrived in Palm Springs in 1952 and lived a decadent, self-indulgent life, accompanied by his chauffeur and live-in lover Scott Thurston and their 26 dogs. The Cloisters was Liberace's fourth and final home in Palm Springs (he also bought two others for his brother George and their mother). It is easily recognized by the gauche candelabra—Liberace's trademark—in the forecourt and a pair of curlicued L's that hang from the gates.

The home was built in 1930 for Alvah Hicks, owner of the Palm Springs Water Company. It had three bedrooms but was later added to in extravagant style by its second owner, Ludvovica Graham, a wealthy socialite. After changing hands twice more, the house was transformed into a Spanish-revival villa with enclosed courtyards with bubbling fountains. The home was run-down when Liberace paid $185,000 for it in 1967. The entertainer lavished huge sums of money in doing up the home, with chandeliers and gold-leafed mirrors, and even a chapel with stained-glass windows. The bedrooms were themed and included a Rudolph Valentino Suite, with a brass sleigh-bed once owned by Valentino; plus a Gloria Vanderbilt Suite; a Zebra Room; another with tiger-skin wallpaper; and the infamous Persian Tent Room, said to have been used for Greek-style orgies. Liberace's own bedroom featured a silk-lined mink bedspread and a red-velvet throne toilet, plus bathroom wallpaper adorned with copulating Greek couples. Liberace, who was greatly appreciated by locals for his philanthropy, was the consummate host: Visitors were gifted with terry robes, slippers, and sandalwood soaps shaped like tiny pianos.

Liberace's mother, Frances Zuchowski, who lived in a studio to the rear of the Cloisters, strongly denied her son's homosexuality and pedophilia, as did the singer himself. Nonetheless, Liberace died here of AIDS on February 4, 1987, as mourning fans gathered

Liberace's home, the Cloisters.

outside for a candlelight vigil and tabloid photographers scaled the walls. His estate—which included no end of kitschy and tacky mementos, not least, apparently, a life-size stuffed doll with erect penis—plus half a million dollars worth of Rolls-Royce and other luxurious automobiles, was auctioned off and the money donated to the Foundation for the Performing and Creative Arts.

"HOUSE OF TOMORROW"

1350 Ladera Circle, Palm Springs, CA 92262
760-322-1192
www.elvishoneymoon.com
E-mail: halcyon180@yahoo.com
Tours Mon.–Fri. at 1 PM, by appointment; $25 per person
This minimalist yet futuristic modernist home was designed in 1962 by Dan Palmer and William Krisel as a personal residence for developer Bob Alexander, who perished along with most of his family in a plane crash on November 14, 1965. The home's greater claim to fame is that this is where Elvis Presley honeymooned with Priscilla Presley after he made her an honest woman (the two had met in Germany when Priscilla Beaulieu was only 14 years old; she claimed that she remained a virgin until her wedding night). In April 1967 the King leased the home for a year in the days leading up to the marriage (Presley's manager, "Colonel" Tom Parker, lived one block away at 1166 N. Vista Vespero). Presley wanted his wedding kept secret. The press was on their scent, however, having been tipped off by gossip columnist Rona Barrett, who lived two doors away and grew suspicious when Elvis's extended family started gathering. On the eve of the wedding, the lovers slipped away through the orchard to the rear and were whisked to the airport, where Frank Sinatra's Learjet was waiting to fly them to Las Vegas, where they married in the Aladdin Hotel on

Elvis Presley's "Honeymoon House."

May 1. The newlyweds then returned to Palm Springs, and Elvis carried Priscilla over the threshold and up the stairs of the Honeymoon Hideaway singing "The Hawaiian Wedding Song."

The spectacular house was built on a sloping site, with four circular rooms at different levels, including a massive living room with a freestanding conical fireplace with a soaring vent, natural peanut-brittle stone, and high clerestory window views of the mountains. The home that *Look* magazine called "House of Tomorrow" boasts the original 64-foot-long built-in banquette couch and foot-deep shag carpet. Fully restored and furnished in period fashion, it now rents out for weddings, honeymoons, fashion shoots, and corporate parties. Quirky interior touches include a leather-jacketed mannequin, a sixties jukebox, and, of course, blown-up black-and-whites of the King.

Little Tuscany District

Immediately north of Las Palmas is Little Tuscany, to the west of the Racquet Club, where expensive custom-built 1950s modernist gems such as the Kaufmann house are built amid natural boulders on the lower slopes of Mount San Jacinto.

The list of Hollywood stars who lived in Little Tuscany is long. Actor **Tom Neal** moved to Palm Springs when his B-movie career washed up. He lived at 2481 Cardillo Ave., where in April 1965 he shot his wife to death. **Marc Lawrence**, star of such film noir gangster movies as *This Gun for Hire* and *Dillinger*, lived one block west at 2200 Vista Grande Ave. Many famous Broadway musical songs ("I Could Have Danced All Night," "Thank Heaven for Little Girls," "On the Street Where You Live," "The Rain in Spain") were penned nearby at 815 Panorama, where Austrian-born composer **Frederick Loewe** lived for 28 years. **Magda Gabor**, the milder-tempered sister of Zsa Zsa, lived a reclusive life farther up the hill at 1090 Cielo Dr. until her death in 1997.

Horsing Around

Palm Springs' adorable climate is tailor-made for exploring downtown with the top down. I'm not talking automobiles. When the stars come out, it's time to hop aboard a horse-drawn surrey for a romantic tour in Cinderella fashion.

Palm Springs Carriages (760-364-4430; www.palmspringscarriages.com) offers three narrated tours of the Palm Springs Strip and historic Tennis Club district, departing from Palm Canyon Drive in front of the Historic Village Green, between Arenas and Baristo. Tours from 10 minutes to 1 hour ($25 to 125 for a party of four) are offered 7–10 PM Mon.–Wed., 7–11 Fri. and Sun., and 7–midnight on Sat.; no reservations are required. In winter, longer tours (90 minutes to 4 hours; $25 to 375) of the Las Palmas area are also offered, by reservation, taking you past the homes of Hollywood celebrities past and present.

Coulson Carriages (951-237-5438; www.coulsoncarriage.com) also offers "Starbound Tours" by horse-drawn carriage on weekends 1–4 PM (winter) and 8–10 PM (summer), departing from E. Andreas Rd. and N. Palm Canyon Dr. Trips range from 15 minutes to 1 hour ($25–45 up to four people).

Palm Springs Carriages' horse-drawn surrey.

The area's most famous resident was **Elvis Presley**, who owned a five-bedroom Spanish-style mansion at 845 W. Chino Canyon Rd. Presley bought the home in 1970 from **Richard McDonald**, co-founder of the hamburger chain. The King made it his western retreat until his death in 1977 and even recorded two of his songs—"Are You Sincere?" and "I Miss You"—after remodeling the living room's vaulted ceilings with acoustic tiles. (In August 2007 new owners announced plans to turn the home into a Graceland West.) Elvis loved Palm Springs and could be seen riding his Harley-Davidson to downtown for ice cream.

TENNIS CLUB AND ART COLONY DISTRICT

The Tennis Club district, west of Palm Canyon Drive between Tahquitz Canyon Road and Ramon Road, was once covered by fruit orchards. It is named for the **Tennis Club** (701 W. Baristo Rd.), a superb modernist exemplar built in 1937 by developer Pearl McManus at the end of Baristo Road. Hard up against the rock-strewn base of Mount San Jacinto, it featured a restaurant that perched on a ledge above an iconic oval-shaped swimming pool pinned by twin palms that were widely imitated by designers around the world. Here Marilyn Monroe famously posed nude for *Playboy*.

Today the Tennis Club district is known for its boutique hotels. The district takes up only four blocks north to south; the two northern blocks are known as the Art Colony. Irish movie star **J. Carrol Naish** (*Beau Geste, House of Frankenstein*) lived in the two-story Mediterranean-style villa at 139 S. Tahquitz Dr. His next-door neighbor was Scottish artist **Gordon Coutts**, a peripatetic member of the Royal Academy of London. In 1924 Coutts settled in Palm Springs and built himself a French-Moroccan style villa at 257 S. Patencio Rd. to remind him of his days in Tangier. He named it "Dar Maroc." Crenellated like a vision from Naish's *Beau Geste*, it fits right in against the palms and craggy mauve mountains. Winston Churchill, who had a great fondness for Morocco, relaxed here with his easel and paints. And, it is claimed, here Rudolph Valentino made love to his domineering to-be-second wife, Natasha Rambova, on a four-poster bed. Today, the Naish and Coutts homes comprise the Korakia Pensione hotel.

MOVIE COLONY

Centered on Ruth Hardy Park, the Movie Colony (the area east of Indian Canyon Drive, extending to Sunrise Way, between Vista Chino to the north and Alejo Road to the south) is named for the Hollywood stars who bought homes here in the late 1930s and '40s, when the area was on the outskirts of town. The flamboyant lifestyle with which the Movie Colony was synonymous was epitomized by the clothing-optional, luxury hotel Casa del Sol that Australian-born bon vivant actor **Errol Flynn** built in 1943 (he kept his name off the legal books for tax reasons). Hollywood's sybaritic crowd flocked to Flynn's wild hotel, which though it burned down in 1990, set a precedent for the Desert Shadows Inn, a nudist-lifestyle resort that currently occupies the same site. Back in the day, the area also had a western ranch—the Ranch Club—where the likes of Jane Wyman loved to ride horses while adorned in cowboy attire.

Among the Who's Who of past residents? Shock-jock novelist **Truman Capote**—author of *Breakfast at Tiffany's* and *In Cold Blood*—wintered at his home at 853 Paseo el Mirador. Capote was a regular at the city's gay nightspots and party scene. Capote's neighbor, bandleader **Lawrence "Ah-one and ah-two" Welk**, lived at 730 Paseo el Mirador, where he parked his car with the license plate A1NA2. Noted local architect **E. Stewart Williams** designed a modernist home for himself at 1250 Paseo el Mirador.

Despite his vast fortune, eccentric billionaire aviator/filmmaker/industrialist/financier **Howard Hughes** tried to keep a low profile in public and had an intimate familiarity with Palm Springs. Hughes rented his first desert home in 1940 "to 'stash' his then 15-year-old acting protégée, Faith Domergue," claims author Howard Johns. In 1957 Hughes moved to another rented pad at 1451 N. Paseo de Anza, where he secretly honeymooned with his second wife, actress Jean Peters. In 1963, during the scandal of his Trans World Airlines antitrust lawsuit, he tried to avoid the press at a modest tract home at 1185 Pasatiempo Rd. Eventually Hughes descended into madness and died in an emaciated state in 1976.

In 1987 cash-skimming televangelists **Jim and Tammy Faye Bakker** also attempted to hide from the paparazzi as helicopters whirred overhead (their Praise the Lord Ministry empire began to fall apart after Jim was caught funneling $265,000 hush money to church secretary Jessica Hahn to cover up an adulterous affair). Their five-bedroom hideout at 688 E. Vereda Sur featured gold-plated fixtures and even an air-conditioned dog kennel.

Kirk Douglas lived at 1069 E. Marshall Way, his first Palm Springs home, in the Tachevah Vista district. **Bob and Dolores Hope** and their four children lived from 1941 to 1946 just two blocks south, at 1014 Buena Vista Dr.—*their* first desert home. The Hopes then moved two blocks south to 1188 El Alameda, where they built a wall so that Bob could serve his famous frozen daiquiris by the pool beyond prying eyes. Hope's inseparable sidekick **Bing Crosby** occupied 1011 E. El Alameda in 1936 with wife, Dixie Lee, and their three children. In 1948 Brazilian bombshell **Carmen Miranda** lived at 1285 E. Verbena Dr.

No end of famous folks are associated with nearby Tamarisk and Via Miraleste roads. The grandiose Spanish colonial revival house at 796 Via Miraleste, on the southeast corner of the two roads, was built by Oklahoma "wildcatter" millionaire **Harry Hanbury**. Famously, **Cary Grant** and **Barbara Hutton** (heiress to the Woolworth fortune) honeymooned here in 1942. In the mid-1950s, Hollywood mogul **David Selznick** (*King Kong, A Tale of Two Cities, The Third Man*) rented the estate, which was later bought by Democratic fund-raiser **Phil Reagan**, who hosted a litany of political luminaries such as President Harry Truman. A neighboring ten-bedroom estate, at 346 E. Tamarisk Rd., passed into the hands of movie mogul **Darryl F. Zanuck**, supposedly in a poker game with United Artists' president Joseph Schenck, who built the home in 1934. Zanuck's walled compound hosted nobles, heads of state, and a rotating list of Hollywood stars attending the 20th Century Fox founder's croquet lawn parties that after lights-out turned into a game of musical beds. "Although we had separate rooms, sometimes at night [Tyrone Power] would sneak into mine," recalled glamour girl Lana Turner. Following her retirement, silent-screen goddess **Gloria Swanson** lived at 635 E. Granvia Valmonte, although she came out of retirement in 1974 for *Airport*.

Zanuck's onetime neighbor, actor **George Montgomery**, built the home at 877 N. Avenida Palos Verde, where he lived with his wife, **Dinah Shore**. And comedic film star **Jack Benny** lived at 987 Avenida Palos Verde, where he hosted Elizabeth Taylor and a rotating list of Hollywood greats. To the east one block, at 899 N. Avenida Palmas, lived **Harold Lloyd**, the bespectacled daredevil comedian of 1920s hits such as *The Kid Brother*. A millionaire at 31, Lloyd could be seen driving around the desert in any of his two Rolls-Royces, or his Cunningham, Pierce-Arrow, blue Chandler phaeton, and other classy cars from his auto stable. And **Cary Grant** lived at the Andalusian-style six-bedroom house at 928 Avenida Palmas. It was here, in 1954, that Alfred Hitchcock famously arrived with a copy of the script for *To Catch a Thief* to talk the debonair actor out of retirement. Grant lived at this rustic home between 1954 and 1972 with third and fourth wives, Betsy Drake and Dyan Cannon.

On the south side of Tamarisk, the gifted dance choreographer **Busby Berkeley** (of *Footlight Parade* and *Babes on Broadway* fame) lived for 18 years at 318 Via Alta Mira. Vaudeville entertainer **Al Jolson** settled at 570 Via Corta (perpendicular to Alta Mira, one block east) in 1946 following many years of peripatetic visits to Palm Springs. Hollywood filmmaker **Kenneth Anger** now lives there and swears that Jolson's ghost wanders the house in blackface. "He points to his mouth like he is saying 'Mammy, Mammy,' but you can't hear a word," Anger told an interviewer with *Grand Street* magazine in 1996.

Frank Sinatra's house, Twin Palms.

The area's most famous resident was undoubtedly **Frank Sinatra**, whose home "Twin Palms" at 1148 E. Alejo Rd. (www.sinatrahouse.com) is one of the most visited sites in Palm Springs (see the special topic, Frank Sinatra's Palm Springs). Sinatra had the house built in 1947. He sold it in 1957. For the next 43 years it was occupied by a Texan couple who let the house go to near-ruin. Bought for the unbelievable price of $135,000 in 1997, it was restored and sold in 2000 for $1,345,000, then again in 2005 for $2.9 million; it now serves as a luxury vacation rental, and visits are permitted by appointment only. After moving on to Rancho Mirage, Sinatra was a frequent guest of **Janet Leigh** and **Tony Curtis** in their post-and-beam modernist home at 641 N. Camino Real, and which the Hollywood dream couple bought in 1960.

PALM SPRINGS CENTRAL

South of Alejo Road and east of Avenida Caballeros, extending all the way to the airport, the residential district known as Palm Springs Central is an eclectic enclave of condominiums, middle-class homes, and fancier houses occupied now, or then, by the rich and famous.

The area was formerly the site of the original Palm

Sinatra's lounge, Twin Palms.

Springs airport. In 1949, construction of a new, larger airport was initiated to the east. In place of the original airstrip, the 20-acre La Mancha estate (444 N. Avenida Caballeros) went up, drawing a revolving door of famous guests, from Elizabeth Taylor to Barbra Streisand.

Clara Bow, the emotionally troubled flapper-actress of *Mantrap* and *It*, and later *Dangerous Curves* and *The Saturday Night Kid*, lived briefly in the 1950s at 200 N. Avenida Caballeros. **Conrad Hilton**, founder of the famous hotel chain, lived at his estate at 1961 E. Desert Palms Dr., along with his temperamental wife Zsa Zsa Gabor.

WARM SANDS PARK, DEEP DISH WELL, AND SOUTH PALM CANYON

The area immediately south of Ramon and east of South Indian Canyon Drive is known as Warm Sands Park and hosts several inexpensive "motels" that were the setting for wild times in the 1980s and '90s, when rowdy spring breakers favored the area. Some have survived in contempo vogue, the spring breakers having been replaced by a mostly gay clientele. Most are clothing-optional, as the names attest: Bacchanal, Inndulge, and Chestnutz.

The area south of Mesquite is known as Deep Well. The area is named for Deep Well Ranch, a horse ranch long since replaced by tract housing, including many California modernist gems. One of the area's most famous residents was **Patrick Macnee**, the dandified English actor who played John Steed in *The Avengers* and who lived (1973–88) at the Spanish-ranch-style home at 748 E. Mesquite Ave. TV glamour legend **Loretta Young** and her husband, Jean Louis, moved into 1075 Manzanita Ave. in 1993, four years after the end of her astounding acting career, which spanned 72 years.

Fruit-wearing Brazilian bombshell **Carmen Miranda** lived at 1044 S. Calle Rolph. One block west, loyal family man **Jerry Lewis**, the klutzy comedic actor, lived for many years at 1349 Sagebrush Rd. with his wife and six sons. A stone's throw west, the Japanese-style house at 1323 S. Driftwood Dr. belonged to peripatetic Hollywood heartthrob **William Holden**, star of *The Bridge on the River Kwai* and *The World of Suzie Wong*. He settled into his permanent home in 1967 after more than three decades of visiting Palm Springs, which he thought "was the place where you could get the cleanest air and an instant suntan for a healthy onscreen look." He lived here a full decade, surrounded by artwork and artifacts from his travels in Asia and Africa.

In 1957 **Liberace** settled in Palm Springs, moving into a house at 1516 S. Manzanita Ave. His flamboyant home featured candelabra-shaped garden torches, a fireplace hood decorated with harlequin diamonds, a rose-pink kitchen, and a swimming pool "flanked by muscular bodybuilders." One block south, the **Biltmore Hotel** opened in 1948 at 1000 E. Palm Canyon Dr. "The World's Finest Desert Resort" was party-central for the Rat Pack and drew a constant parade of Hollywood stars and starlets for 40 years, until Palm Springs' decline did the grande dame in. It closed in 1988 and gathered dust until razed in 2003.

South of Warm Sands and Deep Dish Well, the South Palm Canyon district is permanent home to longtime Palm Springs resident **Barry Manilow** (2196 S. Camino Barranca), whose hilltop home offers spectacular views; no surprise, access is denied by security gates. Nearby, and reached by a private funicular, the pink French-style mountainside home known as Les Baux de Palm Springs (385 Alta Vista Rd.) is the prime residence of actress-turned-self-help-guru **Suzanne Somers**. In January 2008 she and her husband, Alan Hamel, put their beloved 65-acre estate (which they bought in 1977) up for sale for $35 million. The couple intend to live in a contemporary custom-built glass-and-stone villa on the north side of the mountain ridge.

Suzanne Somers's house.

CINEMA

There's no shortage of cinemas in Palm Springs, although none of the grand movie house variety you might expect from the heyday when every Hollywood star caroused here.

PALM SPRINGS

Camelot Theatres (760-325-6565; www.camelottheatres.com; 2300 E. Baristo Rd., Palm Springs, CA 92262) State-of-the-art movie theater. Shows mainly independent films, as well as occasional blockbusters. It also hosts the Palm Springs International Film Festival.

Regal Palm Springs Stadium 9 (760-323-4466; 789 Tahquitz Canyon Way, Palm Springs, CA 92262) This modern nine-screen cinema even offers 3-D viewing (for an extra charge).

PALM SPRINGS VICINITY

Century Theaters (760-862-9997; 71-800 Hwy. 111 and Bob Hope Dr., Rancho Mirage, CA 92270) Has twin theaters: the 15-screen Century 15, showing mainstream movies; and the Cine Arts@The River, which shows art and independent films. Also shows simulcast presentation of the Metropolitan Opera and major concerts.

Desert IMAX Theater (760-324-7333, www.desertimax.com; 68-510 Hwy. 111, Cathedral Canyon, CA 92234) This state-of-the-art cinema has a six-story-high screen that draws you right into everything from *Harry Potter* to documentaries. It offers both two-dimensional and 3-D projection screens.

Mary Pickford Stadium 14 Cinemas (760-328-7100; www.northamericancinemas.com;

There are 14 screens at the Mary Pickford cinemas.

36-850 Pickfair St., Cathedral City, CA 92234) On Town Square, this elegant 14-screen theater has up-to-the-minute surround-sound and spacious seating.

Regal Cinemas (760-322-3456; 72-777 Dinah Shore Dr., Rancho Mirage, CA 92270) This complex has 14 screens for first-run movies. Some screenings are in digital 3-D.

SOUTHERN DESERT RESORTS

Cinemas Palme d'Or (760-779-0730; www.thepalme.com; 72-840 Hwy. 111, Palm Desert, CA 92270) In Westfield Shopping Center, it has 15 screens.

Regal Metro 8 (760-342-8451; 81-725 Hwy. 111 at Monroe, Indio, CA 92201) This cinema has eight screens.

GALLERIES

Sophisticated diversity sums up the valley's gallery offerings, with everything from mid-century abstraction to cutting-edge contemporary on view. The list of galleries is as astounding as the wealth of art they display. El Paseo, in Palm Desert, is a veritable art haven, and not just in its trove of upscale galleries lining the boulevard—in fact, the Strip itself is a paean to creativity, with several dozen sculptures along its mile-long median.

A specialty of the desert is plein air, outdoor paintings evoking impressionistic images

Art Festivals to Know

Desert Arts Festival, Francis Stevens Park.

The La Quinta Arts Foundation (760-564-1244) sponsors the weeklong **Annual Desert Plein Air** exhibition the third week in January.

The **Desert Arts Festival** (818-709-2907, Frances Stevens Park, 538 N. Palm Canyon Dr., Palm Springs, CA 92262) is held in late January.

The two-day **Rancho Mirage Art Affaire** (760-324-4511; Whitewater Park, 71-560 San Jacinto Dr., Rancho Mirage, CA 92270), a free fine-art and jazz festival, is hosted every early November.

of stark local landscapes and spectacular spring blooms. Gordon Coutts, John Frost, and Paul Grimm are world-recognized names among the many early 20th-century artists who set up their easels and studios in the Coachella Valley. Although the plein air movement was eclipsed in popularity by the conceptual and abstract art of the 1930s onward, it is now back in vogue.

Palm Springs

DESERT ART CENTER

760-323-7973
www.desertartcenter.com
550 N. Palm Canyon Dr., Palm Springs, CA 92262
Open: Tues.–Sun. 10–4
Admission: Free
This co-operative represents over 140 local artists working in all mediums. It offers classes six days a week and has bimonthly gallery openings. There are guided tours 6–10 PM nightly during the holidays.

"ROBOT HOUSE"

760-323-2828
1077 Granvia Valmonte, Palm Springs, CA 92262
Open: By appointment, except self-guided tours 7–10 PM daily, Dec.–Jan.
Admission: By donation
"Surreal" best describes the home—known as the "Robot House" (corner of Arquilla and Valmonte)—of eccentric sculptor Kenny Irwin Jr. Covering almost 4 acres, the family estate displays more than 200 metal statues, most of them humanoid and nonhumanoid robotic

Kenny Irwin's sculptures at the "Robot House."

sculptures made from discarded metallic junk painted in gaudy primary colors. Many are humongous (one is 48 feet tall). Some are animated. At year's end Kenny, who began creating his sculptures as a child, turns the "Robot House" into a Christmas village replete with Santa's workshop and Rudolph's barn with robotic reindeer. The Christmas display, which also includes more than 100 inflatables, among them a 50-foot rooftop Santa, is illuminated by more than *one million* twinkling lightbulbs!

SOUTHERN DESERT RESORTS

WALTER N. MARKS CENTER FOR THE ARTS
760-776-7278
www.collegeofthedesert.edu/visitors/Marks/index.asp
E-mail: artgallery@collegeofthedesert.edu
43-500 Monterey Ave., Palm Desert, CA 92260
Open: Tues.–Fri. noon–4
Admission: Free
In the College of the Desert, this arts center offers classes and lectures spanning ceramics and drawing to photography and performance arts. You can explore a sculpture garden plus three galleries hosting revolving exhibitions ranging from Early Desert Painters to Art of the Olympics.

Path of the Bighorn

Two centuries ago, between 1.5 and 2 million bighorn sheep roamed the mountains of North America. Today fewer than 70,000 remain. Of these, a mere 800 or so are Peninsular bighorn, a subspecies found only in California, from Palm Springs south to the Mexican border. After hitting a low of 280 individuals in 1996, the endangered Peninsular bighorn population is rising.

"Path of the Bighorn" sculpture, Rancho Mirage.

Their preferred habitat is rugged mountain terrain between 400 and 4,000 feet elevation. While seeing one in the wild would be cause for celebration, spotting a life-size facsimile is easy. More than a hundred 71-inch fiberglass rams, each weighing 350 pounds, stand at museums, tourist attractions, and other public places throughout the greater Palm Springs region, including the one that greets visitors at Palm Springs International Airport. The rams are sponsored (and some are even hand-adorned) by such celebrities as Chevy Chase, Cher, Tony Curtis, Phyllis Diller, Stefanie Powers, Anjelica Huston, and Sidney Sheldon, as well as local artists. Some are painted in colorful landscapes. Others bear Native American motifs. Some are inscribed with messages. The original was sculpted by Palm Springs artist Joe Wertheimer.

Proceeds from the "Path of the Bighorn" public art project benefit the nonprofit Bighorn Institute (760-346-7334; www.bighorninstitute.org; P.O. Box 262, Palm Desert, CA 92261), a conservation organization that launched the project to raise awareness of the plight of the endangered Peninsular bighorn.

Other Galleries

Palm Springs

Adagio Galleries (760-320-2230; www.adagiogalleries.com; 193 S. Palm Canyon Dr., Palm Springs, CA 92262) Specializing in Southwest and Hispanic art of the West Coast, this store represents many of the leading artists of the genre, such as Michael Atkinson.

Backstreet Art District (760-328-1440; 2688 Cherokee Way, Palm Springs, CA 92264) Eight artists' studios and galleries, including a warehouse space shared by a handful of talented artists. An Art Walk evening is offered the first Wednesday of each month.

The Carlan Gallery (760-322-8002; 1546 N. Palm Canyon Dr., Palm Springs, CA 92262) This light and bright gallery-museum displays works by leading 20th-century European masters, including Day-Glo bright works by Jean-Claude Tron and Olivier Tramoni.

Evocative Arts (760-327-7111; 170 E. Tahquitz Canyon Way, Palm Springs, CA 92262) Evocative contemporary art with an emphasis on figurative works.

Palm Springs Wine & Art Bistro (760-325-9991; www.palmspringswineandart.com; 242 N. Palm Canyon Dr., Palm Springs, CA 92262) This lively wine bar features local artwork with revolving exhibitions, plus it serves tapas and cocktails and has live jazz on Friday and Saturday nights.

Slaughterhouse Gallery (760-324-3320; www.slaughterhouseps.com; 2608 S. Cherokee Way, Palm Springs, CA 92264) Represents the works of three leading contemporary resident artists, including abstract photographer Karl Hatrak, plus revolving exhibitions by guest artists.

Southern Desert Resorts

El Paseo has more than 20 commercial galleries. On the first Thursday of each month, Oct.–May, they stay open late for the **El Paseo Art Walk** (1-877-735-7273; 5–9 PM). Free shuttle service is offered. And **The Art Place** (760-776-2268; 41-801 Corporate Way, Palm Desert, CA 92260) art and interior design complex showcases paintings, photography, and sculptures on the evening of every first Friday, Oct.–June.

A Gallery Fine Art (760-346-8885; www.agalleryfineart.com; 73-956 El Paseo, Palm Desert, CA 92260) Permanent collections by Erica Hopper and Jeffrey Jon Gluck, plus other paintings, glasswork, sculptures, and jewelry by emerging and established artists.

Coda Gallery (760-346-4661; www.codagallery.com; 73-151 El Paseo, Palm Desert, CA 92260) A remarkable collection of contemporary art from dozens of leading artists.

Desert Art Collection (760-674-9955; www.desertartcollection.com; 45-350 San Luis Rey Ave., Palm Desert, CA 92260) Contemporary fine art by several dozen leading artists, plus a sculpture garden.

Edenhurst Gallery (760-346-7900; www.edenhurstgallery.com; 73-655 El Paseo, Palm Desert, CA 92260) This gallery displays early California and American impressionists, such as Conrad Buff and William Wendt, plus modernist and contemporary works.

Eleonore Austerer Gallery (760-346-3695; www.austererfineart.com; 73-660 El Paseo, Palm Desert, CA 92260) Specializes in original works by modernist masters such as Chagall, Miró, Picasso, and Henry Moore, plus limited-edition graphics by Klee, Kandinsky, et al. Contemporary artists are also represented in their own exhibition space.

The Hart Gallery (760-346-4243; www.hartgallery.com; 73-111 El Paseo, Palm Desert, CA 92260) Owner Eva Hart's wide-open gallery exhibits an eclectic collection of contemporary European art, including sculptures.

Imago Galleries (760-776-9890; 45-450 Hwy. 74, Palm Desert, CA 92260) A top gallery with works by such legendary contemporary artists as Hans Hoffman and Mel Ramos, the Pop artist known for his erotic photorealistic nude pinup girls associated with retroculture icons, such as inside a martini glass. Noted glass artist Dale Chihuly, known for his riotous blown glass flowers, is a featured exhibitor. The gallery—a sublime piece of contemporary architecture—includes a library and adjacent sculpture garden.

Modern Masters Fine Art (760-341-1056; www.modernmastersfineart.com; 73-200 El

Art in Public Places

Palm Springs

Palm Springs isn't shortchanged for public art. A brief downtown tour should start with the *Agua Caliente Women* (Tahquitz Canyon Way and Indian Canyon Dr.), a huge patinated bronze by Nez Perce artist Doug Hyde. One block west, at the corner of Palm Canyon Drive, look for the life-size bronze of Lucille Ball sitting on a bench; while a stone's throw south, Emmanuil Snitkovsky's lifelike statue of Sonny Bono surveys the scene from his seat beside the fountain in Plaza Mercado. Various other Hollywood Sculptures, life-size painted steel likenesses of stars, can be seen in various locations downtown. And Steve Tyree's *Crouching Cougar* seems set to leap at folks passing by the Convention Center (277 N. Avenida Caballeros), where John Kennedy's slender *The Entertainer* stands in the lobby.

By far the most moving piece—a must-see—is *Help Is on the Way*, outside the police headquarters (200 S. Civic Dr.). This memorial, created in 1998 by Jeffrey Fowler, honors fallen officers Lyle Wayne Larrabee and Gale Gene Eldridge, and other police officers killed in the line of duty. It shows a policeman helping a fellow stricken officer.

Palm Springs Vicinity

Cathedral City's "Old Firehouse" (Cathedral Canyon Dr. and Commercial Rd., Cathedral City, CA 92234) is graced with a trompe l'oeil mural by artist Jerry High as part of the city's "Paint the Town" program.

Southern Desert Resorts

Palm Desert's city fathers also proudly sponsor public art and have invested no small sum to grace several boulevards and city parks with top-class pieces that are the envy of far larger cities. Palm Desert's Art in Public Places (760-568-5240; www.palmdesertart.org) requires developers to place art in parks, street medians, or even private buildings.

More than 150 unique works of art decorate Palm Desert, including at the Palm Desert Public Library—home to more than a dozen art pieces. The works are grouped into four-self-guided tours. The El Paseo Tour runs along the grassy median of El Paseo and features 18 exhibits—floodlit at night—that change every two years. Following Fred Waring Boulevard, the Fred Waring Corridor Tour passes bighorn sheep sculptures, bas-relief murals, and even a colorful obelisk. And Civic Center Sculpture Walk is a highlight of the 72-acre Civic Center Park (760-568-9697; Fred Waring Dr. and San Pablo Ave.), with 25 sculptures, including second-grader Bernice González's prize-winning, larger-than-life bronze sculpture of a mother and daughter holding hands, surrounded by terrazzo desert animals. Among the most

Paseo, Palm Desert, CA 92260) Roy Lichtenstein, Rufino Tamayo, Marc Chagall, and Justin Love are among the masters represented in this contemporary fine art gallery.

Historic Sites

PALM SPRINGS VICINITY

BLUE SKIES VILLAGE MOBILE HOME PARK

760-328-2600
70-260 Hwy. 111, Rancho Mirage, CA 92270
Open: Mon.–Thurs. 8–noon; call in advance for access
Admission: Free

This gated mobile home park introduced the notion of a luxury planned trailer park to America when it opened in 1955. Bing Crosby, who had a home at the nearby Thunderbird

interesting pieces are Gordon Huether's 12-foot-tall polished aluminum *Agave* (Fred Waring Dr., 50 yards west of Portola Ave.), made from salvaged aircraft fuel tanks; and David Phelps's *The Dreamer* (Civic Center Park), showing a barefoot worker—14 feet long!—reclining on the lawn, as if taking a bath. Nearby, *Midstream*, a life-size painted bronze sculpture of a fisherman standing over the lake, delights passersby. Also in Civic Center Park is the haunting bronze and granite Holocaust Memorial (see Military Sites, this chapter, for full details). Ross Andrews's Peace Memorial (Magnesia Falls Dr. and Fred Waring Dr.) is graced with the names of desert residents who lost their lives defending freedom. And *For Our Freedom* (Freedom Park, 77-400 Country Club Dr.), a Veterans Day tribute dedicated on 11 November 2007, is a beautiful bronze sculpture by father-and-son artists Jesus and Adam Romo; it depicts a woman on her knees, clutching a folded flag and flower bouquet while her young son looks on.

Agua Caliente Women, *by Nez Perce artist Doug Hyde.*

Before exploring, pick up a copy of *Palm Desert Art & Architecture*, a small guide to the art and architecture of the city published by the city of Palm Desert. Free docent tours are given on the second Saturday of each month (except July and August).

Seven colorful murals grace historic downtown Indio, painting a big picture on the city's past. Guided **Indio Mural Walks** (760-347-0676; www.indiochamber.org) led by museum docents interpret the murals, which include *History of Transportation* (Indio Blvd. and Sun Gold St.) *Life in an Indian Village* (Indio Blvd. and Towne St.), and *The History of the Date Industry* (Miles Ave. and Oasis St.). Sponsored by the city of Indio, Indio Chamber of Commerce, and Coachella Valley Museum & Cultural Center; free.

Country Club, was the major investor, took a hand in design, and even named it for one of his hit songs (the park began as a spin-off from the temporary movie-set trailers that housed actors, directors, and others during filming of a movie on Crosby's property). The park featured landscaping, a dance hall designed by William Cody, and a nine-hole pitch-and putt-golf course. The narrow streets (which were made for golf carts, first introduced next door at the Thunderbird Country Club) were named for Bing's fellow entertainer investors, such as Danny Kaye and Jack Benny, who attended community functions here. Blue Skies opened when the new highway network spawned interstate tourism by vacation trailers, and before the taboo against prefab homes took hold. The comedy *The Long, Long Trailer*, starring Lucille Ball and Desi Arnaz, helped make vacation homes respectable, while Bing's popularity added to the respectability of Blue Skies.

Through the decades the basic trailer homes have been turned into a hodgepodge of global housing. One has an Oriental motif, with Chinese-dragon front door and Japanese landscaping. Another is themed like the Karnak temples in Egypt, with King Tut hiero-

Lucille Ball sculpture.

glyphics. A third resembles Tara, from *Gone With the Wind*.

The only parking meter in Rancho Mirage is within the park. It's a monument to Jack Benny the actor (and Blue Skies investment partner), whose TV persona was a penny-pinching spendthrift.

"THE COMPOUND"

70-588 Frank Sinatra Dr., Rancho Mirage, CA 92270
Closed to the public
In 1957 Frank Sinatra left Palm Springs for "The Compound," his new full-time home in Rancho Mirage. Designed by William Cody and spread over 2 acres on the 17th fairway of the Tamarisk Country Club, the home featured two pools, a movie theater, and even a barbershop. The residence (once identified by the sign reading "Forget the dog. Beware of the Owner") is hidden from view from the road, except for the tops of the five guesthouses that Sinatra added and named for his songs.

A helicopter pad and special presidential guesthouse were added in 1962 in anticipation of a visit by President John F. Kennedy, on whose behalf Sinatra had campaigned and even performed at the inaugural ball. Sinatra saw his home as a potential western White House. The visit never happened, however. At the time, Attorney General Robert Kennedy was concerned about Sinatra's ties to mobsters, not least Sam Giancana, with whom JFK shared a mistress (Judith Campbell, to whom he had been introduced by Sinatra) and who had been a guest at Ol' Blue Eyes' home. Thus, JFK instead chose Republican crooner Bing Crosby's house during his visit of March 24–26, 1962 (and famously made love to Marilyn Monroe while there). When Peter Lawford broke the news, Sinatra became enraged. Forsaking the Democrats, he nurtured his ties with Richard Nixon and vice president Spiro

Midstream, *by J. Seward Johnson Jr., Palm Desert Civic Center Park.*

Agnew, and renamed the "Kennedy Mansion" as "Agnew House."

Mia Farrow lived here for two years following her marriage to Sinatra on July 19, 1966. Ten years later, her place was taken by Sinatra's final wife, Barbara Marx, the former Las Vegas showgirl who had married Zeppo Marx, of the Marx brothers.

Today the home (which sold for $4.3 million in 1996 and has a 12-car garage) is owned by a Canadian company, the Jim Pattison Group (604-688-6764; www.jimpattison.com), which rents it for corporate retreats under the new moniker, the "Honeymoon Hideaway." The various guest bungalows include The Caboose, a converted train caboose (Sinatra's former gym); adjoining, another bungalow is filled with hundreds of electric trains—a passion of Ol' Blue Eyes—including eight that chug around a huge table in the center of the room.

SUNNYLANDS ESTATE

267-738-2933
www.sunnylandstrust.org
c/o The Annenberg Foundation Trust at Sunnylands. Frank Sinatra Dr., Rancho Mirage, CA 92270

Nope, you can't visit (yet), but this vast estate occupying the entire quadrant along Bob Hope Drive between Frank Sinatra and Bob Hope drives is perhaps the most important piece of turf in the valley. "Sunnylands" was the home of Walter Annenberg (1908–2002), billionaire publisher of *The Philadelphia Inquirer*, *TV Guide*, and *Seventeen*. Annenberg, the U.S. ambassador to Great Britain during the Nixon era, created the 208-acre walled compound with a private nine-hole golf course in the 1960s, when it became the largest single-family residence in Riverside County. Walter and Leonore Annenberg's home became known as "the western White House." President Dwight Eisenhower stayed here. Nixon wrote his last State of the Union address here and went into seclusion here following his humiliating resignation in 1974. The Reagans were regular visitors. Presidents Ford, Carter, Clinton, and George W. Bush have all been guests. President George Bush and Japanese prime minister Toshiki Kaifu ensconced themselves here in 1990 for their official summit. Queen Elizabeth visited in 1984. Sunnylands hosted the Shah of Iran following the Iranian revolution in 1980. And Frank Sinatra and Barbara Marx were even married here in 1976. Annenberg's widow, Leonore (President Reagan's former chief of protocol), still lives at the private estate, which was named a historic site in 1990. The house itself sprawls over 32,000 square feet (the living room alone measures 6,400 square feet). The compound—ringed by a pink wall—is heavily, albeit discreetly, guarded.

After selling most of his business empire to Rupert Murdoch for $3 billion in 1998, Annenberg dedicated himself to philanthropy and gave away an estimated $2 billion. His stunning $1 billion art collection that includes works by Van Gogh, Gauguin, Renoir, Monet, and a portrait of Annenberg himself by Andrew Wyeth, was bequeathed to the New York Metropolitan Museum of Art. The estate he willed to the city of Rancho Mirage, which eventually hopes to turn it into a "Hearst Castle in the Desert."

In November 2007 the Annenberg Foundation Trust at Sunnylands announced plans to open a visitor center, museum, and conference center in 2010 on property adjoining the estate. The center will eventually host public tours of the Sunnylands estate.

Libraries

The Palms Springs region has two distinguished libraries. The **Palm Springs Public Library** (760-322-7323; www.palmspringslibrary.org; 300 S. Sunrise Way, Palm Springs, CA 92262), with 172,000 volumes, is the leading library in the desert. It also has a large collection of videos and DVDs. Public lectures are hosted. Opened in 2006, the **Rancho Mirage Public Library** (760-341-7323; www.ranchomiragelibrary.org; 71-100 Hwy. 111, Rancho Mirage, CA 92270) is a spectacular architectural statement with state-of-the-art facilities and 62,000 volumes. The library also hosts music events, programs, and exhibits for all ages.

Smaller venues include the **Welwood Murray Memorial Library** (760-323-8296; 100 S. Palm Canyon Dr., Palm Springs, CA 92262), in downtown Palm Springs. It opened as the first permanent home of the Palm Springs Public Library in February 1941 and today is operated and maintained by volunteers. The **Cathedral City Library** (760-328-4262; 33-520 Date Palm Dr., Cathedral City, CA 92234) is a 20,000-square-foot facility housing art and historical collections along with 43,000 books. And **Palm Desert Library** (760-346-6552; 73-300 Fred Waring Dr., Palm Desert, CA 92260) partners with the **College of the Desert Library** (760-773-2563; www.collegeofthedesert.edu; 43-500 Monterey Ave., Palm Desert, CA 92260) in a community lending partnership. The college's library has a renowned collection of books about the local desert and deserts of the world, plus the Winston S. Churchill Collection (with 1,000 books relating to the great British statesman) available for public perusal.

B-17 Flying Fortress, Palm Springs Air Museum.

Military Sites and Museums

PALM SPRINGS

PALM SPRINGS AIR MUSEUM

760-778-6262 ext. 223
www.palmspringsairmuseum.org
745 Gene Autry Trail, Palm Springs, CA 92262
Open: Daily 10–5; closed Thanksgiving and Christmas Day
Admission: $10

Although it also boasts several recent-era military jets, such as the McDonnell Douglas F-4 Phantom and Grumman Tomcat, plus Soviet MiGs, this spectacular museum is "dedicated to the preservation, presentation and interpretation of the Air Power of World War Two." And what a superb job it does! Three air-conditioned hangars measuring 67,000 square feet contain bombers, fighters, and trainers that together add up to the world's largest collections of airworthy World War II aircraft, including such rarities as a Bell King Cobra, a Curtiss Kittyhawk, a Republic Thunderbolt, a P-51 Mustang, a Supermarine Spitfire, and a B-17 Flying Fortress. More than half the aircraft are in flyable condition, and flight demonstrations are frequently offered.

One hangar displays planes from the European theater of operations, and a second displays aircraft from the Pacific theater, including a Grumman F4F Wildcat, Grumman F6F Hellcat, Grumman TBF-1 Avenger torpedo-bomber, and Douglas A-26 Invader attack bomber, plus a twin-engine Grumman F7F Tigercat. You can even explore inside a C-47, a PBY Catalina "Flying Boat," and the B-17. There's an original Jeep, too, plus all manner of

World War II–era military motorcycles, as well as classic automobiles of the era and miscellaneous memorabilia such as original photography, military uniforms, and weapons.

Scale-model aircraft seem to roar by overhead. Splendid wall murals and 3-D dioramas add to the drama, not least a narrated diorama of the fateful attack on Pearl Harbor. And a "warship row" displays large-scale cutaway models of everything from a U.S. World War II submarine to the USS *Missouri* battleship. Upstairs, the library boasts an impressive collection of books and magazines on aviation and military history, and movies are shown in the Buddy Rogers "Wings" Theater, which has an astonishing collection of aviation-related CDs, DVDs, and videos. There are even computer flight simulators! Commemorative lectures are presented on Sat., Sept.–May.

You can rent a self-guided audiotape, and docents give guided tours.

Palm Springs Vicinity

PATRIOT PARK

Corner of Dinah Shore Dr. and Date Palm Dr., Cathedral City

Appropriately named, this park hosts a 9-foot-tall bronze statue (imported to the city from China) that honors U.S. Army Pfc. Ming Sun, a Cathedral City soldier, killed in Iraq on January 9, 2007. The plaque reads: "There is no greater sacrifice from a person than to give his life in the service of others."

Southern Desert Resorts

COACHELLA VALLEY CEMETERY VETERANS MEMORIAL

Coachella Valley Cemetery, 82-925 Ave. 52, Coachella, CA 92236

Dedicated in 2007, this veterans memorial and monument honors Coachella Valley service personnel who lost their lives serving their country. A black granite "Wall of Honor" and a "Wall of Ultimate Sacrifice" bear the names of local war veterans and the honored war dead. Film director Frank Capra is also interred in the cemetery, shaded by trees.

DESERT HOLOCAUST MEMORIAL

Civic Center Park, Fred Waring Dr. and San Pablo Ave., Palm Desert, CA 92270

Undoubtedly the Palm Springs region's most emotionally moving site, this spectacular bronze and granite monument is a ghostly memorial to the tragedy and horror that befell Europe's Jews, trade unionists, and leftist intellectuals at the hands of the Nazi regime. Created in 1994 by local artist Dee Clements, it consists of seven larger-than-life human figures mounted on a double-tiered black granite Star of David, plus 11 bas-reliefs that depict death-camp scenes including sleeping quarters, gas chambers, and crematoriums. The human figures include a rabbi praying, a "lost boy of the ghetto," and an emaciated man, alone and dying on the ground; the faces and representations are all taken from actual photographs. Measuring 88 feet long, the cobblestone site entry is overhung by light standards that replicate those at Auschwitz. For more information contact the Jewish Federation of Palm Springs (619-325-7281).

EISENHOWER WALK OF HONOR AND VETERANS MEMORIAL

Hwy. 111 and Eldorado Dr., Indian Wells, CA 92210

A memorial to General Dwight D. Eisenhower stands on the front lawn of the Indian Wells

Holocaust Memorial.

City Hall (760-346-2489; 44-950 Eldorado Dr., Indian Wells, CA 92210). Shaded by palms, the 1.5-times-life-size bronze bust of Eisenhower—depicted saluting—rests upon a red granite pentagonal base, backed by flags representing the five branches of the armed services. Plaques to each side profile Eisenhower's achievements as Supreme Allied Commander during World War II, and as the 34th president of the United States. Nearby, two 7-foot granite walls form a memorial inscribed with the names of more than 500 Indian Wells residents who served in the armed forces.

GENERAL PATTON MEMORIAL MUSEUM

760-227-3483
www.generalpattonmuseum.com
Chiriaco Summit, I-10, 30 miles east of Indio
Open: Daily 9:30–4:30
Admission: $4; children and military in uniform free

In 1942, during the dark days of World War II, Maj. Gen. George S. Patton Jr. set up and oversaw the Desert Training Center to prepare army troops and tank battalions for the coming confrontation with German field marshal Erwin Rommel's Afrika Korps. Headquartered at Chiriaco Summit (a 20-minute drive southeast from Indio), the training camp eventually stretched over 18,000 square miles of desert—the world's largest military installation in both size and population. More than 1.5 million troops were rotated between 1942 and 1944. While troops slept in about 100,000 tents in 10 massive camp cities, Patton billeted in La Quinta Resort & Club, which closed for the duration of the war.

Thousands of tanks, self-propelled artillery units, and trucks thundered through the desert. Tank tracks from these maneuvers are still visible today, and a Sherman and Stuart tank are among the various tanks, armored cars, and other equipment displayed at the museum. Visitors view a 30-minute movie and learn astounding trivia, such as that troops were expected to survive on one canteen of water a day in the sizzling summer heat! Exhibits include memorabilia from the life and times of General Patton, as well as memorabilia spanning U.S. military conflicts from the Civil War to Operation Iraqi Freedom. The main focus, however, is World War II, with an astounding and fascinating array of wartime miscellany, from carbines, machine guns, and mortars, to medals, maps, and uniforms, representing both Allied and Axis forces.

A West Coast Vietnam Wall honors all veterans who served in Vietnam, with names etched on black granite plaques.

Museums

Palm Springs

AGUA CALIENTE CULTURAL MUSEUM

760-778-1079
www.accmuseum.org
219 S. Palm Canyon Rd., Palm Springs, CA 92262
Open: Wed.–Sat. 10–5 and Sun. noon–5 in winter; Fri., Sat. 10–5 and Sun. noon–5 in summer
Admission: Free

The tiny tribal museum of the Agua Caliente band of Cahuilla Indians, downtown in the historic Village Green Heritage Center, educates visitors about the local native Indian culture. The rather meager exhibits include baskets, ceramics, and stone utensils used for food preparation, plus profiles on petroglyphs and pictographs. Do take time to watch the fascinating video narrated by a female elder recalling life of her youth. You'll gain an appreciation for the Cahuillas' resourcefulness, imagination, intelligence, and hard work once required to make a good life for their families in this rugged desert country.

Traditional skills workshops are taught in the patio to the rear, including "Preserving the Spirit" classes that teach basketry, pottery, fry bread cooking, gourd art, and more. You can even learn how to build a *kish*—a traditional home of the Cahuilla Indians. A gift store sells native crafts and books. A bighorn ram sculpture that stands in the lobby is named for Pemtemwhaha, the Indian guardian of hoofed animals.

The museum will relocate to a stunning, 88,000-square-foot new facility to open in 2009 at Tahquitz Canyon Way and Hermosa Drive.

PALM SPRINGS ART MUSEUM

760-325-7186; fax: 760-327-5069
www.psmuseum.org
E-mail: info@psmuseum.org
101 Museum Dr., Palm Springs, CA 92262
Open: Tues., Wed., Fri., Sat., Sun. 10–5, Thurs. noon–8, closed Mon.
Admission: $12.50; $5 to students and military personnel; free Thurs. evenings
Special Features: Auditorium, café, nature trail

Earning laurels as one of California's top regional art venues, the museum was founded as an educational institution in 1938 (when it was mainly a collection of stuffed wildlife),

Humanlike sculptures at the Palm Springs Art Museum.

though its current home dates from 1970. Set against a boulder-strewn backdrop, the museum is housed in a striking, block-style modernist building designed with a volcanic cinder veneer by local architect E. Stewart Williams. The main block is surrounded by a sunken sculpture garden moat and architecturally is as striking and inspirational as the collection within.

Dedicated to promoting understanding of the arts, the museum is publicly supported by private contributions and has traditionally focused its exhibits on desert themes. Its permanent art collection includes works spanning the past two centuries, from pre-Columbian and Native American to contemporary Californian themes. The collection of Native American basketry is particularly impressive, as are the galleries of classic western American paintings by such early masters as Maynard Dixon, Charles M. Russell, Frederic Remington, and Joseph Henry Sharp.

In recent years the museum has expanded to become an oasis for contemporary arts, with sculptures and paintings by current leading exponents. Not least, Duane Hanson's 3-D life-size images of humans will make you do a double-take. Much of the artwork was donated by author Sidney Sheldon and by actor Kirk Douglas and his wife, Anne, all three longtime Palm Springs residents and art collectors.

In 2004 the wildlife dioramas were replaced by the Steve Chase Art Wing and Education Center. The wing houses a permanent collection of art from throughout Asia, Africa, and Europe bequeathed by two other local residents, actors William Holden and George Montgomery, whose self-cast bronze effigy resides in one of two sculpture gardens. And the Kaplan/Ostergaard Glass Center, opened in 2007, features contemporary glass art, including the spectacularly weird creations of Dale Chihuly. Children in particular will admire the Miniature Wing, in the northwest corner, displaying a permanent collection of miniature dioramas by Eugene J. Kupjack (1912–91) that show period slices of life, from "Chinese Laundry, circa 1910" to "Backstage at the Circus, 1915." A photographic gallery focuses its lens on desert photography.

Art workshops for adults and children are held October through May. Also here is the 450-seat Annenberg Theater, which hosts lectures and dance, musical, and theatrical performances.

RUDDY'S 1930S GENERAL STORE MUSEUM

760-327-2156
221 S. Palm Canyon Dr., Palm Springs, CA 92262
Open: Thurs.–Sun. 10–4, Oct.–June; Sat. and Sun. 10–4, July–Sept.
Admission: 95 cents
This genuine 1930s general store, in the Village Green Heritage Center in the heart of downtown, is stocked with original products offering a piece of pure nostalgia. Sarsaparilla, Father John's Medicine, Uneeda biscuits in their old cracker barrel—the museum has these and more than 6,000 other individual yesteryear products displayed on original shelving and fixtures from the era.

Palm Springs Vicinity

CABOT'S INDIAN PUEBLO MUSEUM

760-329-7610; fax: 760-329-2738
www.cabotsmuseum.com
67-616 E. Desert View, Desert Hot Springs, CA 92240
Open: Fri.–Sun. 11–3, Oct.–May
Admission: $6 adults, $5 seniors, $4 for students and military personnel
An official State Historic Site, this Hopi-style pueblo was originally homesteaded by Cabot Yerxa, who discovered the hot mineral springs of Miracle Hill and Mission Springs in 1914. Yerxa began building his 35-room pueblo in 1941 and continued in haphazard fashion over two decades, his structure growing by accretion into a rambling oddity made from items that he found in the desert. Now restored, it serves as a trading post, museum, and art gallery. Don't miss—you *can't* miss—the 43-foot-tall "Waokiye" monument carved by sculptor Peter Toth from a 750-year-old sequoia redwood. Guided tours are offered on weekends, as are special lectures and art classes. Tours run about 30 minutes.

CHILDREN'S DISCOVERY MUSEUM OF THE DESERT

760-321-0602; fax: 760-321-1605
www.cdmod.org
71-701 Gerald Ford Dr., Rancho Mirage, CA 92270
Open: Tues.–Sun. 10–5
Admission: $8
If you like the idea of your children honing their intellectual curiosity while they learn and have fun, then this museum is a must. Even adults will enjoy it. Focusing on the natural environment, the interactive exhibits and programs encourage children to learn about

themselves and the world around them. Science, archaeology, the human body, physics, and the arts are some of the themes covered in over 50 hands-on exhibits, many of them highly amusing and sure to keep kids and the kid within entertained.

Other Museums

Cabazon Band of Mission Indians Cultural Museum (760-268-5770; www.cabazonindians-nsn.gov; 84-245 Indio Springs Pkwy., Indio, CA 92201) Dedicated to telling the story of the local Cabazon Band of Cahuilla Indians (now numbering only about 55 members), the museum, across from the Fantasy Springs Resort Hotel, north of I-10, displays artifacts and hands-on exhibits and interpretive scenes. Call for hours of operation. Admission is free. It hosts the three-day Indio Powwow in late Nov.

Coachella Valley Museum & Cultural Center (760-342-6651; 82-616 Miles St., Indio, CA 92201) Housed in a mid-1920s adobe doctor's home and medical center, this tidy little place displays Native American basketry and artifacts and has exhibits on valley pioneer families, plus local railroad and agricultural memorabilia, including two 1923 Fordson tractors. It even has a blacksmith shop and sawmill, plus the city's original 1909 schoolhouse.

Heartland (760-324-3278; 39-600 Bob Hope Dr., Rancho Mirage, CA 92270) Located at Eisenhower Medical Center, this small museum is designed to get your heart racing with fun exhibits and a "Happy Heart Cinema." Open Mon.–Sat. 7:30–7.

Jude E. Poynter Golf Museum (760-341-0994; College of the Desert Campus, Fred Waring Dr. and San Pablo Ave., Palm Desert, CA 92260) In the Victor J. LoBue Institute of Golf, this shrine to the valley's favorite pastime exhibits celebrity memorabilia, golf gear through the ages, and photographs and more that trace the history of the sport. Open daily 7–10.

Historical Society of Palm Desert Museum (760-346-6588; 72-861 El Paseo, Palm Desert, CA 92260) This little museum in the Old Palm Desert Firehouse, complete with an old fire engine, has eclectic exhibits, mostly relating to Palm Desert's past. Historical photos and newspaper and magazine archives include aerial views of the valley through half a century. You'll learn about the early days of the Indians, and how the Coachella Valley gets its water. If you get caught short, there's even a large collection of chamber pots. Open Mon.–Sat. 10–3.; closed June 15 through Sept. 15.

Shields Date Gardens (760-347-0996 or 1-800-414-2555; www.shieldsdates.com; 80-225 Hwy. 111, Indio, CA 92201) A visit is worth it simply to watch *Romance and Sex Life of the Date*, a multimedia presentation that traces the life cycle of this meaty fruit for which Indio is famed. A store sells fresh dates and gift boxes, and you can't leave without tasting its renowned date ice cream and milk shakes. It has an original 1950s soda fountain. Open daily 9–5.

Classical Venues

You'd expect a place with so much highfalutin money to be a great sponsor of classical music, and you wouldn't be wrong.

The big enchilada is the **Coachella Valley Symphony** (760-360-2222; www.coachellavalleysymphony.com; 38-180 Del Webb Blvd., Palm Desert, CA 92255). Since 1995, music director and conductor Christian Chalifour has revitalized this 70-piece orchestra, which performs six main concert events each season and offers a wide variety of classical and pops music. Its winter season of performances might range from Mozart to the Russian masters, plus "The Nutcracker," plus its special concerts such as the annual Easter Irish Italian Dinner Concert. Its Buddy Rogers Youth Symphony, composed of aspiring and promising youngsters, offers more than two dozen public and private performances each season. Venues vary.

The **Palm Springs Opera Guild** (760-325-6107; www.palmspringsoperaguild.org) performs at the Annenberg Theater and McCallum Theatre, Nov. through Apr.

On the choral scene, watch for performances by **Caballeros: The Gay Men's Chorus of Palm Springs** (760-322-3112; www.pscaballeros.org). Having grown from a five-man ensemble into a full-blown, 75-member men's choral group, it is acknowledged as one of the premier singing groups in the Coachella Valley. And **California Desert Chorale** (760-346-4933; www.californiadesertchorale.org), comprising both professional and amateur singers under artistic director Tim Bruneau, performs throughout the valley—ranging from baroque to the Beatles!

Joshua Bell performing at the McCallum Theatre. Timothy White

Music

There's no shortage of opportunity to hear great music in the Coachella Valley, be it R&B, jazz, rock 'n' roll, or classical. While at first the scene seems low-key, with most venues being pubs and clubs (Palm Canyon Drive, in Palm Springs, has at least two dozen live-music venues), the valley is blessed with world-class auditoriums where you can listen to top-flight performers.

Yesteryear favorites are a steadfast feature of the **April Musical Chairs Concert Series** (760-416-5353 or 1-866-760-2828; www.musicalchairs.us), held in top theaters throughout the valley. Every three months the themes change. The 2008 series presented the songs of the Big Band era; a tribute to the great variety shows; the songs of Livingston and Evans; and "Richard Rodgers Revisited."

Despite their young age, the **Desert Youth Ballet** (760-341-0122; www.desertyouthballet.org; 71-711 San Jacinto Dr., Rancho Mirage, CA 92270) have even performed with the Moscow Ballet!

The **Palm Springs Friends of Philharmonic** (760-341013; www.psfp.org) sponsors classical music concerts that have brought most of the world's preeminent orchestras to the valley. The 2008 season, for example, included the Los Angeles Philharmonic, Czech Philharmonic, and the Royal Philharmonic Orchestra.

Palm Springs Community Concerts (760-322-6132; www.psconcerts.org; 2248 Ramon Rd., Palm Springs, CA, 92262) sponsors a series of classic concerts held in the Palm Springs High School Auditorium, Jan.–Mar.

And the annual **Virginia Waring International Piano Competition** (760-773-2575; www.vwipc.com) is held in Palm Desert, with competitions for three different age groups of pianists from around the world.

Palm Springs

When the third Sunday in April comes around, take your beach chairs and picnic baskets to Sunrise Park for **Opera in the Park** (760-325-6107; Sunrise Way, Palm Springs). This all-day free concert features music from opera arias to Broadway show tunes. No dressing up in a tux and gown needed . . . although the singers do! It has a Funzone for the kids, and umbrella rentals.

The **Church of St. Paul in the Desert** (760-320-7488; 125 W. El Alameda, Palm Springs, CA 92262) offers concerts during the school year, with national choirs, pianists, organists, and small ensembles. The series includes a Festival of Christmas Lessons and Carols.

Palm Springs Vicinity

The **Rancho Mirage Public Library** (760-341-7323; www.ranchomiragelibrary.org; 71-100 Hwy. 111, CA 92270) sponsors its annual ongoing International Classical Concerts of the Desert, Great American Composers Performance Series, and Friends of the Library Piano Recitals.

The **Desert Friends of Music** (760-346-2697; www.stmargarets.org; St. Margaret's Episcopal Church, 47-535 Hwy. 74, Palm Desert, CA 92260) has a six-month choral season, Nov–Mar., that has featured such outstanding performers as the American Boychoir, the Vienna Boys' Choir, and the Westminster Choir. The annual Chanticleer Christmas concert is not to be missed (the Chanticleers have been hailed by the *New Yorker* magazine as "the world's reigning male chorus."

Other Music

PALM SPRINGS

Azul (760-325-5533; www.azultapaslounge.com; 369 N. Palm Canyon Dr., Palm Springs, CA 92262) No cover charge at this tapas lounge with a tremendous lineup of performing talent Thurs.–Sat.

Blame It on Midnight (760-323-1200; www.blameitonmidnight.com; 777 E. Tahquitz Canyon Way, Palm Springs, CA 92262) This bar and grill popular with a mostly gay clientele has live entertainment Thurs.–Sat. and a piano bar on Sun. Gennine Jackson and Karen Cobb are among the recent performers. It has great dining, too.

Blue Guitar (760-327-1549; www.blueguitarpalmsprings.com; 120 S. Palm Canyon Rd., Palm Springs, CA 92262) Tremendous blues and jazz club with contemporary decor, dance floor, and great cocktails. Stanley Butler leads the Dean, Alan and Stanley Band on Thurs.;

Bob Zinner leads a Sun. Pro-Jam Session; and you can warble to your heart's content during karaoke sessions that follow Monday Night Football.

Cascade Lounge (760-883-1000; www.sparesortcasino.com; Spa Resort Casino, 401 E. Amado Rd., Palm Springs, CA 92262) The spicy-hot house band, Quinto Menguante, plays every Sun. night at the Spa Resort Casino's Cascade Lounge. Also live entertainment Mon.–Sat.

Las Casuelas Lounge & Patio Bar (760-325-2794; 222 S. Palm Canyon Dr., Palm Springs, CA 92262) One of the most popular live entertainment spots in town, although the light rock music always seems out of place at this hacienda-themed Mexican restaurant. The patio has misters.

Peabody's (760-322-1877; www.peabodyspalmsprings.com; 134 S. Palm Canyon Dr., Palm Springs, CA 92262) The place to come to try for a moment of fame, this is *the* karaoke nightspot in town, Thurs.–Sat. evenings, when patrons wail out everything from 50 Cents to Willy Nelson.

Shanghai Reds (760-322-9293; 235 S. Indian Canyon Dr., Palm Springs, CA 92262) Live R&B music by the Barry Baughn Blues Band on Fri. and Sat. nights in the intimate open-air courtyard of this hole-in-the-wall bar serving oyster shooters, fish tacos, steamed clams, and other delicious dishes from Neptune's larder. Late-night happy hour 9–midnight.

Village Pub (760-323-3265; 255 S. Palm Canyon Dr., Palm Springs, CA 92262) One of the liveliest spots on the Strip, with live rock, four bars, a dance floor, and pub food from

Bing Crosby's.

pizzas to steaks and seafood. Happy hour 3:30–6 daily, with Ron James on piano, Wed.–Sun. Various artists perform at night.

PALM SPRINGS VICINITY

Live music is offered free every Sat. night at **The River amphitheater** (71-800 Hwy. 111, Rancho Mirage). Expect to hear everything from top-40 tunes to Cuban jazz. Closed Jul. - Aug.

Jazz lovers can delight in the **Jazz Concert Series**, with live music outdoors at The Gardens, on El Paseo, each Sat. evening Feb.–Apr.; the valley's premier jazz aficionado, Jim "Fitz" Fitzgerald, presides. And the **Rancho Mirage Public Library** (760-341-7323; www.ranchomiragelibrary.org; 71-100 Hwy. 111, Rancho Mirage, CA 92270) hosts "Jazz in the Afternoon" musical lectures.

Agua Caliente Casino (760-321-2000; www.hotwatercasino.com; 32-250 Bob Hope Dr., Rancho Mirage, CA 92270) Eclectic describes the weekly program in the Lounge. On "Sassy Salsa Wednesdays," Latin dance lessons (6:30–8:30 PM) precede *caliente* rhythms from the Ritmo Caliente Orchestra. Country-western fans flock for "Two-Step Thursday." "Smooth Sundays" feature live entertainment by the Mike Costley Band. And live bands perform on Fri. and Sat. nights, with dancing until 1:30 AM.

Bing Crosby's (760-674-5764; www.bingcrosbysrestaurant.com; 71-743 Hwy. 111, Rancho Mirage, CA 92270) A pianist and a medley of other fine performers entertain at this classic yesteryear-themed supper club.

Paseo Palms Bar & Grill (760-837-3800; 73-040 El Paseo, Palm Desert, CA 92260) Erik Frankson tickles the ivories every Thurs. and Fri. evening. Musicians in a mood to jam are welcome.

SOUTHERN DESERT RESORTS

Palm Desert hosts a **Summer of Fun Concerts & Movies** (760-346-0611; www.palm desert.org) held at the Palm Desert Civic Center Amphitheater. Bring your lawn chair, blankets, and picnic baskets to enjoy cartoons, movies, and music from classical orchestras to rock—all for free. August.

Although it's way above the valley in Idyllwood, **Jazz in the Pines** (951-500-3200; www.idyllwildjazz.com) is considered an integral part of the Palm Springs music scene. Jazz lovers relax in the crisp mountain air for two days in late Aug.

Fantasy Springs Casino (760-342-5000 or 1-800-827-2946; www.fantasysprings resort.com; 84-245 Indio Springs Pkwy., Indio, CA 92203) Live performances by big bands and singers, most of whom have been around a few years. The Scorpions. Diana Ross. Kenny G. They perform in the Special Events Center.

McCormick's Live Entertainment (760-340-0553; 74-360 Hwy. 111, Palm Desert, CA 92260) This lively nightclub features the Brad Mercer Band on Thurs. nights (no cover), and the Michael James Band on Fri. and Sat. (no cover before 9 PM).

Vineyard Lounge (760-341-2200; 45-000 Indian Wells La., Indian Wells, CA 92210) Fans of Spanish guitar should make a beeline to Miramonte Resort & Spa, where Rafael Soto strings together a mean repertoire every Thurs. evening, and there's live jazz Fri. and Sat. nights.

Nature Parks

The desert's spectacular natural environment can be experienced close-up at several educational facilities. For wilderness parks, see Hiking, in the Recreation chapter.

In December 2007, **Wildlife WayStation** (www.wildlifewaystation.org), one of the nation's largest animal rescue facilities, signed a lease to move to a parcel adjoining Salvia Road, off Gene Autry Trail near I-10, in Palm Springs. The facility cares for injured, abandoned, and abused tigers, bears, baboons, alligators, and more. The largest primate center in the country is planned.

PALM SPRINGS

MOORTEN BOTANICAL GARDENS

760-327-6555
E-mail: clarkmoorten@yahoo.com
1701 S. Palm Canyon Dr., Palm Springs, CA 92264
Open: Mon.–Sat. 9–4:30, Sun. 10–4, closed Wed.
Admission: $3 adults, $1.50 children

This desert-themed private arboretum features more than 3,000 varieties of desert plants, from succulents to shrubs and trees. A nature trail weaves through the small, compact garden packed with desert specimens nurtured over decades by Patricia and Chester "Cactus Slim" Moorten (she a botanist, he one of the original Keystone Cops) and now in the care of their son, Clark Moorten. The cacti and other desert plants are grouped by geographic regions spanning Arizona, Baja California, California, Colorado, the Mojave Desert, the Sonoran Desert, South Africa, arid South America, and Texas. Be sure to visit the "Cactarium," with a remarkable collection of unusual cacti in a Quonset hut greenhouse. Note the Moortens' Mediterranean-style home, called Cactus Castle, in the Palm Grove.

Moorten Botanical Garden.

Cheeta the Chimp

There's nothing unusual about aged Hollywood stars retiring to Palm Springs to paint and enjoy their retirement in the sun. Even chimpanzees do it.

Cheeta, the chimpanzee co-star to Johnny Weissmuller in 12 Tarzan movies and to Ronald Reagan in *Bedtime for Bonzo* (and Rex Harrison in *Doctor Doolittle*), lives at the **CHEETA Primate Sanctuary** (www.cheetathechimp.org; 1033 E. Francis Rd., Palm Springs, CA 92262; not open to the public). And, yes, he paints! In fact, Cheeta is a wonderful abstract artist and true Renaissance "man"—his trademarked "ape-stract" paintings can even be bought on the Web site ($135, including shipping and handling). He's also probably the world's oldest chimp (born April 9, 1932) and has even been honored with a star on the Palm Springs "Walk of Stars."

Cheeta and Dan Westfall.

The sanctuary is in the home of former singer-comedian Dan Westfall, who got custody of Cheeta in 1991. Westfall runs the sanctuary out of his three-bedroom house on this otherwise normal residential street. The caged facility out back houses five other primates (including a rhesus monkey and two orangutans). All are homeless or unwanted ex-showbiz hands, including Jeeter—Cheeta's grandson—who even enjoys swimming in Westfall's pool.

"Casa de Cheeta" is closed to the public, but you can see a bronze statue of Cheeta in front of the house-turned-sanctuary. And, who knows? With luck you might even spot the real Cheeta riding shotgun in Westfall's golf cart.

PALM SPRINGS VICINITY

BLIXSETH MOUNTAIN PARK

Indian Trail and Mirage Rd., Rancho Mirage, CA 92270

Accessed by a wooden bridge across the flood-control channel, this park is designed with primitive walking trails and stone benches for quiet contemplation of the desert landscape and mountain vistas. Native vegetation—barrel cactus, cholla cactus, creosote bush, and paloverde—push up from the sandy earth.

SOUTHERN DESERT RESORTS

AERIE ART GARDEN

760-568-6366

(http://aerieartgarden.com)

71-255 Aerie Rd., Palm Desert, CA 92260

Open: By appointment, Sep.–May
This landscaped garden showcases the beauty of desert flora, including various cacti. Artists Clonard and Bruce Thomas have also prepared a sculpture garden in their 20-acre wilderness estate (which once belonged to matinee screen idol Tom Mix) at the base of the Santa Rosa Mountains. Many of the sculptures are made from discarded items, including the remnants of an airplane cockpit.

COACHELLA VALLEY WILD BIRD CENTER

760-347-2647
www.coachellavalleywildbirdcenter.org
46-500 Van Buren St., Indio, CA 92201
Open: Daily 9–noon
Admission: Free
The rehabilitation and release center cares for wild birds such as owls, ospreys, and kestrels, as well as hummingbirds, mockingbirds, and quail. Wetlands with observation towers provide for bird spotting in a natural setting; scores of species flock in during migration. Call for bird watch appointments. Two-hour Bird Walks are offered the first Sat. of each month.

LIVING DESERT ZOO & GARDENS

760-346-5694
www.livingdesert.org
47-900 Portola Ave., Palm Desert, CA 92260
Open: Daily 9–5, Sept.–mid-June
Admission: $11.95 adults, $7.50 children (3–12) winter; $8.75 adults, $4.75 children summer
One of the highlights of any visit to the desert region, this zoo and botanical garden astounds. Established in 1970 as a 360-acre wilderness preserve, it is the only zoological and botanical park specializing in one ecosystem, interpreting and conserving deserts of the world. Today sprawling over 1,200 acres, it exhibits nearly 400 species of animals, from oryx and zebras and meerkats to local favorites such as bighorn sheep and coyotes. The Discovery Room provides a complete introduction to desert ecologies. Hiking trails lead through specialized botanical gardens, including the Upper Colorado Garden and Cahuilla Indian Ethnobotanical Garden (you can also buy desert plants at the Palo Verde Garden Center).

The main trail leads to Eagle Canyon, exhibiting local desert animals, including bobcat, mountain lion, desert badger, coyotes, and various foxes, viewable through walls of glass in spacious enclosures that are re-creations of the animals' natural habitats. One exhibit, built around a rocky mountain, is dedicated to the bighorn sheep. The birds are there, too, including golden eagle, and don't be surprised to see an owl perched in the palms overhead. Foreign animals are also well represented, including endangered Mexican wolves.

You can't help but thrill to the site of giraffe and ostrich strutting their stuff in the section dedicated to African desert wildlife. Oryx, camels, cheetahs, and zebras also kick up the dust or spend long hours snoozing in the shade. There's even a re-creation of a 19th-century Nigerian village called Wa Tu Tu, with a petting kraal with sheep, goats, and Ankole cattle.

You can even watch animals being treated in the veterinary hospital, where a wall of glass and TV monitor permit close-up viewing. Treatment schedules are posted.

The Living Desert supports conservation programs around the world, including efforts

Checking out the giraffe at the Living Desert.

to protect the pronghorn antelope of Baja California's Vizcaíno Biosphere Reserve. It even has an in-vitro fertilization program, such as for endangered sand cats of North Africa. In 2007 an exhibition was added dedicated to educating patrons on the current extinction crisis of amphibians worldwide.

OASIS DATE GARDENS

760-399-1068 or 1-800-827-8017
www.oasisdategardens.com
59-111 Hwy. 111, Thermal, CA 92274
Open: Mon.–Sat 8–5; guided tours at 10:30 and 2:30
Admission: Free
Established in 1912, this 175-acre date-palm farm offers tours that provide a fascinating introduction to the production and history and lore of dates. You'll explore the arboretum and packing house, where dates are cleaned and graded, plus view a video about how dates are grown. The rancho produces mostly Medjool dates.

Nightlife

There's heaps to do in Palm Springs and the valley when the sun goes down, with something for every age and taste. Many bars and clubs in Palm Springs cater to a primarily gay clientele, but most welcome patrons of any persuasion. Things really begin to sizzle in winter, but these days Palm Springs is happening year-round. The other cities are less gay-focused. Venues down valley range from down-to-earth beer halls to full-on nightclubs, such as in the major casinos.

Wind Turbines

Wind turbines with Mount San Jacinto behind.

Strong winds howl through the San Gorgonio Pass, spinning the turbines of the world's largest wind farm. California produces about three-quarters of the world's wind-generated electricity, and a good portion of it comes from the valley between Palm Springs and Desert Hot Springs, where a forest of gigantic wind turbines spin silently overhead. The largest of these windmills stand 150 feet tall, with rotor blades half the length of a football field.

The more than 4,000 windmills collectively produce enough electricity to power a city the size of San Francisco. The electricity is sold principally to Southern California Edison and is sufficient to power Palm Springs and the entire Coachella Valley. Since the electricity generated cannot be practically stored, it is transferred by underground cable to a Southern California Edison substation, from where it is distributed to consumers. At peak efficiency, each windmill generates enough energy to power 1,500 homes.

Windmill Tours (760-251-1997; www.windmilltours.com) offers educational guided tours that include the Southern California Edison facility on the North Frontage Road, near the intersection of Indian Avenue and Interstate 10. Visitors board electric-powered vehicles (recharged directly from the windmills) to tour the facility, including the wind turbine generators *whooshing* overhead. The tour introduces visitors to the history of wind power development, meteorology, and the place of windmills in global ecology; Wed.–Sat. 9, 11, and 2; $25 adults, $10 children.

The Entertainer is a great source for what's happening, as is the *Desert Sun*. Also see the Music section.

Palm Springs

The happening nightclub in town is **Zelda's** (760-325-2375; 169 N. Indian Canyon Rd., Palm Springs, CA 92264), a hip disco with two dance rooms with separate DJs spinning tunes into the wee hours; one spins salsa to hip-hop, while the other plays '70s, '80s and '90s classics. The Men of the Hollywood Strip—an all-male revue—take it off for the ladies on Thurs. and Fri.

Exuding yesteryear decor with its Polynesian tiki vibe, the hip **Reef Tiki Bar** (760-327-1391; 411 E. Canyon Dr., Palm Springs, CA 92264), at the Caliente Tropic Resort, grooves to live music by night, and it's a great spot to relax with a specialty cocktail beneath the stars by the pool.

Serving cooling beers for hot nights, the **Hair of the Dog English Pub** (760-323-9890;

Hair of the Dog pub.

238 N. Palm Canyon Dr., Palm Springs, CA 92262) packs 'em in for the open mike, electronic darts, and pool tables. This no-frills and rather cramped bar was formerly Ruby's Dunes, which opened in 1941 and became *the* hangout for Hollywood stars and entertainers, not least of all Frank Sinatra, Burt Lancaster, and Kirk Douglas. Beer lovers will appreciate the Guinness plus real British beer on tap, including some rare treats.

Havana Restaurant & Club (760-323-4870; 155 S. Belardo Rd., Palm Springs, CA 92262), at the Palm Mountain Resort & Spa, has dancing every Fri. and Sat. night for 21s up. Intended to re-create the ambience of Hemingway's Havana, it almost delivers on the promise. At least the music is good. Dress to impress.

Want to dine with Elvis? Or maybe Michael Jackson? Or Cher? Head to **CopyKatz Showroom & Backstage Bistro** (760-864-9293; www.copykatzentertainment.com; 200 S. Palm Canyon Dr., Palm Springs, CA 92262), a cocktail lounge—formerly the hot-spot Muriel's supper club—where nightly shows by look-alikes of stars past and present will have you firmly believing that Elvis really is alive and kicking. The "Celebrity Revue" is held Tues.–Sun. at 8 PM. Monday night is Comedy Night. Movable walls push open to the sidewalks for alfresco dining.

Fun, fun, fun is also the name of the game at **Heaven** (760-416-0950; 611 S. Palm Canyon Dr., Palm Springs, CA 92264), hosting a different theme nightly, from drag to karaoke.

Palm Springs Vicinity

On Fri. and Sat. nights, Las Casuelas Nuevas restaurant metamorphoses into **Caramba's MusiCantana** (760-328-8844; 70-050 Hwy. 111, Rancho Mirage, CA 92270), the hottest

Palm Springs actively promotes gay tourism. Palm Springs Desert Resorts Conventions & Visitors Authority

Gay Palm Springs

The Palm Springs community may be politically conservative, but the region's welcome to gays dates back to Hollywood's heyday, when gay and bisexual stars could indulge their lifestyles beyond prying eyes. In the past decade the scene has picked up. Dozens of hotels now cater to a gay and/or lesbian clientele. And the city has witnessed an explosion in the resident gay population, which has lent it an exciting, more liberal pizzazz. In 2003 Palm Springs residents even elected an openly gay mayor.

Palm Springs actively promotes gay tourism: The city's Bureau of Tourism (www.gayguidepalm springs.com) publishes the annual *Palm Springs Official Gay & Lesbian Visitors Guide*.

Several local gay publications are good resources. Try *The Bottom Line* (760-323-0552; www.psbottommline.com) and *Gay Yellow Pages of the Desert* (www.psgayyellowpages.com), and the Desert Gay Tourism Guild Web site (www.palmspringsgayinfo.com) and Palm Springs Gay Information Line (1-877-980-INFO).

The annual Easter weekend **White Party** (www.jeffreysanker.com) draws 25,000 gays. It features spectacular live performances, top-notch DJ talent, and cutting-edge lighting and special effects. The White Party is preceded by the similarly exciting **Dinah Shore Weekend** (www.thedinah.com), for lesbians.

Nightlife: Arenas Road is Palm Springs' gay-focused center of action, full of honky-tonk and leather bars. The colorful **Hunters Video Bar** (760-323-0700; www.huntersnightclubs.com; 302 E. Arenas Rd., Palm Springs, CA 92262) gets the gay crowd onto the dance floor with techno and world beat. Nearby, the **Rainbow Restaurant & Piano Bar** (760-325-3868; 212 S. Indian Canyon Dr., Palm Springs, CA 92262) draws a mostly monied gay crowd who hang on every word as a pianist tickles the ivories.

Toucans Tiki Lounge (760-416-7584; www.toucanstikilounge.com; 2100 N. Palm Canyon Dr., Palm Springs, CA 92262), loosely themed on Disneyland's Enchanted Tiki Room, is the liveliest gay club in town and has drag shows, male striptease, disco, and heaps of titillating fun. Straights of both genders are welcome.

Gays break out the leathers or cowboy gear for a visit to the, er, **Tool Shed** (760-325-3686; www.toolshed-ps.com; 600 E. Sunny Dunes Rd., Palm Springs, CA 92262); and to **Sidewinders** (760-328-9919; www.sidewinders-ps.com; 67-555 E. Palm Canyon Dr., Cathedral City, CA 92234) for a whopping, stomping good time dancing to country and western. Karaoke fans won't be disappointed at Sidewinders, which has pool, darts, and video games, plus free hot dogs, and burgers with all the fixins' 4–8 PM.

Oasis Nightclub & Lounge (760-416-0950; 611 S. Palm Canyon Dr., Palm Springs, CA 92262) appeals to a mixed crowd but takes a heavily gay and lesbian slant. Closed Mon. and Tues.

Latin scene for miles. Two dance floors, plus live entertainment in the restaurant. Open 10–2, Fri.–Sun.

A 15-minute drive north of Palm Springs, the multilevel **Vibe** nightclub (951-755-5555; www.morongocasinoresort.com; Morongo Casino, Resort & Spa, 49-500 Seminole Rd., Cabazon, CA 92230) has four bars plus private skyboxes that overlook an elevated dance floor. The main bar features water-filled banquettes and is popular with twenty-somethings in body-clinging (or body-revealing) lycra tops swaying to the sounds of Kanye West and quaffing Grey Goose. Also here is the **360 Spacebar**, on the 26th floor, with a fantastic view of the desert through walls of glass. Try the bar's signature "Lost in Space" cocktail. A DJ spins tunes.

For a more sedate evening, try **The Yard House** (760-779-1415; 71-800 Hwy. 111, Rancho Mirage, CA 92270), a massive and classy bar in The River complex. It serves only draft beers—a whopping 150 or so, from all corners of the globe. Confused by your choices? Then opt for a "flight" of six small glasses with samples. New beers are rotated in and "old" beers rotated out on a weekly basis.

BUDDY GRECO'S

760-883-5812
www.buddygreco.com
68-805 Hwy. 111, Cathedral City, CA 92234
Closed: Mon.
Price: Expensive
Credit Cards: AE, D, MC, V
Cuisine: International
Serving: L, D
Reservations: Recommended
Handicapped Access: Yes
Special Features: Live music

Buddy Greco's Nightclub. Palm Springs Desert Resorts Conventions & Visitors Authority

Another classic supper club in yesteryear tradition, this one is owned by jazz and pop crooner legend Buddy Greco, who delights patrons with dinner shows Thurs.–Sat. nights, plus a Sun. matinee luncheon show. The seductively intimate ambience takes you back down Memory Lane with memorabilia from Greco's long career, including a wall festooned with 40 of his albums. And, of course, there's Buddy himself, singing his smash hits such as "The Lady Is a Tramp" and "Around the World." Opened in 2006, the supper club seats a mere 70 patrons. Chef Isabel Talamantes does a bang-up job in the kitchen, delivering consistently superb gourmet treats such as lamb braised in Rutherford merlot and assorted fresh herbs, and pecan-crusted baked salmon and a medley of berries with a dash of Jack Daniels and pomegranate. Leave room for the dessert liquors, such as martini of chocolate Grand Marnier mousse with cinnamon ice cream. Dinner shows $45 ($60 with cocktails).

SOUTHERN DESERT RESORTS

The **Velvet Palm Night Club** (760-342-5000; www.fantasyspringsresort.com; 84-245 Indio Springs Pkwy., Indio, CA 92203), on the 12th floor of the Fantasy Springs Resort Casino Hotel, hops on Wed.–Sun. nights. It also hosts top-flight comedy at the **Improv Comedy Club**; and the **Special Events Center** is one of the valley's premier venues for concerts by international superstars such as B. B. King, Willie Nelson, and local legend Barry Manilow.

Stepping upmarket, the fun, party-hearty club of choice has to be **Red 74** (760-568-6774; 72-990 El Paseo, Palm Desert, CA 92260), a sultry, red-decorated spot that hops with trendy young club-goers in body-hugging attire. A DJ spins retro tunes on Wed. night, drawing an older crowd, and the gals get preferential treatment on Tues. (glow bracelets identify "single to mingle") and Thurs. ("Girls Night Out").

Giving Red 74 a run for its money is **South Beach Nightclub** (760-773-1711; 72-191 Hwy. 111, Palm Desert, CA 92260), a high-energy, Miami Beach–themed nightclub that draws a sophisticated young-at-heart 30-plus crowd prior to 10:30 PM, when the dancing begins and a younger crowd flocks. The dance floor is ringed by booths, chaise longues, and couches. Romantics can cool off on the outside decks with water features, and fire pits for cool nights. It hosts live music Thurs.–Sun., and the management bills Monday Night Football as "where women go to watch men watch football."

Everyone agrees that the classiest place to dance is **Costas Nightclub** (760-341-2211; 74-855 Country Club Dr., Palm Desert, CA 92260), at the Desert Springs JW Marriott Resort & Spa. Open Thurs.–Sat. nights, it draws a monied younger crowd for hit tunes from hip-hop to yesterday hits spun by DJs.

If T-shirts and flip-flops are your preferred attire, head to **The Beer Hunter** (760-564-7442; 78-483 Hwy. 111, La Quinta, CA 92253). With 30 beers on tap and some 150 in bottles, this is a place for serious sudsters. Almost 50 labels are imported. It has pool, darts, shuffleboard, and serves burgers, steaks, salads, etc.

Parks and Plazas

PALM SPRINGS

Palm Springs does not lack for public greenery. The largest of its several well-manicured community parks is 61-acre **DeMuth Park** (4375 Mesquite Ave., Palm Springs, CA 92262), with picnic areas, four night-lit tennis courts, baseball diamonds and batting cages, plus picnic tables, drinking fountains, and restroom. **Ruth Hardy Park** (N. Avenida Caballeros and E. Tamarisk Rd., Palm Springs, CA 92262) likewise has picnic areas, eight lighted tennis courts, and a children's jungle gym and water fountain play area. Tiny **Frances Stevens Park** (555 N. Palm Canyon Dr., Palm Springs, CA 92262) has picnic tables and drinking fountains. **Sunrise Park** (S. Sunrise Way between Ramon Rd. and Baristo Rd., Palm Springs, CA 92262) has picnic areas and a playground. And **Baristo Park** (Calle Segundo and Saturnino) has picnic tables, a basketball court, children's playground, barbecue grills, and drinking fountains. Also see Fitness Facilities, in the Recreation chapter, for public parks.

PALM SPRINGS PLAZA

128 S. Palm Canyon Dr., Palm Springs, CA 92262

The heart of downtown Palm Springs, this plaza linking Palm Canyon and Indian Canyon was completed in 1936 and built for Julia Carnell, owner of the National Cash Register

Martini Bars

Chilled martinis are the drink of choice in Palm Springs and the desert resorts, where bartenders shake and stir these classic cocktails with style and aplomb at almost every restaurant and bar in town. Frank Sinatra tunes add to the jazzy finger-snapping style of the valley's finest 'tini bars, most of which offer their own specialty versions of the classic martini.

Smoking martini at The Falls. Palm Springs Desert Resorts Conventions & Visitors Authority

The Falls Martini Bar (760-416-8664; 155 S. Palm Canyon Dr., Palm Springs, CA 92262) is known for its signature "smoking" martinis, with dry-ice mist curling up from the drink. The bar, which draws a blend of hip young singles and mature professionals, is open-air, so if you like cigars, bring your favorite stogie. Its sibling Falls Prime Steak House, down valley in La Quinta, also has the **Martini Dome** (760-777-9999; 78-430 Hwy. 111, La Quinta, CA 92253), drawing the desert "in crowd" to savor from a list of 35 smoking hot martinis, from the green apple to the cosmopolitan. It has a patio bar with water features and views of the Santa Rosa Mountains.

Melvyn's (760-325-0046; 220 W. Ramon Rd., Palm Springs, CA 92264), at the Ingleside Inn, was once a favored hangout for Sinatra and still serves an amazing martini to sequined seniors. The timeless Casablanca Room is *the* piano bar for those seeking a classic retro experience and has a live jam session every Sun. afternoon, but you can trip the light fantastic seven nights a week.

To mix it up with a younger, high-end, and oh-so-chic crowd, head to **The Parker Palm Springs** (760-770-5000; 4200 E. Palm Canyon Dr., Palm Springs, CA 92264), with its retro decor and infused (and pricey) vodka 'tinis. Other good 'tini spots include **Coral Sea Lounge** (760-866-1952; www.thetropicale.com; 30 E. Amado Rd., Palm Springs, CA 92262), in the Tropicale restaurant.

Down valley, **Fusion One II** (760-341-5903; www.fusiononeII.com; 73-850 Hwy. 111, Palm Desert, CA 92260) is a hip addition that opened in 2007. It serves more than 20 tapas to accompany the 20 specialty martinis. The chic bar at **Pacifica Seafood Restaurant** (760-674-8666; www.pacificaseafoodrestaurant.com; 73-505 El Paseo, Palm Desert, CA 92260) serves more than 125 premium vodkas from around the world—all for a very reasonable $6. Here, martinis come with a regional twist. And the **Yard House** (760-779-1415; The River at Rancho Mirage, CA 99270) has a martini and beer happy hour, 3–6 Mon.–Fri.

Company (the wealthy industrialist made her winter home here in the 1930s). It was designed in Spanish colonial style with colorful tile-work by Ohio architect Harry Williams, who integrated a theater, shops, apartments, and parking into his multiuse plaza—one of the first such plazas in America oriented to the car. Jack Benny broadcast his national radio program from the Plaza Theatre throughout much of the 1930s and '40s, projecting Palm Springs into the national consciousness. For the past decade the theater has played host to Palm Springs' spectacular vaudeville act, the Fabulous Palm Springs Follies.

Sonny Bono and his star.

"Walk of Stars"

More than 250 personalities who have lived, loved, and played in Palm Springs are commemorated in pink granite stars embedded in the sidewalks along Palm Canyon Drive between Alejo and Baristo roads. From singer Al Jolson (No. 222) and actor Lon Chaney (No. 157), who helped start the escape to the desert in the 1920s, to later luminaries such as Elizabeth Taylor (No. 5) and Rock Hudson (No. 109), the star-studded cast is seemingly endless. Frank Sinatra's star (No. 49) is on the west side of the street, in front of the former Chi Chi Club, which stood at 271 Palm Canyon Dr. Elvis Presley (No. 209) lives on, at least in memory, on the southeast corner of Palm Canyon Dr. and Tahquitz Canyon.

For more information call 760-416-5811 or visit the Walk of Stars Web site at www.palmsprings.com/stars, which lists some of the most important stars in walking order.

VILLAGE GREEN HERITAGE CENTER

760-323-8297
www.palmspringshistoricalsociety.com
221 S. Palm Canyon Dr., Palm Springs, CA 92262
Open: Wed. and Sun. noon–3; Thurs.–Sat. 10–4; closed June–mid-Oct.
This lovely little park one block south of Palm Springs Plaza plays host to two 19th-century pioneer homes, including the **McCallum Adobe**, the oldest remaining building in Palm Springs. It was built of adobe (mud and straw) bricks in 1884 by settler John Guthrie McCallum, the first permanent white settler, who came to the desert to help his son recover from typhoid. A 24-minute film on the history of Palm Springs loops continuously, and you can peruse paintings, photographs, and miscellaneous artifacts from the earliest days of Palm Springs.

Adjacent, **Miss Cornelia's "Little House"** was constructed in 1893 of railroad ties from the defunct Palmdale Railway. Built by the city's first hotel proprietor, Dr. Welwood Murray, it was later purchased by Cornelia White and her sister Dr. Florilla White. Today it is furnished in period fashion with antiques from Palm Springs' pioneer era.

The park, maintained by the Palm Springs Historical Society, features a fountain fabricated in Mexico and Felipe Castaneda's *Standing Woman* bronze sculpture.

PALM SPRINGS VICINITY

CANCER SURVIVORS PARK

69-825 Hwy. 111, Rancho Mirage, CA 92270
Adjacent to City Hall, at the junction with Frank Sinatra Drive, this moving tribute to survivors of cancer features tiled benches, ponds, a hillside waterfall, and bronze sculptures. Most notable is the *Cancer . . . there's hope* sculpture by Mexican artist Victor Salmones, showing eight life-size bronze figures negotiating metaphorical cancer treatments. The **Positive Attitude Walk** has meditative places and 14 plaques designed to inspire hope.

DESERT MEMORIAL PARK

760-328-3316
31-705 Da Vall Dr., Cathedral City, CA 92234
Palm Springs' cemetery has no fanciful mausoleums or ancient headstones à la old English graveyards. In fact, this unassuming place comprises little more than palm-shaded lawns studded with symmetrical rows of identical, tiny, pavinglike tombstones sunk into the ground. But it *is* a Who's Who of stars laid to rest. The main draw is Frank Sinatra's tomb. He was buried here on May 20, 1998, next to his parents, Dolly and Marty (Dolly was killed when her plane hit San Gregorio Mountain after taking off from Palm Springs en route to Las Vegas, where she was to attend a show by her son). Sinatra's own simple flat tombstone is inscribed with the words "Francis Albert Sinatra, 1915–1998" and "The Best Is Yet to Come," from his song. Beneath, his lead-lined casket contains a bottle of Jack Daniel's, his favorite tipple, along with his cigarette lighter and a roll of dimes.

Salvatore Phillip "Sonny" Bono (of Sonny and Cher fame) also has a place of honor. And actors Cameron Mitchell and William Powell, star of the great "Thin Man" movies, also lie here. So, too, Busby Berkeley, director of Hollywood's splashiest musicals; composer Jimmy Van Heusen (born Edward Chester Babcock); Jolie and Magda Gabor, mother and sister respectively of Zsa Zsa; and Brooklyn Dodgers great "Pistol" Pete Reiser.

A map at the cemetery office shows the location of the key graves. Open 7 AM–5 PM daily.

HOT SPRINGS PARK

760-329-6411
Palm Dr. and 8th St., Desert Hot Springs, CA 92240
Desert Hot Springs' fabled mineral springs are celebrated in this interactive educational park, featuring a beautiful fountain gushing forth fresh thermal water. It also displays a manmade "fault line" and a mini date grove to illustrate the relationship of fault, water, and palms.

MICHAEL S. WOLFSON PARK

Frank Sinatra Dr. and Da Vall Dr., Rancho Mirage, CA 92270
This small park is landscaped with cactus and palms and manicured lawns and makes a lovely place to stretch your legs and relax. A braille trail leads through a fragrance garden, and there's a fountain, decorative lighting fixtures, plus benches. If you hit the red button on the pedestal near the entrance, Ol' Blue Eyes greets you with: "Hi, this is Frank Sinatra."

TOWN SQUARE

68-700 Ave. Lalo Guerrero, Cathedral City, CA 92234

Cathedral's City's once-moribund downtown has been revitalized by this landscaped park fronting the Civic Center and flanked by the IMAX and Mary Pickford theaters. The wide-open plaza, between Hwy. 111 and Ave. Lalo Guerrero, and Glenn Ave. and Monty Hall Dr., centers on the **Fountain of Life**. This almost surreal yet award-winning sculpture by artist Jennifer Johnson is made of adoquin stone adorned with hand-cut mosaic tiles and glass. Vibrant with native Indian and desert symbolism, the multitiered fountain incorporates sculptures of native desert animals: bighorn sheep, tortoises, lizards, fishes, birds, and other creatures that exist under cascades of water.

Nearby, note the life-size bronze statues of trombone-playing musician Buddy Rogers and cowboy film star George Montgomery, cast by the artist-actor himself.

WHITEWATER PARK

71-560 San Jacinto Dr., Rancho Mirage, CA 92270

This recreational facility tucked out of sight a sling-shot north of Hwy. 111 features walking paths with a fitness trail, a children's playground, picnic facilities, and a classic fire engine. Sports facilities include two basketball courts, two racquetball/handball courts, four lighted tennis courts, and an informal play field. Ranchito Chiquito, the city's oldest house (it was built in 1934 as a date ranch), was relocated here in 2004. It's also a venue for concerts and several annual events, including Art Affaire (760-568-9351; www.ci.rancho-mirage.ca.us)—a two-day arts, jazz, and food and wine festival held each Nov.

Trina Parks, of the Fabulous Palm Springs Follies. Ned Redway

SOUTHERN DESERT RESORTS

CIVIC CENTER PARK

760-568-9697

Fred Waring Dr. and San Pablo Ave., Palm Desert, CA 92260

One of the largest city parks in the valley, this grassy 72-acre space is a great place to stroll and relax. It's also blessed with an astounding collection of public sculptures, including *The Dreamer*, the Holocaust Memorial, and the Peace Memorial. Fitness freaks also love it for its recreational amenities, including four baseball fields, three basketball courts, a skate park, and tennis and volleyball courts. There's also a kiddy playground plus a dog park. The city's Fourth of July celebration and many other special events are held here.

Theater

The valley's monied class includes plenty of culture vultures with a strong appreciation for the theater. In fact, they're major sponsors, not least because a good many residents have had or continue to have ties to the dramatic arts. The **Desert Theater League** (760-200-0897; www.deserttheatreleague.net; P.O. Box 2675, Palm Springs, CA 92263) is the major umbrella sponsor.

PALM SPRINGS

ANNENBERG THEATER

760-325-4490
www.psmuseum.org
E-mail: info@psmuseum.org
101 Museum Dr., Palm Springs, CA 92262
Season: Year-round
Tickets: Call for prices
Recently refitted to the latest standards, this sumptuous, acoustically perfect 450-seat theater within the Palm Springs Art Museum hosts a wide range of dance, music, and theater (everything from traditional musicals to avant-garde productions). The theater also hosts lecture and film series and is a venue for the Palm Springs International Film Festival.

FABULOUS PALM SPRINGS FOLLIES

760-327-0225 or 1-800-967-9997
www.palmspringsfollies.com
Plaza Theater, 128 S. Palm Canyon Dr., Palm Springs, CA 92262
Season: Nov.–mid-May
Performances: Varies by month
Tickets: $48–90
This Broadway-caliber vaudeville extravaganza, held from Nov. to May in the Historic Plaza Theater (which opened its doors in 1936), presents the "timeless music and magic of the '30s and '40s," although the sets, costumes, and musical numbers change every year and are as hip and as sophisticated as anything Vegas can offer. The general theme of the show harks back to Palm Springs' heyday as a playground of the stars.

The cast of Long-Legged Lovelies and Follies Gentlemen are old enough to remember the Folies Bergère and Ziegfeld Follies that inspired the show. Yes, the long-legged lovelies have to be 50 years or older to kick up their heels in the chorus line! The entire cast is 50 to 80 years young. The oldest member, Dorothy Kloss, was still performing in 2007 at the age of 84 (yet looking 30 years younger), 60 years after she performed in swanky Chicago nightclubs, proving beyond a doubt Florenz Ziegfeld's quip that "Age doesn't matter unless you're a cheese." And no amateurs, these. All were once top-notch professional performers who years later found themselves missing the applause.

The show is surprisingly hip, and the ladies' flamboyant costumes are a spectacle unto themselves as the gals sashay and shake in sequined bikinis, ruffled frills, sensational headdresses, and feathers more ostentatious than peacocks' (some costumes cost $35,000 apiece).

The show's creator, Riff Markowitz, emcees the Follies with a cutting wit. Be warned: the show is three and a half hours long, with two intermissions! But it's worth every cent.

Fountain of Life, Town Square, Cathedral City.

Each season sees a roster of international guest stars, and in Nov. and Dec. the Follies presents a lavish holiday spectacular, with a matinee and evening show most days.

PLAYWRIGHT'S CIRCLE
760-327-4877
www.playwrightscircle.com
Email: info@playwrightscircle.com
457 N. Palm Canyon Dr., Suite C, Palm Springs, CA 92262

Billing itself as "the birthplace of new works," this organization is dedicated to giving new plays their first moment on stage before live audiences. International in scope, it promotes and introduces new works from around the world. It gives stage readings of original scripts at three local venues: the Annenberg Theater and Black Box Theater, and adjoining Palm Springs High School Auditorium. It also sponsors the Palm Springs National Short Play Festival.

Southern Desert Resorts

THE MCCALLUM THEATRE
760-346-6505
www.mccallumtheater.com
73-000 Fred Waring Dr., Palm Desert, CA 92260
Season: Sept.–June
Tickets: $25–100

The McCallum Theatre. McCallum Theatre.

This stunning, state-of-the-art 1,127-seat theater is the valley's main performance venue, hosting top-ranked musicians and other performers. During its two decades in existence, its list of performers reads like an entertainment industry Who's Who. The McCallum presents premier theatrical and artistic productions, with the eclectic menu spanning local faves Barry Manilow and Jack Jones to the Moscow Classical Ballet and the Peking Acrobats.

Other Theater

Palm Springs

Palm Canyon Theater (760-323-0739; www.palmcanyontheatre.org; 538 N. Palm Canyon Dr., Palm Springs, CA. 92262) This decade-old company performs in its eponymous 230-seat proscenium theater at Francis Steven Park. Musicals to Shakespeare. Also shows movies and is a Palm Springs Film Festival venue.

Palm Springs High School Theater Company (760-778-0419; www.pshsdrama.com; 2401 E. Baristo Rd., Palm Springs, CA 92262) Performs at the Palm Springs High School Auditorium.

Pavilion Theater (760-778-5715; www.pspavilion.com; 123 N. Palm Canyon Dr., Palm Springs, CA 92262) This 1,000-seat canopied theater opened in late 2005 and folded its tent two years later. The theater still stood at press time, when its future was uncertain. It initially served as home to *Cirque Dreams*, a spellbinding combination of amazing performance artistry and quixotic design that had you breathless on the edge of your seat.

Thorny Theater (760-325-0853; www.thornytheater.com; 2500 N. Palm Canyon Dr., Palm Springs, CA 92262) This gay and lesbian theater puts on prize-winning plays and musicals funded by grants from the Arch and Bruce Brown Foundation (www.aabbfoundation.org) to playwrights and novelists who deal with LGBT issues. Mid-Sept.–mid-June.

Southern Desert Resorts

College of the Desert Performing and Visual Arts (760-346-8041; www.collegeofthedesert.edu; 43-500 Monterey Ave., Palm Desert, CA 92260) performs in the college's Pollock Theater. Everything from opera to Molière.

The Joslyn Players (760-340-3220; www.joslyncenter.org; Joslyn Senior Center, 73-750 Catalina Way, Palm Desert, CA 92260) Formed in 1999, this company of actors, singers, and dancers puts on plays, musical revues, and book musicals at the Joslyn Senior Center. It offers a six-production season incorporating comedy, musicals, and drama.

Indio Performing Arts Center (760-775-5200 or 760-564-3112; www.indioperformingartscenter.org; 45-175 Fargo St., Indio, CA 92201) Comprises three theaters. Eclectic offerings in any one year might include barbershop singing, comedy, jazz, off-Broadway musicals, and magic. Season runs Oct.–Mar.

La Quinta Playhouse (760-360-9191; www.laquintaplayhouse.com; La Ranchita at Calle Estado, La Quinta, CA 92247) Performs at diverse venues in La Quinta, Nov.–mid-Mar.

Theatre 29 (760-361-4151; www.theatre29.com; John Calveri Theatre, 73-637 Sullivan Rd., Twentynine Palms, CA 92277) A local community theater serving Twentynine Palms with family-oriented productions, from Rodgers and Hammerstein to rock 'n' roll musical *Grease*.

Seasonal Events

Palm Spring residents are party-hearty and like nothing more than to throw a good bash. Many of the festivals and fairs fill out the winter months, when the local populace swells and the climate is more conducive to outdoor events. Given the area's decades of ties to Hollywood, it's no surprise that film is the city's forte, while the large gay population loves any reason to host a bash. Here we list some of the more popular events.

American Heat—Palm Springs Motorcycle Weekend (1-800-200-4557) Bikers pour in from across the nation to roar their Harleys down Palm Canyon Drive. This Oct. event features stunts, a ride-in show, and no shortage of leather and skin.

The Art of Food & Wine Festival (1-866-968-2783; www.artoffoodandwine.com; Palm Desert) A four-day event held at various venues, with food and wine tastings, celebrity chef demonstrations, and culinary and lifestyle seminars. The Grand Tasting Venue, held over two days on the lawns of the Desert Springs JW Marriott Resort & Spa, provides a chance to sample delicacies from dozens of the finest local restaurants, with signature samplers prepared in front of your eyes by the chefs themselves. And such celebrities as legendary Thai chef Tommy Tang will show you how to cook up a mean grill Thai eggplant with Kaffir lime sauce. Acclaimed sommeliers demonstrate the fine arts of wine appreciation. Select wineries also serve their best. Musicians perform. November.

Bob Hope Desert Chrysler Golf Classic (760-346-8184; www.bhcc.com; 39-000 Bob Hope Dr., Rancho Mirage, CA 92270) Held over five days on four separate championship courses in La Quinta and Rancho Mirage, this annual golf championship pairs golf pros and famous entertainers (from actor Andy Garcia to rock superstar Alice Cooper). Mid-Jan.

California Date Chef's Competition (760-347-4510 or 1-800-223-8748; www.datesaregreat.com; P.O. Box 1736, Indio, CA 92202) Top chefs from around the nation compete to produce the most creative and delicious meals using the desert's favorite local ingredient. Each year a different venue hosts the event. Mid-Apr.

Coachella Valley Fiesta of Chilies and Chili Cook-Off (760-398-3502 ext. 102; Veterans Memorial Park, 1515 Sixth St., Coachella, CA 92236) Inaugurated in 2007, this daylong festival features music and dancing in addition to salsa and chili competitions. Mid-Nov. Admission.

Coachella Valley Music and Arts Festival (1-800-537-6986; www.coachella.com; Empire Polo Field, 81-800 Ave. 51, Indio, CA 92201) Billed as the largest music festival in

Distinguished Speaker!

The Palm Springs region punches well above its weight as a powerhouse of movers and shakers. Former president Gerald Ford lived here. So, too, former ambassador Walter Annenberg, who hosted every U.S. president since Eisenhower, who was a regular to the desert. With keen intellects and an interest in current affairs, the worldly valley populace is a tailor-made audience for distinguished speakers.

The **World Affairs Council of the Desert** (760-322-7711; www.worldaffairsdesert.org; P.O. Box 467, Palm Springs, CA 92263), a nonpartisan and nonprofit organization, provides a monthly speaker/dinner event, Oct.–May. Ambassadors, academics, and other authorities speak on timely national or international issues that have significance to the foreign policy of the United States.

The **Desert Town Hall** (760-416-3400 or 1-800-224-4991; www.deserttownhall.org; 500 S. Palm Canyon Dr., Suite 215, Palm Springs, CA 92264) hosts the world's top speakers in an annual four-speaker series, Jan. –Apr. The list of past speakers includes James Baker III, Tony Blair, William F. Buckley Jr., Rudy Giuliani, Benjamin Netanyahu, Henry Kissinger, Lady Margaret Thatcher, and George Tenet, to name a few.

The Art of Food & Wine Festival.

California, this three-day multimedia mega-concert held in mid-Apr. is the biggest thing since Woodstock and spans several musical genres. The 2007 lineup featured more than 100 acts, from Air and the Arctic Monkeys and Red Hot Chili Peppers to Rage Against the Machine. From $85. Purchase tickets via Ticketmaster (1-866-448-7849; www.ticketmaster.com).

Crossroads Renaissance Festival (1-800-320-4736; www.renaissanceinfo.com; 538 N. Palm Canyon Dr., Palm Springs, CA 92262) Dust off your Elizabethan costume for this fun-filled faire with professional actors but where everyone is encouraged to play the part. Three days in late Mar.

Desert Circuit Horse Show (760-399-9200; www.hitsshows.com; HITS Desert Horse Park, 85-555 Airport Blvd., Thermal, CA 92274) This eight-week equestrian show circuit takes place in Thermal, Jan.–Mar. More than 25,000 spectators attend the event—the pre-eminent U.S. winter show circuit and the largest show-jumping event west of the Mississippi—which features 18 grand prix events worth nearly $2 million in prize money.

Dinah Shore Weekend (415-596-8730 or 1-888-923-4624; www.thedinah.com; 1410 N. Poinsettia Place, Los Angeles, CA 90046) The biggest lesbian bash on the planet offers three days of entertainment, from comedy to pool parties.

Dinner in the Canyons (760-778-1079 ext. 111; www.accmuseum.org) The Agua Caliente Band of Indians' annual dinner features a cocktail reception, traditional native entertainment, and a live auction under the stars in Andreas Canyon.

Fashion Week (760-325-2333; www.fashionweekelpaseo.com; El Paseo, Palm Desert, CA 92260) Inaugurated in 2006, this weeklong celebration sees haute couture designers showing off their latest moods and trends of the moment at runway and fashion-related events. Various venues. Mid-Mar.

Festival of Lights Parade (760-325-5749; www.paradesofpalmsprings.com; S. Palm Canyon Dr., Palm Springs, CA 92262) Adorned with thousands of lightbulbs, fire engines and dozens of other vehicles parade through town accompanied by equestrians and high school marching bands. A Christmas-week evening.

Film Noir Festival (760-325-6565; www.palmspringsfilmnoir.com; Camelot Theatre, 2300 Baristo Rd., Palm Springs, CA 92262) Held in June, this festival revives movies from the '40s and '50s. Tickets $11.50 to 13.50.

Frank Sinatra Celebrity Invitational Golf Tournament (760-674-8447 or 1-800-377-8277; www.sinatragolf.com; Indian Wells Country Club, Indian Wells, CA) Amateurs tee off alongside top celebrities each Feb. Social events include a fashion show hosted by Barbara Sinatra.

Gay Pride Weekend (760-416-8711; www.pspride.org; 611 S. Palm Canyon Dr., Suite 7436. Palm Springs, CA 92264) Each Nov. more than 30,000 gays and lesbians flock to make merry and celebrate. There's scads of music, food, wine tastings, and even an art festival.

Gay Singles Weekend (760-320-1928; www.gaysinglesweekend.com) This four-day event hosted by the Desert Gay Tourism Guild in mid-Dec. includes a street fair, cultural events that include wine tasting, and even hiking in Indian Canyon.

Golf Cart Parade (760-346-6111; www.golfcartparade.com; Palm Desert) Whimsically decorated golf carts trundling down El Paseo draw more than 25,000 spectators every fourth Sun. in Oct. Each year a different theme is selected. The parade started when star residents Phil Harris, Alice Faye, and other celebrities with homes in Palm Desert wanted something fun to do.

Indio Powwow (760-238-5770; www.cabazonindians-nsn.gov; Fantasy Springs Casino Special Events Center, 84-245 Indio Springs Pkwy., Indio, CA 92203) Held over Thanksgiving weekend, this annual three-day cultural festival hosted by the Cabazon Band of Mission Indians draws more than 40 different tribes to the sacred powwow grounds next to Fantasy Springs Casino.

International Hispanic Film Festival of Greater Palm Springs (760-325-6565; Camelot Theaters, Palm Springs, CA 92262) Held each Oct., this festival shows films and documentaries by Hispanics and/or about Hispanic culture. Admission.

International Tamale Festival (760-342-6532; www.tamalefestival.net; 100 Civic Center Mall, Indio, CA 92201) Spicing up the historic streets of Old Town Indio, this annual festival is one of the great all-American food festivals. Every Dec.

Jacqueline Cochran Air Show (760-863-8247; www.jacquelinecochranairshow.org; Jacqueline Cochran Regional Airport, 56-850 Vic Higgins Dr., Thermal, CA 82274) Spectacular air show featuring the Patriots in dazzling formation flight, plus World War II aircraft, team parachute displays, helicopters, and more. First week of Nov.

Kraft Nabisco Championship PGA Golf Tournament (760-324-4546; www.kncgolf.com; 34-600 Mission Hills Dr., Rancho Mirage, CA 92270) Held every spring since 1972 at the Mission Hills Country Club, this prestige event (formerly the Dinah Shore Golf Classic) is the "Masters" of women's golf and by default has become a major event on the national lesbian calendar. Mar.

La Quinta Arts Festival (760-564-1244; www.lqaf.com; 78-150 Calle Tampico, Suite 215, La Quinta, CA 92253) Sponsored by the La Quinta Arts Foundation, this annual festival is held in and around La Quinta Civic Center Park and features works by more than 200 artists. Gourmet food and wines are served. Mid-Mar.

Festival of Native Film & Culture (760-778-1079; www.accmuseum.org; Camelot Theaters, 2300 E. Baristo Rd., Palm Springs, CA 92262) An annual Mar. event focusing on films about native cultures. The Native American Storytelling Festival is held in conjunction. Admission.

Pacific Life Open (760-200-8400, or 1-800-999-1585; www.pacificlifeopen.com; Indian Wells Tennis Garden, 78-200 Miles Ave., Indian Wells, CA 92210) One of North America's premier tennis championships, hosted every Mar. at the Indian Wells Tennis Garden. More than 250 of the world's finest players usually compete.

Palm Springs International Film Festival (760-322-2930; www.psfilmfest.org; 1700 E. Tahquitz Canyon Way, Suite 3, Palm Springs, CA 92262) A highlight of the year, drawing Hollywood and international stars. More than 200 films unspool at theaters around town. Private parties are hosted for those in the know. Every Jan. Admission.

Palm Springs International Festival of Short Films (760-322-2930; www.psfilmfest.org; 1700 E. Tahquitz Canyon Way, Suite 3, Palm Springs, CA 92262) North America's largest short-film festival, showing cutting-edge productions from around the globe. Sept. Admission.

Palm Springs Restaurant Week (www.palmspringsrestaurantweek.com) Inaugurated in 2008, this six-day culinary event showcases the talents of chefs from some 40 or so of Palm Springs' premier restaurants, which will offer prix fixe three-course menus. Mid-June.

Brad Pitt at the Palm Springs International Film Festival. Palm Springs International Film Festival

Red, White, and Blue Polo and Balloon Festival (760-777-8081; www.poloamerica.com; Eldorado Polo Club, 50-950 Madison St., Indio, CA 92201) Celebrities clash for charity on the polo fields, while hot-air balloons take to the air. The event is the third-largest special shape balloon festival in the country, drawing 50,000 attendees. Entry by donation. Jan.

Riverside County Fair & National Date Festival (760-347-0676 or 1-800-811-FAIR; www.datefest.org; Riverside County Fairgrounds, 82-503 Hwy. 111, Indio, CA 92201) This hugely popular festival, held mid-Feb., features camel and ostrich racing, a rodeo, carnival rides, and a monster truck show, but everyone is really there for the outrageous date milk shakes. Admission.

Stagecoach (http://stagecoachfestival.com; Empire Polo Field, 81-800 Ave. 51, Indio, CA 92201) Billed as "California's Country Music Festival," with a jam-packed musical lineup that in 2008 included country superstars Tim McGraw and Rascal Flatts. You can also thrill to hayrides, mechanical bulls, a lasso and roping clinic, and more.

Summer of Fun (760-346-0611; Civic Center Park Amphitheater, 73-510 Fred Waring Dr., Palm Desert, CA 92270) Free movies (at 6:30 PM) and concerts (at 7:30 PM) alfresco. Bring a blanket, chairs, and a picnic. Every Thurs., July–Aug.

Tour de Palm Springs Bike Event (760-770-4626; www.tourdepalmsprings.com; 36-665 Bankside Dr., Suite C, Cathedral City, CA 92235) A charity ride. Amateur and professional cyclists from around the world gather each Feb. to compete (or simply have fun) in 5-, 15-, 25-, 50-, and 100-mile events in and around Palm Springs. Admission.

Villagefest (760-320-3781; S. Palm Canyon Dr., Palm Springs) The Strip—Palm Canyon Drive—is closed to traffic every Thurs. night and throngs to pedestrians. Street stalls sell everything from fine art and jewelry to tacos and hot dogs. Musicians and magicians entertain.

White Party (323-653-0800; www.jeffreysanker.com; 8344 Melrose Ave., Suite 20, W. Hollywood, CA 90069) *The* gay event of the year. Four days of sensational parties (including a white underwear party), plus mixers, and events with top entertainers draw more than 25,000 gay attendees each Apr.

Wildlights Holiday Light Festival (760-346-5694; www.livingdesert.org; 47-900 Portola Ave., Palm Desert, CA 92260) Six-week-long Christmastime light festival at the Living Desert, with various animals depicted.

Beyond the Valley

To the South

ANZA-BORREGO DESERT STATE PARK

760-767-5311
www.anzaborrego.statepark.org
P.O. Box 299, Borrego Springs, CA 92004
Open: Visitor center open daily 9–5, Oct.–May; 10–3 June–Sept.
Called the "capital of desert botanica," this 600,000-acre park—California's largest state park—is renowned for the spectacular spring bloom of wildflowers, which draws thousands of flower lovers (Spring Wildflower Hotline: 760-767-4684). The bloom begins in

Feb. and peaks in Apr. The park, abutting the southern end of the Santa Rosa National Scenic Area, in one of the most remote areas of California, is named for the *borrego*, or bighorn sheep. It is accessed via Borrego Springs, at the southern end of the Coachella Valley.

The visitor center, built into a rocky hillside, has a cactus garden and a desert pupfish pond. It features a slide show, and exhibits include mammoth fossils, Native Indian artifacts, and a re-created *Aiolornis incredibilis*, a stalking bird with a 17-foot wingspan from the Pleistocene era.

The park has 110 miles of hiking and riding trails. The 1.5-mile-long **Borrego Palm Canyon Trail** begins 1 mile from the visitor center, winds through a grove filled with bamboo and Indian grinding rocks, and ends at a waterfall in the midst of palms. Bighorn sheep are often seen. And lucky visitors might spot roadrunners, golden eagles, kit foxes, and mule deer, as well as desert iguanas, chuckwallas, and four species of rattlesnake.

SONNY BONO SALTON SEA NATIONAL WILDLIFE REFUGE

760-348-5278
www.fws.gov/saltonsea
Sinclair Rd. and Gentry Rd., Niland, CA 92254
Open: Dawn to dusk daily; visitor center open Mon.–Fri. 7–3:30, Apr.–Sept.; Sat. and Sun. 8–4:30, Oct.–Mar.
Admission: Free

At the southern end of the Salton Sea at the southern end of the Coachella Valley, this refuge is one of California's premier birding sites. The freshwater wetland habitats that border this vast, highly saline body of water are a habitat for more than 400 bird species. Pelicans. Cormorants. Black-necked stilts. Clapper rails. Cinnamon teal and ruddy ducks. Egrets and great blue herons. Gulls and grebes. From the Arctic come snow geese and Ross's geese, while blue-footed boobies fly in from equatorial South America. All probing for pile worms—*Pick! Pick! Pick!*—or stabbing at fish amid the rustling reeds.

The visitor center has a bird diorama and bookstore, plus an observation tower and picnic area. A self-guided trail will introduce you to the various habitats found in desert ecosystems.

Elite Land Discovery Tours (760-318-1200; www.elitelandtours.com; 555 S. Sunrise Way, Suite 200, Palm Springs, CA 92264) offers tours by Humvee, including visits to mud volcanoes spewing bubbling, superheated mud.

To the East

The east side of the Coachella Valley is framed by the Little San Bernardino Mountains, gateway to the high desert terrain of Joshua Tree National Park via California Highway 62 and the towns of Yucca Valley, Joshua Tree, and Twentynine Palms. These relatively sleepy places have a Wild West feel and no shortage of artifacts and mementos to pioneering days.

In fact, one of the local attractions is **Pioneer Town**, built in 1946 as a set for western movies. The Hayden Movie Ranch included homes for actors and Hollywood staff to live on-site during filming. Remarkably, the set is now a lived-in "museum." Mane Street has real-life functioning western saloons, an antique bowling alley, and a genuine old western motel (Pioneertown Motel; 760-365-4879; www.pioneertownmotel.com; 5040 Curtis Rd., Pioneertown, CA92268). The Pioneertown Posse (760-228-0494; www.pioneertown-posse.org) gives Old West reenactments at 2:30 on weekends, Apr.–Oct. Driving up

The Salton Sea

One of the world's largest saltwater seas and California's largest lake, the 38-mile-long by 15-mile-wide, below-sea-level sea is also one of the world's most unusual bodies of water.

A century ago, developers tapped the Colorado River to turn the river's then bone-dry ancient delta—the Salton Sink—into an agricultural Eden. Today, thanks to irrigation, the Imperial Valley supports a billion-dollar farm economy spanning half a million acres of well-watered land nicknamed the "winter salad bowl of the nation." The runoff feeds the sea, which came into being in 1905 when the Colorado River blew out a poorly constructed levee for the Imperial Canal. The river poured unchecked into the valley. It took two years to fix the riverbanks and force the river back into its former channel, by which time a 500-square-mile sea had been created. Under natural conditions, the lake would have evaporated in the 115-degree summer heat. But the runoff from ongoing irrigation has fed the Salton Sea, which has no natural outlet.

By the 1950s the sea had also become a popular tourist attraction. Hollywood stars filtered down from Palm Springs to the luxurious North Shore Yacht Club, designed in 1958 by Albert Frey with a nautical motif and circular windows hooded like traffic lights to protect against glare. Dean Martin and Frank Sinatra water-skied. The area witnessed a short-lived real estate boom. Fishermen were in their element. Campers jammed the shores. In its heyday, the Salton Sea even drew more visitors than Yosemite National Park. But the popularity was short-lived and by the 1960s had faltered.

The shores are hardly inviting. For a start, the "sand" actually comprises billions of barnacles and bone fragments from fish that have expired in mass die-offs. There's no escaping the fish die-offs, which result from midsummer algae blooms that float atop the surface in great blobs, drawing oxygen from the water and causing a horrible stench. In the 1930s the California Department of Fish and Game introduced pile worms to eat the algae that had bloomed. In the 1950s saltwater fish were introduced, including corvina and sargo. Soon enough, pelicans, cormorants, and dozens of other fish-eating birds began to flock. To millions of birds, this giant stagnant lake is an all-you-can-eat buffet of pile worms and fish—mostly tilapia, considered a fish pest (this hardy freshwater African fish appeared mysteriously in the lake in the 1970s; it thrived and multiplied, providing further nourishment for large birds).

No waterway carries away the salts and minerals, which build up year by year due to evaporation. Today, the sea has a salinity of 41 parts per million (the Pacific Ocean has about 35 parts per million).

Pioneertown Road you'll pass through a fantastical desert landscape that causes déjà vu for anyone familiar with Gene Autry and Hopalong Cassidy movies.

Yucca Valley, at 3,300 feet elevation, is the setting for antiques stores, western-style saloons, plus three sites of interest. The family-run **Hi-Desert Nature Museum** (760-369-7212; www.hidesertnaturemuseum.org; Community Center Complex, 57-090 Twentynine Palms Hwy., Yucca Valley, CA 92284) explores the art, culture, and flora and fauna of the high desert, including an educational hands-on area for children, plus mini-zoo with desert animals. Open Tues.–Sun. 10–5. Nearby, the **High Desert Living Art Center** (760-369-5040; 55-840 Twentynine Palms Hwy., Yucca Valley, CA 92284) is a cooperative gallery and learning space, with art and crafts classes. Open Daily 11–6. And motorcycle fans might stop in at **Hutchins Harley-Davidson Museum** (760-365-1877; 55-405 Twentynine Palms Hwy., Yucca Valley, CA 92284), displaying vintage Harleys and memorabilia harking back to the early days of motorcycling.

It's not the Dead Sea. Nonetheless, the salinity makes these waters extremely buoyant. The salt concentrations are increasing, with severe ecological consequences.

In 2003 a huge gulp of Colorado River water was transferred from the Imperial Valley farms to San Diego. Twenty percent less water now flows into the sea. Environmentalists fear that the Salton Sea will eventually shrink to virtually nothing, exposing all manner of dangerous dust to the wind, turning the area into the nation's next toxic Dust Bowl (the fertilizer- and pesticide-laden irrigation waters have deposited billions of tons of toxic chemicals, heavy metals, and salts). In recent years the sea has suffered from mass fish and bird kills, thought to be a result of poisoning and oxygen depletion caused by agricultural runoff. The rotting fish carcasses produce botulism, which is taken up by feeding birds, which then die. For example, in 1992 more than 150,000 eared grebes died from avian botulism. Mass fish die-offs have gotten larger by the year: 14 million in 2000, 21 million in 2001. Fishing season is Oct. through May (there is no limit on how many tilapia can be caught, but state health officials warn that Salton Sea fish now contain too much selenium and have advised people to limit their consumption).

A development plan (www.saltonsea.ca.gov) intended to save the lake includes construction of a dike with an 8-mile-long causeway. The Torres-Martinez Indians will run a lakeside casino. New marinas will open, as will golf courses, bringing the old seaside developments back to life, while new canals will help channel both inflow and outflow to maintain an ecological balance so that the wetlands and sloughs can thrive.

The land north and south of the sea is intensively farmed (the Imperial Valley, which extends south from the sea all the way to the Mexican border, soaks up more water than Los Angeles and Las Vegas combined). Heat-loving fruits and vegetables, such as grapes, citrus, dates, tomatoes, and avocados, thrive here.

A curiosity worth the visit is **Slab City**, a former World War II-era U.S. naval base 3 miles east of Niland, along Hwy. 111, beyond the flyspeck desert communities of Thermal and Mecca. Every year as many as 6,000 squatters arrive with their RVs to form an itinerant community of desert dwellers. They set up home atop the 640 acres of concrete slabs without water and electricity, although natural hot springs provide alfresco showers. The main entrance to Slab City is marked by **Salvation Mountain**, a series of hills emblazoned with art by Leonard Knight, a septuagenarian who has been at work on the artwork for almost two decades. And Slab City's makeshift Sidewinder Golf Course has no greens fees, nor greens. All that's required is a sand wedge and a sharp eye for rattlers.

The town of Twentynine Palms is the setting for the **Old School House Museum** (760-367-2366; www.msnusers.com/29palmshistoricalsociety; 6760 National Park Dr., Twentynine Palms, CA 92277), housed in the original schoolhouse. It displays memorabilia relating to the area's history and culture. The main point of interest for visitors, however, is the **Oasis of Murals** (760-361-2286; www.oasisofmurals.com; 6455 Mesquite Ave., Twentynine Palms, CA 92277). This historic project was begun in 1994 and today features 18 spectacular murals on the exterior walls of commercial buildings. The murals depict the rich history and culture of the area. The chamber of commerce has a free self-guided tour map and sells limited-edition prints of the art.

BIG MORONGO CANYON PRESERVE

760-363-7190
11-055 East Dr., off Hwy. 62, Morongo Valley; P.O. Box 780, Morongo Valley, CA 92256

Open: 7:30–sunset
Admission: Free
Run by the Bureau of Land Management, this desert oasis nestles in the Little San Bernardino Mountains and spans 31,000 acres, ranging in elevation from 600 feet on the canyon floor to 3,000 feet. It is a transition zone spanning both the Colorado Desert and Mojave Desert. Seven distinct trails offer a wide variety of landscapes and habitats that include wetland, woodland, and grassland.

The half-mile-long **Marsh Trail** is a wheelchair-accessible boardwalk through marsh that comprises one of the 10 largest cottonwood and willow riparian (stream) habitats in California. The mile-long **Desert Trail** follows desert meadow with fall-blooming alkali goldenbush, drops into a wash, and leads to an overlook above the riparian systems. The **Yucca Ridge Trail** offers some spectacular geological formations and links to both the Desert Trail and streamside **Mesquite Trail** (0.5 miles). The longest trail, the 5.5-mile-long **Canyon Trail**, follows a canyon from high desert to low desert.

The preserve is renowned as one of California's best birding spots, particularly during migration season. More than 245 bird species have been observed, including yellow-billed cuckoo, the endangered least Bell's vireo, and the vermilion flycatcher (the preserve's signature bird). Other denizens include bighorn sheep, bobcats, coyotes, raccoons, and all manner of snakes and other reptiles.

Free guided early-morning birding walks are offered by the **Friends of Big Morongo Canyon** (760-363-7190; P.O. Box 780, Morongo Valley, CA 92256) every Wed. and Sat., except the first Sat. of each month.

The preserve has restrooms, drinking water, and parking. Dogs not allowed. Kickapoo Trail, in Little Morongo Canyon, is the only trail open to off-road vehicles.

JOSHUA TREE NATIONAL PARK

760-367-5500
www.nps.gov/jotr
74-485 National Park Dr., Joshua Tree, CA 92277
Open: Oasis Visitor Center, daily 8–5; Joshua Tree Visitor Center, daily 8–5; Cottonwood Visitor Center, daily 9–3; Black Rock Nature Center, Sat.–Thurs. 8–4 and Fri. noon–8, Oct.–May only
Admission: $10 per vehicle
Spanning 1,240 square miles of the Mojave and lower Colorado deserts, Joshua Tree protects one of the most spectacular desert regions in North America. It is named for the peculiar Joshua trees, with their multiple armlike branches, that grow here in abundance. In fact, the park owes its existence to one woman's effort to save the tree from Los Angelenos, who descended on the desert to poach cactus. The problem became so severe that the flora was threatened. It was a Pasadena matron named Minerva H. Hoyt who initiated a campaign to gain government protection. Her almost single-handed effort succeeded when the Joshua Tree National Monument was created by the Roosevelt administration in 1936. In 1994 it was elevated to national park status.

The park lies at the junction of three ecosystems. The Colorado Desert, a western extension of the vast Sonoran Desert, occupies the southern and eastern parts of the park and is characterized by stands of spikelike ocotillo plants and "jumping" cholla cactus. The southern boundary of the higher, moister, and slightly cooler Mojave Desert reaches across the northern part of the park and is the habitat of the park's namesake, the Joshua tree.

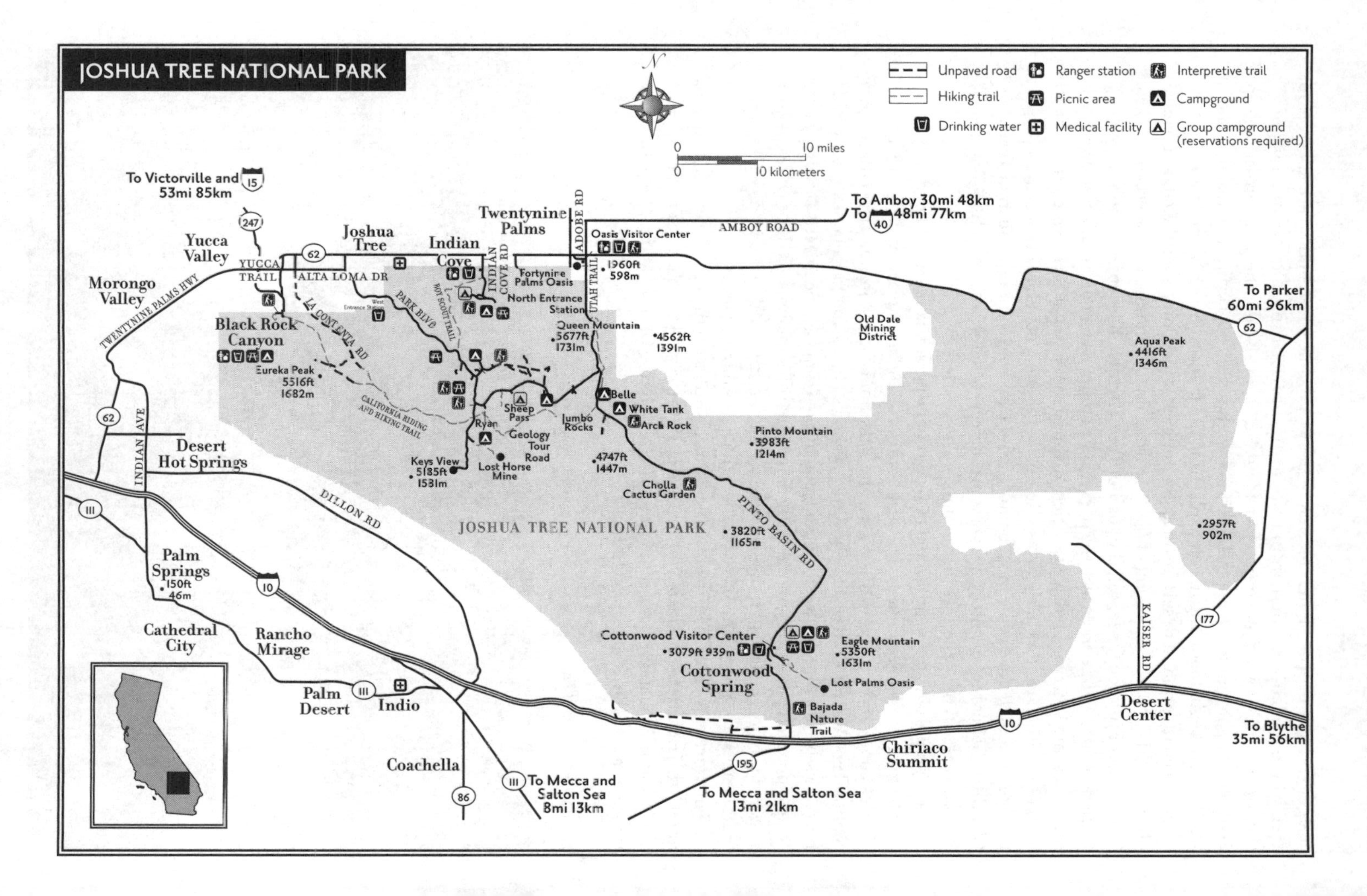
JOSHUA TREE NATIONAL PARK
Unpaved road
Hiking trail
Drinking water
Ranger station
Picnic area
Medical facility
Interpretive trail
Campground
Group campground (reservations required)
0 10 miles
0 10 kilometers
To Victorville and 15 53mi 85km
To Amboy 30mi 48km
To 40 48mi 77km
To Parker 60mi 96km
To Blythe 35mi 56km
To Mecca and Salton Sea 13mi 21km
To Mecca and Salton Sea 8mi 13km
Morongo Valley
Yucca Valley
Joshua Tree
Indian Cove
Twentynine Palms
Desert Hot Springs
Palm Springs 150ft 46m
Cathedral City
Rancho Mirage
Palm Desert
Indio
Coachella
Chiriaco Summit
Desert Center
TWENTYNINE PALMS HWY
INDIAN AVE
DILLON RD
YUCCA TRAIL
ALTA LOMA DR
LA CONTENTA RD
PARK BLVD
BOY SCOUT TRAIL
INDIAN COVE RD
ADOBE RD
UTAH TRAIL
AMBOY ROAD
PINTO BASIN RD
KAISER RD
CALIFORNIA RIDING AND HIKING TRAIL
Black Rock Canyon
Eureka Peak 5516ft 1682m
West Entrance Station
Keys View 5185ft 1531m
Lost Horse Mine
Ryan
Geology Tour Road
Sheep Pass
Jumbo Rocks
Belle
White Tank
Arch Rock
Queen Mountain 5677ft 1731m
North Entrance Station
Fortynine Palms Oasis
Oasis Visitor Center
1960ft 598m
4562ft 1391m
4747ft 1447m
Cholla Cactus Garden
JOSHUA TREE NATIONAL PARK
Pinto Mountain 3983ft 1214m
3820ft 1165m
Old Dale Mining District
Cottonwood Visitor Center 3079ft 939m
Cottonwood Spring
Lost Palms Oasis
Bajada Nature Trail
Eagle Mountain 5350ft 1631m
Aqua Peak 4416ft 1346m
2957ft 902m
62
247
10
111
86
195
177

Joshua Tree's third ecosystem is located in the westernmost part of the park above 4,000 feet, where the Little San Bernardino Mountains provide habitat for a community of California juniper and piñon pine. Five fan palm oases also dot the park, providing especially good opportunities for spotting kit fox, bighorn sheep, coyote, and badger. And wildflowers begin blooming in Feb., splashing the landscape with Monet colors.

If you chance upon a desert tortoise, do not pick it up. Doing so is illegal, as tortoises often void their water supply out of fear—a virtual death sentence for the creature. If you find a sick or injured turtle, call the **Joshua Tree Tortoise Rescue** (760-369-1235).

Self-guided nature trails lace the park, and a spider web of dirt roads is accessible to dirt bikes and four-wheel-drive vehicles. Joshua Tree National Park, which receives more than one million visitors per year, is also one of the most popular rock-climbing areas in the world. Indian Cove is the most popular center for rock-climbing. **Joshua Tree Climbing School** (760-366-4745; www.joshuatreerockclimbing.com; HCR Box 3034, Joshua Tree, CA 92252) offers instruction.

Take plenty of water—a minimum of 1 gallon per person is recommended.

The park has four entrances. The main entrance and headquarters is the West Entrance, 5 miles south of the junction of Hwy. 62 and Park Boulevard at Joshua Tree Village. Here, **Joshua Tree Visitor Center** (760-366-1855) shows videos and has a bookstore. While here, be sure to visit Keys West (a 20-minute drive from Park Boulevard down Keys View Road), perched on the crest of the Little San Bernardino mountains. It provides panoramic views of the Coachella Valley, the Santa Rosa and San Jacinto Mountains, as well as the Salton Sea and—quite plain to view below—the San Andreas fault.

The North Entrance is in Twentynine Palms, 3 miles south of the junction of Hwy. 62 and Utah Trail. Here the **Oasis Visitor Center** (760-367-3300) has park exhibits, plus maps and information, and a trail leads from here to the Oasis of Mara. The palm oasis was long a home to the Chemehuevi Indians.

Joshua Tree National Park. Palm Springs Desert Resorts Conventions & Visitors Authority

Jazz in the Pines. J. Hocker & Associates

The **Black Rock Nature Center** (760-367-3001), in the northwest corner of the park, is 4 miles south of Yucca Valley. Hiking trails that lead through the hills behind the Black Rock Canyon campground include the easy 1.3-mile Hi-View Nature Trail. And the trailhead for a 35-mile section of the California Riding and Hiking Trail begins here.

The southern entrance is on Cottonwood Springs Road, off I-10, about 25 miles east of Indio; the **Cottonwood Visitor Center** is 7 miles from the southern entrance to the park. The oasis here is a superb birding site. It was once a center for gold mining, and evidence of prospecting can still be seen. Hikes here include the easy Cottonwood Wash walk; it leads to a dry falls that gushes in wet years, drawing bighorn sheep in the early hours. The 3-mile loop trail to Mastodon Peak offers spectacular views. And the Lost Palms Oasis trail (8 miles round-trip) for those looking for a longer hike—and the largest stand of fan palms in the park—is a sure winner.

Elite Land Discovery Tours (760-318-1200; www.elitelandtours.com; 555 S. Sunrise Way, Suite 200, Palm Springs, CA 92264) and **Adventure Hummer Tours** (760-285-0876 or 1-877-656-2453; www.joshuatreetour.com; 42-335 Washington St., #F121, Palm Desert CA 92211) offer tours by Humvee.

The **Desert Institute of Joshua Tree National Park** (760-367-5535; www.joshua tree.org) is a tremendous resource.

To the West

The Palms to Pines Scenic Byway (California Highway 74) leads west from Palm Desert and climbs steeply into the Santa Rosa Mountains. It's a stupendously scenic drive that leads to **Idyllwild**, an alpine village set among tall pines, sweet-smelling cedars, and legendary rock formations. Idyllwild is a gateway for hikes to Mount San Jacinto (10,804 feet), and miles of other Forest Service trails are popular with hikers and mountain bikers. Tahquitz and Suicide Rocks are legendary among rock climbers. And there are dozens of campsites and cozy bed-and-breakfasts.

Idyllwild is also famous as an arts center, with more than a dozen galleries open to view (1-866-439-5278; www.artinidyllwild.com). Try to visit on Sun. morning for the May–Sept. Art Café, when local artists offer informal educational demonstrations.

The annual Art Walk and Wine Tasting, in Oct., is a magnet for visitors—besides the art and wine, there are horse-drawn carriage rides and entertainment. And the two-day **Jazz in the Pines festival** (951-500-3200; www.idyllwildjazz.com) in late Aug. is a fun-filled event featuring some of the world's top jazz musicians.

Contact the **Idyllwild Chamber of Commerce** (951-659-3259 or 1-888-659-3259; www.idyllwildchamber.com) for information.

Lamb dish at the Viceroy Palm Springs. Viceroy Palm Springs

5

Restaurants and Food Purveyors

Bon Appétit!

From cozy cafés to ritzy recherché restaurants, Palm Springs and neighboring cities offer a complete spectrum of dining experiences. In fact, mile for mile it must rank as one of the world's great culinary havens. Steakhouses are the valley's forte, but you'll also find world-class Chinese, French, Italian, Japanese, Mexican, and you-name-it fare. Wherever you dine, you're pretty much guaranteed fresh produce straight from the Imperial Valley, a few miles away. And dates, the local signature crop of choice, turn up on menus in the most inspired ways, paired with game dishes, meats, and seafood, as well as delicious desserts such as brie cheesecake with date compote, or Deglet date pudding with toffee sauce. The annual California Date Chef Competition, in April, lures chefs from throughout North America.

Take a deep breath before dining, as the desert region doesn't come cheap. In fact, it can be plain expensive! It's hard to find a good breakfast for under $10, and sushi is charged at twice the price you'll pay in Los Angeles or San Francisco. But that's what you pay for quality, as the desert resorts are simply overflowing like a soufflé with fine-dining outlets run by chefs who care for the quality of the cuisine they serve.

Every year sees a stellar crop of new restaurants opening, while inevitably one or two gems fall by the wayside. A fistful of chef-owned restaurants have opened up in recent years, many of them exuding star quality with their superlative decor and nouvelle cuisines capped off with incomparable settings, including the beautiful San Jacinto Mountains.

Look for *Palm Springs Life: Dine Out*, a glossy full-color magazine available in the arrivals lounge at Palm Springs International Airport.

Restaurants in Palm Springs

BILLY REED'S

760-325-1946
1800 N. Palm Canyon Dr., Palm Springs, CA 92262
Price: Moderate
Credit Cards: AE, D, MC, V

Cuisine: American
Serving: L, D
Reservations: Not required
Handicapped Access: Yes

Billy Reed's is a Palm Springs institution named for the vaudeville performer who "tiptoed through the tulips" in *Gold Diggers of Broadway*. Its yesteryear "grandma's parlor" ambience (floral wallpaper, brass pots, red velvet chairs, lamps straight out of a western movie) isn't for everyone. The vast comfort-food menu ranges from burgers and sandwiches to meat loaf, pot roast, and chicken pot pie, all at one set price. Most dishes are rather bland, and few stand out. Billy Reed's, however, is known for its scrumptious desserts, including "top hat" pastries and fresh fruit pies. Evening midweek specials are a bargain and include prime ribs on Mon. and filet mignon on Thurs. The beer selection, alas, is limited to U.S. staples, hinting at the down-income clientele for whom this restaurant remains a firm favorite, thanks primarily to its great prices.

BLUE COYOTE GRILL

760-327-1196
www.bluecoyote-grill.com
455 N. Palm Canyon Dr., Palm Springs, CA 92262
Price: Moderate
Credit Cards: AE, MC, V
Cuisine: Tex-Mex
Serving: L, D
Reservations: Recommended
Handicapped Access: Yes
Special Features: Outdoor dining

A favorite of youngish local patrons who enjoy outdoor dining under umbrellas and misters or heat lamps (depending on season), this local institution is as much bar as restaurant—the "Wild Coyote" margaritas are the drink of choice. The mood is inviting, though the kitchen earns no prizes for gourmet cuisine, which cross-breeds Mexican staples with American favorites. Expect to see chipotle baby back ribs, Cajun salmon, even southwestern meat loaf complementing burritos, enchiladas, etc. Service is friendly but less than polished. Treat this as a great place for comfort food and a lively ambience.

CITRON

760-320-4117
www.viceroypalmsprings.com
415 S. Belardo Rd., Palm Springs, CA 92264
Price: Expensive
Credit Cards: AE, CB, D, DC, MC, V
Cuisine: California modern
Serving: B, L, D
Reservations: Recommended
Handicapped Access: Yes
Special Features: Hip bar

Decor is "Hollywood Regency." The color scheme is clinically white with lemon yellows. The mood is romantic. The ambience is classy and chic. Mirrored panels reflect the white marble-tiled floor. In all, a superb package that puts a satisfied smile on the face of (predominantly young) sophisticates. Romantics can choose banquette seating or a candle-lit table under the stars; misters and heaters are provided according to season.

Trained in French-American techniques at the prestigious California Culinary Academy in San Francisco, executive chef Stephen Belie delivers consistently superb California modern cuisine. A typical dinner might include seared foie gras with apple-scented sweet potatoes, apple frites, and sorrel; blue-eyes panna cotta with Tuscan melon soup and tea brittle; and pumpkin-seed crusted Chilean sea bass with lobster-asparagus ravioli and uni butter. Divine desserts include a chocolate mousse as soft as a cloud.

The chic, minimalist bar is a cool spot for pre- or postprandial cocktails, notably the house *mojitos* infused with your fresh

Risotto at Citron. Viceroy Palm Springs

fruit juice of choice. Citron gets packed for Sun. brunch—a relative bargain at $35, including free-poured champagne or mimosas.

DALE'S LOST HIGHWAY

760-327-2005
(http://daleslosthighway.com)
125 E. Tahquitz Canyon Way, Palm Springs, CA 92262
Price: Moderate
Credit Cards: AE, D, MC, V
Cuisine: Eclectic American fare
Serving: B, L, D
Reservations: Not required
Handicapped Access: Yes
Special Features: Movies screened alfresco

Comfort food pure and simple. Come for the cozy outdoor bistro ambience lent a unique twist by the movies screened onto the wall. The place is totally laid-back, including the service. The menu features burgers and Tex-Mex favorites, plus such roadhouse specials as green bean casserole ($9.95) and 8-ounce flat-iron steak ($16.95) marinated with chili, garlic, olive oil, and Worcestershire sauce, served with mesquite-grilled vegetables and rice. French-born chef Denis Sibee puts a Gallic touch to classic American cuisine such as Alabama fried chicken, Louisiana crab cakes, Tacoma ahi, Memphis coleslaw, and Fort Worth barbecue. Every evening features a special: Mon. for $3 well drinks and $1.50 drafts; Wed. for all-you-can-drink beer ($10); Thurs. for bottomless margarita ($12). And the "Morning-After Gospel Brunch" is a winner with its bottomless champagne and mimosas. The indoor section has a piano bar.

EL MIRASOL

760-323-0721
140 E. Palm Canyon Dr., Palm Springs, CA 92262
Price: Inexpensive to Moderate
Credit Cards: AE, MC, V
Cuisine: Mexican
Serving: L, D
Reservations: Not required
Handicapped Access: Yes
Special Features: Patio dining

A no-frills, down-home Mexican eatery that draws mostly from a dedicated local crowd, El Mirasol delivers filling and satisfying fare. The menu includes the to-be-expected *chile rellenos*, burritos, etc., as well as such specialties as *machaca* with cheese, and a superb *pollo en mole poblano* with ground pumpkin seeds and chiles and a deliciously sweet, mildly spiced chocolate *mole*. Another winner here is the jumbo shrimp *doña diablo* sautéed in hot garlic oil with chipotle (smoked jalapeño) and chili sauce with lime juice. And meat lovers will find satisfaction in the steak *picado* sautéed with bell peppers, onions, and tomatoes. The homemade corn tortillas are first rate, as is the ceviche (weekends only). Service is on the ball, but the huge margaritas are often weak. Choose from somewhat ascetic interior dining, or a roadside patio with cowhide seats, heaters, and a great view of the San Jacinto massif.

EUROPA RESTAURANT

760-327-2314 or 1-800-245-2314
www.villaroyale.com
1620 S. Indian Trail, Palm Springs, CA 92262
Price: Moderate to Expensive
Credit Cards: AE, D, MC, V
Cuisine: Mediterranean
Serving: D
Reservations: Required
Handicapped Access: Yes

Kindling an incomparably warm Tuscan ambience, this exquisite European-style restaurant in the Villa Royale Inn appropriately serves some of the finest Mediterranean cuisine in town. Whether you opt to dine fireside or under the desert stars, the experience is romantic to a T, much thanks to sponge-washed walls, glowing wall sconces, antique mahogany furniture, and Wedgwood china and real silverware. Twirled pilasters frame the draped windows. The Provençal-inspired food here doesn't always live up to the lovely ambience, but the dishes do usually satisfy, including a fabulous melt-in-your-mouth pâté. The menu includes other to-be-expected offerings such as rack of lamb (served with lavender rather than mint); crab cakes (on a spicy red-pepper coulis); and a tender duck confit with a Grand Marnier bigarade. The wine list impresses.

THE FALLS PRIME STEAK HOUSE

760-416-8664
www.thefallsrestaurants.com
155 S. Palm Canyon Dr., Palm Springs, CA 92262
Price: Expensive
Credit Cards: AE, D, MC, V
Cuisine: Meats and seafood
Serving: L, D
Reservations: Recommended
Handicapped Access: Yes
Special Features: Martini bar

Named for the signature waterfall behind the lively bar, this chic contemporary American steakhouse has a favored position directly above Palm Springs' downtown plaza. Aggressive promotion has succeeded in packing the joint on weekend evenings, although most patrons seem to be out-of-towners come to see what the fuss is all about. The menu is heavily laden with well-recognized favorites (crab cakes, Caesar salad, Colorado rack of lamb, and porterhouse steak), although with some intriguing twists. Portions are generous, but quality varies, and many patrons depart disappointed. The balcony tables (with heaters and misters) offer a fun perspective over the street action below. The restaurant hosts special events, such as special wine-tasting evenings, and the bar—where service is friendly and fast—is renowned for its "smoking" martinis.

FISHERMAN'S MARKET & GRILL

760-327-1766
www.gotofishermans.com
235 S. Indian Canyon Dr., Palm Springs, CA 92262
Price: Inexpensive to Moderate
Credit Cards: AE, MC, V
Cuisine: Seafood
Serving: L, D
Reservations: Not required
Handicapped Access: Yes
Special Features: Patio dining with misters and heaters

Serving fresh catches from King Neptune's larder, this seafood restaurant draws a fiercely loyal clientele who know a good thing when they see it. The menu plays a calliope on the fish scales, from clam chowder, crab cakes, and a charbroiled

Fisherman's Market & Grill.

swordfish taco plate to ahi sashimi and good ol' English-style fish-and-chips (a half order is quite sufficient). A self-service bar offers all the condiments you could hope for, along with to-be-expected malt vinegar. Wines and beers are served, but on hot days you'll want to try the all-you-can-drink colas and lemonade. Everything here is fresh as fresh can be, thanks to owner Louis Pagano's appreciation of how to ensure the best flavors: He grew up crewing on his father's fishing boat.

Choose from the matter-of-fact, air-conditioned interior or the shaded patio with misters and heaters. Oh, and the prices are fair.

To the rear, Shanghai Red's (4–midnight) hideaway bar offers live R&B music from 8 to 11 PM on Fri. and Sat., and on Sun. afternoons. It also serves pastas, and even steaks, but really you should try the oyster shooters, fish tacos, or calamari *fritti*, all served until midnight.

JOHANNES

760-778-0017
www.johannesrestaurants.com
196 S. Indian Canyon Dr., Palm Springs, CA 92262
Closed: Mon.
Price: Expensive
Credit Cards: AE, MC, V
Cuisine: California fusion
Serving: D
Reservations: Recommended (required Dec.–Apr.)
Handicapped Access: Yes
Special Features: Specialty cocktails

Sophisticated without being pretentious, this is one of the classiest acts in town. Better yet, it offers consistently superb nouvelle fusion cuisine at fair prices. Just one block from the Strip in the heart of downtown, the restaurant looks quite tiny from outside, and with its black curtains drawn across much of the frontage, many locals aren't even aware of its existence. Their loss; our gain. Being on the corner of Arenas, the city's gay boulevard, Johannes is popular with a gay clientele. The restaurant makes efficient use of its limited space without feeling crowded, although romantics preferring to dine alfresco on the tiny road-front patio are squeezed in a tad too close for comfort. The chic decor is appeal-

Johannes.

ingly retro-modern, with the accent on rich orange tones. Industrial piping and tiny halogens run along the lofty, white-painted ceiling, while the floor of glazed concrete adds to the sense of hip.

Austrian-born Chef Johannes Bacher helped pioneer fusion cuisine in the valley. His imaginatively cosmopolitan menu uses unfailingly fresh ingredients and features specialty Austrian dishes while drawing on Herr Bacher's many years worldly experience on cruise ships and with Hilton Hotels. For starters we like the curried lump crab, and you can't go wrong with the fabulous wild mushroom soup or the roasted beets with Wisconsin Blue Billy goat cheese, hazelnut oil, organic pistachios, pink grapefruit, and yellow bell pepper puree. A great entrée pick is the house special Wiener schnitzel served with a separate bowl of deliciously creamed cucumbers. Another wise option is the grilled Irish organic salmon with olive oil–braised tomatoes, fresh crisp veggies, and apple balsamic reduction. Feeling adventurous? Go for the prosciutto-wrapped U10 Maine scallops with yellow mustard seed, lemon parsley *gremolata*, and sautéed spinach. Leave room for the divine desserts.

Dishes come from the kitchen with Swiss-watch precision and attention to detail and are delivered by wait staff sharply dressed in all black and attentive to a fault. The robust wine list circles the globe, with an excellent selection by the glass. And the specialty "contemporary" martinis—coconutini, anyone?—are served in large glasses, adding to the overall sense of value for money.

KAISER GRILLE

760-323-1003
www.kaisergrille.com
205 S. Palm Canyon Dr., Palm Springs, CA 92262
Price: Expensive
Credit Cards: AE, MC, V
Cuisine: Steaks
Serving: L, D
Reservations: Recommended
Handicapped Access: Yes
Special Features: Patio dining with misters and heaters

One of five restaurants in the local Kaiser group, this one occupies a premium position on a main intersection in the heart of downtown. The misted and heated elevated patio offers a great vantage for perusing the street action, although the traffic noise can detract. It specializes in rotisserie and charbroiled meats prepared in a wood-burning oven, but it also serves fresh seafood, pastas, and more, all of it prepared in an uncomplicated fashion by European-trained chefs. We like the hazelnut salmon, but carnivores also rave about the black Angus steak. Alas, the vast menu (Chinese and Mexican dishes are also featured) is perhaps *too* broad to ensure consistent quality, and even the Caesar salad is lackluster. Penny-pinchers should dine early: The Kaiser Grill offers an early bird special (you need to ask for the menu).

KALURA TRATTORIA ITALIANA

760-323-4748
www.kaluratrattoria.com
124 S. Palm Canyon Dr., Palm Springs, CA 92262
Price: Moderate
Credit Cards: AE, D, DC, MC, V
Cuisine: Italian
Serving: D
Reservations: Not required
Handicapped Access: Yes
Special Features: Patio dining with misters and heaters

If people-watching and a sense of being in the thick of the Palm Springs action are foremost, then this is the place to be. The patio is a wonderful spot from which to watch the comings and goings along Palm Canyon Drive, although the crowds flocking in and out of the adjacent Plaza Theater make for a nightly commotion—but that's half the fun of being here. A warmly rustic interior space permits you to escape the throng. The menu features classic Italian favorites. Spaghetti bolognese. Thin-crust pizza. Grilled calamari. A satisfying risotto with white truffle oil and porcini mushrooms. And my favorite—grilled salmon. Chefs Enzo Amodea and Ignazio Battaglia do a fine job preparing consistently satisfying, rather than gourmet, fare supported by hearty pourings of wine.

LAS CASUELAS TERRAZA

760-325-2794
www.lascasuelas.com
222 S. Palm Canyon Dr., Palm Springs, CA 92262
Price: Moderate
Credit Cards: AE, D, MC, V
Cuisine: Mexican
Serving: L, D
Reservations: Recommended
Handicapped Access: Yes
Special Features: Patio dining with live music and dancing

Las Casuelas has endured for many years as a Palm Springs institution—a festive, always-packed place where patrons come to idle on the terrace with an oversize margarita. The rambling, redbrick hacienda-style establishment has several indoor rooms with wrought-iron lanterns and to-be-expected Mexican-themed decor: piñatas, bull's head, and wide-brimmed sombreros. A narrow, bougainvillea-shrouded dining terrace opens onto Palm Canyon Drive and is cooled by misters in summer and warmed by heat lamps in winter. The adjacent outdoor patio with *palapa* bar hosts live music and dancing. The nightly entertainment, however, tends toward rock rather than mariachi and is definitely a mood spoiler for diners hoping to savor the south-of-the-border ambience.

The burritos, enchiladas, and other staples will fill you up, but don't expect gourmet fare—there are far better Mexican options in town. This is comfort food, and the salads are consistently ho-hum. However, a few dishes stand out, including the lunch specials such as chimichangas and spicy pork fajitas, and the *pollo asado* (marinated chicken) and *pescado greco* (fish in garlic and wine) dinner entrées. For dessert, try the strawberry margarita cheesecake or the Mexican chocolate, Kahlúa, and fudge brownie. The margaritas will put you on your back. You can choose from three dozen tequilas!

LG'S PRIME STEAKHOUSE

760-416-1779
www.lgsprimesteakhouse.com
255 S. Palm Canyon Dr., Palm Springs, CA 92262
Price: Very Expensive
Credit Cards: AE, D, MC, V
Cuisine: Steaks
Serving: L, D
Reservations: Recommended
Handicapped Access: Yes
Special Features: Patio dining with misters and heaters

OK. We agree. It's probably the best steakhouse in the desert, and, yes, the steaks are cooked to perfection, and the service is top-drawer. But is that the reason the prices here verge on robbery? Still, this restaurant's popularity with monied patrons is well founded (LG's owner, Leon Greenberg, even gets his own plaque on the town's Walk of Stars). The classy ambience combines a contemporary refit to a traditional Spanish frame, evoking a 21st-century take on the Santa Fe style. Executive chef Maura Tello waves a magic wand in the kitchen, and the 100 percent prime meat dishes verge on faultless, as do the genuine full-flavored Caesar salad and the Australian lobster tail. All the steaks here are corn-fed Kansas USDA prime beef aged to perfection. The Rolls-Royce of LG's dishes is the 20-ounce dry-aged porterhouse—the meat alone will set you back over $50. With everything here à la carte, it's hard to conceive of a couple surviving a three-course dinner with wine for less than $100 apiece. The large wine selection offers bottles ranging from $30 to $3,000.

LOOK

760-778-3520
www.lookpalmsprings.com
139 E. Andreas Rd., Palm Springs, CA 92262
Price: Moderate
Credit Cards: AE, MC, V
Cuisine: International
Serving: L, D
Reservations: Not required
Handicapped Access: No
Special Features: Video lounge

Barely a country in the world has been left off the menu at this quaint restaurant, popular with a gay clientele. Crab and artichoke dip . . . sashimi ahi . . . quesadillas . . . French onion soup . . . Cobb salad . . . artichoke and feta pizza . . . and entrées ranging from peppercorn steak to seafood crepes. Its strong suit is the long list of wraps, sandwiches, and panini (the roasted chicken panini is our favorite). Sun. brunch includes the classics. And late-night appetizers are served until 1 AM. The wine selection is rather meager, and the sole house red is frequently delivered overly chilled. All is forgiven, however, due to the 10-ounce martinis (!) for $5 on "Absolute Tini Tuesdays." Most patrons opt for patio dining beneath misters and heaters, depending on season.

MATCHBOX

760-778-6000
www.matchboxpalmsprings.com
155 S. Palm Canyon Dr., Palm Springs, CA 92262
Price: Moderate
Credit Cards: AE, D, MC, V
Cuisine: Pizzas
Serving: L, D
Reservations: Not required
Handicapped Access: Yes
Special Features: Giant-screen TV in the bar

Even in the thick of a chill winter night, dining out on the mezzanine open-air terrace at this classy pizzeria is a treat, thanks to flaming gas burners at the poured cement bar overlooking Mercado Plaza. And in summer, of course, there are misters, while if you simply must dine indoors there are spacious air-conditioned rooms to suit. And couples can opt for a private balcony overhanging Palm Canyon Drive.

You're here for the wood-fired, thin-crust pizzas prepared by chef Kevin Sharkey. Try the spicy Fire & Smoke pizza heaped with fire-roasted red peppers and smoked Gouda cheese with whole basil, which I like to wash

Matchbox pizzeria. Palm Springs Desert Resorts Conventions & Visitors Authority

down with a cool pint of Fat Dog ale or robust winter ale. Carnivores might go for the Matchbox Meat pizza with sweet Italian sausage, crispy bacon, pepperoni, mozzarella cheese, and tomato sauce, perfectly complemented by a boutique brew, such as a full-bodied dark, knock-you-on-your-back Delirium Tremens. (Matchbox also has a robust wine list). Chef Sharkey also delivers bistro-style California-fusion entrées such as crab cakes baked in crisp phyllo pastry served over wilted spinach with roasted pepper rémoulade and fresh chives; and a delicious pepper-crusted yellowfin tuna on sesame sticky rice with stir-fried veggies. Note the eclectic matchboxes from around the world embedded in the handmade tables. Serves until 1 AM Thurs.–Sat., and large pizzas are half-price on Mon. evenings.

mister parker's. The Parker Palm Springs

MISTER PARKER'S

760-321-4629
www.theparkerpalmsprings.com.
4200 E. Palm Canyon Dr., Palm Springs, CA 92264
Closed: Mon. and Tues.
Price: Expensive
Credit Cards: AE, D, DC, MC, V
Cuisine: French-inspired fusion
Serving: D
Reservations: Recommended
Handicapped Access: Yes
Special Features: Live piano music

Self-described as a "deconstructed formal hangout for fops, flaneurs and assorted cronies," this dark-lit fine-dining establishment in the oh-so very-hip Parker Palm Springs exudes clubby atmosphere. In complete contrast to Norma's, its sibling restaurant, this one is done in Elizabethan English vogue with a hip twist. Think beamed-and-mirrored ceiling; dark wood-paneled walls festooned with a miscellany of old prints and contemporary art (mostly Pop Art and kinky surreal pieces); and traditional Elizabethan-style studded chairs with chic modern fabric. A pianist tickles the ivories by the oversize fireplace.

The menu is avant-garde. You might start with escargots with hazelnut garlic butter, or smoked monkfish with caviar crème fraîche and roasted red pepper gratiné. And the sautéed duck foie gras is sublime. To follow? The butternut squash ravioli in vin blanc sauce is divine. The sautéed duck confit with thinly sliced truffled potatoes is a dish made in heaven. And the Australian rack of lamb served with risotto and merlot-and-meat-stock reduction is intensely delicious (although perhaps *too* intense for some tastes). Some traditional favorites pop up on the dessert menu, including profiteroles and good ol' banana split. Puerto Rican chef Rosio Varela's masterly creations don't come cheap, alas—expect to pay upward of $200 for dinner for two.

PEABODY'S CAFÉ BAR & COFFEE

760-322-1877
www.peabodyspalmsprings.com

134 S. Palm Canyon Dr., Palm Springs, CA 92262
Price: Moderate
Credit Cards: AE, D, MC, V
Cuisine: American
Serving: B, L, D
Reservations: Not required
Handicapped Access: Yes
Special Features: Karaoke

A great spot to breakfast on the sidewalk patio, this slightly Bohemian homegrown café with sidewalk patio is strategically located a stone's throw from the downtown plaza. Unpretentious and fun, it draws as eclectic a crowd as you'll find in the desert. Service is on the ball, even when packed, which is often—especially on Thurs.–Sat. night when patrons put on their "wannabe rock star" hats for karaoke. Overseen by owner Debbie Alexander, the kitchen delivers great omelets, burgers, and salads, and the tempting café drinks range from chai cappuccino to root beer floats. Not fine dining, for sure, but you're here for the setting and laid-back mood perfectly suited to Sun. brunch.

PEAKS
760-325-4537
www.pstramway.com
Top of the Tram, 1 Tramway Rd., Palm Springs, CA 92262
Closed: Sep.
Price: Moderate to Expensive
Credit Cards: AE, D, MC, V
Cuisine: California fusion
Serving: L, D
Reservations: Recommended
Handicapped Access: No
Special Features: Stunning views

Truly one of a kind, Peaks perches at 8,516 feet at the top of the aerial tram, three-quarters way up Mount San Jacinto. Talk about staggering views! Anyone who remembers this as the uninspired Mountain Station Restaurant will be delightfully surprised by the upgrading under new owners and new chef David Le Pow. The restaurant is an integral part of the E. Stuart Williams–designed Mountain Station, with soaring beamed ceilings, heaps of natural stone, and massive panoramic windows for enjoying the views down over the desert floor spread out below. Le Pow's California fusion menu shows originality and superb execution. Why not start with scallops and butternut squash risotto with corn emulsion and balsamic syrup, or a carpaccio of fresh tuna, thin-sliced raw filet, and roasted yellow beets? To follow, we recommend the rack of lamb with fresh peach compote and truffled mashed potatoes.

PEPPER'S
760-322-1259
396 N. Palm Canyon Dr., Palm Springs, CA 92262
Price: Moderate
Credit Cards: AE, MC, V
Cuisine: Thai
Serving: L, D
Reservations: Not required
Handicapped Access: No

Peaks restaurant, at the top of the aerial tram. Palm Springs Aerial Tramway

A no-brainer for a good meal for less than ten bucks, this bargain-priced restaurant offers Thai cuisine with a Polynesian and French twist. It serves gourmet vegetarian dishes along with staples such as pad thai and a delicious lemony chicken noodle soup. Seafood dishes are a specialty, including filet of sole pan-fried with ginger and garlic sauce. All dishes are made to order according to your tolerance of spices and herbs. And the sweet sticky rice dessert with fresh mango is delicious. Service is efficient and comes with a smile.

RICK'S

760-416-0090
1973 N. Palm Canyon Dr., Palm Springs, CA 92262
Price: Inexpensive to Moderate
Credit Cards: AE, D, MC, V
Cuisine: American
Serving: B, L
Reservations: Not required
Handicapped Access: Yes
Special Features: Counter dining

Considered by unpretentious locals as *the* place for weekday brunch, or for breakfast and lunch any other day of the week, this is one of Palm Springs' most popular eateries. Ostensibly a Cuban restaurant (the menu features *ropa vieja*, a Cuban national dish, and other Cuban treats), this good ol' American diner has a vast menu spanning omelets, corned-beef hash and eggs, pancakes and fruit, hot meat loaf sandwich, and a superb ahi tuna salad. Oh, and all-you-can-drink coffee or deliciously cooling lemonade. It draws a large gay clientele. Decor is light and airy, and the staff is superfriendly. It has banquette booths, or you might prefer to sit at the counter . . . but please don't take *my* seat!

SHERMAN'S

760-325-1199
www.shermansdeli.com
401 Tahquitz Canyon Rd., Palm Springs, CA 92262
Price: Inexpensive to Moderate
Credit Cards: AE, D, MC, V
Cuisine: American
Serving: B, L, D
Reservations: Not required
Handicapped Access: Yes
Special Features: Bakery

Billing itself as a "Kosher-style Family Restaurant," this flashback to the 1960s is a local institution, especially for Sun. brunch, when the place hums with the lively buzz of a packed house, despite its plain decor. The modernist deli-bakery offers a huge menu that spans the spectrum of American favorites, with all the staples included. BLT special. Turkey burger. Caesar salad. Grilled Reuben. My breakfast favorite is the fresh-sliced nova lox and soft cream cheese platter, and if you're not fearful of your weight, knock yourself out with the corned beef, pastrami, knockwurst, and eggs. There are a few weak links, however: The omelets and scrambles, for example, are consistently delivered floating in butter. For light lunches, try the intriguing soups, such as mushroom barley, and cold beet borscht; while night calls for heartier fare such as calf's liver and onions, rotisserie chicken, and choice New York steak.

The separate bakery, by the entrance, offers a tantalizing selection of fresh-baked breads, bagels, and scrumptious desserts such as tiramisu, strawberry shortcake, and homemade apple strudel. The airy interior is air-conditioned, and misters (in summer) and heaters (in winter) make sitting out on the long, shaded patio facing Tahquitz Canyon Road a pleasure.

SPENCER'S AT THE MOUNTAIN

760-327-3446
www.spencersrestaurant.com
701 W. Baristo Rd., Palm Springs, CA 92262

Price: Expensive
Credit Cards: AE, D, MC, V
Cuisine: Pacific fusion
Serving: B, L, D
Reservations: Recommended
Handicapped Access: Yes
Special Features: Live piano music; outdoor fire pit

Fusing a Japanese-inspired minimalism into a remodeled modernist shell, this sophisticated restaurant at the Palm Springs Tennis Club caters to a monied and discerning clientele. Its magnificent, calming aesthetic combines extensive use of natural teaks and natural stone with *en vogue* taupe and black color schemes. Design guru Dodd Michell designed the Zen-modernist interior. James Beard Award–winning chef Urs Balmer takes care of the equally scintillating California-Pacific cuisine. Balmer's menu is slanted toward surf and turf combos, although risottos, pastas, and poultry dishes are represented, alongside such flavorful seafood dishes as Chilean sea bass with baby artichokes and crispy leeks in a light saffron sauce. The wine cellar offers a choice of 200 labels. The prix fixe three-course dinner is a bargain at $39. Anyone with back problems should avoid the bench seats, which are too far from the tables for comfort—I finished my meal with an aching back. The small bar has room for half a dozen people, and a patio overlooks the courts of the Palm Springs Tennis Club. Pianist Patrick Karst tickles the ivories Sun.–Thurs.

THE STEAKHOUSE AT SPA RESORT CASINO

1-888-999-1995
www.sparesortcasino.com
401 E. Amado Rd., Palm Springs, CA 92262
Price: Very Expensive
Credit Cards: AE, D, DC, MC, V
Cuisine: Steaks
Serving: B, L, D
Reservations: Recommended
Handicapped Access: Yes
Special Features: No one under 21 allowed

Dark wood accents enhance the stylish decor of this upscale casino restaurant, where Sandy Josephson, director of food and beverage, oversees a menu heavy with steak dishes using completely organic beef aged to perfection. Take your pick. Prime rib. A 16-ounce New York sirloin. Even a 24-ounce porterhouse. All served with a choice of Yukon garlic mashed potatoes, sautéed asparagus, curried cauliflower, and other savory sides. The entrée menu also highlights succulent triple-cut lamb joint, and even fresh oysters, Australian lobster tail, and wild salmon. Start out, however, with the caramelized onion Gorgonzola potato tart, or the jumbo shrimp cocktail. So far so good. And portions are ample. However, gourmands complain that many of the dishes arrive carbonized, while the sauces (béarnaise, bordelaine, Dijonnaise, au poivre, and wild mushroom) don't always live up to expectations—a big letdown at prices that aim to recoup the winnings of gamblers who hit the jackpot.

TONY'S PASTA MIA

760-327-1773
E-mail: tpastamia@aol.com
360 N. Palm Canyon Dr., Palm Springs, CA 92262
Price: Moderate
Credit Cards: AE, MC, V
Cuisine: Italian
Serving: L, D
Reservations: Not required
Handicapped Access: Yes
Special Features: Live music nightly

The hearty New Jersey Italian fare here rarely rises above average, but so what? You come for a savory taste of the past, courtesy of faux marble columns and pink stucco walls hung with giant black-and-white prints of Marilyn Monroe, Frank Sinatra, and scenes from *The Godfather*, plus an oversize photo of owner Tony himself with the cast of *The Sopranos*. The crowd fits right in: the males with slicked-back blue-rinse hair and their spouses with soufflé hairdos. This joint is Rat Pack redux. Twice weekly, Mike Costley croons Sinatra favorites (his voice is a dead ringer for Ol' Blue Eyes), and local residents and regulars Jack Jones and Trini Lopez are sometimes called up from the audience to perform as the patrons shuffle around the dance floor in nostalgic ecstasy. The martinis are made the way martinis *should* be made. If you don't like to sit at floral fabric banquettes, you can sit at the white baby-grand piano with its blue-lit glass bar, or outside on the tight patio facing onto Palm Canyon Drive. As to the food . . . the stuffed artichoke appetizer earns two thumbs up; the pizzas are gourmet; and you can't go wrong with the eggplant parmigiana.

The bar at the Tropicale.

TROPICALE

760-866-1952
www.thetropicale.com
Email: info@thetropicale.com
30 E. Amado Rd., Palm Springs, CA 92262
Price: Expensive
Credit Cards: AE, D, MC, V
Cuisine: Caribbean-Pacific fusion
Serving: D
Reservations: Recommended
Handicapped Access: Yes
Special Features: Outside bar

This sensational newcomer took Palm Springs by storm when it opened in late 2007. I love its aesthetic and ambience—part Polynesian, part Cuban, and wholly Palm Springs—and so do the city's gay fashionistas. The 1950s modernist structure was given an exciting 21st-century face-lift that pays homage to the tiki-and-'tini era while being as hip as hip can be. Key elements? Pink-and-gray checkered tile floor. Walls paneled in stone, cream textured fabric, and mahogany. Pea-soup-green leather banquette seating. And a ceiling wrapped in a pink glow from all-around recessed lighting. The open Coral Sea Lounge bar with classy charcoal leather high chairs is overhung by a sloping mural (the focal point of the restaurant) of an idyllic Polynesian scene. The bar is echoed in the rear dining patio—a fantastic place to sip and chat beneath heat lamps or misters. Cuban music adds to the lively ambience lent by the gay party crowd.

The Caribbean-Pacific fusion menu doesn't quite live up to the setting, alas, but is more than passable. For appetizers consider Asian crisp-fried baby squid ($8.95) or Hawaiian *poko* with macadamia nuts and scallions and chili sesame ($10.95). And for main course, you can't go wrong with either Kahlúa-BBQ pork porterhouse chop with mashed plantains, sautéed peppers and Maui onions ($19.95), or the superb sesame-grilled Hawaiian ono filet with lime butter and coconut rice, stir-fried veggies, and gingered tomatoes ($22.95). The Chilean sea bass disappoints and should also be avoided, as this species is endangered. The cocktails here excel. Who can resist a Silk Stocking? Or a desert pear margarita, or spicy mango *mojito*?

Oh, and the fireplace in the small but relaxing waiting area is actually a flat-screen TV screening a dancing faux-fire!

LE VALLAURIS

760-325-5059
www.levallauris.com
385 W. Tahquitz Canyon Way, Palm Springs, CA 92262
Price: Expensive
Credit Cards: AE, D, DC, MC, V
Cuisine: French
Serving: L, D
Reservations: Recommended
Handicapped Access: Yes
Special Features: Valet parking

The patio at Le Vallauris. Le Vallauris

One of the pioneers of fine French cuisine in the valley, this landmark restaurant (named for a Provençal hill town) is beloved of discriminating diners and is run with loving care by owner Paul Bruggemans. Located in the historic Roberson House, built by George B. Roberson (son of Palm Springs pioneer Nellie Coffman), Le Vallauris successfully re-creates a luxurious provincial French ambience with its cozy fireplace, Flemish tapestries, and Louis XV furniture. Most diners prefer the leafy outdoor patio, with venerable ficus trees wrapped in twinkling fair-lights.

Chef Jean Paul Lair oversees a French menu of superlative dishes that include such appetizers as sautéed foie gras, escargots in garlic and parsley butter, and crab cakes with whole-grain mustard sauce on mixed greens in balsamic vinegar. The seared Lake Superior whitefish with mustard sauce served on a bed of shiitake mushrooms and spinach is a divine entrée, but you won't regret the Maine lobster ravioli with basil cream, or the roast rack of lamb with thyme and garlic. Alas, the huge wine list will give you sticker shock; the $30 corkage fee is no less outrageous.

WANG'S IN THE DESERT

760-325-9264
www.wangsinthedesert.com
424 S. Indian Canyon Dr., Palm Springs, CA 92262
Price: Moderate
Credit Cards: AE, D, DC, MC, V
Cuisine: Asian
Serving: D
Reservations: Recommended on weekends
Handicapped Access: Yes
Special Features: Koi pond with bridge in the main dining room.

Not sure if you're in the mood for Chinese or Thai? Then head to Wang's, serving pan-Asian fare blending spices and styles from throughout the Orient. Opened in 2004 by restaurateurs Joel Herzer and Alford Harrison, this bistro-style restaurant has lived up to the buzz surrounding its launch. Decor is sublimely elegant and contemporary and features original art on the walls. Service is on the ball. And the cuisine is as good as you'll find in the valley. I recommend either the Cantonese seafood (with mussels, scallops, shrimp, and fresh fish) sautéed in a mildly spicy Chinese black bean sauce; or the house specialty spicy pork chops with jalapeño and salt and pepper seasonings with Hoisin sauce. The dessert menu is limited to cheesecake, chocolate ganache torte, crème brûlée, and mango sorbet. No dish tops $20. Gays hang at the bar on weekends.

Restaurants in the Palm Springs Vicinity

DESERT HOT SPRINGS

SOUTH OF THE BORDER

760-251-4000
11-719 Palm Dr., Desert Hot Springs, CA 92240
Price: Inexpensive to Moderate
Credit Cards: AE, D, MC, V
Cuisine: Mexican
Serving: L, D
Reservations: Not required
Handicapped Access: Yes
Special Features: Full bar

Seeking authentic Mexican fare? Then you can't do better than this local favorite, which has been around for two decades and packs patrons in on weekends, when a half-hour wait is typical and well worth it. Decor is suitably themed, the pueblo-style building having cheery green and red decor, Mexican colonial hand-painted benches, and walls festooned with paintings and photos of bullfights reflecting Ecuadorian owner Fernando Guerrero's status as a former matador. The menu features the to-be-expected favorites, plus vegetarian dishes such as spinach enchilada, and sweet corn and cheese-filled tamales served with rice and beans. A full bar serves favorite Mexican and U.S.-brand beers.

CATHEDRAL CITY

TOOTIE'S TEXAS BARBECUE

760-202-6963
www.tootiesbbq.com
68-703 Perez Rd., Cathedral City, CA 92234
Closed: Sun. and Mon.
Price: Moderate
Credit Cards: AE, D, MC, V
Cuisine: Barbecue
Serving: L, D
Reservations: Not required
Handicapped Access: Yes
Special Features: Ice-chilled beers

Sure, it's no-frills, but you don't expect fancy surrounds when it comes to ribs. Seating comprises simple wooden benches and bare-wood chairs. But the food is something else if you're a barbecue lover. Specializing in East Texas barbecue (yes, barbecue from the Lone Star state really does vary by east, north, west, and south), Texan co-owners Steven Vinson and Willard Sterling stay true to their roots, despite their long pedigrees of professional culinary training and expertise at some of the best restaurants in California. That means slow cooking, indirect smoking, and genuine Texas sauces on their beef brisket, barbecued pork, pork ribs, plus chicken, turkey, and sausage dishes, all served with a choice of baked beans, cowboy beans, creamed corn, dirty rice, macaroni, potato salad, or—recommended—Texas caviar (black-eyed peas). This duo treats the fine American tradition of barbecue with culinary dignity. No wonder Tootie's earned *Sunset* magazine's laurels as one of 10 restaurants in their Barbecue Hall of Fame.

Rancho Mirage

BABE'S BAR-B-QUE GRILL & BREWHOUSE

760-346-8738
71-800 Hwy. 111, A-176, Rancho Mirage, CA 92270
Price: Moderate to Expensive
Credit Cards: AE, MC, V
Cuisine: American
Serving: L, D
Reservations: Not required
Handicapped Access: Yes
Special Features: Outside dining with fire pit

We were at a loss when the fabulous turkey meat loaf disappeared from the menu, but there are more than enough delicious comfort dishes to compensate at this cozy faux-western restaurant and brewpub, in The River, in Rancho Mirage. With its stone fireplace, lofty ceiling, and mezzanine level, the air-conditioned interior offers a pleasant ambience, with the copper brewing paraphernalia open to view. You can also eat at the curving bar with sports channels on TV. I prefer the shaded patio with its roaring fire pit, especially on cool winter nights when overhead heaters also kick in (misters cool things down in summer).

The menu offers tremendous comfort food. Not gourmet, but tasty and filling for sure (you'll need a doggy bag). You can't go wrong with appetizers such as Bar-B-Que wings ($6.95) and Cajun popcorn crawfish ($7.95), such intriguing salads as apricot Stilton jubilee salad ($9.95), such lunch entrées as BBQ chicken thighs ($9.95), and dinner entrées such as Babe's Big Beef Platter ($20.95) and the more-than-satisfying hickory-grilled salmon ($24.95). The hickory-smoked ribs here disappoint, however, for their sweetness and lack of spicy tang. Entrées come with two sides: Choose from beans, coleslaw, fries, or sweet potato fries. And the flavorful corn bread here is divine. For suds, select from the pub's half-a-dozen fresh (and excellent) microbrews, from pale ale to a dark and hearty Nipster Winter Ale.

BEEFSTEAK FINE FOOD & WINE

760-328-9814
www.beefsteakfinefood.com
69-930 Hwy. 111, Rancho Mirage, CA 92270
Closed: Tues.
Price: Expensive to Very Expensive
Credit Cards: AE, D, MC, V
Cuisine: California fusion
Serving: L, D
Reservations: Recommended
Handicapped Access: Yes
Special Features: Live music on Sun.

Opened in late 2006 in The Atrium by Wisconsin-born owner/chef Eric Wadlund (formerly of Azur, at La Quinta Resort & Club), this chic, contemporary upscale restaurant echoes many of the signature dishes for which Wadlund made a mark at Azur. Rusted iron features, tweed carpeting, and chocolate brown sofas combine to form an inviting ambience (Wadlund calls it "museum modern"), but the star of the show here is Wadlund's winning regional American cuisine. Local ingredients find their way into some irresistible dishes, such as the seared scallops on a bed of tapioca drizzled with local date reduction. Sea scallop ceviche or lobster chunks poached in anise broth make for fabulous appetizers, perhaps followed by Lake Superior whitefish on a black truffle–infused wild mushroom risotto and butternut squash puree. Carnivores might opt for the espresso-and-cocoa-rubbed filet mignon with sweet cherry sauce, shiitake mushrooms, *cipollini* onions, and potato puree. The wine menu is biased toward Napa and Sonoma labels.

BING CROSBY'S RESTAURANT & PIANO LOUNGE

760-674-5764

www.bingcrosbysrestaurant.com
71-743 Hwy. 111, Rancho Mirage, CA 92270
Price: Expensive
Credit Cards: AE, MC, V
Cuisine: Californian
Serving: D
Reservations: Recommended
Handicapped Access: Yes
Special Features: Live music

A hip retro newcomer in 2007, this upscale supper club harks back to the heyday of Crosby and Hope, rekindling a glamorous era. An immediate warm rush of nostalgia hits patrons, not least thanks to walls festooned with photos from Bing Crosby's life. While this plush place successfully captures the glories of the 1930s, the chocolate-green-and-cream decor is chicly contemporary: Think dark brown carpeting, travertine fireplace, high-back booths, chocolate high-back leather chairs, and pendulous contemporary cubist lamps.

Executive chef Scott Kendig is in charge of the innovative California country club cuisine, featuring fish, shellfish, and meat and game dishes that include such treats as Dungeness crab cakes, baked fresh goat cheese, veal scallopine with lemon caper sauce, porterhouse, and cornmeal-crusted sea bass with herb gnocchi. A few yesteryear favorites have made a comeback, such as oysters Rockefeller and Waldorf salad. Room for dessert? The banana bread pudding is a no-brainer. The wine labels are prejudiced toward California's finest. The bar serves classic cocktails, and live entertainers keep patrons in high spirits until closing. Crosby-style golf togs are not required, but a dress code *is* enforced.

BLUEMBER
760-568-2727
www.dinebluember.com
Rancho Las Palmas Resort & Spa, 41-000 Bob Hope Dr., Rancho Mirage, CA 92270
Price: Expensive
Credit Cards: AE, D, MC, V
Cuisine: Nouvelle Californian
Serving: L, D
Reservations: Recommended
Handicapped Access: Yes
Special Features: Outdoor dining

A classy entrée launched in November 2007, this suavely contemporary eatery exudes an irresistibly inviting ambience. The recipe is well known. Plenty of refined, deep-red hardwoods. Gold and taupe color schemes. Subdued lighting. A sophisticated lounge-bar. And the option for patio dining beside a blazing fire. Live music adds vitality Wed.–Sat. evening.

Hawaiian-born executive chef Leanne Kamekona and chef de cuisine Todd Claytor combine skills to craft local ingredients into mouth-watering California fusion cuisine inspired by Asian, Middle Eastern, and Mediterranean flavors. For lunch, try the turkey and brie panini with dried peaches, with a baby green salad featuring California figs and goat cheese. Two of my favorite dinner entrées are the grilled organic chicken with artichokes, grilled scallions, and preserved lemon risotto, punctuated by an unexpected olive broth ($22); and the pan-roasted California sea bass with braised Napa cabbage, cardamom, and crisp fried leeks ($29), best accompanied with truffle mashed potatoes.

THE CHEESECAKE FACTORY
760-404-1400
www.thecheesecakefactory.com
71-800 Hwy. 111, Rancho Mirage, CA 92270
Price: Moderate
Credit Cards: AE, D, MC, V
Cuisine: Eclectic
Serving: L, D
Reservations: Not required
Handicapped Access: Yes
Special Features: Three-dozen cheesecakes

Huge portions of comfort food in a kitschy chain-brand concoction in The River.

That's the motif. Families (or at least the kids) love the Las Vegas-meets-Babylon movie-set ambience, including animal hide upholstery and a Brobdingnagian menu literally too big for the kids to handle. The eclectic offerings range from pastas and pizzas to steaks and seafoods. In fact, the menu runs to more than 200 entrées! As you'd expect, cheesecake (more than 30 varieties) is a signature. Doggy bags are sure to be required, but meals here don't come cheap, considering that this is far from gourmet.

THE DANCING GREEK

760-202-0092
www.dancinggreek.com
69-600 Hwy. 111, Rancho Mirage, CA 92270
Price: Moderate
Credit Cards: AE, D, MC, V
Cuisine: Greek
Serving: L, D
Reservations: Recommended
Handicapped Access: Yes
Special Features: Belly dancing

One of the most fun dining spots in the valley, this Hellenic-themed option is as much a nightclub as restaurant, and tables surround a U-shaped stage. Decor is suitably iconic blue-and-white throughout; Greek travel posters adorn the walls; and Corinthian columns (yes, I know, they should be Doric) add to the Aegean mood. The to-be-expected favorites are featured, including familiar Greek appetizers such as dolmathes (grape leaves stuffed with rice and beef), spanakopita (spinach and feta pies of phyllo dough), *saganaki* (cognac-flamed fried cheese), and hummus. However, anyone who has delighted in genuine Greek fare will be disappointed, not least with the moussaka (eggplant, beef, and spicy béchamel sauce). Still, let's face it, you're here mostly for the rip-roaring fun of nightly live entertainment. Sometimes the entire restaurant is coaxed to join in raucous "Zorba the Greek"–style dancing, yelling *"Opa! Opa!"* as if Anthony Quinn himself were rousing everyone to jump to their feet in applause. On Fri. and Sat., Nika swirls her way among the tables, sensuously writhing her bare belly. A Family Feast—a two-course meal with 15 plates—is guaranteed to satisfy groups.

FLEMING'S PRIME STEAKHOUSE & WINE BAR

760-776-6685
www.flemingssteakhouse.com
71-800 Hwy. 111, Rancho Mirage, CA 92270
Price: Moderate to Expensive
Credit Cards: AE, D, MC, V
Cuisine: Steaks
Serving: L, D
Reservations: Not required
Handicapped Access: Yes
Special Features: Separate bar

Classic steakhouse fare artfully prepared is

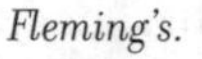

Fleming's.

the name of the game at Fleming's, where elegant contemporary decor featuring rich hardwoods and subdued lighting adds to the memorable experience. Fleming's is all about meats—specifically, steaks. The inventive menu offers such succulent temptations as prosciutto-wrapped filet mignon with green pepper sauce, and New York strip au poivre. While carnivores are in heaven, fish lovers aren't forgotten. Australian lobster tails, New Zealand king salmon, and Alaskan king crab legs all feature, as do mouth-watering seared scallops in lobster cream sauce with a puff pastry of sautéed fresh vegetables. Wines are extremely important here, and more than 100 wines are served by the glass! The wine staff are well trained (Fleming's has its own in-house 25-hour intensive sommelier course), and sommelier Wayne Hanseth is usually on hand to assist with decisions.

Fleming's hosts popular "Nights of Discovery," with five wines paired with cheeses and hors d'oeuvres, and six wine-tasting dinners each year (reserve early to avoid disappointment). And the annual "All Red 90+ Wine Dinner" in mid-Nov. draws gourmands from far and wide for a sensory treat, with red wines rated 90-plus by *Wine Spectator*. The 2007 dinner paired a 2005 Juliénas Château des Capitans 2005 with grilled vegetable bruschetta and garlic and chervil shrimp on lotus root hors d'oeuvres; Clancy's Barossa 2004 with lobster ravioli with lavender cream sauce; a Whitehall Lane Napa Valley merlot 2004 with petit filet mignon on thyme-scented potatoes and truffle butter; and a 2004 Tuscan Il Borro with New York strip with morel and shiitake ragout with rosemary veal demi-glace; and—phew!—a 2000 Cockburn vintage port with triple-layer chocolate mousse with raspberry sauce. Need I say more?

HALEIWA JOE'S
760-324-5613
www.haleiwajoes.com
69-934 Hwy. 111, Rancho Mirage, CA 92270
Price: Moderate
Credit Cards: AE, D, DC, MC, V
Cuisine: Pacific Rim
Serving: L, D
Reservations: Not required
Handicapped Access: Yes
Special Features: Live music every Fri.

Bringing a spirit of aloha to the desert, this remarkable architectural landmark built into the rocky hillside looks like a set for *Voyage to the Bottom of the Sea*. Part of the eponymous award-winning restaurant chain, it adopts their trademark Polynesian-theme decor (including lava-rock fireplace plus surfboards suspended from the ceiling), right down to the pretty female waitresses in orchid-patterned miniskirts and spaghetti-strapped shifts. The menu tips a hat to other Pacific Rim influences: China, Japan, Korea, and Thailand. There's even a Sumatran grilled beef salad. Locally purchased seafood? Forget it! Fresh fish is flown in daily from the Honolulu Seafood Auction. Still, most dishes are merely satisfying rather than scintillating. One of my faves is the fresh grilled mahimahi on Asian slaw in a soy hot-pepper vinaigrette, but you can't go wrong with the grilled Atlantic salmon, crunchy coconut shrimp, or premium ahi served with island beurre blanc on udon noodles. Meat-lovers aren't forgotten. Filet mignon. Slow-roasted prime rib with garlic mashed potatoes. And an always-satisfying certified Angus prime steak with ginger papaya salad and wasabi cream sauce. After dining, why not settle into the lounge bar (where surfing videos air on TV) for a specialty cocktail, such as the Sandy Snorkel or Clark's Special Mai Tai? Better yet, call in at the Aloha Hour (4:30–6:30 PM daily) for half-price pupus.

Kobe Japanese Steak House.

KOBE JAPANESE STEAK HOUSE

760-324-1717
www.koberanchomirage.com
69-838 Hwy. 111, Rancho Mirage, CA 92270
Price: Moderate
Credit Cards: AE, MC, V
Cuisine: Japanese
Serving: L, D
Reservations: Not required
Handicapped Access: Yes
Special Features: Hibachi, sushi bar

Transporting patrons metaphorically to the Orient with its authentic Japanese decor, this replica of a Japanese country inn features an authentic wooden *mon* gateway and little red bridge spanning a koi pond. The various dining rooms are adorned with genuine Japanese artwork and artifacts—a perfect mood-setter. For three decades, this local landmark has delivered real Japanese teppanyaki, prepared at your table by a knife-wielding chef whose slicing-and-dicing training extends to culinary acrobatics. Fresh, quality beef, chicken, and seafoods go into the menu, which ranges from the to-be-expected sushi (best enjoyed at the sushi bar) to New York steaks and filet mignon. The teppan combination dinners are a great bargain. This being the martini-loving desert, we suggest you try the saketini, made of gin and sake.

LAS CASUELAS NUEVAS

760-328-8844
www.lascasuelasquinta.com
70-050 Hwy. 111, Rancho Mirage, CA 92270
Price: Inexpensive to Moderate
Credit Cards: AE, D, DC, MC, V
Cuisine: Tex-Mex
Serving: L, D
Reservations: Not required
Handicapped Access: Yes
Special Features: Live music

A recent addition to the Delgado family's Las Casuelas chain (now comprising five restaurants in the desert), this one melds a colonial Mexican hacienda ambience with contemporary California tastes. Seeking family favorites? They're here, including crab enchiladas, chicken *en mole,* spicy pork fajitas, and fajitas *camarones* (succulent grilled shrimps with bell peppers and onions). The menu also has some creative surprises, such as *camarones con fideos*—Mexican shrimp sautéed in a tomato basil pesto sauce served on a cilantro angel hair pasta. Fireplaces provide the perfect spot to nestle down to savor the margaritas, and a garden patio is perfect for Sun. champagne brunch, or for dining under the stars as strolling mariachis serenade. Most dishes are bland. Come for the fun and touristy ambience.

LORD FLETCHER'S

760-328-1161
70-385 Hwy. 111, Rancho Mirage, CA 92270
Closed: Mon.
Price: Expensive
Credit Cards: AE, D, MC, V
Cuisine: English-American
Serving: L, D

Reservations: Recommended
Handicapped Access: Yes
Special Features: Waitresses dressed as Old English wenches

Decked out in Merry Olde England fashion, Lord Fletcher's specializes in lamb roasts and prime rib, but you'll also find northern halibut and Lake Superior whitefish dishes. Opened by Ron Fletcher in the 1960s, this family-run restaurant is now managed by son Michael Fletcher, who hasn't changed a thing. The decor is classic old England, right down to the sooty redbrick fireplace with copper kettles and Toby mugs (all the bric-a-brac, including the grandfather clock, are genuine English antique imports). An original A. Egerton Cooper portrait of Sir Winston Churchill even hangs in the entryway, and the Shakespearean Room is hung with 18th-century etchings depicting scenes from the Bard's plays.

This blast-from-the-past was for three decades a favorite restaurant of Frank Sinatra (he even celebrated his 70th birthday here in 1985). You can ask to sit at Sinatra's corner table and even order his favorite dish—pot roast and potato pancakes—washed down by a glass of Château Lafite, his favorite wine. Other choice selections include fresh Atlantic king salmon, roast prime rib beef with Yorkshire pudding and red cabbage, and—my favorite—roast rack of lamb prepared "Canterbury-style" with steamed veggies and potatoes. Consider this comfort food, rather than gourmet. And for dessert? Why, sir, nothing but the English rice pudding with raspberries, or cinnamon and whipped cream.

MIDORI
760-202-8186
www.midorijapanese.com
36-101 Bob Hope Dr., Rancho Mirage, CA 92270
Price: Expensive
Credit Cards: AE, D, DC, MC, V
Cuisine: Japanese
Serving: L, D
Reservations: Recommended
Handicapped Access: Yes
Special Features: Sushi and martini bar

In the Pavilion shopping center, this contemporary-themed Japanese restaurant owned by Ako Hiroto has been a Highway 111 institution for two decades. Painted a cool apple green reflecting its name—*midori* means "a green place"—it offers polished teak tables and charcoal accents, and there's a patio with wrought-iron tables under umbrellas. Comfy teak bar stools are drawn up to the split-level granite-topped sushi and martini bar, where favorite drinks include the Geisha (martini with pineapple juice) and the Samurai (with orange juice and peach schnapps). Midori offers some of the freshest sushi in the desert. The restaurant's signature Midori roll features fried calamari and green beans topped with fresh avocado and freshwater eel; and the Rainbow roll has seven fish species. Of course, tempuras, steamed dishes, and noodle specialties are also served, as are lunch specials.

P. F. CHANG'S
760-776-49112
www.pfchangs.com.
78-800 Hwy. 111, Rancho Mirage, CA 92270
Price: Moderate to Expensive
Credit Cards: AE, D, MC, V
Cuisine: Chinese
Serving: L, D
Reservations: Recommended
Handicapped Access: Yes

In The River, this popular Asian bistro—part of the famous cookie-cutter national chain—is known for its elegant contemporary styling, reasonable prices, and consistently outstanding fare. First, the decor. A huge horse guards the entrance, Xian-style Chinese warriors feature inside, and a vast

Oriental mural adorns the semicircular bar. Nonetheless, the overall theme is distinctly Moderne. The menu features Cantonese, Mandarin, and Szechuan options—the latter can be particularly spicy (so heed the "warnings")—including signature dishes such as Cantonese scallops, Chang's chicken in soothing lettuce wraps, and orange peel beef. For a delicious dessert? I can't resist the banana spring rolls and (but not together!) the Great Wall of Chocolate. The menu also boasts an extensive wine list. And service is on the ball.

RISTORANTE VITTORIO

760-776-7535
73-375 El Paseo, Rancho Mirage, CA 92270
Closed: Mon.
Price: Inexpensive to Moderate
Credit Cards: AE, D, MC, V
Cuisine: Italian
Serving: B, L, D
Reservations: Recommended
Handicapped Access: Yes
Special Features: Patio sidewalk dining

For genuine Italian fare, chef Vittorio Virgili's spacious and airy Ristorante Vittorio ranks right up there with La Spiga. It offers a graceful blue-themed contemporary motif, with walls of glass. Raviolis, classic pasta dishes, and bargain-priced wood-fired pizzas highlight the menu. Dishes are graced by light sauces, such as the scaloppine alla piccata (veal sautéed in white wine, capers, and lemons, with angel hair pasta) and the ravioli with butternut squash, ricotta cheese, parmesan cheese, and tomato sauce. Leave room for a homemade cannoli dessert, or gelato ice cream imported from Italy. The wine list includes a large selection of Italian vintages, and generous portions when ordered by the glass. Service is top-notch, with Vittorio's family in attendance.

ROY'S

760-340-9044
www.roysrestaurant.com
71-959 Hwy. 111, Rancho Mirage, CA 92270
Price: Expensive
Credit Cards: AE, D, DC, MC, V
Cuisine: Hawaiian fusion
Serving: D
Reservations: Recommended; required in winter
Handicapped Access: Yes
Special Features: Full bar

Roy is Roy Yamaguchi, Tokyo-born maestro of Hawaiian fusion cuisine and owner of the world-wide, eponymous chain that counts almost three dozen outlets. Nonetheless, this is no cookie-cutter chain, and the elegance of the quasi-Polynesian ambience is equally matched by the superior quality of the cuisine, which focuses on seafoods. Appetizers include such standards as lobster pot stickers, and seared tiger shrimp in wasabi cocktail sauce. Recommended entrées? Either the saffron-infused scallops with gnocchi, mushrooms, and basil balsamic; or the roasted macadamia mahimahi with garlic mashed potatoes. Roy's is renowned for its signature melting chocolate soufflé, made of semisweet chocolate, creamy unsalted butter, sugar, and fresh eggs. Opt for a scoop of rich vanilla bean ice cream on top. The high prices here reflect the restaurant's premier location smack center in an ocean of wealth.

WALLY'S DESERT TURTLE

760-568-9321
www.wallys-desert-turtle.com
71-775 Hwy. 111, Rancho Mirage, CA 92270
Price: Expensive
Credit Cards: D, DC, MC, V
Cuisine: Continental
Serving: D
Reservations: Recommended
Handicapped Access: Yes
Special Features: Live piano

If you ever wondered what dining at Versailles—the palace outside Paris—might be like, then Wally's comes close with its beveled mirror ceilings and glittering chandeliers. Actually there are several dining rooms, each with its own mood and decor, but lavish elegance is the watchword throughout. Even before eyeing the menu, you sense why this place has won more awards than any other restaurant in the valley, including both the coveted AAA Four Diamond Award and Mobil Travel Four Star Award. Still, it could be a tad OTT (over the top) for some tastes. Wally is founder Wally Botello, who opened the doors on this twinkling gem in 1978. Now under the purview of his son Michael, the restaurant delivers consistently exquisite French-inspired cuisine, courtesy of executive chef Pascal Lallemand.

Such choices! Perhaps *escargots chablisienne* to begin, or vine-ripened tomato and sweet onion, followed by seared bluefin tuna and caviar with Tahi chili dressing and wasabi; or the pan-broiled Lake Superior whitefish, with mussels, leek fondue, and lemon beurre blanc apricot soufflé. One of my favorites is the roasted half-duck with Medjool date sauce.

Semiprivate dining is available in the intimate Sable Room, with its fanciful medievalist artwork; and the Foyer, adorned with hand-painted murals of idyllic Moroccan scenes. If you're seeking a more contemporary mood, the 90-seat Mirage Room was recently remodeled to that purpose. Live piano entertainment adds to the engaging mood. Wally's Desert Turtle is renowned for its Christmas Day dinner and New Year's Eve Gala Celebration.

Although not obligatory by any means, dusting off your most sophisticated duds wouldn't hurt. Oh, and you'll need a *very* fat wallet to dine here.

Restaurants in the Southern Desert Resorts

Palm Desert

CASTELLI'S

760-773-3365
www.castellis.cc
73-098 Hwy. 111, Palm Desert, CA 92260
Closed: July and Aug.
Price: Expensive
Credit Cards: AE, D, MC, V
Cuisine: Italian
Serving: D
Reservations: Recommended
Handicapped Access: Yes
Special Features: Full bar

You could be forgiven for thinking that you've stepped through the doors of Castelli's into a real-life piece of romantic Tuscany, thanks not least to trompe l'oeil murals and walls of natural stone. Aiding the romance are soft lighting, fresh-cut flowers, and lacy curtains. Brothers Jon and Michael Castelli are usually on hand to guide you personally to your table. The restaurant is known for its award-winning pastas, seafoods, and veal and lamb dishes. The fettuccine Alfredo house special is guaranteed to please, but you also can't go wrong with a 10-ounce charbroiled filet mignon topped with marsala wine sauce and portobello mushrooms. Those in a seafood mood might opt for a three-course lobster ravioli appetizer, linguini with clams, followed by the spumoni dessert, perhaps washed down with a hearty classic Sassicaia—one of several dozen Italian labels on the exclusive wine list. Chef Brian Altman prepares seasonal specials. A "Celebrity Room" posts photos of the rich and famous who've dined here. Joe Jaggi entertains nightly. Reservations are wise, especially on weekends when a fun-loving local crowd descends.

CORK TREE

760-779-0123
Desert Springs Marketplace, 74-950 Country Club Dr., Palm Desert, CA 92260
www.thecorktree.com
Closed: Mon.
Price: Expensive
Credit Cards: AE, D, MC, V
Cuisine: California nouvelle
Serving: L, D
Reservations: Recommended
Handicapped Access: Yes
Special Features: Bar

A rich, warm ambience awaits at this sophisticated restaurant, opened in 2007, handily just a five-minute stroll from the Desert Springs JW Marriott Resort. Dark hardwoods, maroon upholstery, a black-painted industrial-style ceiling with open beams, plus banquette seating and a wine cellar open to view combine to evoke a classy, clubby atmosphere. Nine-feet-tall lamp standards act as a room divide, as does a wall of glass separating the dining area from the chic convex bar. Chef Hervé Glin's nouvelle menu offers a feast for the senses. I recommend the roasted organic beets appetizer with goat cheese and shaved fennel drizzled with a shallot sauce; or the foie gras and wild mushroom crème brûlée with poached pear in Muscado and warm brioche. For the main course, you can't go wrong with seared scallops, rock shrimp artichoke orzotto, with whole grain mustard emulsion; or the pork shank with roasted garlic mashed potatoes, asparagus, and baby carrots in a merlot reduction.

CUISTOT

760-340-1000
72-595 El Paseo, Palm Desert, CA 92260
www.cuistotrestaurant.com
Closed: Sun. L and Mon.
Price: Expensive
Credit Cards: AE, D, MC, V
Cuisine: French
Serving: L, D
Reservations: Recommended
Handicapped Access: Yes
Special Features: Huge wine list; fire pit

One of the desert region's finest of fine-dining establishments, this invitingly warm restaurant is the brainchild of owner and chef Bernard Dervieux, who apprenticed with the legendary Paul Bocuse. In fact, Dervieux designed the restaurant himself in grand architectural style to replicate a French stone farmhouse of his native Lyon, right down to the trellised ivy clambering over the tower porte cochere entrance with arched parapet. The main dining room, done up in charcoal and copper and gold decor, boasts a beamed cathedral ceiling, massive stone fireplace, and an equally massive open island kitchen. Outside, a spacious patio features its own vast fire-place, plus a water cascade with boulders.

The cuisine is delicate and delectable, subtle and sensuous. Monsieur Dervieux has devised an irresistible menu drawing on traditional French dishes, such as rabbit (here in Dijon mustard sauce with a sorrel-frisée chiffonade and rainbow rice), while other dishes infuse local ingredients with creative French-inspired touches, such as artichoke-filled escargots and Dover sole with hazelnut lemon sauce; or sea bass in light pastry shell, with chervil sauce and baby tomatoes. And who can resist a fresh strawberry cake with strawberry sorbet and crème anglaise? In summer, Dervieux features a Tour de France prix fixe menu with cuisines from a different region of France each weekday evening. The wine list runs to 23 pages!

THE ELEPHANT BAR RESTAURANT

760-340-0456
www.elephantbar.com
73-833 Hwy. 111, Palm Desert, CA 92260
Price: Moderate
Credit Cards: AE, D, MC, V
Cuisine: International

Serving: L, D
Reservations: Not required
Handicapped Access: Yes
Special Features: African-themed decor

Appealing to families—the kids love the elephant heads and zebra stripes—this California chain restaurant has a casual tropical atmosphere that transports you metaphorically to Africa. Fresh produce and fish, and USDA choice beef go into the international dishes. The menu spans the globe. Wok-seared pan-Asian chicken and lettuce wrap. Fire-grilled smokehouse chicken sandwich. Blackened catfish with langostinos and shrimp jambalaya. Get the picture? Not gourmet fare, to be sure, but filling and satisfying.

FUSION ONE II

760-341-5903
73-850 Hwy. 111, Palm Desert, CA 92260
www.fusionone11.com
Closed: Sun. and Mon.
Price: Expensive
Credit Cards: AE, MC, V
Cuisine: Tapas
Serving: L, D
Reservations: Recommended
Handicapped Access: Yes
Special Features: Martini bar

Sibling chefs Rob and Steve opened their newest tapas-only bistro in 2007, and despite decades of restaurant experience on Chesapeake Bay they opted for an unusually sterile industrial motif with lots of gun-metal grays and post-modernist decor. The menu features more than 20 "fusion" tapas, including pan-fried lump cakes, roast duckling, and such entrée-style winners as bourbon-marinated pork loin with mashed potatoes, and a delicious pepper-seared North Atlantic salmon between puff pastry, layered with artichoke, flash-fried spinach, and wild rice. Some dishes are sublime, but a few of these tapas you might think mis-matched and overly expensive. The bar menu lists 20 specialty martinis, of which half a dozen are real martinis. I find the gray decor a bit cold.

KEEDY'S FOUNTAIN & GRILL

760-346-6492
73-633 Hwy. 111, Palm Desert, CA 92260
Price: Inexpensive
Credit Cards: AE, D, MC, V
Cuisine: American
Serving: B, L, D
Reservations: Not required
Handicapped Access: Yes
Special Features: 1950s Americana

A Palm Desert staple for half a century, this classic American diner echoes back to 1957, when it first opened its doors. Over the years it has served celebrities such as Marlon Brando, Lawrence Welk, and Lucille Ball, and Arnold Palmer likes to breakfast here when in town. "Keedy's Fix" has remained virtually unchanged, down to the well-worn Formica counter and the retro soda fountain. For breakfast try the famous pancakes or huevos rancheros. You'll also find all the American classics, such as BLTs, triple-decker burgers, and tuna melts, alongside house specials such as country fried steak.

LA SPIGA

760-340-9318
72-557 El Paseo, Palm Desert, CA 92260
Closed: Mon.; Aug.
Price: Expensive
Credit Cards: AE, D, MC, V
Cuisine: Italian
Serving: B, L, D
Reservations: Recommended
Handicapped Access: Yes
Special Features: Full bar

A genuine and superb *ristorante italiano* run by owner-chef Vince Cultraro, who worked his way up from washing dishes in Sicily (Cultraro now has five restaurants under his belt, including his original La Spiga, in

Edmonton, Canada). Anyone familiar with the small, hard-to-get-into "old" restaurant will be delighted by the new, very Tuscan-looking location—which opened for Christmas 2007—beside the Palm Desert Visitors Center just off Hwy. 111. While larger, it retains a warm, friendly, family feel and offers a wall-enclosed herb and flower garden plus an outdoor wood-burning pizza oven.

Cultraro is a true master of his craft, and his culinary genius is evident in even the simplest dishes, such as the cold potato-zucchini soup infused with fennel and a dash of olive oil and topped with a dollop of cream. Even vegetarians might swoon over the filet mignon with green peppercorn demi-glace wine reduction, dwarf peach in truffle oil, and deep-fried croquette of risotto plus blanched baby veggies. The venison with mushroom is no less divine. And traditionalists will find pasta al dente and calamari. However, La Spiga is a true fine-dining experience, so don't come expecting spaghetti and pizza. *Buon appetito!*

LE BASIL

760-773-1112
72-695 Hwy. 111, Palm Desert, CA 92260
Price: Moderate
Credit Cards: AE, MC, V
Cuisine: Asian
Serving: L, D
Reservations: Not required
Handicapped Access: Yes

A newcomer to the desert in 2007, this pleasant, contemporary-themed Thai restaurant (run by friendly owners Orn and Thom Chotiyanonta, from Thailand) has quickly proved popular. Service can be excruciatingly slow on busy weekends. The menu features contemporary Southeast Asia cuisine with light sauces. It offers five dozen choices, from appetizers to noodle dishes. Go for the Bo-Lulac—cubed flank steak stir-fried with garlic, onions, and butter and served over a green salad. Also recommended: the delicious Panang curry with tofu, red coconut peanut-flavored curry, bell pepper, and Thai lime leaves.

PACIFICA

760-674-8666
www.pacificainthedesert.com
The Gardens, 73-505 El Paseo, Palm Desert, CA 92260
Closed: L, Oct.–May
Price: Expensive
Credit Cards: AE, D, MC, V
Cuisine: Seafood
Serving: B, L, D
Reservations: Recommended
Handicapped Access: No
Special Features: Vodka bar

Upstairs at The Gardens, this edgy, suavely contemporary restaurant is one of the valley's most popular venues. A high point is the chic bar, renowned for its 125 premium vodkas from 20 countries. Bar foods are served at half price on the last Wed. of every month. You can dine out on the terrace overlooking El Paseo, or indoors beneath a ceiling of canvas "sails." Pacifica specializes in fresh seafood dishes. Former chef Brett Pollock had a tendency to marry seemingly incongruous elements into his fusion dishes, and not always successfully. His recent successor, California Culinary Academy in San Francisco graduate Kelly Walling (formerly of Casa Madrona and Pacifica del Mar) has elevated standards. How does Maine black mussels steamed with white wine, garlic, chili flakes, and whole grain mustard sound? The cuisine here is more than satisfying, and fairly priced.

RATTLESNAKE

760-775-2880
www.rattlesnakeclub.com
75-200 Classic Club Blvd., Palm Desert, CA 92211
Price: Expensive
Closed: Mon.

Credit Cards: AE, D, DC, MC, V
Cuisine: Californian
Serving: L, D
Reservations: Recommended
Handicapped Access: Yes
Special Features: Martini bar

Considered by many gourmands as the top restaurant in the valley, Rattlesnake guarantees nothing less than a superb experience, well worth the journey (in late 2007, it relocated from the Spotlight Casino to the ritzy new Classic Club, handily situated just off I-10). The "Award of Excellence" from *Wine Spectator* magazine is the tip of the iceberg of awards heaped upon this luxurious steakhouse, with its rich black and red decor, sumptuous leather banquette booths, glowing hardwoods, and black-and-white prints of desert scenes.

Chef Jimmy Schmidt, three-time James Beard Award winner, loaded his low-carb, four-course-based menu with a tornado of creative new dishes. How does jumbo Gulf shrimp martini appetizer sound? I thought so. Or a cold terrine of foie gras roasted in sauterne and chilled, served with honey crisps in sweet pomegranate and blackberry marmalade . . . or roast sweet pepper "rooster" sauce with horseradish cream? Schmidt loves his meat dishes (my favorite is the pistachio-crusted rack of mountain meadows baby lamp with Syrah-berry *jus*), but seafood dishes are well represented, too. Take the moist and flaky Atlantic swordfish topped with caramelized pineapple on a vanilla bean skewer, garnished with Asian basil oil and spicy ginger froth. The treats are as much a feast for the eyes as the palate: The braised prime Angus beef short ribs, for example, is served on a bagged platter, and you'll want your camera to record the fun and artsy display of the popcorn parfait made with buttered popcorn ice cream served with caramel, chocolate fudge, and cream soda.

So don some nice duds and make the drive. You won't regret it.

RISTORANTE MAMMA GINA
760-568-9898
www.mammagina.com
73-705 El Paseo, Palm Desert, CA 92260
Closed: L Sun.
Price: Moderate to Expensive
Credit Cards: AE, D, MC, V
Cuisine: Italian
Serving: L, D
Reservations: Recommended
Handicapped Access: Yes
Special Features: Extensive wine list

Focusing on Florentine and Tuscan dishes, this northern Italian restaurant is the pride of owner Piero Pierattoni, who chose a subdued contemporary aesthetic for his locally popular *ristorante*. Longtime server Anthony Cascio-Mariana and Chef Tony have been here for more than two decades since the restaurant opened. Not all dishes thrill, but those recommended here will leave you more than delighted. *Do* try the Gorgonzola gnocchi appetizer; the magnificent *Brodello di pesce fresco cioppino*; and the ravioli stuffed with lobster and ricotta cheese in squid ink and tomato cream sauce.

TUSCANY'S
760-311-5828
74-855 Country Club Dr., Palm Desert, CA 92260
Price: Expensive
Credit Cards: AE, DC, MC, V
Cuisine: Italian
Serving: L, D
Reservations: Recommended
Handicapped Access: Yes
Special Features: Full bar

An Andrea Bocelli CD—a great start!—was playing when I dined in travertine-clad Tuscany's, a cavernous space in the Desert Springs JW Marriott Resort. The decor here is a tad formal, with Pompeiian trompe

Singing waiter at Café Italia.

l'oeil murals and Vegas-style columns and faux Roman kitsch. The menu aims for high cuisine—consider it nouvelle Italian—with great success. I reveled in the yellowtail carpaccio appetizer . . . mushroom leek risotto . . . and semolina dusted scallops. Simply divine! The four-course tasting menu is a bargain at $65 ($95 with wine), and the ravenous can choose up to seven courses ($100).

INDIAN WELLS

CAFÉ ITALIA

760-773-3080
74-901 Hwy. 111, Indian Wells, CA 92210
www.cafeitaliaindianwells.com
Price: Moderate to Expensive
Credit Cards: AE, D, MC, V
Cuisine: Italian
Serving: L, D
Reservations: Recommended
Handicapped Access: Yes
Special Features: Singing waiters

Singing waiters? *Ma sì!* Yes, of course. That's what makes this small, cozy, entirely unpretentious Italian restaurant unique. You're enjoying your pasta and *vino* when the waiter comes up and begins belting out an aria as if he were Andrea Bocelli. All the waiters sing. And not just Italian. Rock staples. R&B. Anything goes. The menu focuses on hearty Italian comfort food, such as spinach salad, linguini *pescatore*, and Sicilian cannoli, the latter with white wine sauce, capers, and lemon. All entrées are served with fresh vegetables al dente, and soup and salad included. Café Italia is tucked into the Village Shopping Center, at the junction of Cook Street and Hwy. 111. You might get lucky with a song or two at lunchtime, but the real fun comes at night.

LE ST. GERMAIN

760-773-6511
74-985 Hwy. 111, Indian Wells, CA 92210
www.lestgermain.com
Price: Expensive
Credit Cards: AE, MC, V
Cuisine: California-French
Serving: D
Reservations: Recommended
Handicapped Access: Yes
Special Features: Private dining rooms

Owners Paul Bruggerman and Michel Despras have tried to replicate the success of the renowned Hollywood restaurant of the same name. This one is huge, with almost 400 seats, albeit divided into six intimate rooms that together attempt to evoke a French provincial feel. Our favorite spot, however, is the patio with fireplace. A few classical French dishes feature, including escargots, and filet mignon with Roquefort and au poivre reduction. But for the most part, chef Didier Tsirony delivers exquisite California-French fusion dishes. Fans of seafood might pair the crab tower appetizer (with avocado, cucumber, peppercorns, and salmon caviar with ginger-sesame sauce) with the salmon with tomato relish on a bed of spinach. And the Australian rack of lamb crusted with pistachios and grilled with cardamom-infused

Amorè Ristorante Italiano.

reduced lamb stock is superb. Among the desserts are some scrumptious French pastries. The extensive wine list features a wide choice of Californian and French labels. The Melrose private dining room has its own bar.

La Quinta

AMORÈ

760-777-1315
www.amoredining.com
47-474 Washington St., La Quinta, CA 92253
Closed: Sun.
Price: Very expensive
Credit Cards: AE, D, MC, V
Cuisine: California fusion
Serving: L, D
Reservations: Recommended
Handicapped Access: Yes
Special Features: Stunning architecture

Perhaps the most architecturally dramatic restaurant in the valley, this magnificent post-modernist palace was designed by Keith Leonhard in 2001, when it opened as Omri & Boni—a temple to fine dining until mid-2006, when it reopened under new owners. With a lofty, slanted roofline, curvilinear wall of glass offering spectacular views of the Santa Rosa Mountains, plus effusive use of bare metal, cement, and frosted glass, this gorgeous structure is as much a work of art as a sensational venue for haute cuisine. I like to dine at the wide-open, trapezoidal bar—a chic, cozy spot that draws monied singles (Amorè caters to the Bentley and Porsche crowd). While tipping its hat toward Italy, the vast menu spans the globe. Many dishes fuse local ingredients. Dates, almonds, and fig essence, for example, find their way into the seven-spice crusted baby lamb chop appetizer. Of the disorienting array of pastas, we recommend the Michelangelo—a creamy fettucini with pancetta, peas, and porcini and shiitake mushrooms. Chef Luis Zamera excels, as does everything about this place.

ARNOLD PALMER'S

760-771-4653
www.arnoldpalmers.net
78-164 Ave. 52, La Quinta, CA 92253
Price: Very expensive
Credit Cards: AE, D, MC, V
Cuisine: Nouvelle
Serving: D
Reservations: Recommended
Handicapped Access: Yes
Special Features: Live music and dancing

Arnold Palmer himself is often on hand to greet patrons at his homey eatery serving his favorite food. With a classic country-club ambience setting the tone, this is a favored place among the local cognoscenti seeking extraordinary comfort food, such as slow-cooked pot roast, chicken pot pie, and traditional meat loaf. Executive Chef Brett Maddock's steakhouse menu really gets the juices flowing with such mouthwatering treats as 14-ounce rib eye steak or the beef medallion in blue cheese, while noncarnivores won't be disappointed with the New Zealand snapper with shimp, wontons, baby bok choy, enoki mushrooms, and coconut Thai broth. There's a nightly featured menu, plus weekend specials, and wine steward Bo Moore oversees the 600-bottle cellar with almost 400 labels. The bar (*do* order a custom martini) is always jammed midafternoon onward, and entertainer Kevin Henry gets things humming at night, when patrons whirl around the dance floor. There's even a putting green—yes, clubs and balls are available at reception. The main downside here is the very steep prices.

AZUR
760-777-4927
www.laquintaresort.com
49-499 Eisenhower Dr., La Quinta, CA 92253
Closed: Sun. and Mon.
Price: Very expensive
Credit Cards: AE, MC, V
Cuisine: California fusion
Serving: D
Reservations: Recommended
Handicapped Access: Yes
Special Features: Live music

You'd expect the signature restaurant at the legendary, historic La Quinta Resort & Club to not disappoint, and in that regard patrons are not disappointed. Let's start with the heart-warming decor. A rough-beamed ceiling and original tile mosaic blend with contemporary art in what was the hotel's original 1926 Mission-style lobby, where bougainvillea spill over the blue shutters and blazing white walls outside. The historic ambience fuses with hip notes, not least those of saxophonist Brian Denigan and pianist John Hardie, who perform Wed.–Sat. evenings in the restaurant lounge.

Signature fine dining at Azur comes with a French twist, courtesy of French-trained award-winning chef William Winthrow, who took over the kitchen here in 2007. The lobster and English pea bisque (with aged sherry and Devonshire cream) makes a superb starter. The perfect meal might comprise pan-seared Hudson Valley foie gras; Dungeness crab beignets; rack of New Zealand lamb; and chocolate symphony dessert. Wine buffs are offered vintages that span the globe, with a noteworthy corps of Burgundy labels, and monthly wine dinners are a specialty drawing discerning cognoscenti. And new for 2008, the Azur sushi bar is presided over by chef Shinya Horiguchi, whose irresistibly creative treats include the signature Azur Roll of shrimp tempura, crab meat, and seared jalapeños.

When a break-the-bank spurge is called for, you won't find a better treat in the desert.

CANTON BISTRO
760-771-9129
79-405 Hwy. 111, La Quinta, CA 92253
Price: Inexpensive
Credit Cards: AE, D, MC, V
Cuisine: Chinese
Serving: L, D
Reservations: Not required
Handicapped Access: Yes
Special Features: Delivers

When your taste buds call out for simple, filling Chinese-American fare, then this family-run no-frills restaurant will fit the bill. Decor combines Oriental chairs with an industrial, black-painted ceiling. The expansive menu has all the to-be-expected dishes. More intriguing specials include pork with scallion; flounder with vegetable; and crispy shrimp and scallop with garlic sauce combination.

THE FALLS PRIME STEAK HOUSE
760-777-9999
78-430 Hwy. 111, La Quinta, CA 92253
Price: Inexpensive

Credit Cards: AE, D, MC, V
Cuisine: Steaks
Serving: L, D
Reservations: Recommended
Handicapped Access: Yes
Special Features: Martini bar

Echoing its sibling in Palm Springs, this restaurant similarly features a signature water cascade. It draws a hip, youngish crowd who come primarily to sip signature "smoking" martinis at the high-energy bar. The menu here is identical to that in Palm Springs, with plenty of seafood and steaks and fusion dishes, all in generous portions. A few dishes raise eyebrows, such as Colorado rack of lamb with roasted red pepper crême brûlée!

HOG'S BREATH INN LA QUINTA

760-564-5556 or 1-866-HOGS-888
www.restaurantsofpalmsprings.com
78-065 Main St., La Quinta, CA 92253
Closed: Mon.
Price: Moderate to Expensive
Credit Cards: AE, D, DC, MC, V
Cuisine: Californian
Serving: L, D
Reservations: Recommended
Handicapped Access: Yes
Special Features: Sports bar

An offshoot of Clint Eastwood's original Hog's Breath Inn of Carmel, and since 2006 part of the Kaiser Group of Restaurants chain, this elegantly rustic movie-themed restaurant upstairs in Old Town La Quinta serves classic American fare that includes the likes of chopped steak with wild mushroom, the Dirty Harry Bacon Cheeseburger, and High Plains Drifter Prime Rib. The menu runs from sand dabs to filet mignon and includes tasty chops and a superb mahimahi in a mild Thai curry sauce. Don't overdo it, as you'll need room for the not-to-be-missed Lady Godiva chocolate mousse cake. The food wins no prizes but is tasty and filling. The decor is classic Californian, with weathered wood beams and fireplaces. Clint Eastwood stares down as you dine, as murals play on Eastwood's movie roles. You can opt to enjoy views of the Santa Rosa Mountains from the second-floor balcony. The wine list impresses. The Sports Bar serves a good selection of draft beers, including draft Guinness and Bass Ale, plus an extensive choice of tequilas for great margaritas, and there's an adjunct piano bar for sing-alongs.

MARIO'S ITALIAN CAFÉ

760-777-4055
49-906 Jefferson St., La Quinta, CA 92253
Price: Moderate
Credit Cards: MC, V
Cuisine: Italian
Serving: L, D
Reservations: Not required
Handicapped Access: Yes
Special Features: Patio

A delightfully homey atmosphere with faux-Italian decor, this simple eatery serves Italian comfort food. Though not gourmet, the piping hot meals are filling. The wide-ranging menu runs from Italian favorites such as antipasto salad (all salads cost $5.75 or 7.95) and eggplant parmigiano ($9.95) to pastas (all $8.95) and crab ravioli ($10.95). It also has sub sandwiches and hand-tossed pizzas cooked in the brick oven. The chicken marsala is a bit heavy: Mine was served floating in butter, with canned mushrooms. You can dine on the patio with misters and heat lamps. The oversize wine glasses are served brim-full. Mario's also has outlets in Bermuda Dunes (42-104 Washington St.; 760-772-6100), Rancho Mirage (42-418 Bob Hope Dr.; 760-341-9941), and Indio (81-939 Hwy. 111; 760-775-2888).

INDIO

EL CAMPANARIO

760-342-3681

44-185 Monroe St., Indio, CA 92201
Price: Inexpensive
Credit Cards: MC, V
Cuisine: Mexican
Serving: B, L, D
Reservations: Not required
Handicapped Access: Yes
Special Features: Mariachis

A great budget option for fans of quality Mexican fare. Fast, friendly service combine with a tremendous selection of specialty dishes, including the signature shrimp-wrapped-in-bacon seafood dinner and a choice of *molcajetes*—various meats (including quail) and seafood in a spicy, salsalike, super-flavorful sauce, accompanied by scallions and fried strips of prickly pear cactus. The kids menu offers half a dozen options for less than a dollar. The clientele here is almost exclusively Hispanic. Service is slow, but the wait is more than worthwhile. Choose from a wide selection of Mexican beers.

MACARIO'S

760-342-5649
80-783 Indio Blvd., Indio, CA 92201
Price: Inexpensive
Credit Cards: MC, V
Cuisine: Mexican
Serving: B, L, D
Reservations: Not required
Handicapped Access: Yes
Special Features: Fireplace

This family-run restaurant, named for owner Macario Tristan, is another local institution and a worthy competitor to El Campanario. You know the fare can be trusted when it's the Mexicans themselves lining up to dine here. The large breakfast menu includes a tremendous huevos rancheros ($3.99), and a whopping dish of *machaca* and eggs with refried beans, potatoes, and tortillas, sufficient to see you through to dinner. It has plenty of seafood options, too. We recommend *camarones Maria's*, the house signature dish of shrimp stuffed with chipotle chile, wrapped in bacon, and lathered with melted cheese.

ROSAMARILLO

760-777-1725
49-900 Jefferson St., Indio, CA 92201
Price: Inexpensive
Credit Cards: MC, V
Cuisine: Mexican
Serving: B, L, D
Reservations: Not required
Handicapped Access: Yes
Special Features: Patio dining

This family-run Mexican restaurant is one of the hidden gems of the desert. Despite its storefront setting in Ralph's shopping center and its rather humble albeit richly colored decor, it serves gourmet Mexican fare at exceptional prices. Owner Christina Tristan fusses over patrons and clearly prides herself on serving only the freshest ingredients, ably prepared by chef Rosario Enriquez. The deep-fried "chips" offer just the right crunchy resistance, and the salsa is truly *fresca*. Enriquez's thick and complex black bean soup is delicious. Patrons rave about the *huachinango frito* (whole deep-fried red snapper with garlic) and the sizzling Veracruz shrimp. And the *mole* here gets five-star reviews. Still, my favorite remains the plump and deliciously succulent (and extremely filling) *burrito Ricardo* stuffed with white-wine-simmered chicken with onions, yellow peppers, garlic, and herbs, served (as are most dishes) with rice and black beans. Rosamarillo offers a choice of Mexican beers, but on hot days try the all-you-can-drink pink lemonade.

FOOD PURVEYORS

Bakeries

There's no shortage of bakeries in the Palm Springs region, with the most well-known being **Sherman's** (760-325-1199; www.shermansdeli.com; 401 Tahquitz Canyon Rd., Palm Springs, CA 92262), with a superb takeout baked-goods section. Find a full review earlier in this chapter.

El Cielo Bakery (760-318-9277; 400 S. El Cielo Rd. # 8, Palm Springs, CA 92262) is highly rated among locals for its custom birthday cakes. Likewise, **Carousel Bakery** (760-324-2420; 35-280 Date Palm Dr., Cathedral City, CA 92234), which can also produce wedding cakes to your specifications; and **Pastry Swan Bakery** (760-202-1213; www.pastryswan.com; 68-444 Perez Rd., Cathedral City, CA 92234) and **La Quinta Baking Co.** (760-777-1699; 78-395 Hwy. 111, La Quinta, CA 92253), both specializing in cakes for all occasions.

Ruby's Diner, Rancho Mirage.

Sure, **Winchell's Donut House** (760-327-4832; www.winchells.com; 2383 E. Tahquitz Canyon Way, Palm Springs, CA 92262) is known for its doughnuts, but it also serves breads, pastries, and more. It also has an outlet at 45-995 Monroe Ave., Indio, CA 92201 (760-342-3287).

Vons (760-322-2192; www.vons.com; 2315 E. Tahquitz Canyon Way, Palm Springs, CA 92262), the grocery chain that specializes in health foods and fine wines, has an excellent bakery section. It has five other outlets in the desert (4733 E. Palm Canyon Dr., Palm Springs, CA 92264; 14-200 Palm Dr., Desert Hot Springs, CA 92240; 36-101 Bob Hope Dr., Rancho Mirage, CA 92270; 42-424 Bob Hope Dr., Rancho Mirage, CA 92270; 72-675 Hwy. 111, Palm Desert, CA 92260; and 78-271 Hwy. 111, La Quinta, CA 92253).

The **Three Dog Bakery on El Paseo** (760-776-9899; 73-255 El Paseo, Palm Desert, CA 92270), in the Jensen's shopping center, is a specialty bakery for dogs and cats. At the weekly "cockertail hour," your pet can belly up to the "bow wow bar" to sample the treats.

Burgers, Etc.

Fatburger (760-323-1492; www.fatburger.com; 451 Paseo Dorotea, Palm Springs, CA 92262) A local institution since 1952. Wins hands-down for a fair-priced quality burger and fries. The meat is fresh. Also chicken burgers and great milk shakes.

Hamburger Mary's (760-778-6279; 415 N. Palm Canyon Dr., Palm Springs, CA 92262) Popular with locals and sought out by visitors, this fun-filled joint delivers double-fisted burgers, plus chicken fingers, fajitas, etc. Patio dining with misters and heaters, and big-screen TV inside.

Ruby's Diner (760-406-7829; 155 S. Palm Canyon Dr., Palm Springs, CA 92262) If it's fresh-baked apple pie you're craving, and the best shake in town, head to Ruby's Diner, a classic fifties-style diner right down to the decor and waitresses in bobby socks and pink-and-white-striped outfits. The burgers here are disappointingly bland, as are the fries, and the salads fare no better. But the desserts make amends. Situated on the downtown plaza, it's a great spot for taking in the scene from the patio. A nice quirk is the model railway supported from the ceiling. It also has an outlet at 71-855 Hwy. 111, Rancho Mirage, CA 92270 (760-836-0788) with three classic cars to draw you in.

Tyler's Burgers (760-325-2990; 149 S. Indian Canyon Dr., Palm Springs, CA 92262) Locals swear that Tyler's—in a cute little cottage between Indian Canyon and South Palm Canyon Drives—delivers the biggest, juiciest, and tastiest burgers in town. Great malt shakes and fries, too. Also hot dogs, if you prefer.

Grill-a-Burger (760-327-8175; www.grill-a-burger.com; 166 N. Palm Canyon Dr., Palm Springs, CA 92262) The menu here has 24 signature burgers, including the "Double Whammy" with two half-pound patties, three slices of bacon, and three pieces of cheese—truly bigger than your stomach! I love the magic mushroom burger with fresh sautéed mushrooms and Swiss cheese ($6.95). Partners Rick Ameil and Dean Talbott have enhanced their burger joint with jungle decor, plus classic rock and Motown tunes. They recently added a second outlet at Plaza de Monterey, 73-091 Country Club Dr., Palm Desert, CA 92260 (760-346-8170).

Coffeehouses

Bad Ass Coffee (760-568-2231; www.badasscoffee.com; 42-464 Bob Hope Dr., Rancho Mirage, CA 92270) Gourmet coffee shop with a fun, Hawaiian theme. Of course, it serves Kona coffee. You can also snatch up chocolates, macadamia nuts, custom-branded mugs, hats, Tshirts, etc.

The Coffee Bean & Tea Leaf (760-325-9402; www.coffeebean.com; 100 N. Palm Canyon Dr., Palm Springs CA, 92262) Delightful, centrally located coffee shop and tea house (formerly LaLaJava's) with cozy sofa, fireplace, and outside misters. Note the life-size bronze statue of Lucille Ball on a bench outside.

Coffee Break (760-564-0226; 78-900 Ave. 47 #100, La Quinta, CA 92253) Handily located just off Hwy. 111, this café serves breakfast and lunch and has a full espresso bar. The "Shepherd's Breakfast" gets rave reviews, and the cappuccinos are yummy.

It's a Grind Coffee House (760-321-2880; www.itsagrind.com; 34-151 Monterey Ave., Rancho Mirage, CA 92270) This chain coffeehouse offers a cozy seating and great blues and jazz music by which to enjoy your cappuccino, espresso, and other quality coffee drinks, hot toasted bagels, muffins, etc. It also has outlets at 36-901 Cook St., Palm Desert, CA 92211 (760-674-0000) and 44-100 Jefferson St., Indio, CA 92201 (760-200-9474).

Koffi (760-416-2244; 515 N. Palm Canyon Dr., Palm Springs, CA 92262) Where the gay crowd comes for their caffeinated pleasure. It has a lovely landscaped garden to the rear.

Peabody's Café Bar & Coffee (760-322-1877; www.peabodyspalmsprings.com; 134 S. Palm Canyon Dr., Palm Springs, CA 92262) A delightful place to chill over morning cup of joe on the roadside patio. Find a full review earlier in this chapter.

The Coffee Bean & Tea Leaf.

Starbucks (760-323-7412; www.star bucks.com; 101 S. Palm Canyon Dr., Palm Springs, CA 92262) A favorite meeting spot for locals on a busy street corner, although inside seating is limited and this coffeehouse lacks the intimacy of most Starbucks outlets. There's another Starbucks at 682 S. Palm Canyon Dr., Palm Springs, CA 92264 (760-323-8023), plus four venues in Cathedral City, three in Rancho Mirage, six in Palm Desert, three in La Quinta, two in Indio, and one in Coachella. See the Web site for contact information and directions.

Deli and Gourmet Shops

Aspen Mills Bread Co. (760-323-3123; 555 S. Sunrise Way, Palm Springs, CA 92264) Known for its delicious box lunches, superb sandwiches, and excellent breads and fruit muffins. And the brownie slab dessert is to die for.

Canyon Italian Deli (760-328-8978; 68-444 Perez Rd., Cathedral City, CA 92234) Evoking memories of a classic New York delicatessen, with fresh meats, cheeses, and hearty sandwiches lavished with toppings.

Einstein Brothers Bagels (760-416-6364; www.einsteinbros.com; 109 S. Palm Canyon Dr., Palm Springs, CA 92262) Bagel omelet sandwiches. Breakfast panini. Schmears. Grilled albacore tuna sandwiches. All this and much more.

Jensen's (760-325-8282; www.jensensfoods.com; 102 S. Sunrise Way, Palm Springs, CA 92262) This well-respected supermarket has a marvelous deli section selling filling sandwiches. It even has a sit-down section with banquette seating. It also has outlets at 69-900 Frank Sinatra Dr., Rancho Mirage, CA 92270 (760-770-3355); 73-601 Hwy. 111, Palm Desert, CA 92260 (760-346-9393); 42-150 Cook St., Palm Desert, CA 92260 (760-837-1877); and 78-525 Hwy. 111, La Quinta, CA 92253 (760-777-8181).

Jet Stream Deli (760-325-6695; 440 S. El Cielo, Palm Springs, CA 92262) Hidden inside Palm Liquor, this is one of the best sandwich shops around. Its wide selection includes capicola, ham, mortadella, roast beef, and salami, plus cheeses and more, all served on fresh Italian bread, pressed and toasted.

Marsh's Desert Deli (760-324-7500; 69-930 Hwy. 111, Rancho Mirage, CA 92270) In the Atrium Design Center, this New York-style deli/restaurant serves homemade soups, salads, and meats

Sossa's Deli Liquor Market (760-323-2700; 3700 E. Vista Chino, Palm Springs, CA 92262) This deli with in-store dining tables is known for its tasty torpedo special—a foot-long sandwich stuffed with bologna, ham, and salami.

Fish and Meat Markets

Sure, you may be a hundred miles from the ocean, but did you know pupfish swim in the desert? This endangered fish is off-limits, but there's plenty of fresh scafood to be bought at local stores.

Owned by former fisherman Louis Pagano, **Fisherman's Market & Grill** (760-776-6533; 44-250 Town Center Way, Palm Desert, CA 92260) is *the* place in the desert to buy your fresh scallops, jumbo prawns, ahi tuna, and other seafoods. Pagano also has outlets at 235 S. Indian Canyon Dr., Palm Springs, CA 92262 (760-327-1766); in Jensen's Shopping Center, at 78-575 Hwy. 111, La Quinta, CA, 92253 (760-777-1601); and Westfield Palm Desert, 72-840 Hwy. 111, Palm Desert CA 92260 (760-779-9724).

Produce

Surprise! Much of the fresh produce for sale in local markets comes from right here. Most of it is produced at the south end of the Coachella Valley, near the Salton Sea. Table grapes, bell peppers, lemons, dates, carrots, romaine lettuce, and broccoli are major crops grown for export. Did we mention dates? They're the local specialty, today associated with Indio, where you can still see entire groves dedicated to growing this delicious fruit (once upon a time, the date groves extended as far north as Indian Wells and Palm Desert before being displaced by urban development). Don't miss the National Date Festival (www.datefest.org), held in Indio each Feb.

Clark's Nutrition Natural Health Foods Market (760-969-6735; 34-175 Monterey Ave., Rancho Mirage, CA 92270) Sells an impressive selection of bulk foods, teas, and organic products. It includes the Organic Café, a perfect spot for veggie or organic meat sandwiches, such as chicken with cranberry.

Hadley's (1-888-854-5655; www.hadleyfruitorchards.com; 48-980 Seminole Dr., Cabazon, CA 92230) Just off I-10, a stone's throw from the Cabazon outlets, this store stocks a tremendous variety of health foods, including dates, nuts, etc. The sandwiches here are to die for. Try the veggie sandwich with whole wheat bread, accompanied by a date shake.

Harvest Health Foods (760-862-1911; 73-910 Hwy. 111, Palm Desert, CA 92260) Mineral supplements and the like. Also here is Luscious Lorraine's Fresh Food Bar—part deli, part juice bar—with a fabulous vegetarian lunch menu (including nonvegetarian sandwiches such as albacore tuna) and killer smoothies, such as Tropical Tango.

Dates and date shake at Oasis Date Gardens.

Health Nutz (760-346-5535; www.deserthealthnutz.com; 74-121 Hwy. 111, Palm Desert, CA 99260) Only the freshest ingredients are sold, but mostly this store is about alfalfa, noni, and wheat grass . . . all in bottled tablet form.

Henry's Farmers' Market (760-771-2485; 79-050 Hwy. 111, La Quinta, CA 92253) Farm-fresh, quality organic fruits and vegetables, plus bulk and packaged natural foods, with roadside quality and pricing.

Native Foods (760-416-0070; 1775 E. Palm Canyon Dr., Palm Springs, CA 92264) Serves vegan fare, from Caesar and Jamaican jerked salads to such creative concoctions as "Iron Yam" (steamed yam on salad greens dressed with balsamic vinaigrette, topped with steamed veggies, tofu, and caramelized onions). Also has an outlet at 73-890 El Paseo, Palm Desert, CA 92260 (760-836-9396).

Nature's RX (760-323-9487; 555 Sunrise Way, Palm Springs, CA 92262) A health food store selling the likes of brown rice and fresh veggies. The store's Café Totonaca is a great place to breakfast on tofu scramble or whole-grain pancakes. Lunch options include vegan fare, hearty vegetarian meals, and ethnic salads. I recommend the Nature's Club Sandwich on nine-grain bread.

Oasis Date Gardens (760-399-5665 or 1-800-827-8017; www.oasisdategardens.com; Thermal, CA 92274) This 175-acre date grove was founded in 1912 and is still going strong, producing Medjool dates. It offers free date tasting and also sells a large selection of nuts, dried fruits, honeys, and preserves. Open Mon.–Sat. 8–5.

Shield's Date Gardens (760-347-7768; www.shieldsdategarden.com; 80225 Hwy. 111, Indio, CA 92201) This date market is a local institution. It sells several varieties of dates, available in a vast assortment of prepackaged presentation boxes. Also date cookies, nuts, grapefruits, and more.

Trader Joe's (760-202-0090; www.traderjoes.com; 67-720 E. Palm Canyon Dr., Cathedral City, CA 92234) This national chain renowned for its fresh, organic produce has three outlets in the greater Palm Springs region, including at 46-400 Washington St., La Quinta, CA 92253 (760-777-1553) and 44250 Town Center Way # C6 Palm Desert, CA (760-340-2291). It covers most needs, from the basics like milk, bread, and veggies to exotic fare like imported cheeses and handtossed Italian pizza.

Villagefest (N. Palm Canyon Dr., Palm Springs) Held every Thurs. night year-round on Palm Springs' main drag. Local farmers set up stalls to sell local products, from dates, almonds, and figs to asparagus, tomatoes, and other fresh fruit and veggies.

Pizzas and Pizzerias

Pizza may not be the obsession it is in many other cities, but when the craving hits, you'll find plenty of excellent options. The chain gang, such as Pizza Hut, are well-represented, but here are some of our favorites among the little guys:

If you like innovative toppings, try **California Pizza Kitchen** (760-322-6075; Desert Fashion Plaza, 123 N. Palm Canyon Dr., Palm Springs, CA 92262). Sure, it's a national chain now, with trademark yellow, black, and white color scheme, but its 9-inch wood-fired pizzas are delicious. Spicy? Try the Jamaican Jerk Chicken.

My favorite pizza place is **Matchbox** (760-778-6000; www.matchboxpalmsprings.com; 155 S. Palm Canyon Dr., Palm Springs, CA 92262), serving fabulously tasty thin-crust pizzas with some unusual specials. I'm addicted to the spicy "Fire & Smoke." Find a full review earlier in this chapter. Other good options include:

Good Stuff Pizza (760-771-4440; www.goodstuffpizza.com; 78-383 Hwy. 111, La Quinta, CA 92253)

Palermo's New York Pizza (760-416-1138; 400 S. El Cielo Rd., Palm Springs, CA 92262)

Papa Dan's Pizza & Pasta (760-568-3267; 73-131 Country Club Dr., Palm Desert, CA 92260)

Rocky's Pizza (760-323-9244; 1751 N. Sunrise Way, Palm Springs, CA 92262)

Shakey's Pizza Parlor (760-325-1521; 999 E. Tahquitz Canyon Way, Palm Springs, CA 92262)

Upper Crust Pizza (760-321-2583; 67-555 E. Hwy. 111, Cathedral City, CA 92234)

Little Caesars Pizza (760-342-3880; 42-065 Washington St., Indio, CA 92201)

Sweets and Treats

You'd expect folks who live in the desert to lap up ice cream like *locos*. And they do. However, there's a surprising dearth of boutique ice cream parlors. The national chains command the scene.

Cold Stone Creamery (760-327-6892; www.coldstonecreamery.com; 155 S. Palm Canyon Dr., Palm Springs, CA 92262) serves the best gelato ice cream in town. This ice creamery is perfectly placed right on Palm Springs Plaza, just a stone's throw from a dozen restaurants. There's a bench outside, and the plaza's fountain has seating so you can people watch while savoring your twin scoops. It also has outlets at 68-718 E. Palm Canyon Dr., Cathedral City, CA 92234; at 72-840 Hwy. 111, Palm Desert, CA 92260; and at 78-380 Hwy. 111, La Quinta, CA 92253.

If you're a fan of **Baskin-Robbins** (www.baskinrobbins.com), you'll find outlets at 31-375 Date Palm Dr., Cathedral City, CA 92234 (760-324-8188); 77-912 Country Club Dr., Palm Desert, CA 92211 (760-200-1501); 78-520 Hwy. 111, La Quinta, CA 92253 (760-771-3131); and 82-158 Hwy. 111, Indio, CA 92201 (760-342-3631).

See's Candies (760-325-6211; 144 S. Palm Canyon Dr., Palm Springs, CA 92262), on Palm Springs' main plaza, has an outlet selling See's famous chocolate candies. Not to be outdone, the **Rocky Mountain Chocolate Factory** (760-346-2929; The River at Rancho Mirage, 71-800 Hwy. 111, Rancho Mirage, CA 92270) sells such melt-in-your-mouth delicacies as buttery toffee and creams, creamy fudges, and nut clusters. Oh, it was voted the best-tasting chocolate in America by *Money* magazine for good reason.

Wine and Beer Shops

Local residents are true gourmands, and there's no shortage of upscale wine shops offering (and serving) a huge variety of often hard-to-find labels.

Larry's Wines, Spirits & Gourmet Deli (760-668-5301; 2781 N. Palm Canyon Dr., Palm Springs, CA 92262) This well-stocked deli at the north end of Palm Canyon Drive has an amazing wine selection, plus about 80 handcrafted and imported beers kept within a humidity and temperature-controlled vault. Larry knows his stuff, too!

Old Town Cellar (760-771-8950; 78,015 Main St. #109, La Quinta, CA 92253) In Old Town La Quinta, this boutique wine shop and tasting room has a wine bar offering 20 selections by the glass. It also has monthly wine events and special tastings.

Palm Springs Wine & Art (760-325-9991; www.palmspringswineandart.com; 242 N. Palm Canyon Dr., Palm Springs, CA 92262) Part wine shop, part wine-tasting bar and part art gallery, this homey place has more than 70 boutique wine labels for sampling. Owner Michael Judson-Carr is dedicated in his passion for fine wines, so much so that he opens seven days a week. Daily tastings include three pours for $6, served at the 23-foot-long custom bar. Jazz riffs provide a mellow ambience as you settle in the sofa salon.

PS Wine and Specialty Foods (760-322-4411; e-mail: pswine@verizon.net; 188 S. Indian Canyon Dr., Palm Springs, CA 92262) Palm Springs' premier wine outlet is run by bon vivant oenophile Paulette Wright and stocks several hundred labels from around the world. She was relocating at the time of writing.

Tastings (760-324-4044; The Atrium, 69-930 Hwy. 111, Rancho Mirage, CA 92270) Owned by gourmand husband-and-wife team Marci Brietling and Bob Finlayson, this chic, well-stocked wine bar exudes a living-room ambience with soft lighting for that familial, even romantic mood. You can sit at the bar on tall, chic leather stools or plump into comfy couches and club chairs. The bar serves some 40 or so wines by the glass, including some rare labels. Two wine flights weekly feature four 2-ounce pours. Small portions of gourmet foods complement the wines: Expect treats from crispy wonton-wrapped tiger prawn (good with the Darioush viognier) to sliced roasted chicken panini with brie, basil pesto, and vine-ripened tomato (a perfect complement to the Cartlidge & Brown pinot noir).

Treasures of the Vine (760-564-4777; www.treasuresotv.com; 78-370 Hwy. 111, La Quinta, CA 92253) Wine manager Dustin Miller is usually on hand to lend his expertise for wine tastings every Fri. and Sat., 12–9. Tastings rotate the labels from among more than 300 wines in stock.

Tulip Hill Winery (760-568-5678; www.tuliphillwinery.com; The River, 71-800 Hwy. 111, Rancho Mirage, CA 92270) This unpretentious place serves award-winning wines from the eponymous winery, 500-plus miles away, delivering 14 varietals and blends. Daily tastings at the marble-topped bar are complemented by wine-and-food pairings plus wine-release parties, when the wines and accompanying food are on the house. Plus, there's an olive oil bar and specialty foods.

Vino 100 (760-321-5478; www.vino100cc.com; 68-718 E. Palm Canyon Dr., Cathedral City, CA 92234) A wine shop and tasting bar in the Pickfair Promenade. Knowledgeable staff support owner Brian Estenson, a passionate wine advocate who hosts complimentary tastings on Fri., Sat., and Sun., when he pours four to six wines. A special tasting for new labels is held every first Friday of the month. As you'd expect, cheeses and other gourmet hors d'oeuvres are served and sold. Estenson also stocks more than 80 bottled beers from a dozen countries.

Wild for the Vine (760-325-9930; www.wildforthevine.com; 390 N. Palm Canyon Dr., Palm Springs, CA 92262) Thank goodness this store is leagues better than its awful Web site! Owner Scott Morgan is a font of knowledge and edifies patrons during the daily wine tastings, accompanied by cheeses. And six-ounce pours costs a mere $10. The shop sells wine accessories.

A Fantasy Balloon over La Quinta.

Recreation

The Great Outdoors

You might be forgiven for thinking that a desert offers little to do and that it's just too darn hot to do it in any event. Wrong on both counts! The greater Palm Springs region is replete with exciting recreational activities. The fabulous winter weather spells nirvana for hikers, rock-climbers, cyclists, and other outdoorsy folks. The scenery is breathtaking, and far more diverse than you might imagine, ranging from below sea level to more than 10,000 feet atop Mount San Jacinto. Hundreds of miles of hiking and riding trails lace the region. There are more golf courses than you can shake a golf club at. More tennis courts, too. And a spa for every day of the year. You get the picture.

The **City of Palm Springs Recreation Division** (760-323-8272; 401 S. Pavilion Way, Palm Springs, CA 92262) is a good resource.

Great Outdoors Palm Springs (GOPS; www.greatoutdoors.org; P.O. Box 361, Palm Springs, CA 92263) sponsors hiking, camping, and other recreational outdoor activities for gays and lesbians. And the **Center for Extended Learning for Seniors** (760-776-8874; www.eldercels.com; 38-994 Desert Greens Dr. East, Palm Desert, CA 92260) fulfills the same function for seniors.

Aerial Tours

Soaring over the valley is a spectacular way to appreciate the beauty of the region and is an experience you won't quickly forget.

Sailplane Enterprises (909-658-6577; www.sailplaneenterprises.com; 4655 Whittier Ave., Hemet, CA 92545) For a bird's-eye view in silence. Offers sailplane—"glider"—rides from Jacqueline Cochran Regional Airport, in Thermal, on Wed. and Fri.–Sun. FAA-certified pilots escort you on a serene and silent motorless tour in one- or two-passenger gliders.

Nostalgic Warbird & Biplane Rides (760-641-7335 or 1-800-991-2473; www.nostalgic warbirdrides.com; 4684 Buena Vista Rd. South, Jefferson, OR 97352) Takes you up in a 1930 New Standard or 1941 Stearman open-cockpit biplane, departing Bermuda Dunes Airport. You get to fly and even have the option to try your hand at some aerobatics, just like Snoopy! Nov.–May.

Elite Land Discovery Tours (760-318-1200; www.elitelandtours.com; 555 S. Sunrise Way, Suite 200, Palm Springs, CA 92264) Has a "Helicopter/Hummer Combo" departing Palm Springs Airport by helicopter. After a thrilling aerial tour you land at Jacqueline Cochran

Regional Airport, in Thermal, for a guided adventure by Humvee to the San Andreas fault.

Platinum Helicopters (760-322-6700; www.platinumhelicopters.com; 145 S. Gene Autry Trail, Palm Springs, CA 92262) Offers 30-minute scenic tours of the Palm Springs region.

All-Terrain Vehicles

With so much sandy wilderness, it's no surprise that the Palm Springs region is a mecca for off-roading. Restrictions are enforced to protect the delicate desert environment: You can't just tear across any old sand dune on your ATV. For example, Edom Hill, the vast sand dune north of I-10 between Date Palm Drive and Palm Drive (and long Coachella Valley's most popular offroad vehicle destination) was placed off-limits in 2005.

OffRoad Rentals (760-325-0376, www.offroadrentals.com; 59-511 Hwy. 111, Palm Springs, CA 92262) rents ATVs for self-guided tours on its private sand dunes, 4 miles north of the city. Also has "dune buggy" tours. Open 10–sunset, daily.

For an all-terrain-vehicle experience with a difference, consider **Covered Wagon Tours** (760-347-2161; www.coveredwagontours.com; P.O. Box 1106, La Quinta, CA 92253), which offers a genuine Old West experience with two-hour tours by mule-drawn covered wagons (with padded seats, thank goodness). Your guides are dolled up in cowboy gear. What better excuse do you need to break out your Stetson, denim shirts, and cowboy boots? There's an educational side to this, too: You'll learn about flora and fauna. The tour ends with a chuckwagon-style cookout with guitar entertainment.

Ballooning

Admit it, you've *always* wanted to ride in a hot-air balloon, a peaceful and exhilarating experience. The Phileas Fogg within can't help but delight at the notion of floating over your neighbor's back yard . . . seeing the country clubs from a new angle . . . thrilling to the spectacular views of the entire Coachella Valley laid out below.

At least three companies offer trips in the Coachella Valley, with winter being the preferred months: In summer, the ambient air temperature is too high, even at dawn, for the hot-air balloons to function efficiently (to rise, they rely on being lighter than the cold air around them). A propane burner heats the air within the balloon to give it loft.

Rides start at sunrise, before winds kick up. Your speed and direction are at the mercy of the breeze, although a skilled pilot can "read" the winds (which vary with elevation) and find different currents to ride. Rarely do you rise more than 500 feet above the ground. Since you're moving with the wind, there's no sensation of movement except for the landmarks passing beneath you. Trips typically last about one hour to 90 minutes before your FAA-certified pilot lets the air in the balloon cool and brings you gently back to earth.

Balloon rides typically cost $150–170.

For a colorful balloon extravaganza, be sure to visit the **Red, White, and Blue Polo and Balloon Festival** (760-777-8081; www.poloamerica.com) in January, when almost 100 balloons—many of them "special shape" balloons—take to the air.

Founded in 1981 by champion balloon pilot Steve Wilkinson, **Fantasy Balloon Flights** (760-568-0997 or 1-800-462-2683; www.fantasyballoonflights.com; 74-181 Parosella St., Palm Desert, CA 92260) offers personalized attention and safety-conscious trips. Wilkinson is one of the foremost balloonists in the world, so you're in capable hands. His balloons are different sizes and can carry 2–10 passengers. Upon landing, Fantasy serves chilled champagne—a 200-year-old ballooning tradition started in 1783, when Frenchman

Steve Wilkinson piloting a Fantasy Balloon.

Jean-François Pilâtre de Rozier launched the first hot-air balloon.

Balloon Above the Desert (760-347-0410; www.balloonabovethedesert.com; 83-232 E. Ave. 44, Indio, CA 92201) and **A Dream Flight** (760-346-5330; www.dreamflights.com; 74-181 Parosella St., Palm Desert, CA 92260) also have trips.

Bicycling

With terrain that varies from little-trafficked flats to meandering steep mountain valleys, Palm Springs has roads and trails to suit everyone from leisurely sightseers to hard-core cycling enthusiasts. Sure, you'll work for your reward. But you'll never get so close to so much beauty from inside a car. And you get great exercise, too, in the crystal-clear desert air.

Winter weather is glorious—tailor-made for cycling, in fact. Even summer is a great time to ride. Desert heat is dry heat. It's relatively comfortable for cycling, even when the temperature hovers close to 100 degrees Fahrenheit. Just be sure to drink *lots* of water to avoid dehydration.

If you're looking to rent some wheels and a helmet, **Tri a Bike Rental** (760-340-2840; www.triabike.com; 44-841 San Pablo Ave., Palm Desert, CA 92260) offers bike rentals ($8–12 hourly, $15–30 daily), including road, mountain, hybrid, cruisers, tandems, and kids' bikes.

Many boutique hotels provide free use of cruiser bikes for tootling around Palm Springs.

Adventure Bike Tours (760-328-0282; www.adventurebiketours.info; 70-250 Chappel Rd., Rancho Mirage, CA 92270) This company offers easy-paced "sightseeing from a bike" three- to four-hour tours suitable to all fitness levels, with tours in Palm Springs, Rancho Mirage, and Palm Desert. Children over 12 are welcome. Also mountain biking adventures.

Bicycling in Big Canyon.

Big Wheel Bike Tours (760-779-1837; www.bwbtours.com; P.O. Box 4185, Palm Desert, CA 92261) Mountain-bike tours, from easy road rides to challenging off-road adventures. The "Earthquake Canyon Express," offered daily at 8 AM and 1 PM, is a magnificent 20-mile, mostly downhill ride through the heart of San Andreas fault country to the heart of grape country near Mecca, ending at the Oasis Date Gardens for a well-deserved iced date shake. It also has road and mountain bike rentals.

Desert Bicycle Club (760-861-7472; www.cycleclub.com; P.O. Box 13382, Palm Desert, CA 92255) This recreational road cycling club welcomes guests riders to join club rides, which begin every Sat. morning (6:30–7:30 depending on season) from the parking lot of Palm Desert Civic Center Park. Also Sun. morning mountain bike rides, plus thrice-weekly fast-paced 20-mile training rides for serious cyclists.

Boating and Water Sports

Surprise! There's more than enough water for boating in the desert. In fact, at 376 square miles, the Salton Sea offers unlimited boating opportunities. By 1958 the sea was so popular that Albert Frey was called in to design the North Shore Yacht Club, one of the largest marinas in Southern California at the time (the Beach Boys, Jerry Lewis, and the Marx brothers kept boats here).

The sea's high salinity makes for great buoyancy, and its elevation (220 feet below sea level) results in low barometric pressure—a combination that makes the lake the fastest body of water in the world for speedboat racing. At 35 miles long and 15 miles wide, there's plenty of room to throttle up and let it rip. Many speed records have been broken here (beginning in the 1920s, the annual Salton Sea Regatta was a record-breaking event sponsored by the Salton Sea Yacht Club).

More placid boaters can anchor and fish, sip cocktails, or do whatever in no particular rush. However, sudden strong winds and swells can kick up here in the afternoon, especially Nov. to Apr.

For information contact the **Salton Sea Authority** (760-564-4888; 78-401 Hwy. 111, La Quinta, CA 92253).

There are several boat launch facilities, but only **Salton Sea Beach Marina** (760-395-5212; http://ssbmarina.com; 288 Coachella Ave., Salton Sea Beach, CA 92257) and **Johnson's Landing** (760-394-4755; 559 Sea Garden St., Salton City, CA 92275) remain of the seven marinas just a decade ago.

Bowling

Folks in the valley have two facilities. **Palm Springs Lanes** (760-324-8204; 68-051 Ramon Rd., Cathedral City, CA 92234) has 28 lanes. Make sure to check for featured nights of laser bowling. Open 9 AM–midnight Sun.–Thurs., and 9 AM–2 AM Fri. and Sat.

Considered the best option, **Fantasy Lanes Family Bowling Center** (760-342-5000; www.fantasyspringsresort.com; 84-245 Indio Springs Pkwy., Indio, CA 92203) is world-class. This fun-filled center connected to Fantasy Springs Resort Casino has 24 lanes with neon pins, plus a video game arcade, snack bar, and lounge. It hosts the **Palm Springs Desert Invitational Classic** (619-665-2045; www.psdesertinvitational.com) bowling championship, in Oct.

Otherwise, it's a long drive to **Yucca Bowl** (760-365-7678; www.yuccabowl.com; 58-146 Twentynine Palms Hwy., Yucca Valley, CA 92284).

Camping and RV Parks

The Palm Springs region is extremely popular among the RV crowd and has a long and storied history as a venue for trailer parks. Tent camping is far less popular and highly seasonal because of the brutal summer heat, but the state parks offer year round facilities. Campsites can fill up quickly "in season" (winter).

Reservations are mandatory at most California state parks (www.parks.ca.gov) and can be made up to six months in advance and as late as two days prior to your planned arrival, subject to availability. For reservations contact **ReserveAmerica** (1-800-444-7275). A $7.50 nonrefundable reservation fee applies for each campsite. Camping fees vary with the park and season but typically range from $9 to 25 ($3–5 more in peak season). Hookups cost $9 additional. Sites listed as "primitive" have pit or chemical toilets, drinking water, and usually tables, bench chairs, and barbecues or fire rings. "Developed" sites additionally have flush toilets and hot showers. State campgrounds are noted with an asterisk (*) in the listing.

Privately operated parks typically charge $15–25 per night for tent camping and $25–50 per night for RV sites with hookups.

If you want to rent an RV when you arrive in Palm Springs, contact **All Valley Rentals** (760-324-0454; 650 S. Eugene Rd., Palm Springs, CA 92264) or **Coachella Valley RV Rentals** (760-347-8266 or 1-800-671-7839; www.cruiseamerica.com; 83-827 Tamarisk Ave., Indio, CA 92201).

Palm Springs

Happy Traveler RV Park (760-325-8518; www.happytravelerrv.com; 211 W. Mesquite Ave., Palm Springs, CA 92264) At the base of the San Jacinto Mountains, near the entrance to Tahquitz Canyon. The 130 sites have hookups, cable TV, and picnic tables. Pool and hot tub, plus laundry.

Palm Springs Vicinity

Cathedral Palms RV Resort (760-324-8244; 35-901 Cathedral Canyon Dr., Cathedral City, CA 92234) Has 155 sites, most with hookups, plus tent spaces. Heated pool and hot tub.

Desert Oasis MH & RV Resort (760-329-7346; www.desertoasisrv.com; 17-850 Corkhill Rd., Desert Hot Springs, CA 92241) Seniors resort with 41 hookup sites, clubhouse, heated pool, and three mineral spring spas.

Desert Springs Spa & RV Park (760-329-1384; www.desertspringsrvpark.com; 17-325 Johnson Rd., Desert Hot Springs, CA 92241) For seniors only. Welcomes tent campers as well as RVs and has 42 sites with hookups, plus hot mineral pool, laundry, and free WiFi.

*** Mount San Jacinto State Park** (951-659-2607; www.parks.ca.gov; P.O. Box 308, 25-905 Hwy. 243, Idyllwild, CA 92549) Drive-in RV camps are available at Stone Creek (primitive) and Idyllwild (developed, with hookups). In addition, four hike-in wilderness camps, by permit only. Permits must be requested by mail up to eight weeks but no later than 10 days prior to arrival. No fires are permitted.

Palm Springs Oasis RV Resort (1-800-680-0144; 36-100 Date Palm Dr., Cathedral City, CA 92234) Has 140 sites with hookups, plus clubhouse, two swimming pools, spa, tennis courts, and an 18-hole executive golf course.

Sky Valley Resorts (760-329-8400; www.skyvalleyresort.com; 74,711 Dillon Rd., Desert Hot Springs, CA 92241) This RV resort has more than 1,700 RV spaces with hookups, plus hot springs, tennis, and free WiFi.

Southern Desert Resorts

Emerald Desert Golf & RV Resort (760-345-4770 or 1-800-426-4678; www.emerald desert.com; 76-000 Frank Sinatra Dr., Palm Desert, CA 92211) Full-service resort with clubhouse, market, gym, laundry, and 592 sites with hookups.

Lake Cahuilla Recreation Area (760-564-4712; 58-075 Jefferson St., La Quinta CA 92253) A 710-acre park surrounded by the stark beauty of the Santa Rosa Mountains. Trout fishing in the 135-acre Lake Cahuilla, constructed in the 1960s and filled by aqueduct from the Colorado River. Swimming pool open to the public mid-Apr.–mid-Oct., Sat. and Sun. only. Equestrian and hiking trails. Camping facilities. Closed Tues.–Thurs., May–Sept.

Shadow Hills RV Resort (760-360-4040; www.shadowhillsrvresort.com; 40-655 Jefferson St., Indio, CA 92201) Has 100 hookup sites with free satellite TV and WiFi, plus laundry, clubhouse, pool, Jacuzzi, and business center. Pet friendly.

Other Campsites

*** Anza-Borrego Desert State Park** (760-767-5311; www.parks.ca.gov; P.O. Box 299, Borrego Springs, CA 92004) This 600,000-acre state park has four campgrounds, including the Vern Whitaker Horse Camp (for horseback riders) and the developed Borrego Palm Canyon and Tamarisk Grove camps for RVs and tents. Borrego Palm Canyon has RV hookups. Also eight hike-in campsites, all primitive. Fires are permitted only within established fire rings.

Bashfords Hot Mineral Spa (760-354-1315; 10-590 Hot Mineral Spa Rd., Niland, CA 92257) Beside the Salton Sea, this small RV campground has 143 sites with hookups.

Joshua Tree National Park (760-367-5500; www.nps.gov/jotr; 74-485 National Park Dr., Joshua Tree, CA 92277) This vast, 794,000-acre park has nine RV campgrounds. Each campsite has a picnic table and fire grate, but only Black Wood and Cottonwood have water and toilets (no showers). Reservations for Black Wood and Cottonwood can be made up to six months in advance (1-877-444-6777; www.recreation.gov). The rest are first-come, first-served. There are no RV hookups. Wilderness camping permitted. Fees range from $10 to 15.

Lazy H MHC & RV Park (760-366-2212; www.lazyhmhp.com; 6426 Valley View St., Joshua Tree, CA 92252) Seniors campground with clubhouse, laundry, and just 17 RV sites.

*** Salton Sea State Recreation Area** (760-393-3052; www.parks.ca.gov; 100-225 State Park Rd., North Shore, CA 92254) There are tent campsites and RV hookups at the headquarters.

The Springs at Borrego (760-767-0004 or 1-866-330-0003; www.springsatborrego.com; 2255 Di Giorgio Rd., Borrego Springs, CA 92004) Splendid resort with 180 RV sites with hookups, plus cable TV, high-speed Internet. Clubhouse, tennis, swimming pool, and nine-hole golf course.

Equestrian Centers

Remember the scenes from *The Last of the Pony Riders* and other Gene Autry—the "Singing Cowboy"—movies? Filmed right here at Pioneertown (see the Culture chapter for full details). Great western screen heroes like Autry, the Cisco Kid, Hopalong Cassidy, and Roy Rogers dusted off their chaps at Hayden Movie Ranch while filming TV episodes and movies. And Disney and pals once hung out in Palm Springs and enjoyed donning their cowboy gear to explore the Indian Canyons, which have more than 150 miles of riding trails. Like Disney, many Palm Springs residents and visitors still saddle up and take to the hills to explore the desert region as early pioneers did before them. Guided trail rides start as low as $65 for one hour and as high as $225 for four hours. Happy trails!

Bath time at Smoke Tree Stables.

Several key national equestrian events take place in the valley, including the **Indio Desert Circuit Horse Show**, which attracts visitors from all over the country (see Seasonal Events, in the Culture chapter, for full details). Humble Indio is, amazingly, California's premier venue for the "Sport of Kings"—polo. Two of the nation's premier polo clubs are here.

Palm Springs

Smoke Tree Stables (760-327-1372; www.smoketreestables.com; 2500 Toledo Ave., Palm Springs, CA 92264) Offers guided tours by the hour or for the entire day. Experienced wranglers will match you to the best horse for your riding level.

Palm Springs Vicinity

Coyote Ridge Stable (760-363-3380; www.coyoteridgestable.com; 50-639 Panorama Dr., Morongo Valley, CA 92256) Guided trail rides for novices through advanced riders. Morongo, northwest of Palm Springs, is a center for horseback ranching as befits a place where the Wild West feel lives on in western-style saloons.

Crazy Horse Ranch (760-831-6450; www.crazyhorseranch.biz; 50-440 Cheyenne Trail, Morongo, CA 92256) Owners Sue Lund and Sally Ellis lead guests on rides into the canyons of Morongo Valley.

Willowbrook Riding Club (760-329-7676; www.willowbrookridingclub.com; 20-555 Mountain View Rd., Desert Hot Springs, CA 92241) This 12-acre club offers lessons for every ability.

Southern Desert Resorts

Eldorado Polo Club (760-342-2223; www.eldoradopolo.com; 50-950 Madison St., Indio, CA 92201) With 14 polo fields, this club hosts national and international competitions and holds polo clinics, Nov.–Apr.

Empire Polo Club (760-342-2762; www.empirepoloevents.com; 81-800 Ave. 51, Indio, CA 92201) Private events facility hosting exhibition polo matches and "golf cart polo," played in a cart instead of on a horse: You wield the mallet while a professional polo player drives the cart. Also four new croquet lawns, plus a venue for concerts, balloon festivals, and rodeos. Not open to the public.

Horses in the Sun (760-399-9200; www.hitsshows.com; HITS Desert Horse Park, 85-555 Airport Blvd., Thermal, CA 92274) Full equestrian facility specializing in jumping. Hosts international competitions.

Pegasus Riding Academy (760-772-3057; www.pegasusridingacademy.org; 35-450 Pegasus Court, Palm Desert, CA 92276) Offers horse-riding for handicapped persons.

Family Fun

Don't forget to bring the kids! The Palm Springs region is family friendly, with plenty of water-focused activities to keep kids cool in summer, plus more intellectual pursuits to challenge their imagination.

The **Howl-o-Ween Spooktacular**, at the Living Desert (760-346-5694; www.theliving desert.org; 47-900 Portola Ave., Palm Desert, CA 92260), is an annual event not to be missed. Held over two nights during Halloween; costumed characters greet you and spook you! In 2007 there was even a Halloween maze.

PALM SPRINGS

Knott's Soak City (760-327-0499; www.knotts.com/soakcity/ps; 1500 S. Gene Autry Trail, Palm Springs, CA 92254) Featuring more than 20 water rides, this park guarantees non-stop fun and is *the* place to beat the heat in midsummer. The seven-story Tidal Wave Tower speed slide will have kids whooping for more. Pacific Spin makes the biggest splash as thrill-seekers plunge 200 feet through a tunnel and funnel, culminating in a waterfall splash. Open Mar.–Oct. Admission: $27.95 adults, children 3–11 $16.95.

Palm Springs Power Baseball Club (760-864-6278; www.palmspringspower baseball.com; 1901 E. Baristo Rd., Palm Springs, CA 92262) Created in 2003, this is a collegiate all-star team composed of top college baseball players from around the country. It plays at Palm Springs Stadium.

Palm Springs Skate Park (760-323-8272; 401 S. Pavilion Way, Palm Springs, CA 92264) Considered one of the best skate parks in California, it has 30,000 square feet of night-lit concrete skating surface designed to challenge skateboarders and in-line skaters alike. All the expected elements are there: a flow bowl with vert-wall, plus hips, pyramids, rails, ramps, quarter-pipes, and stairs. Lockers, restrooms, and spectator seating. Helmets, knee pads, and elbow pads are compulsory. Open Mon.–Thurs. 3–8, Fri. 3–10, Sat. 9 AM–10 PM, Sun. 9 AM–8 PM. Admission $5 per nonresident ($10 annually for Palm Springs residents)

PALM SPRINGS VICINITY

Boomers! (760-770-7522; www.boomersparks.com; 67-700 E. Palm Canyon Dr., Cathedral City, CA 92234) From lightning-fast go-karts to go-slow bumper boats, this family-fun center promises a great experience for kids of all ages. It has miniature golf, a rock-climbing wall, video games, and more. "Twelve buck Tuesday and Thursday" offers unlimited rides for $12. Open daily. Admission: $25 half-day, $28 full-day, $18 weekend special.

Children's Discovery Museum (760-321-0602 ext. 103; www.cdmod.org; 71-701 Gerald Ford Dr., Rancho Mirage, CA 92270) More than 50 hands-on exhibits to educate and enthrall everyone from elementary age up. It has more than 8,000 square feet of exhibition space dedicated to a broad range of subjects, from the physical world to principles of physics. A favorite is the "Dig It," an archaeological dig where kids can sift for Cahuilla Indian artifacts. Shaded picnic areas. Open Tues.–Sun. 10–5. Admission $8, children under 2 free.

SOUTHERN DESERT RESORTS

GarganOptics (760-238-4584; www.garganoptics.com; 40-251 Gold Hills St., Indio, CA 92203) This private observatory utilizes a 14-inch Schmidt Cassegrain computer-controlled telescope to show you the wonders of the universe at night. Located in the foothills of Shadow Hills, astronomer William Gargan's fixed observatory accommodates up to eight people. He also has a mobile

GarganOptics' private observatory. GarganOptics

observatory. Viewing lasts 2 to 3 hours. Complimentary shuttles for "An Evening with the Stars." Open Thurs.–Sun. 7:30–10:30 PM, winter. Admission: $150 adult, $75 children.

Palm Desert Skate Park (760-346-0611, ext. 480; Civic Center Park, 43-900 San Pablo Ave., Palm Desert, CA 92260) More than 20,000 square feet of sculpted runs, with beginners and advanced sections. The main skate park includes a bowl, fun-boxes, pyramids, snake-run, square and round rails, stairs, and drop-ins. The beginner's area also includes a pyramid, box, rails, and drop-ins. Helmets, knee pads, and elbow pads are compulsory. Open daily 6–10.

Palm Desert Soccer Park (760-346-0611; 74-735 Hovley La., Palm Desert, CA 92260) A 21-acre park boasting five full-size soccer fields, plus a basketball court and three shuffleboard courts.

Starry Safari Overnight Camping Adventure (760-346-5694; www.thelivingdesert.org; 47-900 Portola Ave., Palm Desert, CA 92260) Grab your backpacks, roll up your sleeping bags, and head to the Living Desert Zoo & Gardens for this after-hours nighttime sleepover for the whole family in four-person tents. You'll listen to a wildlife and animal presentation, take a nighttime guided walk, eat dinner, then listen to tales told around the campfire before coyotes, and perhaps even the Mexican wolves, sing you to sleep. Admission: $120 adults; $90 children 5–12.

Fitness Facilities

PALM SPRINGS

Highland Park (760-323-8271; 480 Tramview Rd., Palm Springs, CA 92262) Public park with a baseball field and basketball courts. The Desert Highland Park Gymnasium provides basketball, volleyball, badminton, and many indoor games. Highland Park is the home of the Desert Highland Unity Center, which provides a weight-lifting area and a community game room. Facility rentals are available. Open until 10 PM.

Palm Springs "Wellness" Park (corner of Via Miraleste and Tachevah Rd.) This beautifully landscaped little park has walkways, a fitness course, park benches, and water fountains.

Swim Center (760-323-8278; Sunrise Plaza, 05 S. Pavilion Way, Palm Springs, CA 92262) An Olympic-size swimming pool with handicapped chairlift. Has an adult lap swim 5:30–8:30 AM plus Mon., Wed., and Fri. 5–6:30 PM, and Sat. and Sun. 9–11 AM. Open for recreational swimming Mon., Wed., and Fri. 11–5, and Tues., Thurs., Sat., and Sun. 11–2:45. Admission: $3.50 adults, $2.50 children 5–12.

PALM SPRINGS VICINITY

Big League Dreams Sports Park (760-324-5600; www.bigleaguedreams.com; 33-700 Date Palm Dr., Cathedral City, CA 92234) Sports complex that replicates Yankee Stadium, Wrigley Field, and Fenway Park in small scale. Also has basketball, soccer fields, sand volleyball, in-line hockey, and batting cages.

SOUTHERN DESERT RESORTS

Cook Street Sports Complex (760-568-9697; Palm Desert High School, 43,555 Cook St.,

Palm Desert, CA 92260) Ten-acre sports complex with three baseball fields and an open turf area. Restrooms.

Freedom Park (760-346-0611; 39-800 Liberty Dr., Palm Desert, CA 92260) Opened in 2007 after five years in the making, this magnificent facility has 26 acres jam-packed with sports fields, courts, and playgrounds, including a skateboard minipark. No matter how hot outside, kids can enjoy the misting feature built *into* the main play structure.

Golf

There is no more quintessential image of the Palm Springs region than an emerald greensward studded by palms and framed by boulder-strewn mountains gloriously snowcapped in winter. The Coachella Valley has earned the distinction of "Golf Capital of the World" and boasts about 120 individual golf courses, alongside practice ranges and putting greens sporting the same kind of military crew cuts popular when Frank Sinatra was crooning the clubs. No surprise then that about 40 percent of visitors to the desert communities play golf.

The first golf course in the valley was laid out in 1928 by cattle baron Prescott Stevens for his El Mirador Hotel, between Tachevah and Vista Chino, in Palm Springs (the Depression sealed the fate of both hotel and golf course). The post–World War II golf boom was launched in 1951, when the western-style Thunderbird Ranch, which featured ranch homes along riding trails, converted to golf. The boom has never receded. Every year sees at least one new course open in the Palm Springs region, which hosts many key golf championships on the PGA circuit. Book your accommodations early for the Skins Game (November), Bob Hope Chrysler Classic (January), Frank Sinatra Celebrity Invitational Golf Tournament (February), or Kraft Nabisco Championship PGA Golf Tournament (March). See the Seasonal Events section, in the "Culture" chapter, for details.

About one-quarter of courses are associated with premier resort hotels—reason enough to book into the likes of the Westin Mission Hills Resort or Hyatt Grand Champions Resort. Although many courses are for members only, some private clubs allow members of other clubs to enjoy the benefits of their own members. And there are plenty of public courses. The list below includes the pick of the litter.

Greens Fee Price Code
Inexpensive: Under $50
Moderate: $50 to $100
Expensive: Over $100

PALM SPRINGS

Indian Canyons Golf Resort (760-327-6550; www.indiancanyonsgolf.com; 1097 E Murray Dr., Palm Springs, CA 92264) 18 holes, par 73; designed by Casey O'Callahan; public course; pro lessons; clubhouse; shop. The course has spectacular mountain vistas, plus four lakes and almost 1,000

Indian Canyons Golf Resort.

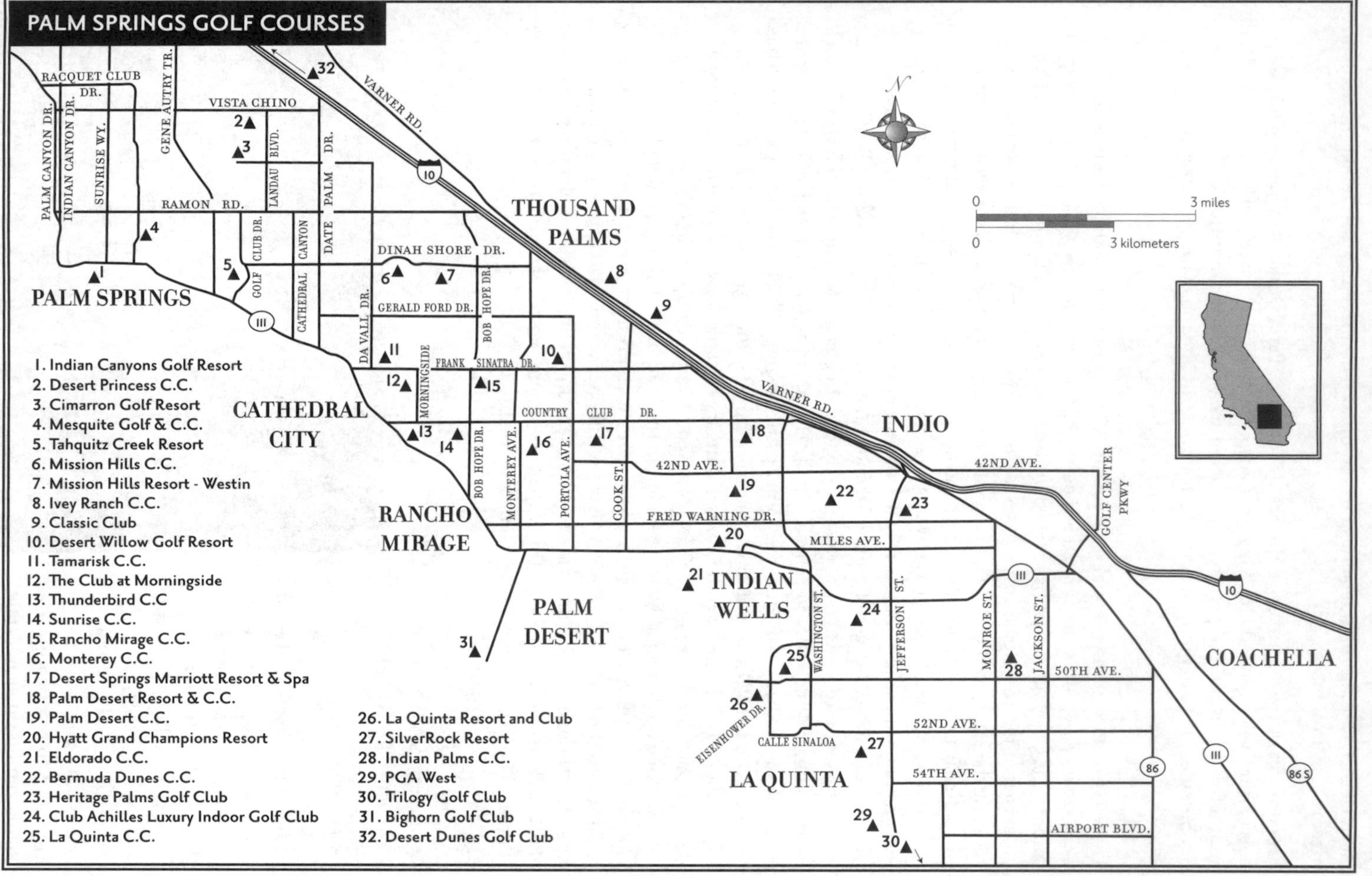
PALM SPRINGS GOLF COURSES
1. Indian Canyons Golf Resort
2. Desert Princess C.C.
3. Cimarron Golf Resort
4. Mesquite Golf & C.C.
5. Tahquitz Creek Resort
6. Mission Hills C.C.
7. Mission Hills Resort - Westin
8. Ivey Ranch C.C.
9. Classic Club
10. Desert Willow Golf Resort
11. Tamarisk C.C.
12. The Club at Morningside
13. Thunderbird C.C
14. Sunrise C.C.
15. Rancho Mirage C.C.
16. Monterey C.C.
17. Desert Springs Marriott Resort & Spa
18. Palm Desert Resort & C.C.
19. Palm Desert C.C.
20. Hyatt Grand Champions Resort
21. Eldorado C.C.
22. Bermuda Dunes C.C.
23. Heritage Palms Golf Club
24. Club Achilles Luxury Indoor Golf Club
25. La Quinta C.C.
26. La Quinta Resort and Club
27. SilverRock Resort
28. Indian Palms C.C.
29. PGA West
30. Trilogy Golf Club
31. Bighorn Golf Club
32. Desert Dunes Golf Club
PALM SPRINGS
CATHEDRAL CITY
RANCHO MIRAGE
THOUSAND PALMS
PALM DESERT
INDIAN WELLS
INDIO
LA QUINTA
COACHELLA
RACQUET CLUB DR.
PALM CANYON DR.
INDIAN CANYON DR.
SUNRISE WY.
GENE AUTRY TR.
VISTA CHINO
RAMON RD.
LANDAU BLVD.
GOLF CLUB DR.
CATHEDRAL CANYON
DATE PALM DR.
DINAH SHORE DR.
GERALD FORD DR.
DA VALL DR.
BOB HOPE DR.
MORNINGSIDE
FRANK SINATRA DR.
COUNTRY CLUB DR.
MONTEREY AVE.
PORTOLA AVE.
COOK ST.
42ND AVE.
FRED WARNING DR.
MILES AVE.
WASHINGTON ST.
JEFFERSON ST.
MONROE ST.
JACKSON ST.
GOLF CENTER PKWY
VARNER RD.
EISENHOWER DR.
CALLE SINALOA
50TH AVE.
52ND AVE.
54TH AVE.
AIRPORT BLVD.
10
111
86
86S
N
0
3 miles
0
3 kilometers

palms. Price: Inexpensive to Moderate.

Mesquite Golf & Country Club (760-323-9377; 2700 E. Mesquite Ave., Palm Springs, CA 92264) 18 holes, par 72; public course once favored by Bob Hope and pals. Price: Moderate.

Tahquitz Creek Resort (760-328-1005; www.tahquitzcreek.com; 1885 Golf Club Dr., Palm Springs, CA 92264) Two 18-hole courses, par 71 and 72; public course; the Legend Course was recently redesigned by Arnold Palmer; the Resort Course is a Ted Robinson links design; pro lessons; putting green; driving range; pro shop. Price: Inexpensive to Moderate.

PALM SPRINGS VICINITY

Cimarron Golf Resort (760-770-6060; www.cimarrongolf.com; 67-603 30th Ave., Cathedral City, CA 92234) Two 18-hole courses, par 56 and 71; public course; pro shop; restaurant. Price: Inexpensive to Expensive.

Desert Dunes Golf Club (760-25-5366; www.desertdunesgolf.com; 19-300 Palm Dr., Desert Hot Springs, CA 92240) 18 holes, par 72; this Robert Trent Jones Jr. course, reminiscent of Ballybunion, in Ireland, has tremendous mountain views; public course; driving range; putting green; clubhouse. Price: Moderate.

Desert Princess Country Club (760-32-2280; www.desertprincesscc.com; 28-555 Landau Blvd., Cathedral City, CA 92234) Three 18-hole courses, par 72; public course; driving range; clubhouse; pro shop. Price: Inexpensive to Expensive.

Mission Hills Country Club (760-324-9400; www.missionhills.com; 34-600 Mission Hills Dr., Rancho Mirage, CA 92270) Three 18-hole courses, all par 72; private course; the private Dinah Shore Tournament Course is site of the Kraft Nabisco Classic; free golf clinics; pro shop. Price: Expensive.

Mission Hills Resort—Westin (760-770-9496; www.starwoodhotels.com; 70-705 Ramon Rd., Rancho Mirage, CA 82270) Two 18-hole courses, both par 72; the Dye Course features very rolling fairways, and the Player Signature Course has 20 acres of lakes, including four waterfalls; driving range; pro shop and lessons. Price: Moderate to Expensive.

Rancho Mirage Country Club (760-324-4711; www.ranchomiragegolf.com; 38-500 Bob Hope Dr., Rancho Mirage, CA 92270) 18 holes, par 70; public course; clubhouse; shop. Price: Inexpensive to Moderate.

Sunrise Country Club (760-328-6549; www.sunrisecountryclub.com; 71-601 Country Club Dr., Rancho Mirage, CA 92270) 18 holes, par 64; private course designed by Ted Robinson. Price: Moderate.

Tamarisk Country Club (760-328-2141; www.tamariskcountryclub.com; 70-240 Frank Sinatra Dr., Rancho Mirage, CA 92270) 18 holes, par 72; private course closed in summer; one of the original courses in the area, associated with many celebrities; clubhouse; restaurant; shop. Price: Expensive.

Thunderbird Country Club (760-328-2161; www.thunderbirdcc.org; 70-612 Hwy. 111, Rancho Mirage, CA 92270) 18 holes, par 72; private course; original site of the Bob Hope Chrysler Classic. Price: Expensive.

Eighteenth hole at the Classic Club, Bob Hope Chrysler Classic.

Southern Desert Resorts

Bermuda Dunes Country Club (76-345-2771; www.bermudadunescc.org; 42-360 Adams, Bermuda Dunes, CA 92203) Three 18-hole courses, all par 72; private course for members and guests only. The courses are known for their huge dunes. Shop; clubhouse. Price: Expensive.

Bighorn Golf Club (760-341-4653; www.bighorngolf.com; 255 Palowet Dr., Palm Desert, CA 92260) Two 18-hole courses designed by Tom Fazio, both par 72; private courses for members and guests. The championship Mountain course is high above the desert floor. Golf lessons; shop; restaurant. Price: Expensive.

Classic Club (760-601-3600; www.classicclubgolf.com; 75-200 Classic Club Blvd., Palm Desert, CA 92211) Spectacular Arnold Palmer–designed course; host for the prestigious Bob Hope Chrysler Classic. Rolling terrain features 30 acres of lakes and water hazards framed by pine, olive, and pepperwood trees—and not a palm tree in sight! The 63,000-square-foot clubhouse hosts Rattlesnake restaurant (see the Restaurant chapter for details) and first-class amenities. Price: Expensive.

Club Achilles Luxury Indoor Golf Club (760-564-9112; www.clubachilles.com; 79-450 Hwy. 111, La Quinta, CA 92253) Part country club, part exercise facility, and part sports bar, this club is *entirely indoors!* It has three practice ranges with instant data feedback, plus golf simulators for a round of virtual golf at over 50 world-renowned courses.

The Club at Morningside (760-324-1234; 39-033 Morningside Dr., Rancho Mirage, CA 92270) 18 holes, par 72; private course; Jack Nicklaus–designed links-type course with huge fairway bunkers. Price: Expensive.

Desert Springs Marriott Resort & Spa (760-341-2211; www.desertspringsresort.com; 74-855 Country Club Dr., Palm Desert, CA 92260) Two 18-hole championship courses; each par 72; designed by Ted Robinson; public course; golf academy and pro lessons; restaurants; shop. The gently rolling Palms has water plays on 10 holes. Price: Moderate to Expensive.

Desert Willow Golf Resort (760-346-7060; www.desertwillow.com; 38-995 Desert Willow Dr., Palm Desert, CA 92260) Two 18-hole courses; chipping and putting greens; pro shop; golf academy and children's classes. The beautiful clubhouse offers stunning mountain vistas.

Eldorado Country Club (760-346-8081; www.eldoradocc.org; 46-000 Fairway Dr., Indian Wells, CA 92210) 18 holes, par 72; private course redesigned in 2003 by Tom Fazio; sponsored guests permitted three days a week. Price: Expensive.

Heritage Palms Golf Club (760-772-7334; www.heritagepalms.org; 44-291 Heritage Palms Dr., Indio, CA 92201) 18 holes, par 72; public course; PGA-certified pro staff. Price: Moderate.

Hyatt Grand Champions Resort (760-341-1000; 1-800-233-1234; http://grandchampions.hyatt.com; 44-600 Indian Wells Lane, Indian Wells, CA 92210) Two 18-hole championship courses; each par 72; designed by Ted Robinson; public courses. Each finishes with a tough dogleg hole. The East layout features waterfalls and a par-3 island hole. The shorter West layout, with multilevel greens, also has a par-4 island green.

Indian Palms Country Club (760-47-2326; www.indianpalms.com; 48-630 Monroe Ave., Indio, CA 92201) Three 18-hole courses, par 71 and 72; recently renovated public course; pro lessons; clubhouse. Price: Moderate.

Ivey Ranch Country Club (760-343-2013; 35-270 San Rock Rd., Thousand Palms, CA 92276) Nine holes, par 70; public course. Price: Inexpensive to Moderate.

La Quinta Country Club (760-564-4151; 77-750 50th Ave., La Quinta, CA 92253) 18 holes, par 72; private course for members and guests only; strategically bunkered with two lakes; hosts the Bob Hope Chrysler Classic; clubhouse. Price: Moderate to Expensive.

La Quinta Resort and Club (760-564-4111; www.laquintaresort.com; 50-200 Ave. Vista Bonita, La Quinta, CA 92253) Two Pete Dye–designed 18-hole courses, both par 72; the private Dunes Course is a difficult links-type play; the public Mountain Course has a spectacular mountainside setting; associated with the world-famous deluxe resort; shop; restaurant. Price: Expensive.

Monterey Country Club (760-568-9311; www.montereycc.com; 41-500 Monterey Ave., Palm Desert, CA 92260) Three 18-hole courses, par 71; private course for members and guests; restaurant. Price: Expensive.

Palm Desert Country Club (760-345-2525; www.theresorter.com; 77-200 California Dr., Palm Desert, CA 92211) 18 holes, par 72; older public course transformed by Cary Bickler in 2006. Tennis courts; clubhouse. Price: Inexpensive to Moderate.

Palm Desert Resort & Country Club (760-772-3880; www.cc-rr.com; 77-333 Country Club Dr., Palm Desert, CA 92211) 18 holes, par 72; public course. Price: Inexpensive to Moderate.

PGA West (760-564-7971; www.pgawest.com; 55-900 PGA Blvd., La Quinta, CA 92253) Six courses, three public and three for private play, all par 72; driving range; pros; shop; clubhouse; lessons; restaurant. The Pete Dye–designed TPC Stadium course is considered one of the U.S.'s most challenging courses and boasts a Scottish links layout that makes

Teeing off at PGA West.

good use of the dunes, as does the Greg Norman course. The Jack Nicklaus course has seven holes with water play. The Arnold Palmer (a host for the Bob Hope Chrysler Classic), Tom Weiskopf, and Jack Nicklaus private courses are for members only. Pro lessons; shop; restaurant. Price: Moderate to Expensive.

SilverRock Resort (760-777-8884; www.silverrock.org; 7979 Ahmanson La., La Quinta, CA 92253) 18 holes, par 72; pubic Arnold Palmer–designed course opened in 2005; golf clinics; shop; restaurant. Price: Moderate to Expensive.

Trilogy Golf Club (760-771-0707; www.trilogygolfclub.com; 60-151 Trilogy Pkwy., La Quinta, CA 92253) 18-hole championship course, par 72; hosted the 2002–2005 Skins Games; restaurant. Price: Moderate to Expensive.

Hiking

Brimming with the glories of nature, the desert defies most people's popular impression and is actually a paradise for anyone who appreciates the rugged outdoors. Abundant rains in winter carpet the desert with wildflowers, and snow crowns the towering San Jacinto Mountains. Even in the brutal heat of midsummer, hiking is joyful, as early morning is usually cool and inviting in the palm-lined canyons—laced with miles of trails—that cut deep into the San Jacintos. Several reserves operated by the Agua Caliente Band of Cahuilla Indians invite you to partake of the canyons' beauty.

Remember to always treat the desert with respect. Use sunscreen, wear a shade hat and sunglasses, and carry plenty of water, especially in summer (the rule of thumb is one quart per person per hour). Long sleeves are a good idea, too, to guard against the harsh desert sun. Mountain lions and bobcats are occasionally seen and should be given a wide berth (if attacked by a mountain lion, do *not* turn your back, crouch down, or run; instead, attempt to appear as large as possible and scream, shout, and otherwise appear threatening). Keep a wary eye out for rattlesnakes and for scorpions, which prefer hideaways in crevices and beneath rocks.

If you plan on hiking a one-way trail, you may need to stage a vehicle at the end of the trail for the ride back to pick up your car at your original trailhead.

The **Coachella Valley Hiking Club** (760-345-6234; http://cvhikingclub.net; P.O. Box 10750, Palm Desert, CA 92255) has over 150 hikes a year, with guided hikes for all abilities on Wed., Sat., and Sun. mornings year-round. Out-of-town visitors are welcome to join on hikes, led by knowledgeable guides. Club membership costs $25 per year.

The **Desert Trails Hiking Club** (760-346-3288; www.deserttrailshiking.com; P.O. Box 10401, Palm Desert, CA 92255) promotes hiking in the valley and offers group hikes three to five times weekly. Nonmembers pay $5 per hike.

The **Coachella Valley Trails Alliance** (760-398-4444; www.cvcta.org; 53-990 Enterprise Way, Suite 9, Coachella, CA 92236) works to promote an ambitious valley-wide trails system that will follow the Whitewater Channel and Coachella Canal, connecting Palm Springs to the Salton Sea, with interconnecting trails off into the mountains on either side of the valley.

Big Wheel Tours (760-779-1837; www.bwbtours.com; P.O. Box 4185, Palm Desert, CA 92261) offers guided hikes throughout the region, including to Joshua Tree National Park, the Coachella Valley Preserve, and San Jacinto Mountains atop the Palm Springs Aerial Tramway.

And **Joshua Tree Hike & Fitness** (760-366-7985; www.joshuatreehike.com; P.O. Box 1088, Joshua Tree, CA 92252) has half- and full-day hiking excursions, from easy to challenging.

Palm Springs

BOGERT TRAIL COMPLEX

Murray Hill, Palm Springs

This complex of eight short, interconnected trails forms a spiderweb along the ridges and plateaus around Murray Hill, at the southeast end of Palm Springs. A good starting point is the 1.6-mile-long **Araby Trail**, which begins at the entrance to the Rimcrest/Southridge development (Southridge Rd. and E. Palm Canyon Dr.); the trailhead is signed on the left side of the road, 20 yards off Hwy. 111; you can park here. The trail gains about 600 feet and takes you right past Bob Hope's turtle-shaped house, plus the homes of Steve McQueen and William Holden. Hence the trail's nickname: "Trail to the Stars." At the top, where you have spectacular views over Palm Springs and the San Jacintos, it links with the Berns, Garstin, Goat, and Henderson trails.

The **Garstin Trail** (S. Barona Rd., off E. Bogert Trail, between Arroyo Seco and Ave. Sevilla) is a moderate to strenuous 2-mile hike that gains about 800 feet as it winds up Smoke Tree Mountain in a series of switchbacks. At the top you're rewarded with fabulous views of Cathedral City and the eastern Coachella Valley; the summit is also a junction for the Berns, Eagle Canyon, Shannon, and Wild Horse trails.

The easy mile-long **Berns Trail** winds over the Smoke Tree Mountain and intersects the Araby Trail. The strenuous, 3.5-mile-long **Wild Horse Trail** climbs to the top of Murray Hill (2,210 feet), the highest peak in the immediate area, offering a spectacular 360-degree view of the Coachella Valley and Little San Bernardino Mountains. The moderate, 7-mile-long **Shannon Trail** begins at the south end of Araby Drive (off Hwy. 111) and gains 1,000 feet to link with the Araby and Garstin trails.

The **Goat Trail**, popular with mountain bikers, begins at the east end of the Von's Rimrock Shopping Center (4771 E. Palm Canyon Dr. at Palm Hills Dr.). It links to the Araby Trail.

The **Alexander Trail** begins at the end of E. Bogert Trail. An easy 1.5-mile hike hugs the base of Murray Hill and the Santa Rosa Mountains.

INDIAN CANYONS

760-325-3400
www.indiancanyons.com
S. Palm Canyon Dr.; 3 miles S. of E. Palm Canyon Dr., Palm Springs

Hikers in Palm Canyon.

Open: Daily 8–5, Oct.–July; Fri.–Sun. only, July–Sept.
Admission: $8 adults, $6 children; $10 with horses
Incising the rugged slopes of the San Jacinto Mountains, these three canyons are nirvana to hikers and equestrians, with 30 miles of trails plus picnic sites. Fed by natural springs, stands of desert fan palms crowd the canyon floors, providing sheltering oases for rabbit and coveys of quail. Roadrunners scurry across the trails. Lizards sun themselves on granite boulders. Agua Caliente Indians once lived in the canyons, now found on the National Register of Historic Places. Ancient petroglyphs and mortar holes where acorns and other seeds were ground can be seen while hiking Andreas Canyon, which has an easy loop trail, a longer, more arduous trail to an abandoned mine, and a short trail connecting with Murray Canyon. Bighorn sheep, bobcat, and mule deer are often spied in Murray Canyon, with its pools succoring cottonwoods, sycamores, and willows. Neighboring Palm Canyon is luxuriantly adorned with the largest palm grove in the Americas, plus sparkling cascades and Indian petroglyphs. After about a mile, the trail rises above the canyon and continues for 14 miles, offering fabulous landscapes down over the valley and across the cactus-strewn mountains: Ranger-led interpretive hikes are offered. No dogs allowed.

TAHQUITZ CANYON

760-416-7044
www.tahquitzcanyon.com
500 W. Mesquite Dr., Palm Springs, CA 92262
Open: Daily 7:30–5, Oct.–July; Fri.–Sun. only, July–Sept.
Admission: $12.50 adults, $6 children
This superstition-filled canyon (pronounced *Tah-kwits*) was recently restored after years of abuse by graffiti-loving vandals. It features a 2-mile, palm-lined loop trail ascending 350 feet in elevation to the spectacular 60-foot Tahquitz Falls, with a swimming hole where Jane Wyatt and Ronald Colman famously frolicked in Frank Capra's 1937 movie version of *Lost Horizon*. The serene canyon is sacred to the Agua Caliente Band of Cahuilla Indians, who oversee visitation. Although you're free to hike alone, it's well worth joining a ranger-led interpretive hiking tour from the visitor center, which shows videos. Steep steps lead to caves—the home, according to Indian legend, of the malevolent spirit Tahquit, who was banished to the canyon and who lures unsuspecting humans to their doom and steals their souls. Rocks can be slippery, and flash floods are a potential danger in winter. Guided hikes are offered four times daily.

MUSEUM TRAIL

101 Museum Dr., Palm Springs, CA 92262
Step out of the museum and step onto this 1.5-mile-long interpretative nature trail that is signed at the museum's north parking lot and ascends the mauve-colored mountain behind the museum. The early section is a steep switchback. The views over the city stagger as you gain almost a thousand feet to a picnic area with benches at 1,400 feet elevation. Here, the trail intersects three other trails:

North Lykken Trail: This moderate 1.5-mile-long trail leads north to Chino Canyon (named for former Indian Shaman Pedro Chino, who lived here) and descends to 780 feet. Superb views of the Chino Canyon alluvial fan.

South Lykken Trail: A relatively easy to moderate trail that connects south to the west end of Ramon Road and offers great views of Palm Springs. It continues south from the Ramon Road trailhead and connects to the Tahquitz Canyon visitor center, at the end of Mesquite Road. A third section leads 2 miles from the Mesquite Road trailhead to the southern trailhead at Canyon Heights Road, off South Palm Canyon Road. You'll get a superb view into Tahquitz Canyon.

Skyline Trail: Not for the faint of heart, this extremely challenging trail—called the "Cactus to Clouds Hike"—leads 10 miles to the top of the Palm Springs Tramway.

Hikers on the Museum Trail.

A Spectacular Ride!

Imagine traveling from Mexico to Alaska in 10 minutes. No joke! You can take the journey metaphorically aboard the Palm Springs Aerial Tramway (760-325-1449 or 1-888-515-8726; www.pstramway.com; 1 Tramway Rd., Palm Springs, CA 92262), which ascends through four life zones—equivalent to a road trip from the Sonoran Desert to Alaska's Transitional Zone.

The road from the Tramway Oasis Gas Station winds up through the scree of the Chino Canyon alluvial fan to the Valley Station, at an elevation of 2,643 feet. From here, the second-steepest ascending tram in the world whisks visitors 2.5 miles to the mountaintop station at 8,516 feet elevation, where the air is 30 or 40 degrees cooler than it is in the desert beneath.

The tram was dubbed "Crocker's Folly" when it was conceived by electrical engineer Francis Crocker in the 1930s. During a long, hot drive, Crocker looked up at the snowcapped summit of Mount San Jacinto and dreamed of how wonderful it must be to be atop the mountain. After years of intense lobbying by Crocker, work on the tram was finally initiated in 1950, funded by private bonds. Completed in 1963 and inaugurated on September 14, the elaborate system of towers, cables, and hanging cars has since safely transported more than 12 million visitors. The current tramcars—the world's largest rotating tramcars, with a capacity for 80 passengers each—were installed in 2000. Each of the two carriages is affixed to a 13,100-foot-long cable pulled by a wheel powered by a 1,100-horsepower motor. Counterweights in excess of 120 tons each keep the cables taut as the cars travel between towers.

Traveling at 21 mph, in 10 minutes you pass from desert to cool alpine terrain. Brace yourself for a stomach-lifting rise-and-dip sway as the carriages pass over the five intermediate towers clinging to the craggy mountainside, generating squeals of delight and trepidation. The trams rotate 360 degrees as they ascend and descend. The cars are actually stationary. It's the floors that rotate, affording passengers a smooth 360-degree view as they ascend the mountain while listening to a recorded narration. Killer views over the Coachella Valley await you from the Mountain Station, which has a natural history museum and fine-dining restaurant.

You are now in Mount San Jacinto State Park. Bring your hiking gear!

The Palm Springs Aerial Tramway. Palm Springs Aerial Tramway

MOUNT SAN JACINTO STATE PARK

951-659-2607
www.parks.ca.gov/?page_id=636
25-905 Hwy. 243, Idyllwild, CA 92549
This pristine, 14,000-acre alpine wilderness (part of the Santa Rosa and San Jacinto Mountains National Monument; see below) is accessed by the Palm Springs Aerial Tramway and enshrines the second-highest mountain range in California, topped by Mount San Jacinto (10,834 feet). The bare granite peak, subalpine forests, and alpine meadows are a delight for hikers. It has 54 miles of hiking trails, most within a designated wilderness area where access (and camping) is by permit only. Free day-use permits are issued at the Long Valley Ranger Station, a short walk from the mountaintop tram station. Application for overnight permits must be made in person or in writing at least 10 days in advance (P.O. Box 308, Idyllwild, CA 92549). During winter, cross-country skis and snowshoes can be rented (snow conditions permitting), and kids can rent inner tubes for sliding. Interpretive specialist Tracy Albrecht leads "In the Woods: Campfire Programs" at Round Valley Campground. Albrecht offer tips on animal tracking, birdcall identification, and other outdoors lore. Admission: Free.

Long Valley has picnic tables, water, flush toilets, and some easy trails that require no permits. Tamarack Valley and Round Valley offer more serious trails and require permits for overnight camping:

Desert View Trail: For fabulous vistas down over Palm Springs and the Coachella Valley as far as the Salton Sea, take this moderate 1.5-mile (2 km) loop trail that leads to a number of scenic overlooks.

Long Valley Discovery Trail: This level and easy 0.75-mile-long loop features educational signs and provides an excellent introduction to the park's plants and animals.

Round Valley: This 2.5-mile-long trail leads to picturesque Round Valley; although fairly level, it has some short, moderately strenuous climbs.

San Jacinto Peak Trail: This strenuous 6-mile (each way) hike gains about 2,600 feet and leads to the second-highest point in Southern California, from where on clear days you can see as far as Catalina Island or even Las Vegas aglow at night.

Pacific Crest Trail: This 2,650-mile-long trail along the entire spine of the western U.S. from Mexico to Canada stretches along the backbone of the San Jacinto Mountains. The 16-mile section within the Santa Rosa and San Jacinto Mountains National Monument has some very steep switchbacks and can be accessed from the trailhead, signed on Falls Creek Road, off Hwy. 111 near the junction with I-10 (turn left off Hwy. 111 onto Snow Creek Rd.). You can also join the trail from Hwy. 74, 20 miles south of Hwy. 111, in Palm Desert. The trailhead is signed and proceeds both north and south of the roadside parking lot. This section of trail lies within the San Bernardino National Forest, and an adventure pass is required: You can buy a permit at the Santa Rosa and San Jacinto Mountains National Monument Visitor Center (760-862-9984; 51-500 Hwy. 74, Palm Desert, CA 92260; $5 day pass, $30 season pass).

PALM SPRINGS VICINITY

BUMP AND GRIND TRAIL

Magnesia Falls Dr., Rancho Mirage
Popular with bikers, joggers, and hikers alike, this 4-mile round-trip jaunt is good for a

leisurely stroll or a morning workout with the bonus of fine views of the central valley. It's actually an old dirt road up the side of Shadow Mountain, rather than a wilderness trail, and is also known by a variety of names: Patton Trail, Desert Mirage Trail, and the ever-popular Dog Poop Trail (for the plastic bags and dog-poop receptacle at the trailhead). It gains 800 feet and links with Desert Drive Trail, which begins on Desert Drive, one block south of Magnesia Falls Drive. This moderately strenuous hike gains about 1,000 feet.

COACHELLA VALLEY PRESERVE

760-343-2733 or 343-4031
www.coachellavalleypreserve.org
Thousand Palm Canyons Rd., north of I-10 in Thousand Palms
Open: Daily 8–5 Sept.–June, 6–10 July–Aug.; visitor center 8–noon Sept., May, and June, 8–4 Oct.–Apr., closed July and Aug.
Admission: Free

This vast preserve—the last undisturbed watershed in the valley—was created in 1984 to protect 20,000 acres of pristine desert that forms a habitat for the endemic, endangered dune-dwelling Coachella Valley fringe-toed lizard. The preserve occupies a zone of the Indio Hills between the Banning and San Andreas faults. It's superb for nature hikes. Some 20 miles of hiking trails penetrate silent canyons, towering sand dunes, and picturesque palm grove oases. Quail, roadrunners, and various lizards (including the fringe-toed lizard, which burrows into sand with its shovel-shaped nose) are among the critters that you might, with luck, spot amid the weirdly beautiful landscape; coyotes, bobcats, gray fox, and rattlesnakes are nocturnal hunters, rarely seen by day. Other critically listed desert species that also live here include the burrowing owl and its prey, the Palm Springs pocket mouse and Palm Springs ground squirrel.

The preserve has a rustic visitor center in a 1930s homestead hut beneath the shade of the Thousands Palms natural palm grove, where mineral springs gurgle forth. Guided hikes and wildlife-spotting trips are offered. The popular mile-long McCallum Trail begins at the visitor center and winds through the Thousand Palms Oasis, with boardwalks to cross the seeping springs; you'll then skirt a marsh as you follow a sandy arroyo to the McCallum Grove. The minnowlike desert pupfish thrive in the ponds and creeks here, alongside bullfrogs. Beyond the grove rise spectacular dunes. More rigorous trails lead to the Indian Palms (1 mile each way), Hidden Palms (2.5 miles), and Horseshoe Palms and Pushawalla Palms (3 miles). The Willis Palms are accessed off Thousand Palms Road.

Trailhead at Coachella Valley Preserve.

The preserve is part of the triptych Coachella Valley Preserve System, comprising three separate units protecting three disparate dune ecosystems. The Coachella Preserve is by far the largest. The other two are the off-limits **Whitewater Valley Floodplains Preserve**, northwest of Palm Springs, and the **Willow Hole–Edom Hill Preserve**, between the other two preserves. The 2,469-acre Willow Hole–Edom Hill Preserve is a unique blow-sand preserve. The westerly, Willow Hill section of the reserve is not open to the public but is accessible with proper permits for scientific research. You can, however, hike to the summit of Edom Hill, the 1,565-feet-high sand dune that dominates the landscape north of the I-10 freeway in Cathedral City. The vast sand dune area is a popular spot for motorcyclists and all-terrain-vehicle enthusiasts. Some 177 acres are protected. You can hike to the top from Varner Road (exit I-10 at Ramon Road; turn east toward Thousand Palms, then north on Varner Road for about 6 miles). The half-hike rises about 1,000 feet—a real challenge in soft sand! Take plenty of water. A crop of antennae pins its sandy peak, which can be reached by vehicle via Edom Hill Road (off Varner Road). You'll have a fantastic view of the valley from the top.

Management of the preserve is a cooperative effort by the U.S. Bureau of Land Management, the California Department of Fish and Game, California State Parks, Center for Natural Lands Management, and U.S. Fish and Wildlife Service, which together own the lands that make up the preserve.

SOUTHERN DESERT RESORTS

COVE OASIS TRAILHEAD

760-777-7090
Calle Tecate between Ave. Ramirez and Ave. Madero, La Quinta
A stupendous trailhead setting at the top (southernmost) of La Quinta Cove, this 114-acre open desert area is a vast alluvial fan that grants access to various trails. It has parking.

The strenuous 4.5-mile-long **Bear Creek Canyon Trail** gains 2,300 feet and offers jaw-dropping views. To reach the trailhead, from the corner of Calle Tecate and Ave. Madero walk south along the arroyo (wash). The trail leads through a narrow canyon to the signed Bear Creek Ridge Trail, by a shady paloverde tree. It's uphill from here, with the panoramic views growing ever more splendid. Midway, the Salton Sea comes into view and the entire Coachella Valley is laid out at your feet. Amazingly, after 4 miles, you come to a lush palm oasis tucked into the head of the canyon. Flourishing in their improbable habitat, these California fan palms brighten the bleakness of the craggy canyons.

For the **Boo Hoff Trail**, head due south from Ave. Ramirez. This trail heads along the wash deep into the Santa Rosas via Martinez Mountain. Soon you're snaking sharply uphill until, after about 3 miles, the trail divides, with the Guadelupe Trail heading west and the Boo Hoff heading east. The latter offers stunning views of the Salton Sea and connects with the Morrow Trail (see Lake Cahuilla Trails, below) and with **Lost Canyon Trail**, a mile-long side trail that leads to a waterfall before descending east out of the Santa Rosas onto a jeep track (2 miles) that leads to the Quarry Country Club and Lake Cahuilla. (The difficult **Guadalupe Trail** leads up the Guadalupe Canyon and Devil's Canyon to link with the **Cactus Springs Trail**, which delivers you after 4 miles at the Sugarloaf Café, on Hwy. 74.)

EISENHOWER PEAK LOOP TRAIL

760-346-5694
www.livingdesert.org
The Living Desert, 47-900 Portola Ave., Palm Desert, CA 92260
This 6-mile-long trail begins near the bighorn-sheep exhibit at the east end of the Living

Desert. After about 1.5 miles of flat, you enter a ravine that requires some scrambling over boulders. Beyond, you begin to ascend Eisenhower Peak, ending at a plateau with a picnic bench and shade awning and great views. Interpretive panels identify desert flora and fauna. (Although it is discouraged by the Living Desert, you can continue to the summit—a steep, demanding scramble rewarded by awesome vistas.) The return loop passes a plaque commemorating the first planting of date palms in the valley; from this point, alas, the view below is of luxury homes, the old date groves having long since been torn up.

LAKE CAHUILLA TRAILS

760-564-4712 or 1-800-234-7175
58-075 Jefferson St., La Quinta, CA 92253
At the south end of La Quinta, hard up against the Santa Rosa Mountains, this 710-acre park centers on Lake Cahuilla. The **Morrow Trail** (aka Lake Cahuilla to La Quinta Cove Connector Trail) snakes up into the mountains along canyons dotted with lacy green desert broom and the scarlet flowers of chuparosa. Higher up, ocotillo stud the slopes like undersea coral in a waterless ocean. The trail links with the Boo Hoff Trail (see Cove Oasis Trailhead, above).

MECCA HILLS WILDERNESS

Box Canyon Rd., Mecca
Admission: Free
The Mecca Hills, in the southern Coachella Valley east of Mecca (about 40 miles southeast of Palm Springs), are undeniably beautiful badlands. Although this federal wilderness, administered by the Bureau of Land Management (760-251-4800; P.O. Box 1260, Palm Springs, CA 92258), comprises 26,036 acres, the main draw is the colorful and geologically dramatic formations associated with labyrinthine canyons. Here, layers of sedimentary rock up to 600 million years old have been upended, squashed, doubled-up, and overturned by the tectonic forces associated with the San Andreas fault. Mother Nature has then eroded the layers into surreal formations (sometimes called the "Mud Hills") tinted by mineral deposits into a rainbow of colors.

The sandy washes are sprinkled with ironwood, paloverde, and tamarisk. In spring the canyons explode in Monet colors, including the lilacs of Mecca aster, a rare bloom resembling a daisy and endemic to the Indio Hills and Mecca Hills. Look for it in the fluvial washes and along the lower slopes. Higher up, ocotillo studs the plateaus and mesas. Desert tortoise, mountain lion, jackrabbit, and the spotted bat are local denizens.

Box Canyon Road (Hwy. 195) snakes up through the hills, linking Mecca to I-10. The road separates the wilderness into two units: Painted Canyon to the west and Hidden Spring Canyon to the east.

Painted Canyon features the most astonishing formations and colors and offers an easy to moderate 5-mile hike (wear ankle-length boots, rather than sneakers, to deal with the soft sand) that begins at the end of unsurfaced Painted Canyon Road (four-wheel-drive recommended). Choose either the **Little Painted Canyon Trail**, which begins on the west of the parking area, or the **Big Painted Canyon Trail**, which leads from the east side and eventually connects with the former trail. The Big Painted trail also offers a fabulous diversion via mile-long **Ladder Canyon**, a slot canyon (partially hidden by rock slides) that is signed about 400 yards along the Big Painted Trail and leads to the junction of the two larger trails. Squeezing into the narrow canyon, you'll find several ladders as hikers' aids to navigate abrupt "dry falls" that can become torrential, muddy waterfalls during flash floods.

Hidden Spring Canyon is signed on the east side of Box Canyon Road. Its draws include marvelous views down over the Salton Sea, the Sheep Hole Oasis (named for the bighorn sheep that sometimes come here to drink), and two rock grotto systems (bring a flashlight).

Each Easter Sunday an estimated 4,000 people (mostly Hispanic families) fill the canyons to celebrate spring with barbecues, volleyball, and music and dancing. To control the invasion, in 2007 the BLM was preparing a management plan to regulate use of the wilderness, which will be renamed the Meccacopia Special Recreation Management Area.

SANTA ROSA AND SAN JACINTO MOUNTAIN MONUMENT

760-862-9984
www.blm.gov/ca/st/en/fo/palmsprings/santarosa.html
Visitor Center, 51-500 Hwy. 74, Palm Desert, CA 92260
Encompassing 272,000 acres within the Santa Rosa and San Jacinto mountains, this huge park was created in October 2000 and is administered by the Bureau of Land Management (760-251-4800; www.blm.gov; 690 W. Garnet Ave., N. Palm Springs, CA 92258) in conjunction with the U.S. Forest Service, California Department of Fish and Game, the California Department of Parks and Recreation, the Agua Caliente Band of Cahuilla Indians, the Coachella Valley Mountains Conservancy, plus the county, adjacent cities, and private owners. It stretches from Mount San Jacinto State Park (which is *within* the monument) in the north, to the Anza-Borrego Desert State Park in the south.

One- to two-hour guided hikes are offered every Thurs. morning from the visitor center, in Palm Desert. Trips depart at 8:30 AM and follow either the Art Smith, Hopalong

Hiking the Mount San Jacinto National Monument in winter.

Cassidy, or Randall Henderson trails, according to visitors' abilities. **Friends of the Desert Mountains** (www.friendsofpalmspringsmountains.org) also offers moderate to strenuous guided hikes along the Cactus Spring Trail.

One of the easiest options is the **Randall Henderson Trail**, a 3-mile loop that ascends 342 feet, with fine views over the valley; the descent leads through a small canyon. It takes about one hour—more for lazing to watch jackrabbits. The trailhead is alongside Hwy. 74, at the beginning of the driveway to the visitor center; peruse the trail map and information panel before setting out. Free.

The 27-acre park **Cap Homme / Ralph Adams Park** (72-500 Thrush Rd., off Hwy. 74) provides access to the dog-friendly Cahuilla Hills Trail System (dogs are not allowed on BLM land) via the **Hopalong Cassidy Trail**. This moderate, 1.75-mile-long trail links to the strenuous 8-mile **Art Smith Trail**, which has only a 1,200-foot elevation gain but traverses the entire ridgeline of the Santa Rosa Mountains, connecting the Palm Desert portion of the monument to the trails of Palm Canyon, in Palm Springs. Horses and mountain bikes also use the trail, which begins opposite the visitor center and passes through several palm oases; there's parking at the trailhead. No dogs are allowed on the Art Smith Trail (in BLM land) because of the bighorn sheep, which are often sighted on the **Hahn Buena Vista Trail**, reached via the Art Smith Trail or directly from the trailhead off Dunn Road.

The **Cactus Spring Trail** snakes for 11 miles to Agua Alta Spring. Rising to 4,000 feet and undulating through transitional desert and pine forest, this strenuous high-desert trail begins on Pinyon Flats Station Transfer Road (off Hwy. 74, 15.6 miles south of Hwy. 111; parking lot). You must register at the trailhead; this is your permit. The **Sawmill Trail**, popular with mountain bikers, is accessed from the same trailhead via a 5-mile dirt road good for four-wheel-drive, horses, and hikers. This trail is within the San Bernardino National Forest, and an adventure pass is required: You can buy a permit at the Santa Rosa and San Jacinto Mountains National Monument Visitor Center ($5 day pass, $30 season pass).

Preserving the Wildlife

The Coachella Valley was once dominated by nearly 100 square miles of sand dunes; today less than 5 percent remains. Over the past century, urban development has blocked the movement of sand vital to keeping the dunes alive. The **Coachella Valley Multiple Species Habitat Conservation Plan** (CVMSHCP; 760-346-1127; www.cvmshcp.org) protects the remaining dunes plus 240,000 acres of open space and 27 threatened or endangered animal and plant species encompassing virtually every environment within the valley. Approved by all eight Coachella Valley cities, the CVMSHCP provides a regional vision for protecting the valley's natural heritage while also fostering a strong economy. It places development constraints on land essential to the survival of vulnerable species such as the desert tortoise, burrowing owl, and desert pupfish (an endemic fish that can tolerate water temperatures of over 100 degrees Fahrenheit and salinity levels up to three times the level of ocean water). The CVMSHCP area incorporates a system of reserves collectively known as the MSHCP Reserve System.

Another good resource is **Friends of the Desert Mountains** (760-568-9918; www.fotdm.org; 45-480 Portola Ave., Palm Desert, CA 92260).

Rock Climbing

With its spectacular geological formations, the desert is tailor-made for folks who like to live on the edge. **Joshua Tree Climbing School** (760-366-4745; www.joshuatreerock climbing.com; HCR Box 3034, Joshua Tree, CA 92252) offers instruction in Joshua Tree National Park, one of the world's premier spots for rock climbing, centered on Indian Cove.

Vertical Adventures Rock Climbing School (949-854-6250 or 1-800-514-8785; www.vertical-adventures.com; P.O. Box 7548, Newport Beach, CA 92658) also offers classes for beginners to advanced climbers at Joshua Tree.

Children can learn the basics at the **Uprising Rock Climbing Center** (760-320-6630; 1500 S. Gene Autry Trail, Palm Springs, CA 92264), in Knott's Soak City Water Park.

Running

With dozens of recreational parks and miles and miles of trails, runners of all ages and abilities will find something to please in the desert. The spectacular winter climate and crystal-clear air are bonuses. Summer is another thing altogether and requires that you drink copious amounts of water while avoiding the brutal heat of midday.

The nine desert cities all have public running tracks (see Fitness Facilities, this chapter).

The **Klein & Clark Sports Palm Springs Half Marathon** (760-324-7069; www.kleinclarksports.com; 80 Via Del Mercato, Rancho Mirage, CA 92270), in mid-Feb., features a half-marathon and 5k runs, beginning at Ruth Hardy Park. And the **Morrow Institute Women Running Wild 5k Run/Walk** also begins at Ruth Hardy Park, in Mar.

In April, Lake Cahuilla (in La Quinta) is the setting for the **Annual Toyota Desert International and Sprint Triathlon**. Less ambitious joggers can try the **Palm Desert Turkey Trot 5K** (760-564-3501), hosted at El Paseo Gardens each Nov.

The **Palm Springs Tram Road Challenge**, held each Oct., is heralded as one of the toughest road races in the world. Despite being only 3.7 miles, the snaking road rises 2,100 feet and has been drawing elite runners from around the world for more than 20 years.

Palm Springs Front Runners & Walkers (www.psfr.org) is a club for gays and lesbians.

Check with Klein & Clark Sports, or the **Palm Springs Desert Resorts Convention & Visitors Authority** (760-770-9000; 1-800-967-3767; www.giveintothedesert.com; 70-100 Hwy. 111, Rancho Mirage, CA 92270) for schedules.

Ice Skating

Ahhh, those were the days . . . when there was an ice-skating rink at the Palm Springs Mall back in the 1960s and '70s, and another in the venerable link at Palm Desert mall (now Westfield Shopping Plaza), but which closed in 2002. Today the valley has just one rink. The coolest place in the desert is the **Ice Garden** (760-770-7046; 68-307 E. Palm Canyon Dr., Cathedral City, CA 92234), which has public skating, plus hockey. It offers lessons. At press time, owner Gary Steven was considering moving to a bigger facility that would include two regulation-size ice rinks, a rollerskating rink, and an Olympic-size pool.

Skateboarding

Skateboarders can get their highs at the superb **Palm Springs Skate Park** (760-323-8272; 401 S. Pavilion Way, Palm Springs, CA 92264), and at the mediocre **Sgt. Frank Hodge Skate Park** (West Dr., Desert Hot Springs, CA 92240), behind the fire station at 65-958 Pierson Blvd.

Palm Springs Skateboard Park.

Down valley, the **Palm Desert Skate Park** (760-346-0611, ext. 480, Civic Center Park, 43,900 San Pablo Ave., Palm Desert, CA 92260) gives the world-class Palm Springs Skate Park a run for its money. **Freedom Park** (760-346-0611; 39-800 Liberty Dr., Palm Desert, CA 92260) has a mini skateboard park. See the Family Fun section, this chapter, for full details.

The **South Jackson Skate Park** (760-347-4263; 83-089 Hwy. 111, Indio CA 92201), behind Thomas Jefferson Middle School off Jackson and Date streets, has facilities for skateboards and roller blades, as do the **Indio Skate Park** (45-871 Clinton St., Indio, CA 92201), behind the Indio Community Center, and **La Quinta Skate Park** (760-777-7000; Fritz Burns Park, Ave. 52 and Bermudas, La Quinta).

Spas

Palm Springs is the proverbial fountain of youth, with enough spas to keep visitors relaxed and rejuvenated year-round. The area's appeal as a healing destination began about 2,000 years ago when the Cahuilla Indians settled the region and established settlements beside sacred hot mineral springs bubbling up from deep aquifers—the Agua Caliente Band of Indians aren't called "Hot Water" for nothing. Geothermal springs burst forth from the northern slope of the Coachella Valley in a constant stream. As its name suggests, Desert Hot Springs is renowned for its curative thermal mineral waters, and for its green "hydroterra" clay that has soaked in the miraculous waters for aeons (when applied to the skin, it is said to absorb toxins and to help restore the natural tone and balance, leaving skin feeling fresh, smooth, and glowing).

The Palm Springs region's spas offer a virtual around-the-world tour of exotic treatments and healing rituals, with something for everyone—from first-time spa-goers to seasoned connoisseurs. Day spas proliferate along El Paseo, in Palm Desert, with more than 50 spas and beauty salons along its 1.5 miles. You'll also find plenty of luxury at destination resort spas where the healthy and wealthy make themselves look good for the society events and pages.

Couples massage. Palm Springs Desert Resorts Conventions & Visitors Authority

PALM SPRINGS

ESTRELLA SPA

760-320-4117
www.viceroypalmsprings.com
415 S. Belardo Rd., Palm Springs, CA 92262
Open: Mon.–Fri. 8–6, Sat. and Sun. 8–8
Credit Cards: AE, CD, D, DC, MC, V
This spa, furnished graciously in "Hollywood Regency" style, defines the ultimate in luxurious resort spa experiences. Sublime treatments in indoor or outdoor settings range from the men's lemon coffee body scrub to a microderm body peel. Try the Estrella Bamboo Ritual Treatment combining shiatsu massage and full-body treatment that starts with a yuzu mimosa sea algae wash, then a ginger grass bamboo exfoliation, followed by a wild cherry blossom rice milk compress, and the massage using wild lime oil, with a plum blossom silk cream to hydrate and soften the skin. Infused with Zen-like sensations of calm, you're good to go.

THE PALM SPRINGS YACHT CLUB

760-770-5000
www.theparkerpalmsprings.com
4200 E. Palm Canyon Dr., Palm Springs, CA 92264
Open: Daily 8–8
Credit Cards: AE, D, DC, MC, V

Notwithstanding its tongue-in-cheek presentations, the spa at the illustrious Parker hotel is a serious affair, with 16 indoor and two outdoor treatment rooms—decked out in crisp whites and blue—under the watchful and skilled care of "Commodore" Wendy Rahier. Its various skin-care treatments, soaks, scrubs, and wraps include the "Creature from the Beautiful Lagoon"—a seaweed wrap preceded by an exfoliation—plus rubdowns, such as "The Wringer," for masochists who like deep tissue, and the "Voodoo We Do," billed as Thai-inspired stretches to refuel your vim and vigor. Guests are encouraged to converse freely, rather than in hushed whispers.

THE SPA RESORT & CASINO

760-778-1772
www.sparesortcasino.com
100 N. Indian Ave., Palm Springs, CA 92262
Open: Daily 8–7
Credit Cards: AE, DC, D, MC, V
Conveniently located downtown, this popular spa for the masses has two outdoor pools fed by real mineral hot springs. Its wide variety of spa treatment packages includes the signature "Taking of the Waters." Admission: $35 hotel guests, $40 nonguests; admission on weekends solely with purchase of a treatment.

THE SPRING

760-251-6700
www.thespringresortandspa.com
12-699 Reposo Way, Palm Springs, CA 92262
Open: Daily 9–6
Credit Cards: AE, MC, V
There are three sparkling mineral pools at this delightful, understated small resort where you can enjoy a Finnish sauna and treatments from an antioxidant salt scrub to deep tissue massage. Also fasting and cleansing retreats.

THE SPRINGS HOTEL AND SPA

760-325-0900
www.thespringsofps.com
227 N. Indian Canyon Dr., Palm Springs, CA 92262
Open: Daily 9–5
Credit Cards: AE, D, DC, MC, V
Right in the heart of town. For the ultimate in decadence, opt for the mint-chocolate defoliating scrub using dark chocolate, butter, peppermint oil, and salts to buff off dead skin, followed by a white chocolate and mint leaf whip massage and milk chocolate cocoon.

PALM SPRINGS VICINITY

DESERT HOT SPRINGS SPA HOTEL

760-329-6000 or 1-800-808-7727
www.dhsspa.com
10-805 Palm Dr., Desert Hot Springs, CA 92240
Open: 24 hours

Credit Cards: AE, CB, D, DC, MC, V
One of the desert originals, this resort spa features treatment rooms surrounding eight mineral spring pools. Massages, facials, and more are offered, but this place is all about the soaking. Day-use fee $3–7.

EL MOROCCO INN & SPA
760-288-2527
www.elmoroccoinn.com
66-810 E. Fourth St., Desert Hot Springs, CA 92240
Open: 8–5
Credit Cards: D, MC, V
Classic *Casablanca* kitsch. The ultimate experience is the two-hour Moroccan Mystical Ritual, which includes a full-body massage, facial, herbal roll, and a dusting with dry, scented powders, then a second massaging with smooth stones, a salt scrub, and ending with a cocoon wrap. Phew!

SWISS HEALTH RESORT
760-329-6912
www.swisshealthresort.com
66-729 Eighth St., Desert Hot Springs, CA 92240
Open: 8–5
Credit Cards: MC, V
The perfect spot to enjoy a guided desert morning walk followed by massage while being cradled and floating in warm water.

TWO BUNCH PALMS RESORT & SPA
760-329-8791
www.twobunchpalms.com
67-425 Two Bunch Palms Trail, Desert Hot Springs, CA 92240
Open: 8–7
Credit Cards: AE, D, DC, MC, V
Celebrities such as Mel Gibson and Goldie Hawn swear by this Rolls Royce of small spas, where 148-degree Fahrenheit waters splash over a rock waterfall and into a grotto pool. Guests cherish the absolute privacy offered. More than 40 treatments, from the spa's legendary mud treatments to the Roman Tub Rejuvenator (an hour-long massage followed by a candlelit

Soaking in thermal mud at Two Bunch Palms Resort & Spa.
Two Bunch Palms Resort & Spa

lavender Epsom salt bath). Not to be missed: the Grape Seed Integrative, with grape-derivative massage followed by wine tasting and dinner. Day pass $25, plus treatment.

WE CARE HOLISTIC HEALTH CENTER

760-251-2261
www.wecarespa.com
18-000 Long Canyon Rd., Desert Hot Springs, CA 92240
Open: 8–5
Credit Cards: AE, MC, V
Wellness extreme, with deep cleansing and detox treatments featuring colonics and all-natural liquid diets. One-day treatments include a Korean Body Splash—a full-body scrub and table bath. Set in lovely grounds, it has cozy and colorful accommodations.

Southern Desert Resorts

ALL ABOUT MASSAGE

760-346-7949 or 1-888-772-2442
www.allaboutmassage.com
74-125 Hwy. 111, Palm Desert, CA 92260
Open: 9–6
Credit Cards: AE, MC, V
Specializes in serious massage, with more than a dozen styles represented, from shiatsu and deep tissue to the de rigueur Desert River Stone Massage. No wonder it's the official massage provider for tennis professionals during the annual Pacific Life Open.

DESERT SPRINGS JW MARRIOTT RESORT & SPA

760-341-1865 or 1-800-255-0848
www.desertspringsspa.com
74-855 Country Club Dr., Palm Desert, CA 92260
Open: Sun.–Thurs. 8–6, Fri.–Sat. 8–8
Credit Cards: AE, D, DC, MC, V
The largest spa in Southern California, this 38,000-square-foot space is nirvana on earth. Reopened in 2007 after being totally remodeled and expanded in lush coral stone and Brazilian ipe wood, it features an aromatic Turkish hammam (a steam chamber infused with fragrance oils), Finnish sauna, heated outdoor lap pool, computer-controlled desert rain showers, and state-of-the-art fitness center among its facilities. The desert-oriented treatment menu is as complete as can be, from desert stone massages and a dermal quench to healing aloe wrap, date scrub, and a self-seducing thermal lavender plunge. Committed sybarites can opt for a full-day (eight-hour) package featuring a private suite rental, champagne, chocolate truffles, and various treatments. And classes range from restorative yoga to mat pilates.

SPA LA QUINTA

760-777-4800
www.laquintaresort.com
49-499 Eisenhower Dr., La Quinta, CA 92253
Open: 8–7

The spa at Desert Springs JW Marriott Resort

Credit Cards: AE, D, DC, MC, V
This hacienda style spa within a lush courtyard sanctuary at the La Quinta Resort & Club is known for its facials, but it also offers a panoply of divine treatments, from sacred stone therapy and mustard bath to desert sun after-care. We suggest the French Body Polish using Saint-Malo–based exfoliants and ending with a relaxing *effleurage* and therapeutic massage.

THE WELL SPA AT MIRAMONTE RESORT

760-341-2200
www.miramonteresort.com
45-500 Indian Wells La., Indian Wells, CA 92210
Open: Sun.–Thurs. 8–8, Fri.–Sat. 8–9
Credit Cards: AE, D, DC, MC, V
This small hotel-based, Mediterranean-themed spa offers a surprisingly large menu, from a tension-relieving seaweed bath with hydro massage to a unique and sensual body-painting party where you get to paint your body—or your significant other's body—into a work of art using colored mineral muds and clays.

Swimming

When the heat is on, Palm Springs cognoscenti slip into their pools to swim, or at least to sip a martini in watery comfort. The place claims to have an astounding 40,000 swimming pools, more per capita than anywhere else in North America. All the hotels and most RV parks have at least one pool. Most of the big resort hotels have multiple pools.

Notwithstanding, you can also get in your laps at the **Palm Springs Swim Center** (760-

Palm Springs Swim Park.

323-8278; 405 S. Pavilion at Baristo Rd., Palm Springs, CA 92262), which has an Olympic-size outdoor pool and lap lanes, and was completely renovated in 2008. Admission: $3.50. **Wardman Park** (Eighth St. and Cactus St., Desert Hot Springs, CA 92240) has a swimming pool operated by the Boys and Girls Club.

The **College of the Desert Swimming Pool** (43-500 Monterey Ave., Palm Desert, CA 92260) is available for public use seasonally, as is the **Palm Desert High School Pool** (760-701-2610; 43-570 Phyllis Jackson Way, Palm Desert, CA 92270).

The Coachella Valley Recreation & Park District (760-347-3484; www.cvrpd.org/facilities/pools.htm) administers the **Bagdouma Community Pool** (760-391-9448; 84-626 Baghdad St., Coachella, CA 92236) and **Pawley Pool Family Aquatic Complex** (760-342-5665; 46-350 S. Jackson St., Indio, CA 92201), both with swim lessons, lap sessions, and open swim time.

Tennis

Palm Springs has been synonymous with tennis since the Hollywood set began cavorting here almost a century ago. Errol Flynn, Jayne Mansfield, Marilyn Monroe, and Bob Hope were among the legends who swung rackets at the infamous members-only Racquet Club, at the north end of town. Though the club is long deceased (in 2008 new owners were planning a comeback), there's no shortage of tennis courts, both public and private. No self-respecting hotel of any size would dare advertise without one: Palm Desert and Indian Wells together claim three of the world's premier tennis resorts. And in a place where the sun shines on average 350 days of the year, you'd expect tennis to be an avid sport.

Semiprivate clubs are private facilities that permit public use for a fee. Reservations are normally required.

PALM SPRINGS

DeMuth Park (760-323-8272; 4375 Mesquite Ave., Palm Springs, CA 92262) Public park with four night-lit courts. Free.

Mesquite Golf & Country Club (760-323-1502; 2700 E. Mesquite Ave., Palm Springs, CA 92262) Known for its lush golf fairways and mountain vistas, this semiprivate club is also acclaimed for its racquet facilities. It has eight tennis and two racquetball courts.

Palm Springs Country Club (760-323-8625; 2500 Whitewater Club Dr., Palm Springs, CA 92262) Two well-kept tennis courts for public use at this semiprivate facility. Free.

The Pacific Life Open at Indian Wells Tennis Center. April Graham

Palm Springs Tennis Club (760-325-1441; www.palmspringstennisclub.com; 701 W. Baristo Rd., Palm Springs, CA 92262) Time was when this was *the* place to play tennis. Since faded, and now a timeshare hotel, the club still has its 11 top-notch courts, thank goodness, available to Joe Public. Reservations essential.

The Plaza Racquet Club (760-323-8997; 1300 E. Baristo Rd., Palm Springs, CA 92262) Has nine lighted courts, plus private lessons, and a ball machine; open 8–6 daily.

Ruth Hardy Park (700 Tamarisk Way, Palm Springs, CA 92262). Eight night-lit public tennis courts with public lessons available. Free.

PALM SPRINGS VICINITY

Canyon Shores (760-328-0032; 35-200 Cathedral Canyon Dr., Cathedral City, CA 92234) This private resort has five semiprivate tennis courts; four are lighted.

Cathedral Canyon Golf and Tennis (760-321-7467; www.cathedral-canyon.com; 68-311 Paseo Real, Cathedral City, CA 92234) Semiprivate. Ten championship tennis courts; seven are lighted. Tennis professionals are available to coach.

Doral Desert Princess Tennis Resort (760-322-2293 or 322-7000; www.doralpalm springs.com; 28-555 Landau Blvd., Cathedral City, CA 92234) Mid-range hotel with 10 courts (5 night-lit), plus pro shop and tennis pros. Tennis instruction at the Moore Tennis Academy (Sept. 1–May 31).

Mission Hills Country Club (760-324-9400; www.missionhills.com; 34-600 Mission Hills Dr., Rancho Mirage, CA 92270) One of the top tennis facilities in the U.S. Has 20 hard courts, 4 clay courts, and 5 lawn tennis courts. Dennis Ralston tennis camp led by the eponymous former U.S. Davis Cup player and captain. Nonmembers by invitation of members only. Dress code.

Rancho Las Palmas Resort & Spa (760-568-2727; www.rancholaspalmas.com; 42-000 Bob Hope Dr., Rancho Mirage, CA 92270) This excellent semiprivate facility has 25 tennis courts; 8 lighted for night play.

Wardman Park (760-329-9147; 8th St. and Cactus Dr., Desert Hot Springs, CA 92240) Two tennis courts, free for public use.

The Westin Mission Hills Resort & Spa (760-770-2199; 71-333 Dinah Shore Dr., Rancho Mirage, CA 92270) Deluxe resort with seven lighted courts, plus a tournament court with stadium seating. The Reed Anderson Tennis School has resident pros.

Whitewater Park (760-324-4511; 71-560 San Jacinto Dr., Rancho Mirage, CA 92270) Four night-lit tennis courts for public use. Free.

SOUTHERN DESERT RESORTS

Cahuilla Hills Park (45-825 Edgehill Dr., Palm Desert, CA 92260) Two courts for public use. First come, first served (pardon the pun). For information, call the City of Palm Desert Parks & Recreation Dept. (760-346-0611).

Civic Center Park (760-773-2326; 43-900 San Pablo St., Palm Desert, CA 92260) Six night-lit courts. Two courts for public use. First come, first served. Free.

College of the Desert (760-341-2491; 43-500 Monterey Ave., Palm Desert, CA 92260) Six tennis courts available free to the public when not in use by staff and students. Free.

Desert Springs JW Marriott (760-341-2211; 74-855 Country Club Dr., Palm Desert, CA 92260) Ranked as one of the top tennis resorts in the world, the Tennis & Lawn Club offers 15 hard-surface courts, 3 clay courts, and 2 stadium grass courts. There's even a computerized hitting wall! Comprehensive tennis programs and clinics, plus private tennis lessons.

Freedom Park (77-400 Country Club Dr., Palm Desert, CA 92260) Two courts for public use. First come, first served. Free.

Fritz Burns Park (760-777-7090; Ave. 52 and Ave. Bermudas, La Quinta, CA 92253) Six courts free for public use.

Hyatt Grand Champions (760-341-1000; http://grandchampions.hyatt.com; 44-600 Indian Wells La., Indian Wells, CA 92210) Only three courts, but Andre Agassi, Boris Becker, Stefan Edberg, Steffi Graf, Pete Sampras, and Monica Seles are among the names who've played here. Tennis instruction. Complete pro shop. Courts are available from 7 AM–10 PM; $20 per hour for public play. Reservations 24 hours in advance.

Indian Wells Tennis Garden (760-200-8200; www.iwtg.net; 78-200 Miles Ave., Indian Wells, CA 92210) This full-service tennis club (home to the prestigious annual Pacific Life Open) boasts the second-largest tennis stadium in the world, with 16,000 seats. The 80-acre facility has 11 sunken championship courts, 6 courts especially designed for clinics, plus 2 Har-Tru clay courts. Reservations up to one week in advance; $20 court fee ($10 June–Sept.) for public play.

La Quinta High School (760-772-4150; 79-255 Westward Ho Dr., La Quinta, CA 92253) Six courts for public use outside school hours. Free.

La Quinta Resort & Spa (1-800-598-3828; www.laquintaresort.com; 49-499 Eisenhower Dr., La Quinta, CA 92253) With 23 courts, La Quinta Resort & Club's world-class tennis club is consistently rated one of the world's premier tennis resorts. Choose 18 hard (night-lit) or 5 clay surfaces, or sunken court. Professional instruction. Open daily 7 AM–10 PM; $25–35 per hour. Dress code.

South Jackson Park (83-100 Date Ave., Indio, CA 92201). Two tennis courts. Free for public use.

Coda gallery on El Paseo, Palm Desert.

7

Shopping

A Shopaholic's Mecca

Where you find serious money, you find serious shops. So it is with Palm Springs and the desert resorts, which draw serious shoppers from far and wide for a dash of retail therapy between their spa treatments. Palm Springs itself is renowned for art galleries and, uniquely, boutique stores specializing in 1950s and 1960s modernist decor. Palm Canyon Drive is a veritable Aladdin's cave of American kitsch. Lava lamps. Velveteen sofas. Tulip-shaped Jackson chairs. Zenith Deluxe Royal 500 transistor radios. There are dozens of thrift stores miraculously unpicked-over. The merchants of Palm Canyon Drive have a Web site: www.palmcanyondrive.org.

For high fashion, the money heads to El Paseo (www.elpaseocatalogue.com), Palm Desert's own take on Beverly Hills' Rodeo Drive. Count the Bentleys parked along its mile length! El Paseo specializes in apparel boutiques, haute couturiers, jewelry stores, and upscale art galleries. It also has plenty of restaurants and bistros. Palm Desert also has a reputation as the desert's retail oasis, thanks to its 14 shopping malls. You can hop a free tour on the **"Shopper Hopper"** (1-800-347-8628), an air-conditioned shuttle that operates every 25 minutes, 10 AM–5 PM, Nov.–May, and every 50 minutes June–Oct., linking the main shopping plazas.

Meanwhile, Cathedral City, for some reason, is carpet central. Rancho Mirage, for all its wealth, is capital of consignment home furnishings. And when it comes to discounts, nowhere beats the factory outlets at Cabazon.

Antiques and Home Furnishings

The nation's unsurpassed repository of mid-20th-century furniture, Palm Springs causes palpitations of glee for *modernistas*. Forget "antiques." The rage here is Rat Pack redux, not Louis XIV. Self-respecting locals decorate with Nelson lamps and Eames and Bertoia chairs and similar vintage-modern furnishings from the seemingly endless supply in local shops. You can even find George Nelson benches and Richard Schultz outdoor furniture. The town is a chic retro outpost of modernist furnishings and memorabilia evoking Hollywood habitués from the old days. A series of vintage and modernist stores is strung along North Palm Canyon Drive. Most pieces are originals, and there are plenty of trend-setting stores selling chic contemporary designs in the modernist spirit. The timing couldn't be better, as Palm Springs' hip custom stores fit right in with the fashionable contemporary stripped-down steel-and-glass style of the 21st century. Genuine modern icons like Eames chairs don't come cheap, however.

Modern Way.

Down valley, the country club style tips its hat to a more traditional style, à la Tommy Bahama.

PALM SPRINGS

111 Antique Mall (760-864-9390; www.info111mall.com; 2500 N. Palm Canyon Dr., Palm Springs, CA 92262) Billing itself as a "supermarket of mid-century furnishings," it has it all, from art and accessories to lighting and jewelry.

The Alley (760-320-5664; 333 S. Palm Canyon Dr., Palm Springs, CA 92262) A local institution, this emporium does a brisk trade serving the undiscriminating shopper with rather hokey decorative ceramics, handcrafted furniture, mirrors, framed prints, and miscellaneous household accessories.

Antiques Center (760-323-4443; 798 N. Palm Canyon Dr., Palm Springs, CA 92262) A mall-style arcade with 35 dealers in vintage wares, from African crafts to jewelry and linens.

Bandini Johnson (760-323-7805; 760 N. Palm Canyon Dr., Palm Springs, CA 92262) A well-stocked warren of eclectic pieces. Specializes in vintage barware, lamps, and ashtrays.

Dazzles (760-327-1446; 457 N. Palm Canyon Dr., Palm Springs, CA 92262) A top-notch collection of authentic retro lamps, vases, and other home accessories, plus classic mid-century chairs, tables, etc.—think orange scoop chairs and amoeba-shaped couches.

Estate Sales Company (760-322-2643; 1554 N. Palm Canyon Dr., Palm Springs, CA 92262) *The* place to buy secondhand furniture and home decor pieces in all genres, although modernist pickings are slim.

LDC Design Studio (760-864-9499; www.ldcdesignstudio.com; 1775 E. Palm Canyon Dr., Suite H-140, Palm Springs, CA 92264) Specializes in custom-designed modernist pieces and reproductions.

Modern Way (760-320-5455; www.psmodernway.com; 745 N. Palm Canyon Dr., Palm Springs, CA 92262) Perhaps the best place in town to find Melmac tableware and Saarinen or Bertoia chairs from the 1950s and '60s. Proprietor Courtney Newman mixes the familiar and quirky, giving the latter labels such as Hollywood Arabian Moderne and Mafia Modern. A rare Knoll sofa might knock you back $5,000.

Music Box & Clocke Shoppe (760-322-6280; 114 La Plaza, Palm Springs, CA 92262) Classic crystal collectibles by Swarovski, porcelain figurines by Lladró, and animated rhythm clocks.

Palm Springs Consignment (760-416-8820; 1117 N. Palm Canyon Dr., Palm Springs, CA

92262) Modern preowned furniture classics at competitive prices, although not all pieces are flawless.

Studio 111 (760-323-5104; 2675 N. Palm Canyon Dr., Palm Springs, CA 92262) Fifties furniture by the classic designers—Bertoia, Eames, et al.—plus modern design, home furnishings, and fine art. Sculpture and ceramics by Stan Bitters.

Palm Springs Vicinity

111 Antique Mall (760-202-0215; 68-401 E. Palm Canyon Dr., Cathedral City, CA 92234) A sister to the Palm Springs outlet of the same name.

Erik's Furniture (760-346-1177; 71-285 Hwy. 111, Rancho Mirage, CA 92270) Tasteful contemporary furniture for sophisticates.

Southern Desert Resorts

Old World Pottery (760-341-9907; www.oldworldpottery-online.com; 73-130 El Paseo, Suite E, Palm Desert, CA 92260) Just the ticket for a charming fine imported Italian majolica piece and other earthenware ceramics to fit the Santa Fe or Tuscan villa mood.

Tabletop Elegance (760-674-9234; www.tabletopelegance.com; 73-470 El Paseo, Palm Desert, CA 92260) Distinctive table settings, gifts, and home accessories by top-of-the-line names such as Hermès, Lynn Chase, and Versace.

Tommy Bahama's Emporium (760-836-0288; www.tommybahama.com; 73-545 El Paseo, Palm Desert, CA 92260) In The Gardens on El Paseo. Sells Caribbean colonial-themed furnishings and decor.

Art Galleries

Bring a fat wallet for browsing the many galleries that line Palm Springs' Palm Canyon Drive and Palm Desert's El Paseo. The range of artworks for sale astounds, from grand canvases by the European masters to masterly works by the desert's own plein-air painters. Also see Galleries, in the Culture chapter, for more details on art galleries.

Palm Springs

Adagio Galleries (760-320-2230; www.adagiogalleries.com; 193 S. Palm Canyon Dr., Palm Springs, CA 92262) Specializing in Southwest and Hispanic art of the West Coast, this store represents many of the leading artists of the genre, such as Michael Atkinson.

Backstreet Art District (760-328-1440; 2688 Cherokee Way, Palm Springs, CA 92264) Eight artists' studios and galleries focused on contemporary art. Includes the Slaughterhouse Gallery (760-324-3320; www.slaughterhouseps.com).

The Carlan Gallery (760-322-8002; 1546 N. Palm Canyon Dr., Palm Springs, CA 92262) Sells works by many leading 20th-century European masters, including Day-Glo bright works by Jean-Claude Tron and Olivier Tramoni.

Imageville (760-416-9825; www.imageville.us; 128 La Plaza, Palm Springs, CA 92262) Framed photographs by Gary Dorothy to bring beauty and boldness (or subtlety) to your walls.

M Modern Gallery (760-325-9135; www.mmoderngallery.com; 2500 N. Palm Canyon Dr., Palm Springs, CA 92262) Specializes in Midcentury Modernist art and objects.

Southern Desert Resorts

El Paseo has more than 20 commercial galleries from which to choose. No schlock here. These galleries represent only top-quality artists. The range of expression is astounding, and there's something for every taste. The galleries are so impressive it's a pity to leave any out, or even to lay stress on any. That said, a spectacular standout is **Imago Galleries** (760-776-9890; www.imagogalleries.com; 45-450 Hwy. 74, Palm Desert, CA 92260), specializing in glass and sculpture. See Galleries, in the Culture chapter, for details on individual galleries.

Books and Music

Notwithstanding the generally high education level of folks in the valley, Palm Springs is poorly served by bookstores. Alas, what was Palm Springs' *only* bookstore, **Peppertree Books** (formerly on Palm Canyon Dr.) shuttered its doors in January 2008, after closing its La Quinta store in 2007. And **Celebrity Books** also closed in 2006. Developers of the proposed downtown Museum Market Plaza are hoping to entice Barnes & Noble to open a store, but that could be several years away.

Meanwhile, serious bibliophiles are now relegated to just two chain bookstores: **Barnes & Noble** (760-346-0725; 72-840 Hwy. 111, Palm Desert, CA 92260) and **Borders** (760-779-1314; 71-800 Hwy. 111, Rancho Mirage, CA 92270). Both have large CD music selections, too. **The Book Rack** (760-771-3449; www.bookrack.org; 78-329 Hwy. 111, La Quinta, CA 92253) specializes in used paperbacks.

On the music front, **FYE** (For Your Entertainment; 760-322-4744; 555 S. Palm Canyon Dr., Palm Springs, CA 92262) is a paradise of rocker junk, including old albums and tapes.

The best all-around music store in the desert, **Musicians Outlet** (760-341-3171; www.musiciansbestfriend.com; 44-850 San Pablo Ave., Palm Desert, CA 92260), can fit you out with everything from a set of drums to a karaoke machine.

Clothing and Accessories

Apparel stores are scattered throughout the valley. Bargain shoppers can choose either of two **Ross Dress for Less** (www.rossstores.com) stores, at 233 S. Farrell Dr., Palm Springs, CA 92262 (760-325-6506) and 72-250 Hwy. 111, Palm Desert, CA 92260 (760-773-9949). Near wholesale prices draw Imelda Marcos wannabes to **E&J's Designer Shoe Outlet** (760-773-5053;www.ejsdesignershoes.com; 44-100 Town Center Way, Palm Desert, CA 92260). Choose from a thousand pairs of shoes. Most of the best designer brands are here, from Cole Haan and Ralph Lauren to Kenneth Cole, and even Nike and Ecco.

Trina Turk's store, Palm Springs.

The Desert Hills and Cabazon factory outlets have dozens of discount clothing stores; see Factory Outlets.

Palm Springs Classic Car Auction.

Classic Automobiles

First-time visitors to Palm Springs can be forgiven for thinking themselves in a 1950s time warp. First, there are the retro modernist homes of the era lining every block. But did you really expect to see a high-finned, voluptuous dowager from Detroit's heyday parked in each driveway? Well, OK, if not every driveway, at least enough to give you a sense of reliving a *temps perdu*. The tail fins of chrome-polished '57 Packards glint in the desert sun. Nearby, perhaps, sits a 1957 Chevrolet Bel-Air convertible, or a Dodge Custom Royal from the same year, inviting passersby to admire the grillwork or run their fingers along a polished tail fin. Cars missing from American highways for decades line every block.

The desert air works wonders for metal, so rust is rare. No surprise, then, that 1950s classics are a dime a dozen in auto showrooms. When you get the mood to show off to your neighbors with a fashionable 1950s T-bird or Corvette in the driveway, head to **Keith McCormick's** (760-320-3290; www.classic-carauction.com; 244 N. Indian Canyon Dr., Palm Springs, CA 92262). There are always precious cars at McCormick's showroom, but the real classics are auctioned the last weekends in February and November. McCormick's also sponsors the annual **Desert Classic Concours d'Elegance**, a two-day event held on the O'Donnell Golf Course in late February and featuring rarely seen automobiles.

Exotic Motor Cars (760-778-5444; www.exoticmotorcars.com; 4525 E. Ramon Rd., Palm Springs, CA 92264) can also fit you out with an E-type Jaguar, Cadillac Calais coupe, or a Bentley S-2 sedan. Lesser selections (in quantity, not quality) are offered at **Mastercraft Classic** (760-324-8016; www.mastercraftclassic.com; 68-333 Perez Rd., Cathedral City, CA 92234); **Zoom Exotic Auto & Cycles** (760-347-1833; 44-919 Golf Center Pkwy., Indio, CA 92201); **Rc Classics** (760-568-3450; 75-135 Sheryl Ave., Palm Desert, CA 92211); and at **Classic Cars of the Desert** (760-322-1101; 548 E. Industrial Place, Palm Springs, CA 92264), which always has a wide selection of rare cars and Rolls-Royces.

If it's fine fashion you're seeking, head to **Trina Turk's** (760-416-2856; www.trina turk.com; 891 N. Palm Canyon Dr., Palm Springs, CA 92262). L.A.-born fashionista Trina Truk's vintage-inspired look fits right in in retro-trendy Palm Springs. Her bold graphic style combines bold, vibrant colors and elegant designs, sold at this stylish clothing emporium. Halle Berry and Julia Roberts are among the fans of Trina's '70s flared fashions.

The Bag Lady (760-202-1866; 68-895 Perez Rd., Cathedral City, CA 92234) will fit you out with distinctive women's accessories, including purses for all occasions and settings, plus wallets for the gents, small luggage items, and jewelry. And cowgirls and wannabe

Ralph Lauren on El Paseo.

cowgirls should check out **Country Club Cowgirl** (760-360-7557; 77-734 Country Club Dr., Palm Desert, CA 92211), a boutique selling contemporary western apparel.

El Paseo (1-877-735-7273; www.elpaseocatalogue.com), in Palm Desert, is where you might spot your favorite movie star while window-shopping. Brooks Brothers, Escada, Gucci, and Ralph Lauren are among the celebrated clothing designers that have boutiques on this mile-long boulevard.

El Paseo

Often referred to as the "Rodeo Drive of the Desert," El Paseo is the Coachella Valley's legendary shopping avenue and features a tree-lined promenade accentuated by contemporary sculpture. Its 300 or so outlets range from art galleries and fashion boutiques to cafés, restaurants, and day spas that provide perfect recuperatives after an hour or two shopping. Shops range from the functional (art, accessories, clothing, home decor) to the luxurious (art, accessories, clothing, home decor).

El Paseo. Palm Springs Desert Resorts Conventions & Visitors Authority

The largest grouping of shops, **The Gardens** (760-862-1990; www.thegardensonelpaseo.com; between San Pablo and Larkspur), is a 200,000-square-foot complex anchored by Saks Fifth Avenue and built around a series of courtyards. It features 45 stores selling the finest in fashions, home furnishings, jewelry, and specialty items, and hosts free outdoor jazz concerts on Sat., Feb.–Apr.; and movies on Fri. in May.

Other key shops to know include:

Belita (760-674-4726; 73-425 El Paseo, Suite 21A, Palm Desert, CA 92260) Fashion for the curvaceous figure. Whether you're seeking casual or cocktail wear, this space will fit if you're size 14 and up. Closed Mon.

Chapmans (760-340-1443; www.chapmanandson.com; 73-470 El Paseo, Palm Desert, CA 92260) Billing itself as selling "Menswear to fit your desert lifestyle," this rather conservative family-run clothing store sells fine duds for discerning males.

Fe Zandi Haute Couture (760-776-6100; www.fezandi.com; 73-111 El Paseo, Palm Desert, CA 92260) The Bentley sure to be parked outside gives a hint of the fashion togs sold here. A favorite of the desert's leading ladies and others on the best-dressed list.

Robert's Fine Shoes (760-340-2929; www.robertsfineshoes.com; 73-725 El Paseo, Palm Desert, CA 92260) When you simply *must* add a pair of Salvatore Ferragamo or Bruno Magli to your closet, this is the place to come. It also sells fine handbags and other accessories by the likes of Judith Leiber and Eric Javits.

Saks Fifth Avenue (760-837-2900; 73-555 El Paseo, Palm Desert, CA 92260) High-quality fashions and accessories, as well as jewelry and perfumes.

Sarit (760-341-0664; 73-130 El Paseo, Palm Desert, CA 92260) This classy boutique specializes in contemporary European silk designs but also sells shoes and accessories.

Crafts and Collectibles

Next time you're seeking a Hopi doll or a pair of genuine deerskin moccasins, check out **Desert Trading** (760-322-6164; 270 N. Palm Canyon, Palm Springs, CA 92262), a family-owned store specializing in Native Indian crafts, including jewelry, rugs, woven blankets, and, yes, Hopi dolls and moccasins.

Diamonds of Splendor (760-568-6641; 73-400 El Paseo, Palm Desert, CA 92260) is a top-of-the-line jeweler selling fine custom designs featuring Fope and Henri Bar, plus unique rare colored stones. El Paseo has no fewer than 21 other fine jewelry stores! Meanwhile, **Fort Knoxx Designer Inspirations** (760-341-4979; 73-101 Country Club Dr., Palm Desert, CA 92260) offers fine-crafted, custom-designed moissanite, zirconia, and other semiprecious stones set in precious metals.

Palm Springs has more cigar stores than you can shake a panatella at. None sell real Cubans (but then again, nowhere in the USA does), but most other famous national brands are represented. **Fame Cigars & Wine** (760-320-2752; 155 S. Palm Canyon Dr., Palm Springs, CA 92262), on

Fame Cigars & Wine.

Palm Springs' main plaza, is a good starting place and is a cozy ambience for sampling a stogie before comparing the goods at **The Tinder Box** (760-325-4041; 245 S. Palm Canyon Dr., Palm Springs, CA 92262), one block south. The latter also sells die-cast Franklin Mint precision World War II aircraft and armor models.

Cohiba Cigar Lounge (760-346-4748; 71-800 Hwy. 111, Rancho Mirage, CA 92270), the premier cigar lounge in the desert, sells a wide selection of premium cigars from the Dominican Republic, Honduras, and Nicaragua, as well as collectors' pre-embargo Cuban cigars. **Palm Desert Tobacco** (760-340-1954; 73-580 El Paseo, Palm Desert, CA 92270) has been selling premium cigars, plus pipes, lighters, and accessories, since 1983. Some 600 varieties are here, including the best Dominican, Nicaraguan, and Honduran smokes you can find.

Factory Outlets

The Palm Springs region is famous for its twinned factory outlets, in Cabazon.

Desert Hills Premium Outlets (951-849-6641; www.premiumoutlets.com; 48-400 Seminole Dr., Cabazon, CA), just a 25-minute drive west from Palm Springs, has 130 outlets representing everything from jewelry and designer fashions to children's goods, housewares, and books. Classy duds are represented by outlets of Giorgio Armani, Burberry, Coach, Eddie Bauer, Escada, Hugo Boss, Gucci, Levi's, Polo, Ralph Lauren, Salvatore Ferragamo, and Yves St. Laurent, to name a few. Nike also has a store in Desert Hills. The long list of outlets reads like a "Who's Who" of high fashion. Open 10–8 Sun.–Thurs., 10–9 Fri., 9–9 Sat.

Adjoining Desert Hills, the compact **Cabazon Outlets** (951-922-3000; www.cabazonoutlets.com; 48-750 Seminole Dr., Cabazon, CA) features Guess, Adidas, Puma, and Reebok among its discount outlets. Extra discounts are offered during its July 4 weekend and Labor Day weekend sales. Golfers should head to the Greg Norman collection. Open 10–8 Sun.–Thurs., 10–9 Fri., 9–9 Sat.

Shopping Malls and Plazas

If you can't fall asleep counting sheep, try counting greater Palm Springs' malls and plazas. Anyone who hasn't traveled down Hwy. 111 in a decade probably won't recognize it today. Here are a few of the standout malls:

The River at Rancho Mirage (760-341-2711; www.theriveratranchomirage.com; 71-800 Hwy. 111, Rancho Mirage, CA 92270) is the class act, with a beautiful setting enhanced by a parklike waterfront along Hwy. 111, with fountains and a sunken amphitheater. The River has 12 restaurants, boutique stores, beauty shops, a chain bookstore, and cinema, plus a 20 percent discount card at select retailers.

A recent $32 million makeover has reinvigorated the formerly jaded and struggling **Westfield Palm Desert** (760-346-2121; 72-840 Hwy. 111, Palm Desert, CA 92260), which now has a Disney Store, Gap, JC Penny, Macy's, Sears, Victoria's Secret, and a beautifully designed Barnes & Noble bookstore and café, plus a food court, and Cinemas Palme d'Or, showing alternative, independent, documentary, and foreign films.

Old Town La Quinta (760-777-1770; www.oldtownlaquinta.com; 78,100 Main St., La Quinta, CA 92253), styled in Santa Fe adobe fashion, offers art galleries, craft stores, and several restaurants. **Indio Fashion Mall** (760-347-8323; www.indiofashionmall.com; Hwy. 111 and Monroe St., Indio, CA 92201) has more than 40 unique shops and restaurants.

Sporting Goods and Sportswear

For sportswear, you can't do better than to head out to the Cabazon factory outlets, where most of the name-brand manufacturers (Adidas, Nike, Reebok, etc.) have discount stores. Otherwise, think *golf!*

In addition to the country club pro shops, several quality stores compete for the golfer's purse. The biggest emporium of golfing goods is **Pete Carlson's Golf & Tennis** (760-568-3263; 73-741 Hwy. 111; Palm Desert, CA 92260), with more than 10,000 square feet stocked with top-quality golf and tennis merchandise. **Lumpy's** has two desert outlets, at 67-625 Hwy. 111, Cathedral City, CA 92234 (760-321-2437; www.lumpys.com) and 46-630 Washington St., La Quinta, CA 92253 (760-904-4911), and includes clearance items as well as a complete range of state-of-the-art golfing equipment and accessories, as does **The Golf Connection** (760-777-1124; www.desertgolfconnection.com; 49-990 Jefferson St., Suite 100, Indio, CA 92201). **California Golf Mart** (760-772-5777; 78-078 Country Club Dr., Suite 210, Indio, CA 92203) competes with everything at discount prices. **Golf Alley** (760-776-4646; 42-829 Cook St., Suite 101, Palm Desert, CA 92211) sells consigned golf equipment, including classic collectors' clubs.

Street Fairs

Every Thurs. night, year-round, locals pour in to Palm Springs for **Villagefest** (www.palmspringsvillagefest.com), when more than 200 stalls selling handmade items (from jewelry to framed prints) are set up along Palm Canyon Drive. Most shops along Palm Canyon Drive stay open late during Villagefest. Held 6–10 PM Oct.–May, 7–10 PM June–Sept.

Similarly, the open-air **College of the Desert Street Fair** (760-568-9921; www.codstreetfair.com; College of the Desert, 43-500 Monterey Ave., Palm Desert, CA 92260) is held every Sat. and Sun. morning on the college campus. From clothing and jewelry to gourmet goodies and unique gifts. Funds raised help finance student scholarships.

The **Indio Open Air Market** (1-800-222-7467; 46-530 Arabia St., Indio, CA 92201) is held in the Riverside County Fair and National Date Festival grounds, 4–10 PM Wed. and Sat.

Villagefest.

Palm Desert police on Segways.

Information

Facts on File

Having the basics at hand provides peace of mind and goes a long way to helping you enjoy the Palm Springs region without worry. The information presented in this chapter covers planning and everyday practical matters, as well as emergencies. Providing information running the gamut from weather reports to visitors bureaus, it serves both the first-time visitor and local residents. Who knows? Like this book's author, you might decide to turn your brief vacation destination into your home.

Ambulance, Fire, and Police

Simply dial 911 for emergency ambulance, fire, or police service. You will reach an operator who will put you through to the correct agency, or will dispatch emergency service.

To report rape or sexual assault, call **Rape Crisis** (760-568-9071; 24 hours).

To report domestic assault, call the **Domestic Violence Hotline** (1-800-339-7233).

To report child abuse, call the **Child Abuse Hotline** (1-800-442-4918).

For the **Regional Poison Control Center**, call 1-800-544-4404.

For non-emergencies, you can contact the following police departments:
California Highway Patrol: 760-345-2544; 79-650 Varner Rd., Indio, CA 92203
Cathedral City: 760-770-0300; 68-700 Ave. Lalo Guerrero, Cathedral City, CA 92234
Coachella: 760-398-0101; 1515 Sixth St., Coachella, CA 92236
Desert Hot Springs: 760-329-2904; 65-950 Pierson Blvd., Desert Hot Springs, CA 92234
Indian Wells: 760-836-1600; 73-520 Fred Waring Dr., Palm Desert, CA 92260
Indio: 760-347-8522; 46-800 S. Jackson St., Indio, CA 92201
La Quinta: 760-836-3215 or 760-863-8990; 82-695 Dr. Carreon Blvd., Indio, CA 92201
Palm Desert: 760-836-1600; 73-520 Fred Waring Dr., Palm Desert, CA 92260
Palm Springs: 760-323-8116; 200 S. Civic Dr., Palm Springs, CA 92262
Rancho Mirage: 760-836-1600; 73-520 Fred Waring Dr., Palm Desert, CA 92260
Riverside County Sheriff: 760-836-1600, 760-328-8871 or 1-800-472-569; 73-520 Fred Waring Dr., Palm Desert, CA 92260
Thousand Palms: 760-836-1600; 73-520 Fred Waring Dr., Palm Desert, CA 92260
Valley Crime Stoppers: 760-341-7867 or 1-800-245-0009; 73-510 Fred Waring Dr., Palm Desert, CA 92260 welcomes anonymous information concerning subjects involved in crime.

Area Codes, Town Government, and Zip Codes

Area Codes

All Coachella Valley cities	760
Idyllwild	951

City Halls and Zip Codes
Cathedral City: 760-770-0340; 68-700 Ave. Lalo Guerrero, Cathedral City, CA 92234
Coachella: 760-398-3502; 1515 Sixth St., Coachella, CA 92236
Desert Hot Springs: 760-329-6411; 65-950 Pierson Blvd., Desert Hot Springs, CA 92240
Indian Wells: 760-346-2489; 44-950 Eldorado Dr., Indian Wells, CA 92210
Indio: 760-391-4000; 100 Civic Center Mall, Indio, CA 92201
La Quinta: 760-777-7035; 78-495 Calle Tampico, La Quinta, CA 92253
Palm Desert: 760-346-0611; 73-510 Fred Waring Dr., Palm Desert, CA 92260
Palm Springs: 760-323-8299; 3200 E. Tahquitz Canyon Way, Palm Springs, CA 92262
Rancho Mirage: 760-324-4511; 69-825 Hwy. 111, Rancho Mirage, CA 92270
Yucca Valley: 760-369-7207; 57-090 Twentynine Palms Hwy., Yucca Valley, CA 92284

Banks

If you have a bank card, you should have no worries about being short of greenbacks, as an automated teller is never far away. The following is a sampling of regional and national banks. Each branch office is equipped with at least one ATM.

Bank of America (1-800-301-3744)
Locations:

83-017 Ave. 48, Coachella	760-342-1000
68-435 Hwy. 111, Cathedral City	760-340-1867
13-210 Palm Dr., Desert Hot Springs	760-251-0854
81-800 Hwy. 111, Indio	760-340-1867
78-400 Hwy. 111, La Quinta	760-340-1867
34-420 Monterey Ave., Palm Desert	760-202-2942
73-820 El Paseo, Palm Desert	760-341-4710
73-766 Hwy. 111, Palm Desert	760-341-4710
42-095 Washington St., Palm Desert	760-340-1867
588 S. Palm Canyon Dr., Palm Springs	760-340-1867
5601 E. Ramon Rd., Palm Springs	760-325-1812
295 N. Sunrise Way, Palm Springs	760-325-1812
1751 N. Sunrise Way, Palm Springs	760-340-1867
1801 E. Palm Canyon Dr., Palm Springs	760-340-1867
71-799 Hwy. 111, Rancho Mirage	760-340-1867
40-101 Monterey Ave., Rancho Mirage	760-340-1867
57-155 Twentynine Palms Hwy., Yucca Valley	760-228-2201

Wachovia (1-800-922-4684)
Locations:

42-420 Washington St., Bermuda Dunes	760-834-2305
4000 Palm Dr., Desert Hot Springs	760-288-7920
74-760 Hwy. 111, Indian Wells	760-340-3200

Washington Mutual (1-800-788-7000)
Locations:

13-000 Palm Dr., Desert Hot Springs	760-329-1442
82-462 Hwy. 111, Indio	760-775-9511
78-805 Hwy. 111, La Quinta	760-564-0351
72-705 Hwy. 111, Palm Desert	760-346-9857
499 S. Palm Canyon Dr., Palm Springs	760-325-1242
36-101 Bob Hope Dr., Rancho Mirage	760-324-9398
57-297 Twentynine Palms Hwy., Yucca Valley	760-365-0683

Wells Fargo (1-800-869-3557)
Locations:

69-255 Ramon Rd., Cathedral City	760-770-2924
46-020 Monroe St., Indio	760-863-5608
78-630 Hwy. 111, La Quinta	760-564-2387
74-105 El Paseo, Palm Desert	760-568-3460
77-952 Country Club Dr., Palm Desert	760-200-3000
1733 E. Palm Canyon Dr., Palm Springs	760-320-4657
1753 N. Sunrise Way, Palm Springs	760-416-1440
1850 E. Del Lago Rd., Palm Springs	760-322-1777
4733 E. Palm Canyon Dr., Palm Springs	760-770-3227
543 S. Palm Canyon Dr., Palm Springs	760-416-3087
42-350 Bob Hope Dr., Rancho Mirage	760-568-0482

BIBLIOGRAPHY

Palm Springs' recent revival has fostered an outpouring of books on the region. "Books You Can Buy" lists titles generally available in bookstores and online. "Books You Can Borrow" lists books that are hard to find, except in libraries, and are no longer available for sale.

Books You Can Buy

Architecture

Coquelle, Aline. *Palm Springs Style*. New York: Assouline, 2006. 192 pages, illustrated. One of several coffee-table books on Palm Springs modernism. Lavish and lovely.

Cygelman, Adele. *Palm Springs Modern*. New York: Rizzoli International, 1999. 192 pages, illustrated. This exquisite coffee-table book examines the impact that Midcentury Modernist architects and designers had on the desert oasis.

Dorran Saeks, Diane. *Palm Springs Living*. New York: Rizzoli, 2007. 224 pages, illustrated. The latest coffee-table book to showcase the inspiring and diverse range of quintessentially Palm Springs exteriors and interiors, including the legendary houses.

Hess, Alan, and Andrew Danish. *Palm Springs Weekend: The Architecture and Design of a Midcentury Oasis*. San Francisco: Chronicle Books, 2001. 180 pages, illustrated. Coffee-table book about the evolution of Palm Springs' eccentric modernist architecture.

Coffee-table

Cornett, James W. *Portrait of Palm Springs*. Helena, MT: Farcountry Press, 2007. 120 pages, illustrated. A captivating portrait of virtually every aspect of Coachella Valley life, illustrated by photographer Tom Brewster.

Lawson, Greg. *Palm Springs Oasis*. El Cajon, CA: Sunbelt Publishing, 1989. 70 pages, illustrated. Captioned in English, Spanish, Italian, German, and Japanese, this collection of full-color images captures the beauty of the region.

Navez, Ren. *Palm Springs: California's Desert Gem*. Englewood, CO: Westcliffe Publishers. 112 pages, paperback. The desert resorts come alive in eye-catching photographs that highlight the unique beauty of the region.

Stringfellow, Kim. *Greetings from the Salton Sea: Folly and Intervention in the Southern California Landscape, 1905–2005*. Chicago: Center for American Places, 2005. 144 pages. Photojournalist essay that eloquently tells the tragic saga of the Salton Sea's decay.

Guidebooks

Fenwick, Henry, and Eric Wadlund, eds. *Palm Springs Flavors: The Best of Desert Eating, with Recipes from the Area's Chefs.* Englewood, CO: Westcliffe Publishers, 2007. 176 pages. Illustrated cookbook featuring top recipes from many of the best kitchens and restaurants of Palm Springs.

Kleven, Robin, ed. *Best Places: Palm Springs and the Desert Communities*. Seattle, WA: Sasquatch Books, 2001. 192 pages. Generic guidebook to the Coachella Valley and surrounding region.

Osbaldeston, Peter. *The Palm Springs Diners Bible*. Gretna, LA: Pelican Publishing, 2007. 352 pages. A comprehensive, opinionated guide to key restaurants throughout the valley. Aims at true gourmands with overly detailed dissections of individual dishes.

Local Histories

Artunian, Judy, and Mike Oldham. *Palm Springs in Vintage Postcards*. Mount Pleasant, SC: Arcadia Publishing, 2005. 128 pages. This collection of 200 vintage postcards tells the story of Palm Springs through the years.

Churchwell, Mary Jo. *Palm Springs: The Landscape, the History, the Lore*. Scottsdale, AZ: Ironwood Editions, 2001. 234 pages. The author acts as knowledgeable guide in this illustrated book, which weaves both social and natural history into a sensual portrait of the Palm Springs region.

DeBuys, William, and Joan Myers. *Salt Dreams: Land and Water in Low-Down California.* Albuquerque: University of New Mexico Press, 2001. 407 pages. An absorbing account of the taming of the Colorado River and transformation of southeastern California desert into an important agricultural region. Also discusses creation of the salt-choked Salton Sea.

Johns, Howard. *Palm Springs Confidential: Playground of the Stars*. Fort Lee, NJ: Barricade Books, 2004. 320 pages; illustrated. Tattletale book spills the beans on shenanigans, from Marilyn Monroe's bedroom antics to Robert Downey Jr.'s drug bust.

Wild, Peter, ed. *The Grumbling Gods: A Palm Springs Reader.* Ogden: University of Utah Press, 2007. 320 pages. An anthology of historical works by authors ranging from explorer Colonel William Banning to former mayor Frank M. Bogert and novelist Raymond Chandler.

Natural History

Anderson, Edward F. *The Cactus Family.* Portland, OR: Timber Press, 2001. 776 pages. Encyclopedic in extent, this massive compendium profiles nearly 2,000 species of New World succulents, illustrated with more than 1,000 photographs.

Bowers, Janice E. *One Hundred Desert Wildflowers of the Southwest.* Tucson, AZ: Western National Parks Association, 1987. 64 pages. Describes and depicts 100 Southwest desert flowers, each shown with two color photographs for easy identification.

Bowers, Janice, and Brian Wignall. *Shrubs & Trees of the Southwest Deserts.* Tucson, AZ: Western National Parks Association, 1993. 140 pages. Illustrated with line drawings, this handy field guide describes 134 common species of the Southwest deserts.

Cornett, James W. *Desert Snakes*. Palm Springs, CA: Nature Trails Press, 2003. 72 pages. Describes 28 different desert snakes, all illustrated.

Davis, Barbara L. *A Field Guide to Birds of the Desert Southwest.* Houston: Gulf Publishing, 1997. 320 pages, illustrated. This field guide for birders covers the deserts and semi-deserts of Arizona, California, and New Mexico.

Dodge, Natt Noye. *Flowers of the Southwest Deserts.* Tucson, AZ: Western National Parks Association, 1985. 136 pages. Field guide to over 100 of the most common flowering desert plants of the Southwest. Detailed line drawings for identification.

Fischer, Pierre C. *70 Common Cacti of the Southwest.* Tucson, AZ: Western National Parks Association, 1989. 76 pages. This valuable guidebook describes and depicts 70 common species of the Southwest deserts. Photos by leading southwestern photographers. Includes index.

Hanson, Jonathan, and Rosanne Beggy. *50 Common Reptiles & Amphibians of the Southwest.* Southwest Parks & Monuments Association, 1997. 64 pages, illustrated. This thoughtful introduction to desert amphibians and reptiles gives the low-down on where to find the desert tortoise, for example, and how to react to encounters with snakes.

Quinn, Meg. *Cacti of the Desert Southwest.* Tucson, AZ: Rio Nuevo Publishers, 2002. 96 pages. Botanist Meg Quinn describes 86 of the most significant cacti of the Southwest deserts. Each is depicted in color photographs.

——. *Wildflowers of the Desert Southwest.* Tucson, AZ: Rio Nuevo Publishers, 2002. 80 pages. Wondering what that gorgeous mauve flower is spreading across the desert floor?

Quinn's handy little compendium describes 85 of the most common and showy Sonoran Desert species, each illustrated with a full-color photograph. Also includes the best locations for specific wildflowers.

Recreation

Ferranti, Philip, and Hank Koenig. *120 Great Hikes in and Near Palm Springs*. Englewood, CO: Westcliffe Publishing, 2003. 216 pages. Descriptions of more than 100 trails throughout the region, from Joshua Tree National Park to the Mecca Hills. Maps and black-and-white photographs.

McMillin Pyle, Linda, and Evelyn Tschida McMillin. *Peaks, Palms & Picnics: Day Journeys in the Mountains & Deserts of Palm Springs and the Coachella Valley of Southern California*. El Cajon, CA: Sunbelt Publications, 2002. 207 pages. A hiker's guide to exploring the region. Each hike is associated with a recipe favored by the author. The anecdotal style detracts, and practical details are lacking.

McKinney, John. *California's Desert Parks: A Day Hiker's Guide.* Berkeley, CA: Wilderness Press, 2006. 263 pages. A comprehensive guide to serve outdoorsy folk. Describes 131 hikes, ranging from Death Valley in the north to Anza-Borrego State Park in the south.

Randall, Laura. *Day and Overnight Hikes: Palm Springs*. Birmingham, AL: Menasha Ridge Press, 2008. 206 pages. Describes dozens of hikes up and down the valley and surrounding area, including detailed maps.

Books You Can Borrow

Bean, Lowell John. *Mukat's People: The Cahuilla Indians of Southern California.* Berkeley: University of California Press, 1974. 201 pages. An excellently researched and highly readable academic text that provides a detailed overview of the Cahuilla culture.

Brumgardt, John R., and Larry Bowles. *People of the Magic Waters: The Cahuilla Indians of Palm Springs*. Palm Springs, CA: Etc. Publications, 1981. 122 pages. An archaeologist and historian chart the history, anthropology, and sociology of the Cahuilla Indians.

Carr, Jim. *Palm Springs and the Coachella Valley*. Helena, MT: American Geography Press, 1990. 112 pages.

Dozier, Deborah. *The Heart Is Fire: The World of the Cahuilla Indians of Southern California.* Berkeley, CA: Heyday Books, 1996. 159 pages, illustrated. Five Cahuilla elders tell their histories and express their fears and thoughts for the future of their culture.

Mungo, Ray. *Palm Springs Babylon: Sizzling Stories from the Desert Playground of the Stars*. New York: St. Martin's Press, 1993. 224 pages. Many of the outrageous claims are to be taken with a pinch of salt, but this tell-all book makes delicious reading nonetheless.

Child Care

Even the most loving parents like to get away from the kids, especially when night calls for sampling a chilled martini. Most resort hotels provide child care facilities, although don't expect the same from small boutique hotels, many of which don't permit children.

For a list of licensed day care providers, contact the California Department of Social Security's **Community Care Licensing Division** (951-782-420; www.ccld.ca.gov; 3737 Main St., Suite 700, Riverside, CA 92501).

For missing children, contact the **Missing Children Hotline** (1-800-222-3463) or **Runaway Hotline** (1-800-231-6946).

Climate, Weather Reports, and What to Wear

Climate

"The desert is a place where you can count the raindrops but not count on them," wrote author Janice Emily Bowers. How true! Palm Springs, with an average of 328 days of sunshine, receives an average of about 5 inches of rain a year. Climate is extremely variable from year to year. Months, or even years, may pass with barely an occasional dew. Then the next winter, a series of Pacific storms may roll over the San Jacinto Mountains, bringing torrents of rain, soaking the desert and causing flash floods. By early spring, the mountainsides and valleys burst into riotous bloom.

In winter, temperatures usually hover in the 70s Fahrenheit (although cooler spells aren't unknown), while spring and fall highs reach the 80s. No wonder Palm Springs' desert resorts are a popular winter destination. It's fabulous to be soaking in an outdoor hot tub or playing a round of golf in the sun while the rest of the country is digging out from under the snow. A social whirl of society events monopolizes the "season" (Nov.–Apr.), with a nonstop calendar of charity parties and golf and tennis tournaments.

Winter nighttimes can be surprisingly cool, however, and a sweater or jacket is required. Freezing nights are frequent in winter, notably at higher elevation, but also in valley bottoms where cold air collects. Winters are almost completely dry, but torrential rains *can* fall, as in January 2008, when the Coachella Valley was deluged by three hefty storms.

Summer sees soaring temperatures, usually well above 100 degrees Fahrenheit, although the nights are delightfully warm. Midsummer thunderstorms sometimes occur, though rain is relatively rare. By June the drought is prolonged, with week after week of cloudless skies. It is not unusual for temperatures to exceed 100 degrees every day for three months, with several weeks in excess of 120 degrees not unknown. The midsummer months can cause a heat-induced stupor, with the sun beating down hard as a nail. The low desert humidity, however, usually makes all but the highest temperatures tolerable.

Whereas resort destinations elsewhere typically spike their summer rates, in the desert resorts rates fall, offering splendid value, especially July–Sept. Many Palm Springs resorts offer incentive packages, such as stay three nights, get one free.

Climate Chart

	Average Daytime Highs	Average Evening Lows
January	69	42
February	74	45
March	79	48
April	87	54
May	94	60
June	103	66
July	108	75
August	107	74
September	102	68
October	92	59
November	79	49
December	70	42

Weather Reports

Desert Sun: www.mydesert.com
DesertWeather: www.desertweather.com
National Weather Service: www.weather.gov
Palm Springs Weather Cam: www.psview.com/weather

GUIDED TOURS

Looking for an expertly guided tour? Maybe a walking tour of Palm Springs, or a Segway tour of celebrity homes? Or perhaps something more adventurous, such as a covered-wagon excursion, or a Humvee tour of Joshua Springs? There's no shortage of options. Also see the Culture and Recreation chapters.

Adventure Hummer Tours (760-285-1608 or 1-877-656-2453; www.adventurehum mer.com; 42-335 Washington St., Palm Desert, CA 92260) Uses open-air Jeeps and open-air, ex-military Humvees for tours into Joshua Tree National Park and canyons along the San Andreas fault. Has morning and afternoon tours daily.

Classicab (760-322-3111 or 1-888-644-8294; 100 S. Sunrise Way, Suite 530, Palm Springs, CA 92264) City and celebrity home tours.

Celebrity Tours (760-770-2700, 1-888-805-2700; www.celebrity-tours.com; 4751 E. Palm Canyon Dr., Palm Springs, CA 92262) City tours taking in Palm Springs to Palm Desert, focusing on homes and other places associated with the valley's celebrities.

Desert Adventures (760-340-2345 or 1-888-440-5337; www.red-jeep.com; 67-555 E. Palm Canyon Dr., Palm Springs, CA 92264) Explore the desert by Jeep Scrambler. A variety of eco-tours, including the popular and fascinating tour along the San Andreas fault to Matate Canyon Ranch, a desert oasis to which Desert Adventures has sole access. It has miles of pristine hiking trails and includes Paltee Wet, a re-created Indian village with *kish* (traditional palm-thatch homes); a replica old mining camp and gold mine; and Hole-in-the-Wall Canyon, a sinuous canyon cut by raging flash floods. It's amazing how much you'll learn about geology and flora and fauna. Ask for Morgan. She's a phenomenal guide. The company also has desert survival tours.

Modernist expert Robert Imber leading a PS Modern Tour.

Elite Land Discovery Tours (760-318-1200; www.elitelandtours.com; 555 S. Sunrise Way, Suite 200, Palm Springs, CA 92264) Offers ecologically sensitive desert tours by air-conditioned Humvee, guaranteeing superb comfort as you explore the remote regions of Joshua Tree National Park, as well as to the Salton Sea and Covington Flats. Co-owners Mark Farley, Jim Trout, and Tia Kennedy run an excellent operation and are the only local operators with a "Night Discovery Tour," utilizing special night-vision scopes to spot wildlife. Knowledgeable guides add immeasurably to the enjoyment of these learning adventures. The price for day trips includes a gourmet picnic lunch (with white tablecloths!) and hotel pick-up.

Palm Springs Architectural Tours (760-341-7330; segwayofthedesert@juno.com; 72-210 E3 Hwy. 111, Palm Desert CA 92260) Specializes in an intimate look at notable architectural sites. Tours by appointment.

PS Modern Tours (760-318-6118, psmoderntours@aol.com) Local man-about-town and modernist expert Robert Imber offers guided tours by both minivan and Segways, focusing on modernist architecture. Imbert is a font of knowledge and has access to many private homes that are 1950s and 1960s gems.

Palm Springs Tours (760-285-1608 or 1-877-656-2453; www.palmspringsfuntrips.com) Acts as a booking agent for local tour companies, including guided nature walks and jeep tours. Every Thurs., "A Taste of Palm Springs" features the best of Palm Springs, including a tour of the homes of the rich and famous followed by a special reserved aerial tram ride for dinner atop the mountain, and ending with a visit to the downtown street fair.

Handicapped Services

The desert resorts are accessible to all—even those in wheelchairs. Hotels are required by law to provide ramp access for wheelchairs, and most restaurants follow suit.

Local organizations that are good resources include **Americans with Disabilities** (760-323-8219; P.O. Box 2743, Palm Springs, CA 92263) and **Desert Blind and Handicapped** (760-323-4414; 800 Vella Rd., Units A&B, Palm Springs, CA 92264). The **Palm Springs Visitor Information Center** (see Tourist Information, below) can supply a coy of *A Mobility Impaired Traveler's Guide to Palm Springs*.

The desert resorts offer a number of solutions to anyone with a handicap to get to and fro:

Desert Health Care (760 862 9843) Provides free rides to/from health-related appointments and services for handicapped people.

Disabled Medical Transportation Service (760 362-068; 44-489 Town Center Way, Suite D, Palm Desert, CA 92260) Provides nonemergency medical transportation 24 hours a day.

SunDial (760-323-6999; Desert Hot Springs; 760-341-6999 Indio) Provides seniors and persons with disabilities with curb-to-curb service along 12 bus routes in the Coachella Valley.

Health and Safety

Don't underestimate the desert! Even lounging around the pool in the shade poses problems in midsummer, when shade temperatures can reach 120 degrees. Humans sweat to cool themselves by evaporation from the skin: In extreme heat, the body can lose more than a liter of liquid per hour. The air is so dry and hot that perspiration evaporates instantly and you may not even realize you're sweating. Unless replenished, this high rate of water loss eventually leads to advanced dehydration. *Drink lots and lots of water—8 pints a day is recommended in midsummer—and avoid alcohol*. Human sweat is also saline, and the salt lost through sweating needs to be replaced. Salt deficiency leads to listlessness. Muscle cramping and headaches are a sure sign of dehydration. If you plan on exploring the remote desert, bring enough water and food for a day or two in the event of a simple emergency.

OK . . . so much for the climate. Now what about those rattlesnakes?

Be cautious when picking up rocks and pieces of wood: Hidden under them might be a scorpion or snake. Most rattlesnake bites occur on the hands and arms. Snakes strike rapidly and often disappear before they can be identified. You may not see them. But they are there, unseen, watching you stride past in daydreaming euphoria. In fact, so well camouflaged are they that it is quite easy to walk right over a dozing, sand-loving rattler—they tend to be inert and sluggish, almost comatose, when the air is too hot or too cold—without waking it from torpor. But if you are unlucky enough to step on it or get too close to one that is fully awake, you are guaranteed to provoke a lightning strike. Even so, less than 3 percent of rattlesnake bites are fatal. If bitten, you should ideally photograph or identify the snake, as the potency of venom differs between the species and may require exact identification. If you plan on hiking or camping out in the desert, carry a rattlesnake kit, and wear loose-fitting boots with ankle protection. When camping, maintain a clean camp, as garbage attracts rodents and rodents attract snakes.

Black widow spiders are also present in large numbers, notably in the hot summer months. They like to hang out in houses, usually in a dark recess, and on the underside of plants and ledges. The females (the smaller males are harmless) are easily identified by their glossy black bodies and the blood-red hourglass mark on their bellies (the mark is easily seen, as the female spider usually hangs upside down). The female's extremely venomous bite—considered 15 times as toxic as the venom of rattlesnakes—can be fatal, although it rarely is, and fewer than 1 percent of bite cases result in death.

Cacti are another potential enemy. *Don't touch cactus!* Once a teddy bear cactus joint attaches itself to your skin or clothing, it is not easily removed. If you try to pluck it loose, the joint merely attaches itself to your other hand, impaling you with a painful palm-full of spines. Your best bet is to brush or lift the joint away using a pair of sticks or stones, and pick out the individual spines, one by one, from your flesh or clothing.

Hospitals

Betty Ford Center (760-773-4100; www.bettyfordcenter.org; 39-000 Bob Hope Dr., Rancho Mirage, CA 92270) Provides alcohol and other drug dependency treatment. Focuses on long-term treatment.

Desert Regional Medical Center (760-323-6511; www.desertmedctr.com; 1150 N. Indian Canyon Dr., Palm Springs, CA 92262) 24-hour emergency care. Physician on duty 24/7. Emergency Dept., 760-323-6251.

Eisenhower Medical Center (760-340-3911; www.emc.org; 39-000 Bob Hope Dr., Rancho Mirage, CA 92270) 24-hour emergency care. Physician on duty 24/7. The EMC has Immediate Care Centers in Cathedral City (760-328-1000; 67-780 E. Palm Canyon Dr.) and La Quinta (760-564-7000; 78-822 Hwy. 111).

Hi-Desert Medical Center (760-366-3711; www.hdmc.org; 6601 White Feather Rd., Joshua Tree, CA 92252) Nonprofit acute care facility. Emergency room.
John F. Kennedy Hospital (760-347-6191; www.jfkmemorialhosp.com; 47-111 Monroe St., Indio, CA 92201) Offers 24-hour emergency care. Physician on duty. Emergency Dept., 760-775-8111.
The following provide valuable information for people with specific health needs:
Cancer Hotline: 760-323-6713
Desert AIDS Project (HIV Health Center): 760-323-2118
Desert Community Mental Health Center Hotline: 1-800-472-4305
Palm Springs: 760-320-0063
Indio: 760-863-8455
Gamblers Anonymous: 760-320-9190
Mental Health Helpline: 1-800-877-7675
Palm Springs Family Care Center: 760-778-2210 or 1-800-720-9553

LATE-NIGHT FOOD AND FUEL

Insomnia after that way-too-late-in-the-day espresso? Or perhaps you're a night bird simply seeking a place to gas up. Here are a few options for night owls.

Gasoline

Pilot: 760-329-5562; www.pilotcorp.com; 6605 N. Indian Canyon Dr., North Palm Springs
Shell Service Station: 760-323-9011; 2796 N. Palm Canyon Dr., Palm Springs
Valero: 3689 N. Indian Canyon Dr., Palm Springs

Restaurants

Blue Coyote Grill: 760-327-1196; 445 N. Palm Canyon Dr., Palm Springs
Las Casuelas Nuevas: 760-328-8844; 70-050 Hwy. 111, Rancho Mirage
Tanpopo: 760-340-1901; 72-221 Hwy. 111, Palm Desert. Late-night sushi Fri. and Sat. 11 PM–1:30 AM.

Stores and Supermarkets

7-Eleven: 760-323-2814; www.7-eleven.com; 2493 N. Palm Canyon Dr., Palm Springs. This 24-hour convenience store has seven other outlets between Yucca Valley and Coachella.
Albertson's: 760-321-0662; www.albertsons.com; 1751 N. Sunrise Way, Palm Springs. This supermarket chain has five other outlets in the Coachella Valley.
Vons: 760-324-4502; www.vons.com; 2315 E. Tahquitz Canyon Way, Palm Springs. This Safeway affiliate has six other stores in the Palm Springs region.

MEDIA

Magazines and Newspapers

The BottomLine (760-323-0552; www.psbottomline.com; 312 N. Palm Canyon Dr., Palm Springs, CA 92262) Biweekly magazine serving the gay and lesbian community.
Desert Entertainer (760-776-5181; www.desertentertainer.com; 41995 Boardwalk, Palm Desert, CA 92211) Covers the entertainment scene with movie and restaurant reviews, spotlight on entertainment venues, plus columns on golf, shopping, and more.

Desert Key (760-346-5998; www.keypalmsprings.com) A visitors' guide with listings and reviews of restaurants, events, shops, and things to see and do. Available at streetside stands.
Desert Magazine (760-322-5555; www.thedesertsun.com; 750 N. Gene Autry Trail, Palm Springs, CA 92262) Monthly full-color, glossy magazine published by the *Desert Sun*.
Desert Post Weekly (760-202-3200; 750 N. Gene Autry Trail, Palm Springs, CA 92262) Free tabloid newspaper available at streetside dispensers. It has excellent restaurant and movie reviews. Published by the *Desert Sun*.
Desert Sun (760-322-5555; www.thedesertsun.com; 750 N. Gene Autry Trail, Palm Springs, CA 92262) Daily newspaper serving the Coachella Valley, with national and international news, plus special sections including business, real estate, sports, etc.
Dune: Desert Life, Desert Style (760-553-9487; www.dunemag.net) Glossy lifestyle magazine spans the spectrum from arts and fine dining to features on fashion and famous folks with desert connections.
Palm Desert Magazine (760-325-2333; www.palmdesertmagazine.com; 303 N. Indian Canyon Dr., Palm Springs, CA 92263) Catering to the monied crowd with personality profiles, photo features on fashion. Published by Desert Publications.
Palm Springs Life (760-325-2333; www.palmspringslife.com; 303 N. Indian Canyon Dr., Palm Springs, CA 92263) Flagship publication of Desert Publications, this slick monthly magazine profiles desert culture and life. The company also prints such specialty publications as *Art & Culture* (quarterly), *Spa Guide*, *Golf Guide*, and *Dine Out* (monthly).

RADIO AND TELEVISION

Radio

Depending on your location, many Los Angeles and San Diego stations may be in range, in addition to the following local stations:
KPSC 88.5 FM (213-225-7400; www.kusc.org; Palm Springs) Classical
KCRI 89.3 FM (310-450-5183; www.kcrw.com; Indio) Public radio
KQCM 92.1 FM (760-361-9200; Joshua Tree) Top 40
KKUU 92.7 FM (760-345-9236; www.927kkuu.com; Indio) Rap, hip-hop
KCLB 93.7 FM (760-391-5252; www.937kclb.com; Coachella) Rock
KLOB 94.7 FM (760-341-5837; Thousand Palms) Spanish
KXCM 96.3 FM (Twentynine Palms) Country
KUNA 96.7 FM (760-568-6830; La Quinta) Spanish
KWXY 98.5 FM (760-328-1104; Cathedral City) Easy listening
KMRJ 99.5 FM (760-778-6995; www.m995.com; Rancho Mirage) Alternative
KPSI 100.5 FM (760-325-2582; www.mix1005.fm; Palm Springs) Eclectic mix
KATY 101.3 FM (951-676-1013; www.1013katy.com; Idyllwild) Adult contemporary
KJJZ 102.3 FM (760-320-4550; www.102kjjz.com; Indio) Smooth jazz
KEZN 103.1 FM (760-340-9383; www.ez103.com; Palm Desert) Soft rock
KDES 104.7 FM (760-325-2582; www.kdes.com; Palm Springs) Oldies
KPLM 106.1 FM (760-320-4550; Palm Springs) Country
KDGL 106.9 FM (760-341-7272; www.theeagle1069.com; Yucca Valley) Classic hits
KCDZ 107.7 FM (760-366-8471; www.kcdzfm.com; Joshua Tree) News and talk
KPSI 920 AM (760-325-2582; www.newstalk920.com; Palm Springs) News and talk
KNWZ 970 AM (760-322-7890; http://knewsradio.com; Coachella) News and talk

KXPS 1010 AM (760-322-7890; www.1010kxps.com; Thousand Palms) Sports
KQYN 1250 AM (760-362-4264; Twenty Nine Palms) News and talk
KWXY 1340 AM (760-328-1104; Cathedral City) Easy listening

Television

The following local TV stations serve the valley:
CBS2 (760-343-5700; www.cbstv2.com; 31-276 Dunham Way, Thousand Palms, CA 92276) CBS's local affiliate news channel.
KESQ News Channel 3 (760-340-7000; www.kesq.com; 42-650 Melanie Pl., Palm Desert, CA 92211) ABC affiliate news channel.
KMIR6 (760-568-3636; www.kmir6.com; 72-920 Park View Dr., Palm Desert, CA 92260) NBC affiliate.
KDFX-CA (760-340-7000; 42-650 Melanie Pl., Palm Desert, CA 92211) This Fox-affiliated station broadcasts on Channel 33.
KVER (760-341-5837; www.kver.entravision.com; 41-601 Corporate Way, Palm Desert, CA 92260) Univision's Palm Springs station broadcasts in Spanish. Soap operas to sports.
Palm Springs Cable Television (760-322-8354; www.psctv.org) Broadcasts City Council and Commission meetings on Channel 17.

PETS

Bringing your dog to the desert is no big deal. Palm Springs residents love their dogs, and dozens of hotels are dog-friendly. Most public parks are off-limits to dogs, but several excellent dog parks have been created just for Fido. The following are useful contacts to know:
Animal Control: 760-323-8151, Palm Springs; 7603478522, Indio
Animal Emergency: 760-343-3438
Animal Medical Hospital: 760-327-1355; 606 S. Oleander Rd., Palm Springs, CA 92264
Animal Samaritans SPCA: 760-343-3477; 72-307 Ramon Rd., Thousand Palms, CA 92276
Guide Dogs of the Desert: 760-329-6257; 60-740 Dillon Rd., White Water, CA 92282
Humane Society of the Desert: 760-329-0203
Pet Sitter Registry: 760-329-0203

Dog Parks

Palm Springs Dog Park (760-322-8362; 222 Civic Dr. North, Palm Springs), behind City Hall, has pooper scoopers, drinking fountains for low-to-the-ground hounds, and antique fire hydrants for pooches to pee. Small dogs get their own fenced area.

Palm Springs Dog Park.

Palm Desert has four dog parks: **Civic Center Dog Park** (73-510 Fred Waring Dr.); **Freedom Park** (77-400 Country Club Dr.); **Joe Mann Dog Park** (77-820 California Dr.); and **University Dog Park** (74-802 University Park Dr.). You can walk or run your dog off-leash at **Cahuilla Hills Park** (45-825 Edgehill Dr.) and **Cap Homme / Ralph Adams Park** (72-500 Thrush Rd.).

Real Estate

A good percentage of snowbirds and others who descend on Palm Springs do so with a view to buying a retro-modernist home, golf course condo, or a plot of land for a future second (or retirement) home. A few years ago they could have snapped up an Alexander designer home for pocket change. By the late 1990s the rush was on, and the millennium brought a few years of astounding appreciation. The steam has since been let off, and housing sales have fallen (as they have across the nation). But to many pundits, Palm Springs' housing prices still seem like a relative bargain. They know they're purchasing more than mere real estate—they're also buying into a California lifestyle, magnificent scenic beauty, and an enviable winter climate.

For information on real estate matters, consult the **California Desert Association of Realtors** (760-346-5637; www.caldesertrealtors.com) and the yellow pages of Palm Springs phone books under "Real Estate Agents."

A good starting point for searching out your dream home is the **Desert Area Multiple Listing Service** (www.desertareamls.com). You can also view listings in the *Desert Sun* classifieds, as well as *Desert Home* (760-325-2333; www.palmspringslife.com; 303 N. Indian Canyon Dr., Palm Springs, CA 92263), a free publication available at the Palm Springs airport and venues throughout the valley.

Religious Services and Organizations

The best source for information about church and synagogue services is the weekend edition of the *Desert Sun* newspaper.

Baptist

Ajalon Baptist Church: 760-325-8195; 433 Tramview Rd., Palm Springs
Central Baptist Church: 760-347-0317; 45-520 Clinton St., Indio
Desert Cities Baptist Church: 760-346-7788; 45-825 Edgehill Dr., La Quinta
First Baptist Church: 760-325-0313; 588 Las Vegas Rd., Palm Springs
Palm Springs Baptist Church: 760-323-1013; 1696 E. El Cielo Rd., Palm Springs
Trinity Baptist Church: 760-347-0604; 44-550 Monroe St., Indio
University Baptist Church: 760-346-3038; 72-700 Fred Waring Dr., Palm Desert

Episcopal

Church of St. Paul in the Desert: 760-320-7488; 320-7488; 125 W. El Alameda Ave., Palm Springs
St. Margaret's Episcopal Church: 760-346-2697; 47-535 Hwy. 74, Palm Desert

Jewish Orthodox

Chabad of Palm Springs: 760-325-0774; 425 Avenida Ortega, Palm Springs

Lutheran

Hope Lutheran Church: 760-346-1273; 45-900 Portola Ave., Palm Desert
Our Savior's Community Lutheran Church: 760-327-5611; 1020 E. Ramon Rd., Palm Springs
Peace Lutheran Church: 760-776-7100; 74-200 Country Club Dr., Palm Desert

St. John's Lutheran Church: 760-345-2122; 42-695 Washington St., Palm Desert
Trinity Lutheran Church: 760-347-3971; 81-500 Miles Ave., Indio

Methodist

First United Methodist Church: 760-347-1046; 45-501 Deglet Noor, Indio
United Methodist Church: 760-327-5931; 1555 E. Alejo Rd., Palm Springs

Presbyterian

Desert Springs Church: 760-568-3646; 43-435 Monterey Ave., Palm Desert
Palm Springs Presbyterian Church: 760-320-2769; 620 S. Sunrise Way, Palm Springs
St. Andrew Community Presbyterian Church: 760-347-5344; 47-192 Monroe St., Indio

Roman Catholic

Our Lady of Guadalupe Catholic Church: 760-325-5809; 204 S. Calle El Segundo, Palm Springs
Our Lady of Perpetual Help: 760-347-3507; 82-450 Bliss Ave., Indio
Our Lady of Solitude Catholic Church: 760-325-3816; 151 W. Alejo Rd., Palm Springs
Sacred Heart Catholic Church: 760-346-6502; 43-775 Deep Canyon Rd., Palm Desert
St. Francis of Assisi Catholic Church: 760-564-1255; 47-225 Washington St., La Quinta
St. Louis Catholic Church: 760-328-2398; 68-333 C St., Cathedral City
St. Theresa Catholic Church: 760-323-2669; 2800 E. Ramon Rd., Palm Springs

ROAD SERVICE

Car overheated because you forgot to top up the water in your radiator? Puncture your tire on a cactus thorn? Help is at hand! For emergency road service from AAA, anywhere in the Coachella Valley region, call 1-800-222-4357; the **AAA-California State Automobile**

Our Lady of Solitude Roman Catholic Church.

Association (760-320-1121) is at 300 S. Farrell Dr., Palm Springs.

For emergency police assistance (including reporting an accident, a crime, or an unsafe driver), call 911. For nonemergencies, contact the **California Highway Patrol** (1-800-835-5247), which has headquarters at 79-650 Varner Rd., Indio (760-772-8911) and 63-683 Twentynine Palms Hwy., Joshua Tree (760-366-3707).

Listed below are companies providing 24-hour emergency road services:

A&A Towing & Recovery: Palm Springs; 760-320-6100
Brothers Towing: Palm Springs; 760-864-1000
Budget Towing: Coachella; 760-345-5227
Dave's Towing: Palm Springs; 760-322-5441
J&S Towing: Palm Springs; 760-325-6904
Plaza Towing: Indio; 760-775-4314 or 760-568-2360
R&R Towing: Indio; 760-775-1433 or 1-800-485-7611
Southwest Towing: Cathedral City; 760-324-1177 or 1-800-286-9776

SCHOOLS

Public School Districts

Desert Sands Unified School District: La Quinta; 760-777-4200; www.dsusd.us
Morongo Unified School District: Twentynine Palms; 760-367-9191; www.morongo.k12.ca.us
Palm Springs Unified School District: Palm Springs; 760-416-6000; www.psusd.us

Private and Religious Schools

Calvary Christian School: Cathedral City; 760-324-2355
Christian School of the Desert: Bermuda Dunes; 760-345-2848
Desert Adventist School: Palm Desert; 760-779-1799; www.desertadventistacademy.com
Desert Chapel Christian: Palm Springs; 706-327-2772
Desert SonShine: Palm Springs; 760-320-9533
Desert Torah Academy: Palm Desert; 760-341-6501
Fountain Christian Academy: Indio; 760-347-0054
Indio Christian Center Academy: Indio; 760-342-1779
Jewish Community School of the Desert: Palm Desert; 760-340-2039; www.jcsdpd.com
Joshua Springs Christian: Yucca Valley; 760-365-3599
King's School of the Desert: Palm Springs; 760-324-7381; www.kingsschools.com
La Quinta Christian Fellowship School: La Quinta; 760-564-9195
Marywood Palm Valley School: Rancho Mirage; 760-770-4541
Montessori School of Palm Springs; Palm Springs; 760-323-2502
Our Lady of the Desert School: Yucca Valley; 760-365-4676
Palm Springs Christian School: Desert Hot Springs; 760-329-5466
Sacred Heart: Palm Desert; 760-346-3513; www.sacredheartpalmdesert.com
St. Margaret's Episcopal: Palm Desert; 760-836-3267; www.stmargarets.org
St. Theresa Elementary School: Palm Springs; 760-327-4919
Xavier College Preparatory High School: Palm Desert; 760-340-9274

Colleges

California State University San Bernardino–Palm Desert Campus: Palm Desert; 760-341-2883; http://pdc.csusb.edu
College of the Desert: Palm Desert; 760-776-0120; www.collegeofthedesert.edu
Maric College: Palm Springs; 1-800-526-0256; www.mariccollege.edu
Milan Institute: Indio; 1-888-207-9460; www.milaninstitute.edu
Park University: Cathedral City; 760-327-5134
Santa Barbara Business College: Palm Desert; 1-866-749-7222

TOURIST INFORMATION

Desert Hot Springs Chamber of Commerce: 760-329-6403 or 1-800-346-3347; www.deserthotsprings.com; 11-711 West Dr., Desert Hot Springs, CA 92240.
Desert Regional Tourism Agency: 760-365-9632; www.desert-regional-tourism-agency.com; 56-711 Twentynine Palms Hwy., Yucca Valley, CA 92284. Based in an official California Tourism Welcome Center.
Palm Desert Visitors Center: 760-568-1441 or 1-800-873-2428; www.palm-desert.org; 72-567 Hwy. 111, Palm Desert, CA 92260. Opened in 2007, the new visitors center features a sculpture garden. Open 9–5 Mon.–Fri. and 9–4 Sat. and Sun.
Palm Springs Desert Resorts Convention and Visitors Authority: 760-770-9000 or 1-800-967-3767; www.giveintothedesert.com; 70-100 Hwy. 111, Rancho Mirage, CA 92270. Promotes tourism to the eight valley cities, including in an excellent printed visitors guide. The headquarters has maps and brochures of CVA members, but it serves more as an administrative center than visitors bureau. Open 8:30–5 Mon.–Fri.
Palm Springs Hospitality Association: 760-835-4957; 100 S. Sunrise Way, PMB 297, Palm Springs, CA 92262. A nonprofit business association working to increase tourism to Palm Springs while representing the interests of its members.
Palm Springs Visitor Information Center: 760-778-8418; www.palm-springs.org; 2901 N. Palm Canyon Dr., Palm Springs, CA 92262. In the historic Albert Frey–designed Tramway Oasis Gas Station, this information center is perfectly positioned at the foot of the tramway access road at the entrance to Palm Springs. Open 9–5 Sun.–Thurs. and 9–5:30 Fri. and Sat. The Palm Springs Bureau of Tourism is headquartered at 777 N. Palm Canyon Dr., Suite 101, Palm Springs (760-327-2828), where it also has an information bureau; open 10–4 daily Sept.–May, and 10–4 Fri. and Sat., June–Aug.
Santa Rosa and San Jacinto National Monument Visitors Center: 760-862-9984; Hwy. 74, Palm Desert, CA 92260. Four miles south of Hwy. 111. Maps, exhibits, and information on the vast National Monument, plus trailheads for exploring the region. Open 9–4 daily.

Palm Canyon.

If Time Is Short

Quick Treats

Hopefully your visit to the Palm Springs region will be long enough to make the most of many of the attractions listed in the Culture and Recreation chapters, and allow for a healthy sampling of restaurants. But if your time is limited and you're scratching your head over so many options, then why not follow an itinerary that samples my personal favorites? Not everyone might pick these particular spots, but I feel confident that you won't go home disappointed.

Places to Stay

La Quinta Resort & Club (760-564-4111 or 1-877-527-7721; www.laquintaresort.com; 49-999 Eisenhower Dr., La Quinta, CA 92253) Go on . . . splurge! Drawing the rich and famous for almost a century, this gracious spa retreat is known for its superb tennis and golf, plus fine-dining restaurants and romantic Mediterranean-themed private cottages.
Two Bunch Palms Resort & Spa (760-329-8791 or 1-800-472-4334; www.twobunchpalms.com; 67-425 Two Bunch Palms Trail, Desert Hot Springs, CA 92240) If it's a classy spa retreat you're seeking, this is as good as it gets. Perched on a hill with vast views, this boutique hotel with period European decor offers the ultimate in privacy and serenity.
Viceroy Palm Springs (760-320-4117; www.viceroypalmsprings.com; 415 S. Belardo Rd., Palm Springs, CA 92264) This gorgeous boutique hotel has a fabulous contemporary aesthetic that wows all comers with its signature black, white, and lemon-yellow motif. The spa is world-class, and the restaurant is one of Palm Springs' finest.

Cultural Attractions: Day

Living Desert Zoo & Gardens (760-346-5694; www.livingdesert.org; 47-900 Portola Ave., Palm Desert, CA 92260) A tremendous place to get close to, and learn about, desert flora and fauna. The kids will love it.
Palm Springs Air Museum (760-778-6262 ext. 223; www.palmspringsairmuseum.org; 745 Gene Autry Trail, Palm Springs, CA 92262) Occupying two hangars at Palm Springs International Airport, the vast collection of *flyable* World War II warplanes includes a P-51 Mustang, a Supermarine Spitfire, and a B-17 Flying Fortress.
Palm Springs Art Museum (760-325-7186; www.psmuseum.org; 101 Museum Dr., Palm

Springs, CA 92262) This modernist gem boasts world-class collections of modern art, Native American displays, plus glass sculptures and photography.

Cultural Attractions: Night

Buddy Greco's (760-883-5812; www.buddygreco.com; 68-805 Hwy. 111, Cathedral City, CA 92234) An intimate supper club in 1950s tradition, this one is owned by, and features, crooner-heartthrob Buddy Greco.
Costas Nightclub (760-341-2211; Desert Springs JW Marriott Resort & Spa, 74-855 Country Club Dr., Palm Desert, CA 92260) Thurs.–Sat. night, Costas is *the* class act in town for sophisticates who like to dress to kill on the dance floor.
Fabulous Palm Springs Follies (760-327-0225 or 1-800-967-9997; www.palmsprings follies.com; Plaza Theater, 128 S. Palm Canyon Dr., Palm Springs, CA 92262) This spectacular Las Vegas–style cabaret features sensational performances by the Long-Legged Lovelies and Follies Gentlemen—all of them over 55 years of age. Where they get their energy I'll never know!

Restaurants

Amorè (760-777-1315; www.amore-dining.com; 47-474 Washington St., La Quinta, CA 92253) Extraordinary contemporary architecture and glitz, not to mention mountain views through a curved floor-to-ceiling glass wall, provide dramatic ambience for enjoying nouvelle Italian fusion dishes. Bring a fat wallet.
Johannes (760-778-0017; www.johannesrestaurants.com; 196 S. Indian Canyon Dr., Palm Springs, CA 92262) Chicly contemporary and beloved of discerning diners, this downtown restaurant delivers consistently superb gourmet nouvelle dishes. Great martinis, too.
Keedy's Fountain & Grill (760-346-6492; 73-633 Hwy. 111, Palm Desert, CA 92260) For breakfast or lunch, you can't go wrong at this classic piece of 1950s Americana. Serves fabulous pancakes and huevos rancheros, plus burgers, tuna melts, and other classics.
Le Vallauris (760-325-5059; www.levallauris.com; 385 W. Tahquitz Canyon Way, Palm Springs, CA 92262) Combining a sumptuous French provincial ambience and mouthwatering French-inspired nouvelle dishes prepared by chef Jean Paul Lair. Choose the leafy outdoor patio on balmy nights.

Recreation

Desert Springs Spa (760-341-1865 or 1-800-255-0848; www.desertspringsspa.com; 74-855 Country Club Dr., Palm Desert, CA 92260) Whether or not you savor spa treatments, *do* take a spa treatment here. This 38,000-square-foot spa offers every relaxing treatment you could wish for, including a sybaritic full-day package.
Fantasy Balloon Flights (760-568-0997 or 1-800-462-2683; www.fantasyballoon flights.com; 74-181 Parosella St., Palm Desert, CA 92260) Let champion balloon pilot Steve Wilkinson take you on a romantic and exhilarating dawn ride over the valley. A great way to start the day.

Indian Canyons (760-325-3400; www.indian-canyons.com; S. Palm Canyon Dr.; 3 miles S. of E. Palm Canyon Dr., Palm Springs) There are dozens of hiking options in the desert, but this remains one of my favorites.
Palm Springs Aerial Tramway (760-325-1449 or 1-888-515-8726; www.pstramway.com; 1 Tramway Rd., Palm Springs, CA 92262) No visit to the Palm Springs region is complete without a revolving tram ride up to the mountaintop station at 8,516 feet. Hike the trails in Mount San Jacinto State Park before descending.
SilverRock Resort (760-777-8884; www.silverrock.org; 7979 Ahmanson La., La Quinta, CA 92253) This golf course owned by the city of La Quinta is one of the most spectacular public courses in the world. Hard up against the base of the Santa Rosa Mountains, it also offers a real challenge without breaking the bank.

About the Author

Christopher P. Baker

Forsaking the San Francisco Bay Area rat race, Christopher P. Baker opted for the calm of Palm Springs in 2005. He first fell in love with the desert region while vacationing at the Hyatt Grand Champions, in La Quinta, in 2002, resulting in his buying a condominium in the deluxe PGA West golf resort and, later, his Alexander-built modernist home in Palm Springs.

Born and raised in Yorkshire, England, Baker earned a bachelor's degree in geography, plus master's degrees in Latin American studies and in education. He settled in California in 1980. Since 1983 he has made his living as a professional travel writer, photographer, and lecturer and has established a reputation as the world's leading guidebook author specializing in Central America and the Caribbean. He has also authored guidebooks on California and Nevada for Frommer's, Prentice Hall, and the National Geographic Society.

Baker is particularly acknowledged as the world's foremost authority on travel to Cuba, about which he has written six books, including *Mi Moto Fidel: Motorcycling through Castro's Cuba*, a two-time national book award winner.

His feature articles have appeared in most major U.S. daily newspapers, as well as in publications as diverse as *Caribbean Travel & Life, Elle, National Geographic Traveler,* and *The Robb Report*. A nine-time Lowell Thomas Award winner, Baker is also an accomplished photographer, with many front-cover credits to his name. His award-winning large-format *Cuba Classics: A Celebration of Vintage American Automobiles* is right at home on the coffee tables of local modernist homes.

A gifted public speaker, he has lectured aboard various cruise ships and has been privileged to address the National Press Club, the National Geographic Society (*Live . . . from National Geographic* series), and the World Affairs Council.

In addition, he has been profiled in *USA Today* and has appeared on dozens of syndicated national radio and TV shows, including on CNN, Fox TV, ABC, NBC, and NPR. In 2005 the Caribbean Tourism Organization named him Travel Writer of the Year.

He promotes himself through his Web site: www.travelguidebooks.com

Index

I

J

K

L

M

N

Q

R

S

T

U

V

W

X

Y

Z

Lodging by Price

Inexpensive: Up to $100
Moderate: $100 to $150
Expensive: $150 to $250
Very Expensive: $250 and up

Palm Springs

Palm Springs Vicinity

Southern Desert Resorts

Dining by Price

Inexpensive: Up to $10
Moderate: $10 to $20
Expensive: $20 to 35
Very Expensive: $35 or more

Dining by Cuisine